TWENTY YEARS AMONG OUR HOSTILE INDIANS

Very Respectfully
J. Lee Humfreville

Twenty Years Among Our Hostile Indians

Describing the Characteristics, Customs, Habits,
Religion, Marriages, Dances, and Battles of the
Wild Indians in Their Natural State,

together with

the Fur Companies, Overland Stage,
Pony Express, Electric Telegraph,
and other Phases of Life in the Pathless
Regions of the Wild West

J. LEE HUMFREVILLE

With a new introduction by Edwin Sweeney

STACKPOLE
BOOKS

New introduction copyright © 2002 by Stackpole Books

Published by
STACKPOLE BOOKS
5067 Ritter Road
Mechanicsburg, PA 17055
www.stackpolebooks.com

Cover design by Tracy Patterson
Cover illustration: "Indian Dancer—Pawnee" from Chapter 35

Printed in the United States of America

10 9 8 7 6 5 4 3 2

FIRST EDITION

Library of Congress Cataloging-in-Publication Data

Humfreville, J. Lee (James Lee), 1841–1916.
     Twenty years among our hostile Indians / J. Lee Humfreville ; with a new introduction by Edwin Sweeney.— 1st. ed.
     p. cm. — (Frontier Classics)
     Originally published: 2nd ed., rev., enl. and improved with many new and rare illustrations selected by the author. New York : Hunter, c1903.
     Includes bibliographical references and index
     ISBN 0-8117-2814-5
     1. Indians of North America—West (U.S.) I. Title. II. Series.

E78.W5 H94 2002
978'.00497—dc21   2002018735

ISBN 978-0-8117-2814-0

TO

JAMES EVERARD,

AS A

SLIGHT TOKEN OF ESTEEM, FOR HIS

STERLING CHARACTER,

AND IN APPRECIATION OF A FRIENDSHIP WHICH
HAS EXISTED FOR MORE THAN
A QUARTER OF A
CENTURY

THIS VOLUME IS DEDICATED

BY

THE AUTHOR.

INTRODUCTION

by Edwin Sweeney

Capt. Jacob L. Humfreville was one of several nineteenth century U.S. army officers to take pen in hand and relate his experiences with the Indian tribes of the American West. The product of his efforts, *Twenty Years Among Our Hostile Indians*, was first published in 1899. Today we can learn from Humfreville's interesting and honest (though frequently ethnocentric) narrative, which was written from the perspective of a cavalry officer who had grown up east of the Mississippi River before the Civil War. His views accord with those of most frontier soldiers and settlers who, appalled by the scalped, mutilated, and butchered victims of the plains warfare, came to hate the Indians. It mattered little to him that the American Indian was defending his cherished way of life, his beliefs, his land, and his loved ones—which is doubtless what Humfreville was doing when he volunteered for service to fight Rebel forces when the Civil War erupted in 1861. To most Americans of the nineteenth century, Indians were subhuman, their way of life savage and uncivilized; they were just another obstacle in the path of the white man's progress and a blur on his vision of a new nation.

It is certainly true that Humfreville never really regarded the matter intellectually or philosophically, that he never saw the Plains Indians as a displaced people. He was generally scornful of the Indian culture and way of life. But he was a soldier, and it is also clear from his narrative that he much admired the courage exhibited by warriors in battle, and that he marveled at their fighting skills and natural cunning. And it must be acknowledged that in his later years Humfreville, as he assumed larger responsibilities and was caused to reflect on the situation of the Indians as wards of the government, did mollify his views. He could appreciate that the Plains Indians had lived a better and more rewarding life in the time before they were made dependent upon corrupt Indian agents and an indifferent Washington, D.C., bureaucracy.

The reader will immediately notice that Capt. Jacob L. Humfreville was not constrained by today's political correctness. His observations account for events just as he remembered them. In his two tours of service in the West, the first from 1862–1866 in the Northern Plains and the second from 1867–1874 in the Southern Plains, he witnessed some of the most brutal fighting that ever occurred between Americans and the Plains Indians. For the Indian it was a struggle born of desperation. After all, the Plains Indians, sustained by the buffalo for generations, were now subject to an onslaught of White encroachment that was threatening to destroy, abruptly and almost totally, their way of life. Trading posts, military forts, emigrant travellers, the transcontinental railroad, buffalo hunters, and finally, the establishment of sprawling ranches and bustling towns, all were damaging to their culture—especially because White frontiersmen had in almost no time virtually exterminated the buffalo. This relentless invasion naturally led to violent clashes between the Plains Indians and the U.S. Army, and to a war that could only mean for the Indian an alien life on the Reservation.

As an officer with the 11th Ohio Cavalry, Humfreville was actively involved in the Indian War of 1864–1865, which erupted after the egregious and shameful Chivington massacre of the Southern Cheyenne at Sand Creek. His narrative contains anecdotal information about his role during the bloody cycle of revenge and retaliation that followed. The Southern Cheyenne enlisted the help of their northern brethren, the Northern Cheyenne, the Arapaho (their erstwhile allies), and the Oglala, Brule, and Miniconjou, the three southern divisions of the powerful Lakota nation, better known as the Sioux. In one skirmish a Sioux arrow point slammed into the knee of Humfreville, leaving him seriously incapacitated and hampering his mobility for the rest of his life.

In contrast, Humfreville in his memoirs virtually ignored his later stint with the 9th Cavalry, the celebrated Buffalo Soldiers, with whom he served from 1867 to 1874 in various forts in Texas. For one-half of this period he acted as the regimental quartermaster. The responsibilities of this staff position were administrative in nature. But for reasons that will later be discussed, Humfreville purposely failed to call attention to his service with the 9th Cavalry.

Jacob L. Humfreville was born on March 18, 1841, perhaps at Piqua, Ohio, according to his enlistment papers. In later years, however, in his request for a pension, he claimed his birth place was Boone County, Kentucky. According to this account, his father worked for the railroad and brought his four sons to Piqua, Ohio, in the late 1840s. Situated on the banks of the Mad River, Piqua had been an important base for the Shawnee Indians, who had established their homes here until frontiersmen under Col. George Rogers Clark destroyed their village in the summer of 1780. As a youth, Jacob undoubtedly heard about the adventures and exploits of the celebrated Shawnee chief, Tecumseh, and the legendary frontiersman of Kentucky, Simon Kenton. Both men had lived near Piqua.

On April 19, 1861, one week after the firing on Fort Sumter that officially began the Civil War, Humfreville, his occupation listed as a "farmer," enlisted for three months as a private in the 11th Regiment of Ohio Infantry at Columbus, Ohio. The state mustered him out on August 18, 1861. About this time William D. Collins, a much-respected lawyer and state representative from Hillsboro, Ohio, wrote a letter to the War Department in which he offered to raise "a regiment in southern Ohio of cavalry" for service in Kentucky or wherever the government needed it. The War Department accepted his offer, and promptly appointed Collins to command with the rank of lieutenant colonel. Shortly after, it merged the 6th and 7th Ohio Volunteer Cavalry into one unit, the 11th regiment, Ohio Volunteer Cavalry. In his hometown of Piqua, Ohio, the twenty-year-old Jacob Humfreville joined Collins's regiment as a private, Company A, on October 23, 1861. He stood five feet, nine inches tall, had blue eyes, and a light complexion. Less than one month later, on November 21, 1861, Humfreville was promoted to sergeant.[1]

In early 1862 Washington ordered the regiment to Camp Denison, Ohio, for training. On February 10, 1862, Lieutenant Colonel Collins, eager to serve the Union cause, travelled to the nation's capital, hoping to receive an assignment to fight Confederates. But, because the Army had transferred east many of its regular troops from the Western Territories, the War Department ordered Collins instead to report for frontier duty to Maj. Gen. Henry Wager Halleck at St. Louis. By this time, a Confederate force from Texas had invaded New Mexico, hoping to gain control of the territory. It was feared that if the Texans were successful, their next target might be Colorado. The Ohio troops reached Benton Barracks, Missouri, on March 18, 1862.

Their time in Missouri would be short. Years later Humfreville would recall that he fought "Bushwhackers" and other "small foraging parties." If so, his experiences fighting the Missouri guerillas were over almost as soon as they began. By mid-April the War Department gave Collins his marching orders. By then, federal and militia forces in New Mexico had driven the Confederates back to Texas, and Gen. James Henry Carleton's California Volunteers were marching to New Mexico with orders to occupy that territory, thus freeing up the remaining regular troops to move east. Because they were no longer needed in the New Mexico Territory, Washington decided to dispatch the Ohio Volunteers to the Idaho Territory, which encompassed then part of what is today southeastern Wyoming, Colorado, and Idaho. Indians living in the Rocky Mountains, in particular

the Shoshone and Utes, had already commenced hostilities against the
stage and telegraph stations, capturing many horses, mules, and supplies.
Though the assignment must have chagrined the Ohio men, who had enlisted to fight against the Confederacy, they understood that they had accepted orders to serve the nation's cause, wherever it might mean. Much of
the credit can be given to the leadership abilities of Lieutenant Colonel
Collins, a man who though little remembered today, was held in high esteem by his contemporaries, soldiers and Indians alike.[2]

As the Ohio regiment journeyed west, Sergeant Humfreville had his
first meeting with the Plains Indians along the trail. In mid-May a group
of two hundred Sioux ventured into Lieutenant Colonel Collins's camp.
Humfreville recalled that they "were decked out in the most fantastic
style . . . many had old discarded white and black plug hats."[3] Collins politely asked them to come in for a talk. Allaying their fears, he carefully explained that he had not come to take their land or to make war upon them
if they remained peaceful. As with every Indian he touched, Collins left a
favorable impression with the Sioux, providing the right dose of greetings,
gifts, and reassurances. In a private letter to his wife he confided: "I am
sure that if the Indian character was better understood and justice done
them respecting their customs, protecting the worthy and punishing the
bad, they would give less trouble." During the long and arduous march,
which was replete with challenges and new experiences, Collins earned his
soldiers' respect and devotion, because of his fair decisions and steadfast
leadership. Tagging along with him was his seventeen-year-old-son, Caspar, whose personality reflected curiosity, impetuosity, and courage. He was
then too young to join the service; yet for the next few years he was constantly at his father's side, absorbing everything, and growing from a boy
into a man under the guidance of the lieutenant colonel. Humfreville knew
both men well.[4]

The regiment reached Fort Laramie in today's southeastern Wyoming
on May 30, 1862. United States troops had first occupied Laramie in
1849, and the army considered it the most important post in the northern
Plains. It was a vital center for emigrants and mail riders travelling along
the Oregon and Bozeman Trails. Here Collins found four companies of
regulars (two cavalry and two infantry) and one infantry company of
Kansas Volunteers. His superiors decided to send the two regular infantry
companies to Fort Kearney, thus leaving him with his four companies of
Ohio Cavalry, two regular cavalry companies and the Kansas infantry.
After a four-day stay at Laramie, he left for the mountains, following the
Overland Mail Route west for three hundred miles to South Pass, where
he established a camp. One of his guides was the legendary scout and

mountain man, Jim Bridger, with whom the youthful Jacob Humfreville would become quite friendly. En route, Collins had detached Company A, to which Humfreville belonged, detailing them as pickets at the various stage stations along the route. According to his recollections, Humfreville was stationed at St. Mary's Station, some forty miles east of South Pass.[5]

Collins had no way of knowing that his Ohio men had been placed into one of the most dangerous parts of Indian country. The Indians committing hostilities in this region were two tribes not usually thought to resist American settlement. According to one respected historian, "The only serious hostilities on the central Plains during 1862 and 1863 centered on the emigrant and mail routes west and south of Fort Laramie. Although some Sioux, Cheyenne and Arapaho warriors may have been involved, the chief offenders were Shoshone and Utes."[6]

On July 11, 1862, mainly because of Indian depredations along the stage route, the Postmaster General ordered that the Overland Mail Company shut down its operations along the Oregon Trail and move them about 150 miles south to a safer and more direct route to Salt Lake City. Collins directed Major O'Farrell to take his Company A to help in the removal. Once the change was accomplished, on July 20, 1862, Gen. James Craig ordered O'Farrell, reinforced by Company D, to construct Fort Halleck as a post to protect the mail route. Situated at the north base of Elk Mountain, the new fort lay in the country of the Northern Arapaho, whom the military believed were at peace. When not occupied in constructing the fort that summer, Humfreville served as the post quartermaster at Halleck.[7]

At some time during that fall season, Company A returned to Laramie. But Humfreville apparently was sent to South Pass for the winter of 1862–63, evidently sharing his quarters with Jim Bridger. During this time, his company skirmished with the Shoshone near the deserted St. Mary's stage station. His performance as a non-commissioned officer must have impressed his ranking officers, for on March 19, 1863, five days after the soldier had turned twenty-two years old, Lieutenant Colonel Collins promoted Humfreville to second lieutenant of Company A and ordered him back to Fort Laramie.[8]

He spent much of the next eighteen months stationed at the fort. Here he came in almost daily contact with a group of Sioux known as the Laramie Loafers, who had become dependent on economic assistance from Americans. Not only did they hunt along the emigrant road, beg food from travellers, and live in a village just outside Fort Laramie, but they also provided female companionship to traders and army officers. Old

Smoke, an uncle of Red Cloud, then the acknowledged war leader of the Oglala, was the leader of the village, which consisted primarily of Northern Oglala but included a few Brule. Besides Old Smoke, Humfreville also met and described other Sioux who would become important historical figures. Among these were the Sioux leaders Little Thunder, Spotted Tail, and Old Man Afraid of His Horses, the Oglala chief who, according to Humfreville, regularly addressed him as "son."[9]

In June 1863, Indian Agent John Loree asked the post commander for an escort of troops to deliver the annual annuity to the Sioux. The distribution point, the ranch of James Bordeau, about eight miles southeast of Fort Laramie, was near the site of the Grattan fight in 1854. Erroneously labelled the Grattan Massacre, in reality it was one of the countless examples of American military men combining shocking misjudgment with a contemptuous disrespect for the fighting abilities of Indians. This mixture proved fatal to the Americans, resulting as it did in the death of Grattan's entire party of twenty-nine soldiers and one civilian interpreter—all because one Sioux had taken a cow that he thought emigrants had abandoned along the trail.[10]

Since Lieutenant Colonel Collins had just returned to Ohio to recruit four more companies of cavalry for duty out West, Major Mackay and Lieutenant Humfreville assisted the agent in issuing the annuities, thus earning a reputation among the Sioux as their "friend and benefactor." According to Humfreville, there were ten thousand Indians present. Though he believed that the distribution was fair (evidently based upon the records that he had), in reality many chiefs and leading men were furious because it seemed to them that the agent substituted farm tools for powder and ammunition, and other goods coveted by them. Moreover, it seemed the Indian agent had doled out less than half the goods intended for the Indians. The Sioux believed that corrupt Indian officials were short-changing them, a suspicion that proved to be correct.[11] Over the next year their fears would simmer and fester until they became a contributing cause of the Indian War of 1864–65. The Indians were made distrustful of all Whites. But because of the relationship that Humfreville enjoyed with the Sioux he was one of the few white men they invited to attend their annual Sun Dance (which he remembered as having occurred in September but likely took place in late June or in July of 1863).

On October 10, 1863, Lieutenant Colonel Collins and his son Caspar, now a lieutenant, returned to Fort Laramie with four companies of new recruits from Ohio. In a report about the fort, Collins wrote that his son Caspar, Lieutenant Humfreville and forty-eight soldiers manned "a howitzer battery consisting of four pieces." He remarked: "Their diligence in drill and rapid improvement does great credit to officers and men."[12] The next spring Humfreville was transferred to Company K and that fall he moved to Fort Halleck, where he would spend most of the next year.

Though Lieutenant Colonel Collins continued to treat the Sioux and Northern Cheyenne near Fort Laramie with consideration and respect, south of him, the civil and military authorities in Colorado, having convinced themselves that an Indian war was imminent, pursued a series of misguided policies that left the Southern Cheyenne and Arapaho wondering about their motives. When the Indians boycotted a treaty council in September of 1863, Gov. John Evans assumed the worst, predicting unbridled hostilities for the following spring. It proved to be a self-fulfilling prophecy.

During the spring of 1864, some of the younger warriors committed a few stock raids, while the military in Colorado attacked Indians whenever they encountered them. Governor Evans and Col. John M. Chivington, a former Methodist minister who would become known as Colorado's "Fighting Parson," sent out detachments to seek out Indian villages, an action which the Cheyenne interpreted as an act of war. In July the Cheyenne struck back, attacking stage coaches, torching ranches, and stealing great numbers of stock. The central part of Colorado was now a war zone as the military beefed up patrols and organized campaigns against the Cheyenne. In September, Maj. Gen. Samuel R. Curtis led a force of more than six hundred men from Fort Kearney against the Cheyenne, but the Indians easily eluded the slow-moving army. Humfreville remembers that he "was ordered to Fort Kearney to accompany Major General Curtis on [the] Smoky Hill Campaign." His detachment, however, did not reach Kearney until shortly after Curtis's departure. He apparently remained at the post until the end of Curtis's expedition, when Humfreville's Ohio men returned to Fort Laramie. On November 3, 1864, he received a promotion to Captain of "K" troop. He then moved back to Fort Halleck, where he assumed command of the post.[13]

These hostilities would soon spread from southern and central Colorado to the Indians living near Fort Laramie. On November 29, 1864, Chivington launched an ignominious attack on Black Kettle's Cheyenne village on Sand Creek, killing as many as one hundred and fifty Cheyenne, most of them women and children. Chivington's surprise assault rivalled, and in fact probably exceeded, in barbarity and savagery, any outrage committed by the Plains Indians. Only a month before this time, Black Kettle, usually a peaceful chief, had solicited peace with Americans at Fort Lyon; but the chief had been told to return to his village until the garrison had received instructions from headquarters. Within weeks, the relatives of the slain Cheyenne dispatched runners to the Indian camps in the north. The normally peaceful Brule, as well as the Oglala, and the Northern Cheyenne and Arapaho, eagerly accepted the war pipes. All agreed to join the Cheyenne to avenge this wanton attack.

In early 1865 the allied Sioux, Cheyenne, and Arapaho launched a series of devastating raids against stage stations and ranches, beginning with Julesburg, Colorado. By the end of January the war party, numbering perhaps one thousand men, began to move northwest to unite with the Northern Cheyenne and the northern groups of Oglala, under Red Cloud and Humfreville's friend, Old Man Afraid of His Horses. En route to the rendezvous, on February 6, 1865, they assaulted the telegraph station at Mud Springs in northwest Nebraska, some 105 miles from Fort Laramie. Two days earlier the telegraph operator at the station had telegraphed Fort Laramie that they expected an attack from a large body of Indians who were lurking in the area. Lieutenant Colonel Collins immediately dispatched reinforcements from Fort Mitchell and then marched from Laramie with 120 men, including Humfreville, arriving at Mud Springs two days later. The following day the Indians called off the engagement and headed north. They had wounded seven men, three seriously.

Collins, electing to follow, finally overtook the Indians near the North Platte River. Observing that the Indians outnumbered him ten to one, he wisely circled his wagons and, after an initial hard fight, the engagement quieted into a sniping duel. The Indians continued their march toward the Black Hills, and Collins decided to retire to Fort Laramie. His pursuit had been a show of force, no more than a warning to the Indians. A month later Collins's enlistment period ended. He left Laramie for Omaha, where he was mustered out of service. His departure left a tremendous void in leadership in the southeastern Wyoming posts.[14]

Meanwhile, things were heating up for Captain Humfreville. His superiors ordered him with the remaining Ohio troops to guard the stage and telegraph stations along the Oregon Trail and the Overland Stage Route. Indian raids, which had begun in April, steadily mounted in intensity through July of 1865.[15]

In his narrative Humfreville describes two of his experiences while fighting the Sioux during this period. On April 21, 1865, Indians assaulted the Deer Creek Station. Soon after, Humfreville, with nine hand-chosen men, each armed with "two six-shooting Colt's revolvers . . . a breech loading carbine slung over our shoulders, and sixty rounds of ammunition," were dispatched on a dangerous mission to seek reinforcements from Fort Laramie, 125 miles to the southeast. Along the march his command perceived unmistakable signs of Indians, but no warriors until some ten miles from Fort Laramie. From here his men engaged in a running fight with thirty to forty warriors. Humfreville, believing that any bloodshed "might cost us our lives," ordered his men to aim at the Sioux's horses. As the Indians became bolder, and tried to prevent his force from reaching Laramie, he issued orders to "put all the lead possible into both horses and Indians." They finally reached the fort and delivered the message—but only after a harrowing thirty-two-hour march that left most of the men emotionally and physically incapacitated.

Humfreville returned to Fort Halleck in early May 1865 to assume command of that post. On June 8, one hundred warriors attacked Sage Creek Station, just west of Fort Halleck on the Overland Stage Route. Humfreville explains how the Indians accomplished their objective. According to his account they first laid siege to the station but when they were unable to inflict any damage on the soldiers, they next employed a plan that today would seem straight out of a Hollywood Western. The Indians "fixed lighted rags to their arrows firing them at the station [which] was built of wood." As the fire engulfed the station, the soldiers were forced to flee the buildings to avoid the blaze. Unfortunately for them, the Sioux were waiting, killing every man but two, who escaped to Fort Halleck. Captain Humfreville promptly assembled a force and rushed to the scene, but the Sioux effectively assaulted his party, wounding the captain with an arrow to his knee, "inflicting a severe and permanent injury."

By then the army had concluded that a major campaign against the allied Arapaho, Cheyenne, and Sioux was warranted and necessary, and Brig. Gen. Patrick E. Connor made plans for simultaneous operations along the Powder River to punish those who were hopeful of sanctuary there. This offensive, launched in the late summer of 1865, would become known as General Connor's Powder River Expedition. It was a three-pronged assault into the country of the hostiles. Captain Humfreville served with General Connor's command, which left Fort Laramie on July 30, 1865, guided by Jim Bridger and Pawnee scouts under Frank North. At daybreak on August 29, 1865, they surprised a large village, consisting primarily of Arapaho with a few Cheyenne, near the Tongue River just south of the Montana border. According to Humfreville, Connor assigned to him the responsibility of leading the morning assault, which he carried out with the support of three howitzers. The Indians fled from their village, which the soldiers then occupied. Next, the Pawnee scouts seized most of their horseherd. By the end of the affair Connor's command had killed an estimated thirty-five Indians and captured twenty-one women and children, whom he released to the Arapaho a few days later.[16]

The following spring Humfreville assumed command of Fort Laramie until the War Department ordered him and his regiment to Fort Leavenworth to be mustered out of service. He departed Fort Laramie on

June 14, 1866, as a seasoned veteran of four years along America's Northern Plains. He took with him the remains of Lt. Caspar Collins, the popular son of Lieutenant Colonel Collins. Indians had slain the courageous young lieutenant the previous July in the battle of Platte Bridge. Captain Humfreville and several other officers of the 11th Ohio Volunteer Cavalry accompanied the remains of Caspar Collins to Hillsboro, Ohio. On June 24, 1866, they attended a poignant service for the lieutenant, who was laid to rest at his family's home.[17]

Yet the twenty-five-year-old captain's military career was not over. At the close of the Civil War, Congress passed an act authorizing the organization of Regular Army units manned by African-American solders, better known today as Buffalo Solders, the nickname given them by the Southern Plains Indians. Initially there were to be two regiments of cavalry and four of infantry, but in 1869 the War Department reduced the infantry to two regiments. The Act also mandated that the officers were to be whites who had served at least two years of active field service during the Civil War. In addition, they had to pass a special examination before a board of officers. Aware that he possessed the necessary qualifications, Humfreville applied, passed the test, and received a commission as second lieutenant, 9th Cavalry, on January 29, 1867. Col. Edward Hatch, a Maine native, who had ended the war as a brigadier general in the 2nd Iowa Cavalry, commanded his regiment.[18]

Unfortunately, Humfreville, seemingly on purpose, wrote little about his years with the 9th Cavalry. But we know something of his activities. In March 1867, the army directed Hatch to take his command to Texas. The responsibility assigned to his twelve companies, which Hatch distributed mainly at Fort Davis and Fort Stockton, was to protect the mail and stage route between San Antonio and El Paso. On May 10, 1867, Colonel Hatch appointed Humfreville the regimental quartermaster, an important staff position that precluded him from taking part in many patrols or campaigns. His post would be at Fort Stockton, where he would remain until early 1870. Though his frontier duty was along the western range of the Mescalero Apache, and in the middle of the Comanche and Kiowa raiding routes into Texas and Mexico, he apparently did not see much of these Indians, unless they came into the post on peaceful visits. On May 30, 1870, he was relieved of his quartermaster duties and returned to his company for regular duty.

After spending most of 1870 at Fort Davis in western Texas, Humfreville, who had been promoted to captain the previous May 31, requested a leave of absence on December 14, 1870, for "60 days with permission to apply for an additional 90 days." His father had passed away, and he needed to return to Ohio to settle his estate. Hatch endorsed the request, noting that "Captain Humfreville has been nearly four years on the frontier without being absent from his command. It is important for himself and family to be allowed to leave." The War Department granted his request and from mid-April 1871 through August 31, 1871, Humfreville was absent on leave. He returned to his regiment at Fort Quitman in September 1871.

In 1872–1873 he was active in patrols against the Southern Plains tribes, primarily the Kiowa and the Comanche. In August 1872 he left Fort Clark with his Company K as escort for a surveying party in south-western Texas. Toward the end of his stint with the surveying party, which lasted until January 1873, Humfreville inexplicably left his command and was absent without permission for more than a week. He also disciplined several of his troopers in such an abusive manner that his superiors filed charges against him. On December 4, 1873, he was "arraigned and tried before a general court martial convened at San Antonio."

Lt. Col. William R. Shafter was the President of the Court, which heard the three charges brought against Humfreville. They were: "First, Conduct prejudicial to good order and military discipline; second, drunkenness on duty; third, conduct unbecoming an officer and a gentleman." The court found him guilty on the first and third charges. It ruled that he had left his command for ten days without leave and that he had "signed and forwarded two false reports." The third count cited several examples of "cruel treatment" of seven African-American soldiers under his command. It found that Humfreville had struck one man "over the head with a carbine" when the soldier was in a "defenseless position" and punched another man "several times with his fist and once with a revolver or a club." On April 3, 1874, the Adjutant General's office announced the verdict of his court martial, and Humfreville was discharged from service.[19]

In late 1874, Humfreville hired a Washington lawyer, George W. Paschal, to review the court's findings. On January 25, 1875, Paschal sent his report, "Remarks upon the Evidence in the case of Captain J. Lee Humfreville," to Joseph Holt, the Judge Advocate General. He requested that the army reinstate his client to his former command. Paschal sought to discredit the testimony of his client's chief accuser, 2nd Lt. Daniel Hezekiah Floyd, a West Point graduate in the class of 1866. His principal argument was that the court had found Humfreville not guilty of the charge of "Drunkenness on duty." Since Floyd was the only witness to have made the accusation of drunkenness, Paschal argued, that judgment must have discredited all his testimony. How could the court accept his testimony on the other two counts? If anything, declared Paschal, Captain Humfreville was guilty of "too great a zeal in the discharge of [his] duties."

The Secretary of War, William Worth Belknap, after discussing the case with President Grant, informed Paschal that the verdict in the case of his client's court martial would stand.[20]

Throughout the 1870s, Humfreville made energetic efforts to rejoin the military but each time, despite the endorsements of several prominent military and civil officials, including Col. Edward Hatch, his petition was rejected. In 1881, Humfreville hired another lawyer to review his court martial. His attorney discovered that the ruling had never become official because the order for Humfreville's "general court martial was not at that time laid before the President," then Ulysses S. Grant. Because of this oversight, on February 7, 1881, Pres. Rutherford B. Hayes revoked the verdict of the court martial, noting that Humfreville should be considered voluntarily resigned from service, effective April 3, 1874, which is what his official military record shows to this day.[21]

This disgrace may be the overriding reason why Humfreville in his narrative neglected to mention much of his service in Texas with the 9th Cavalry. Despite the repeal of the initial judgment, he did not wish to call attention to a period in his life that was both embarrassing and humiliating. His misconduct, if such it was, was evidently a one-time mistake, but it was a blunder that haunted him for the rest of his life. The court martial certainly sullied a reputation built over the previous thirteen years, one that presented him as an honorable man. His lawyer noted that Humfreville had not had one complaint "against his integrity, his propriety, and his gentlemanly manner. In every relation he had won the character of a patriot, an honest man and a faithful soldier."[22]

Most historians have discounted Humfreville's book as an important primary source of information about the Northern Plains Indians in Colorado and Wyoming. Perhaps one reason they disregard his work is the lack of specific dates in his narrative, which makes a researcher's task more daunting and brings the writer's credibility into question. Humfreville's sometimes slanted views and occasional incorrect assumptions and statements are definitely additional factors that have caused writers to view his book with a jaundiced eye. Yet, the historical record suggests that he did play a consequential role in the events that he describes. And there is no convincing reason to doubt or question the validity of his interesting anecdotes, insightful vignettes of prominent Indians and Whites, and his observations about Indian culture and military life on the frontier.

Humfreville forged important friendships with several Sioux chiefs, including two of the most important Oglala leaders of the 1850s and early 1860s: Old Smoke, and Old Man Afraid of His Horses (whom he referred to as a Miniconjou). The Oglala referred to the latter, their beloved chief, as "Our Brave Man." Humfreville, as before noted, claimed that his relationship with Old Man Afraid of His Horses was so close that the warrior called him "son." Some of the most interesting chapters and anecdotes in this volume were a result of this friendship. One evening the two men discussed the possibility of life on the moon. The chief explained that he had heard that the moon contained rivers and mountains. If so, the chief thought, "there must be white men there." Humfreville was surprised at the Sioux's explanation: "Where there are rivers and mountains there must be beavers and otters, and where there are beavers and otters white men surely go." Humfreville agreed that it was a logical conclusion. The Oglala leader even explained to him how he received his colorful name, which agrees with the impressions of many historians (though one, George Hyde, suggests it was simply a family name that dated from the mid-eighteenth century).[23]

It was probably his relationship with Old Man Afraid of His Horses that made it possible for Humfreville to witness the annual Sun Dance (held by the Sioux nearly every summer) in July 1863 near Fort Laramie. Humfreville was so impressed by the spectacle that he described the ceremony in detail, devoting some nine pages to the last four days of the twelve-day occasion. In many cases those men who underwent this excruciating ritual through torture were sacrificing in order to benefit others. The participant frequently would have a vision that would guide or influence his behavior in the future. Although Humfreville may not have realized the cultural and religious significance of the practice, his version accords in many ways with ethnological accounts of the early twentieth century.[24]

Shortly before Humfreville left Fort Laramie for the east, Old Man Afraid of His Horses honored the captain with a dog feast, although he likely meant a "puppy" feast, as the Sioux much prefer the tender meat of the young canine. At about this time, Humfreville also experienced a most moving and heartfelt moment when he witnessed the Brule leader Spotted Tail conveying the body of his daughter to Fort Laramie for interment. His description of this event is consistent with other published accounts.

This volume also contains descriptions of important Americans, among them the legendary frontiersman and mountain man, Jim Bridger. Noted historian Stanley Vestal found Humfreville's book an important source for his biography of Bridger.[25] Another featured personality, Lt. Caspar Collins, the aforementioned son of Humfreville's Ohio Cavalry commander, died in an heroic (perhaps "suicidal" is a more appropriate word), charge against a huge war party of Sioux, Cheyenne, and Arapaho warriors (one of the leaders was Old Man Afraid of His Horses.) in July 1865. Humfreville's characterization of Lieutenant Collins's courage, "brave to a rashness," was right on the mark. His assertion, however, that young Collins "allowed the wily savages to out general him" was patently unfair. Collins had willingly taken the command of a mission that several senior officers had refused to carry out. He knew that his chances of returning alive were slim. Yet he unflinchingly accepted the assignment and honorably performed his duty against impossible odds. Inevitably, the horde of warriors overwhelmed his party, killing the young lieutenant (last seen with an arrow embedded in his forehead with blood streaming down his face) and several other men.[26]

In addition to its accounts of interesting individuals, this book furnishes insight into several other topics.

Humfreville's reasoned explanation of Indian sign language and its usefulness to the Plains Indians is invaluable. After all, each of the allied tribes of the Northern Plains (the Sioux, Northern Cheyenne, and Northern Arapaho) and each of those of the Southern Plains (Southern Cheyenne, Southern Arapaho, Comanche, Kiowa, and Kiowa-Apache) spoke different languages. Humfreville explains "that the sign language enabled each nation of Indians to converse with one another intelligently." In fact, as he points out, it was a most efficient means of communication. An Indian using sign language could "express a great deal more in a shorter time than by word of mouth." Yet, Humfreville suggests that it could be a demanding task, "for the wrong interpretation of a single sign was sufficient to break the whole chain of thought."

His observations regarding the Indian and his mode of warfare are also important. He clearly admired the Indian's fighting ability and courage, which "cannot be disputed." In combat, warriors fought with the "ferocity of a tiger." Unlike what we see in those battles depicted by Hollywood, the Indian would strip to his breechcloth generally wearing nothing that might be an "encumbrance while fighting." Only a few "distinguished" warriors or chiefs wore a war bonnet in a fight, but even "this was rare." His narrative further debunks the "modern literature" of the nineteenth century which suggests that Indians were expert marksman, regarding this as a "romantic delusion." His explanation makes perfect sense, for Indians lacked the ammunition for target practice ("absolutely necessary to make a fine marksman"). He did allow that by the 1870s they had "begun to make progress in the use of modern arms."

Perhaps the one feature of Indian warfare that Humfreville most respected was the skill of the warriors in "seizing and carrying off a wounded comrade from the field of battle to safety." He correctly noted that troops rarely captured a wounded Indian, and he could have added that Indians rarely left a wounded or dead comrade where he fell. In fact, a warrior would take enormous risk to retrieve a fallen friend and give the body a proper burial to ensure that it did not fall into the hands of their enemies.

This volume also contains detailed information on such other important Indian customs as birth, child raising, the bond between parents and
child, marriage ceremonies, infidelity, torture, death, and burial practices.
Humfreville also examines the Indians' ability to adapt to their environment, citing the ingenuity and creativity that produced such noteworthy
features of Indian life as the teepee, snowshoes, and canoes.

In addition to the Captain's particular discussions of military strategy
and tactics and the necessity of cavalry rather than infantry against nomadic Indians, this narrative contains an assessment of the army's large
role in the trans-Mississippi West. Humfreville, who had risen in the ranks
from private to captain, made an observation that today seems clairvoyant
if not prophetic. Americans, he believed, because of their "high sense of
duty . . . can be taken from almost any walk in civilized life and made into
the best soldier, in the shortest time, of any man in the world." He also
stressed the importance of soldiers learning how to cook well and to follow
a nourishing diet. When it is otherwise, he declares, "disease is sure to follow," and able-bodied men are forced to care for the sick, which reduces
the effective fighting force. Finally (conveniently neglecting to mention his
court martial), he praised both soldiers and officers for respecting each
other and performing their duty. Unlike the armies of Europe, in which
officers held their rank because of "noble lineage, social caste, or wealth,"
most of America's forces were led by military commanders who had earned
their rank through performance on the job.

The principal historic value of this book is to be found in Humfreville's experiences with the Southern tribes of the Lakota Sioux, Northern
Cheyenne, and Northern Arapaho. He also met the tribes of the Rocky
Mountains, the Utes, and Shoshone, the southern Plains Indians, Comanche, Kiowa, Kiowa-Apache, Southern Cheyenne, and Southern Arapaho, and allies of American troops such as the Pawnee and Crow. Yet his
account suffers when he discusses other American Indian groups with
whom he never actually came into contact, such as the Apache tribes of
the Southwest, the Indians of California, and those of the Pacific Northwest. In these impressions we must assume that Humfreville relied upon
other published sources, which, in the 1890s, tended to be somewhat unreliable. It should be pointed out that at the time Humfreville produced
this narrative anthropologists had not had the opportunity to study, much
less to understand, the cultures of many Indians tribes who had resisted
American expansionism though the late nineteenth century.

Besides Humfreville's ethnocentric views, which many will find regret-
table, this book contains various errors and flaws, some based on obvious
misconceptions and some disclosed as research and information became
known only after the publication of this narrative.

Some of his errors are simple mistakes. He incorrectly states that the Zuni and Mohave were of Athapaskan stock (page 135). Zunis were unique in that they had their own language (Zunian) and Mohaves were of the Yuman linguistic family. In another chapter, page 235, he erroneously states that the Kiowa were members of the Shoshone nation, and on page 255, he calls the Navajos "Cliff Dwellers," a term usually applied to the Pueblo Indians. On page 236, he refers to Santanta [Satanta] and Big Tree as Comanche, when in fact both men were Kiowa leaders. He also has confused the Uncpapa [Hunkpapa] with either the Brule or Oglala when he states, on page 268, that the Uncpapa travelled great distances to fight the Pawnee. On page 287 his discussion of the first battle between Nez Perce Indians and American soldiers at White Bird Canyon is confusing and garbled. Published sources in the twentieth century, relying upon Nez Perce accounts, clearly reveal that an American scout fired the first shot in the battle that led to the Nez Perce War of 1877.

Other, more significant errors occur on page 151 when he declares that the Dog Soldiers, a Sioux society, was the "only society of any kind among the wild Indians in those days." In this case he was wrong on two counts: First, the Dog Soldiers were a military society of the Cheyenne, not the Sioux, though Humfreville may have reached this conclusion because some Sioux did intermarry with the Cheyenne Dog Soldiers; second, almost every Plains Indian tribe consisted of civil and military societies.

One of the more glaring errors occurs in his discussion of the Chiricahua Apache leader Mangas Coloradas (page 195–196). Humfreville declared that Mangas "frequently led the allied bands of Comanches, Apaches, and Kiowas on the path of plunder and pillage. It was he who commanded the Indians in their attack on Fort Lancaster." To begin with, the Chiricahua Apache were not allies of either the Kiowa or the Comanche during the lifetime of Mangas Coloradas. Moreover, Mangas Coloradas never led an attack against Fort Lancaster in Texas.

Humfreville also adopted the late nineteenth century view of many American civil and military officials that lessened Sitting Bull's importance among the Sioux. He incorrectly declares that Sitting Bull was not present at Custer's defeat on the Little Big Horn, and mixed up the roles of Gall and Sitting Bull, ostensibly based on information given him by Rain-in-the-Face, whom Humfreville met in the 1880s.

Finally, the most egregious statement, one that proves Humfreville's disdain of Indians was his belief that Indians were incapable of undying loyalty to their homelands. On page 47, he suggests that the notion that "wild Indians were fighting for their homes . . . belongs to fiction rather than to fact." Of course, in the literal sense, Indians were not fighting for their homes, because most of them did not have fixed residences. Yet—and this is an important distinction not recognized by the author—they were fighting for their country and for their land. There are countless examples of this attitude during Humfreville's lifetime. In fact, nearly every Indian War in America's history occurred because Indians were determined to preserve their homeland. It would be impossible in this space to mention every occasion. But a few instances that Humfreville certainly knew about could be cited. The Sioux War of 1876–77 took place because the Indians, led by Crazy Horse and Sitting Bull, refused to sell the Black Hills and settle upon reservations. The Nez Perce War of 1877 came about when the government insisted that the Nez Perce relocate from their traditional homes to another reservation. Their leader, Joseph, did not want to abandon the country in which his father had lived and his bones were buried. Victorio, the Chiricahua Apache patriot leader of the Chihenne band, battled American and Mexican troops from 1879–1880 because Indian officials removed him from his beloved ancestral grounds at Ojo Caliente in south-central New Mexico to the dreaded San Carlos Reservation in Arizona. After a short and miserable stay there, he returned to his homeland in New Mexico, vowing to die rather than return to San Carlos. Fate would honor his wishes.

Humfreville's chapters on individual Indian tribes are sometimes subjective and uninformed. He failed to appreciate the culture of each tribe as something unique and admirable. He failed to recognize that each tribe's society had a defined sense of values and mores (love of life, family, and home) that in many ways was not all that different from the values important in his Anglo-Saxon upbringing. For example, he liked and respected the Cheyenne, "a brave and intelligent people . . . the finest specimen of wild men in the world." Yet he found their allies, the Arapaho, to be "dirty and poverty stricken, shiftless and lazy." As far as he was concerned perhaps the only Indians lower in stature than the Arapaho were the Apache, whose culture was an example of "all that was bad" and the Shoshone, who excelled in "nothing but vice." He respected the Kiowa, who were responsible for more deaths "per capita than any other tribe" and were "experts in sign language and trailing." He also discussed the pernicious consequences that smallpox had on many Indian tribes, especially the Blackfoot and Mandan Indians.

Despite his obvious contempt for the Indian way of life before subjugation of the tribes, Humfreville clearly believed the Indians were better off in their "aboriginal condition" when they were "free and independent." Then they were "their own masters, while at present they are almost entirely under the supervision of the United States Government." Indian agents and reservations had reduced them to "miserable specimens of humanity, with hardly enough to eat, not enough clothing to cover their bodies, and with inadequate means of shelter."

After Humfreville left the army he moved to New York and worked as a broker selling stocks and bonds. In 1881, he applied to have his first name changed from Jacob to James, preferring the latter because of its "Christian name." In late 1893, he apparently had a mild stroke that left him paralyzed on his left side. By this time he was also suffering from diabetes and chronic diarrhea. From this time forward he lived in New York City, where the family of Emma Hunter cared for him. He died in New York City on New Year's Eve, December 31, 1916.

In 1946, one reputable historian, Stanley Vestal, had this assessment of Humfreville's *Twenty Years Among Our Hostile Indians*: "Now Humfreville had a flair for romantic—not to say sensational—yarns, but apparently based his stories upon actual stories."[27] The *New York Times*, though troubled by Humfreville's lack of empathy with Indians ("the author has no trace of liking his once savage foe"), praised the book for its "graphically described" coverage of "noted encounters between troops and Indians." It also pointed out that the two hundred or so photos "are of unusual interest."[28] Today this book, scarce and out of print for many years, has been accessible only to serious collectors willing to pay a hefty price. Thus this new printing, as part of Stackpole's "Frontier Classic" series, makes this book available to new readers to enjoy for the first time in a century.[29]

NOTES

1. National Archives (cited hereafter as NA), Jacob (James) L. Humfreville ACP file; Pension File, number 1157743; Agnes Wright Spring, *Caspar Collins*, (Lincoln: University of Nebraska Press, Bison Books, 1969), 31–32, 36–37.
2. NA, Humfreville ACP file; Spring, *Caspar Collins*, 32–33, 36.
3. James L. Humfreville, *Twenty Years Among Our Hostile Indians* (New York: Hunter & Co., 1899), 84.
4. Remi Nadeau, *Fort Laramie and the Sioux* (Lincon: University of Nebraska Press, 1967), 148–49; Spring, *Caspar Collins*, 109.
5. Spring, *Caspar Collins*, 115–16, 118–19,
6. Robert M. Utley, *Frontiersmen in Blue: The United States Army and the Indian, 1848–1865* (Lincoln: University of Nebraska Press, 1967), 281.
7. NA, Humfreville ACP File; Spring, *Caspar Collins*, 42–43.
8. NA, Humfreville ACP File.

9. Ibid.; George E. Hyde, *Red Cloud's Folk: A History of the Oglala Sioux* (Norman: University of Oklahoma Press, fourth printing, 1976), 86–87.

10. Hyde, *Red Cloud's Folk*, 72–77.

11. Nadeau, *Fort Laramie and the Sioux*, 162–53.

12. Spring, *Caspar Collins*, 30–31, 146.

13. NA, Humfreville's ACP files; Utley, *Frontiersmen in Blue*, 284–89.

14. Spring, *Caspar Collins*, 61–63; Hyde, *Red Cloud's Folk*, 112.

15. Utley, *Frontiersmen in Blue*, 319.

16. Utley, *Frontiersmen in Blue*, 325–26; Virginia Cole Trenholm, *The Arapahoes, Our People* (Norman: University of Oklahoma Press, 1970), 207–08; George Bird Grinnell, *The Fighting Cheyennes* (Norman: University of Oklahoma Press, fifth Printing, 1971), 205–07.

17. Spring, *Caspar Collins*, 97–99.

18. William H. Leckie, *The Buffalo Soldiers* (Norman: University of Oklahoma Press, 1067), 5–9; NA, Humfreville ACP File.

19. NA, Humfreville ACP file.

20. Ibid.

21. Ibid. For example, Francis B. Heitman, *Historical Register and Dictionary of the United States Army* (Urbana: University of Illinois Press, 1967), 544, has Humfreville resigning April 3, 1874.

22. NA, Humfreville ACP file.

23. Hyde, *Red Cloud's Folk*, 68.

24. Royal B. Hassrick, *The Sioux: Life and Customs of a Warrior Society* (Norman: University of Oklahoma Press, eighth printing, 1989), 281–288.

25. Stanley Vestal, *Jim Bridger: Mountain Man* (Lincoln: University of Nebraska Press, 1972), 215–16.

26. Spring, *Caspar Collins*, 86–89.

27. Vestal, *Jim Bridger*, 215–16.

28. *New York Times*, December 15, 1900.

29. I would like to express my gratitude to Scott Forsythe and Sue Mc-Donough of the National Archives for providing Humfreville's pension records, and Dr. William (Bill) Betts of Indiana, Pennsylvania, for kindly reviewing my efforts and making many important suggestions that have enhanced the final product.

TO THE READER.

As this is the last book that can ever be written from actual personal experience and contact, on these, the greatest and most interesting of all savages in their wild state, and also realizing that wild Indian life in all its phases is fast disappearing, THE PUBLISHERS *have gone to great expense and labor to secure for this volume the choicest photographs obtainable of Indians and their belongings, as well as their primitive customs, thus making the book of great historical pictorial interest.*

Tree and scaffold graves no longer exist, and the buffalo skin-covered lodges are no more; even Indians in native dress are rare, and they will soon be curiosities, as the following extract from a letter speaks for itself:

> DEPARTMENT OF THE INTERIOR,
> OFFICE OF INDIAN AFFAIRS,
> WASHINGTON, July 31, 1902.

CAPTAIN J. LEE HUMFREVILLE,
      New York:

SIR: The Office has, from time to time, issued general instructions to the agents and superintendents in charge of the Indians, admonishing them to use their best efforts in persuading the Indians to abandon their savage dress and customs and to follow the best customs of the white people. On quite a number of the reservations, the Indians dress entirely in citizens' clothing; on other reservations the Indians appear to be backward in adopting the customs of the whites. Generally those Indians who have lived in contact with white people for a number of years are further advanced in civilization, and do more towards their own support than the Indians on the more isolated reservations.

Very respectfully,
      A. C. TONNER,
          Acting Commissioner.

AUTHOR'S PREFACE.

APACHE BOY.

OF the small number of white men who were on the Great Plains, or in the mountains of the Far West many years ago, when each nation of Indians in its primeval state occupied its own territory or hunting ground, very few are left who knew the Indian in his absolutely wild condition; and as none of them have described him in his untutored state, as he actually lived in his original home, I have ventured to give in this volume some of my experiences among the many nations and tribes with which I came in contact— sometimes in friendly intercourse, often in deadly strife. These experiences covered a period of twenty years immediately preceding the time when civilization had begun to exercise an influence over their manners and customs; during this time I knew the Indian intimately, saw Indian life in all its phases, and had abundant opportunity to study Indian character thoroughly and exhaustively.

My twenty years of life among the Indians, beginning forty years ago, embraced the entire territory from the Saskatchewan River in British America, south to the central portion of Mexico, and from the Mississippi and Sioux Rivers west to the Pacific Ocean, which area covers, as the reader knows, a large portion of our country's vast domain. It was then, except to the Indians who roamed over its far-stretching prairies and followed the windings of its rivers and streams, or climbed its mountain heights in quest of game, almost *terra incognita*.

It seems to me, therefore, that in describing the characteristics, habits, customs, traits, religion and mode of life of a race of people of whose original condition comparatively little is now known beyond vague traditions, fragmentary descriptions, and more frequently untrustworthy or misleading reports, that I might interest at least a portion of the present generation, as well as those to follow, in portraying the inner life, as it then existed of a savage people who, practically, have now disappeared forever.

In this work I shall endeavor to give an accurate account of the daily life of the wild Indians, as I knew them in their natural state. I have often been impressed with the fact that, both in their character and manner of life, they have been grossly misrepresented by modern writers, many of whom evidently depended upon vivid imaginations to furnish what personal experience and knowledge could not supply. The Indian as a wild man lived in a state of nature and followed his natural impulses. He neither dwelt on the past nor anticipated the future. He lived solely in the present, and his life and actions were controlled by the primeval laws of necessity. Before coming in contact with the white man he had neither the virtues nor the vices of civilization. After coming in contact with white traders and others, he had all the vices of civilization but none of its virtues. The first thing he learned from his civilized brother was his vices; these he acquired and retained with wonderful proficiency and tenacity, and instead of improving degenerated.

In the following chapters I shall describe the Indian as he was, when I first knew him, at which time he was absolutely a wild man. I shall endeavor to give a truthful account of what came under my personal experience and observation. It will be my aim to state the truth impartially, and nothing but the truth, to portray the Indian of fact, and not the Indian of fiction. If my experience and views are at variance with preconceived ideas of wild Indian life and character, my readers may rest assured that I am testifying to what I have seen or of which I have personal knowledge, unless otherwise stated.

If I assert that I know as much of Indian life and character as any man now living, the reader may reasonably ask upon what I base so pretentious a claim. My answer is simple. During my experience with the many nations and tribes with which the duties of army life threw me in contact, I was generally protected by troops or other armed bodies of sufficient strength to enable me to enter Indian camps and there observe the inner life and study the character of the Red Man in comparative safety.

Some apparent repetitions may be noticed in the text; but the reader must not forget that while the customs, characteristics, religious belief, and personal traits of the Indian nations and tribes were nearly identical in **many** respects, yet some of them differed in a variety of interesting ways. Hence in portraying the everyday life of so many nations and tribes, I could not avoid at times a certain sameness of ideas and expression, which, however, is more apparent than real. I have also briefly described some noted Indian massacres and battles, because they illustrate certain phases of Indian character better than they could be shown in any other way.

The reader will observe that I use the words nations and tribes frequently, and in a very distinctive manner. This I do for the following reason: I class as nations all those Indians who *spoke a language of their own;* and as tribes, those bodies that formed only a *part of a nation.* A *band* of Indians, as they were known on the frontier, was a party or body composed of allied nations or tribes, which might, or might not, speak different languages or dialects. They banded together for specific purposes, and when these were accomplished they separated, each nation or tribe returning to its own hunting ground or territory.

It was my original purpose to confine this volume to a description of the wild Indians as I knew them, and the animals upon which they depended for subsistence, as well as those they killed for pelts for barter with white traders; these animals at that time roamed over the plains and mountains in countless numbers, but like their pursuers have almost entirely disappeared.

There were other phases of life in the almost pathless West at the time I was there, which deserve mention. These were the Pony Express, Overland Stage and Fur Companies, all of which are things of the past. I have given a brief description of them, as well as an account of a few famous mountaineers, trappers, and guides, who spent their lives among the savages. They were at that time as much a part of the Wild West as the Indians themselves, and it was they who paved the way for civilization as it trended westward, at the imminent peril of their own lives.

J. Lee Humfreville

CONTENTS.

CHAPTER I.

THE PATHLESS WEST OF YEARS AGO—THE NATURAL HOME OF OUR SAVAGE
INDIANS—ROVERS AND FIGHTERS.

PAGE

The Natural Home of the Indians—Their Numbers when I first knew them—Their
Superstition against being counted—Keeping a Roster of their Fighting Men—
The Terrible Scourge of Small-pox—Indian Dread of this Disease—Leaving the
Afflicted to Suffer and Die—An Imposing Body of Warriors—A Treacherous and
Vicious Lot—Visiting the Great Father at Washington—Stories told by them on
their Return—Starting a War Party..................................... 45

CHAPTER II.

THE COURAGE AND FIGHTING QUALITIES OF THE WILD INDIANS—FOES THAT
ASKED AND GAVE NO QUARTER.

Going into Battle—How the Indians Planned a Massacre—Methods of Surprising
their Enemies—How we Defended Ourselves against Sudden Attacks—Description of a Real Battle with Indians—Hardships of an Indian Campaign—Indian
Courage and Ferocity in Battle—Personal Experiences—How we Felt in an Indian Battle—Nerved to Desperation—Mounted Indian Warriors—Their Personal Appearance and Peculiar Fighting Tactics—Fight to the Death—Giving
and Asking no Quarter—Pursuing the Indians—Indian Wiles and Treachery
—A Lurking Foe—Indian War Horses—How the Indians Scalped their Enemies
on the Battlefield—Burial of the Bodies of Troopers—Burial of Indians who
Fell in Battle—Mourning for the Slain—The Safest Place after a Massacre...... 50

CHAPTER III.

THE INDIAN'S MENTAL FACULTIES—HIS PERFECT PHYSICAL SENSES AND
BLUNTED MORAL NATURE—HIS GREAT CRUELTY—
SCALPS AND SCALPING.

The Indian's Preternatural Cunning and Stunted Intelligence—His Highly Developed Physical Senses—His Perfect Vision and Acute Hearing—Vanishing like
an Apparition—His Keenness in following a Trail—His Untiring Patience—His
Intractable Nature—His Instinctive Cruelty—His Suspicious and Distrustful

CHAPTER IV.

INDIAN SMOKES AND SMOKERS—QUEER CUSTOMS AND SUPERSTITIONS—
HOW ANIMALS WERE AFFECTED BY THE UN-
SEEN PRESENCE OF INDIANS.

CHAPTER V.

INDIAN INQUISITIVENESS AND CUNNING—CRUEL TREATMENT OF PRISON-
ERS—THE FATE OF WHITE CAPTIVE WOMEN.

CHAPTER VI.

THE INDIANS' STRANGE IDEAS OF THE HEAVENS—INDIAN CAMPS—SIGNIFI-
CANCE OF SIGNS—WONDERFUL SKILL IN TRAILING—
THE INDIAN AS A PLAINSMAN.

CHAPTER VII.

HOW INDIANS COOKED AND ATE—THEIR LOVE OF FINERY AND PERSONAL ADORNMENT—PAINTING THEIR FACES AND BODIES— MAKING A WILL— PLAINSCRAFT.

CHAPTER VIII.

INDIAN WOOING AND MARRIAGE CUSTOMS—BIRTH OF AN INDIAN BABY— INDIAN WIDOWS AND WIDOWHOOD—NIGHT IN AN INDIAN LODGE.

CHAPTER IX.

INDIAN AMUSEMENTS AND PASTIMES—THEIR THIRST FOR GAMBLING— THEIR GAMES OF SKILL AND CHANCE—EXPERTNESS IN THROWING A KNIFE.

CHAPTER XVII.

STILL AMONG THE SIOUX—THE MANDANS—INDIAN FREE MASONS—THE ASSINIBOINS—THE GROS VENTRES, OR THE BIG BELLIES, CUISSES BRULES OR BURNT THIGHS.

CHAPTER XVIII.

THE COMANCHES—FIERCE TRIBES OF THE SHOSHONEE NATION—GUARDING AGAINST AMBUSH AND SURPRISE—THRILLING INCIDENTS.

CHAPTER XIX.

THE COMANCHES CONTINUED—PUNISHMENT INFLICTED ON THEIR WOMEN— STEALING CONSIDERED A FINE ART.

CHAPTER XXX.

THE DIRTY AND POVERTY-STRICKEN ARAPAHOES—A SHIFTLESS AND LAZY PEOPLE—HOW THEY LIVED—BEGGARS, MENIALS, AND THIEVES.

CHAPTER XXXI.

CLIFF DWELLERS—THE NAVAJOES AND THEIR COUNTRY—THE TONKAWAYS —THEIR WARS AND WANDERINGS—CANNIBALISM AMONG THE INDIANS.

CHAPTER XXXII.

THE PUEBLOS AND ZUNIS—HIDEOUSLY UGLY GODS AND IDOLS—CUSTOMS OF A STRANGE PEOPLE.

CHAPTER XXXVII.

THE COLUMBIAN GROUP—THE STORY OF AN INDIAN QUEST FOR THE WHITE MAN'S BIBLE—INDIAN ATROCITIES.

CHAPTER XXXVIII.

THE GREAT INDIAN NATIONS.

CHAPTER XXXIX.

THE SUN DANCE OF THE SIOUX—THE GREATEST OF ALL INDIAN CEREMONIES—SELF-INFLICTED WOUNDS AND AGONIZING TORTURE—A TERRIBLE ORDEAL.

CHAPTER LIII.

WILD ANIMALS AND REPTILES OF THE PLAINS AND MOUNTAINS—THE DEADLY RATTLESNAKE AND ITS HABITS—FUR-BEARING ANIMALS AND THEIR WAYS.

CHAPTER LIV.

BEARS AND THEIR WAYS—ADVENTURES WITH GRIZZLIES—AN EXCITING FIGHT AND A RACE FOR LIFE.

CHAPTER LV.

JIM BRIDGER, FAMOUS SCOUT, GUIDE, FRONTIERSMAN, AND INDIAN FIGHTER —PERSONAL EXPERIENCES WITH HIM.

CHAPTER LVI.

A FAMOUS FRONTIERSMAN, TRAPPER, SCOUT AND GUIDE—A WHITE MAN WHO HAD A SNAKE WOMAN AND LIVED THE INDIAN LIFE MANY YEARS—HIS ADVENTURES AND EXPLOITS.

LIST OF ILLUSTRATIONS.

TWENTY YEARS AMONG OUR HOSTILE INDIANS.

CHAPTER I.

THE PATHLESS WEST OF YEARS AGO—THE NATURAL HOME OF OUR SAVAGE INDIANS—ROVERS AND FIGHTERS.

The Natural Home of the Indians—Their Numbers when I first knew them—Their Superstition against being counted—Keeping a Roster of their Fighting Men— The Terrible Scourge of Small-pox—Indian Dread of this Disease—Leaving the Afflicted to Suffer and Die—An Imposing Body of Warriors—A Treacherous and Vicious Lot—Visiting the Great Father at Washington—Stories told by them on their Return—Starting a War Party.

THE majority of people to-day little realize that only a few years ago that tract of country lying west of the Mississippi and Missouri Rivers and the Sioux River from its mouth to its source, north into the British possessions, as far west as the Pacific Ocean, and as far south as the central portion of Mexico, was a trackless waste, but little known to the white man, and inhabited by various nations and tribes of savage Indians, who lived almost exclusively by the chase.

When I first went to this wild country the Indian population was almost entirely confined within the boundaries I have described. There were living there at that time, as nearly as could be estimated, between three hundred and fifty thousand and four hundred thousand Indians. These estimates were based solely on information that came from traders, trappers, and chiefs of friendly nations, of which there were only a few. This information was of course, vague, but I have little doubt of its approximate correctness. The Indians had a superstition against being counted, and as white men were seldom permitted to enter their camps, no accurate computation of their numbers could be made. Each chief, however, kept himself informed as to the number of warriors in his tribe upon whom he could rely should occasion arise to go on the war-path. Horses and mules, too, were important factors, and the chiefs carried the number of them in their memories with the same accuracy that they kept a roster of their fighting men.

In their aboriginal condition each tribe occupied its own hunting ground, and was, so to speak, a free and independent sovereignty. The remnants of these once powerful peoples are now kept on "Indian Reservations," there literally cabined, cribbed and confined. Formerly they were their

JUMPING DOG—OGALALA SIOUX.

own masters, while at present they are almost entirely under the supervision of the United States Government. Then they had arms, horses and mules, and hunted and lived on the choicest game. To-day they have no arms, no horses, no mules, and subsist on rations doled out to them with niggardly hand by government agents. They have become what they are in many portions of the country where they have been partly civilized, or an effort made to civilize them, namely, miserable specimens of humanity, with hardly enough to eat, not enough clothing to cover their bodies, and with inadequate means of shelter. The Indian population has been greatly reduced during the past forty years. There have been various causes for this reduction, the principal being small-pox and warfare among themselves. It is a well-authenticated fact that this dread disease is responsible for more deaths among our wild Indians than any other cause. When this scourge once got into an Indian camp it played havoc among the occupants, those who were well fleeing and leaving the afflicted to suffer and die. The appearance of small-pox would not unreasonably throw any tribe into the utmost consternation; as they had no means of combating it the disease was generally fatal.

Our wild Indians had no idea of the ownership of land, either individually or collectively. Like most nomadic people they roamed within a certain territory, ill-defined in most instances, which they regarded as the exclusive hunting ground of their nation or tribe. As they did not till the soil they placed no value on any particular spot or locality, save for the game it afforded for the time being. With the advent of the whites they gradually realized that the lands they claimed as their hunting grounds had a value of which they had never dreamed. The white man was anxious to secure what the Indians considered a small portion of their land to settle on, and would pay for it in money or valuables. They accordingly bartered away their lands on the best terms and conditions they could obtain, which were usually any offer that the white man chose to make.

The idea propagated by some modern sentimentalists that in resisting the march of civilization, the wild Indians were fighting for their homes and firesides, belongs to fiction rather than to fact. In the first place they had no home and no fireside, in the civilized sense of these terms. They had no regard whatever for home as a locality and no conception of a fireside as we understand the term. Their home was wherever they could secure food, and when roaming over the prairies and mountains, or hunting game, fear alone kept them on their own territory. They had no conception of either individual or common rights, outside of their own nation or tribe. There have been many instances where one tribe or nation appropriated the hunting ground of another, driving the weaker people from their territory, and adding the seized tract of land to their own. They did not do this for the purpose of owning territory, as we understand it, but from a spirit of resentment, or, if I may be allowed the expression, from pure cussedness.

About 1855 the Government sent several parties of Indians to Washington to visit the Great Father, that they might see for themselves the great number of white people in the East, and, returning to their people, tell them what they had seen. They would always compare the number of whites to the grasses on the prairie. For a long time those who had remained at home were disbelievers, and said those who had gone East were bewitched by the whites who had escorted them, and that they were great liars. It required persistent effort on their part to make their friends believe the statements they made in regard to the number of people they had seen; but as the Government sent many of these parties to Washington, at different times, who corroborated what had already been told by former visitors, the skeptics were finally compelled to accept these wonderful stories as true.

It may seem strange that a people so vicious and murderous should pray —nevertheless the custom obtained among nearly all Indians, and it was by no means uncommon for some of them to pray many times each day. They scarcely did anything of importance without addressing a crude petition to their Great Creator, for it was to him that the prayers of nearly all the wild Indians of North America were directed. They prayed to him because he was good, and had made so much in the world for which to be thankful; for all were worshippers of some kind after their own fashion.

On rare occasions, when there were important subjects to be discussed, the Indians met in council, at which the most prominent, one after another, arose, and in a standing position, addressed the assembly. These " big talks " were generally in relation to the fitting out and starting of a war party, although other matters of importance might be discussed as well. When a war party was to be made up, it was formed of all the available fighting material of the nation or tribe. Sometimes two or three tribes of the same nation joined together to make the war party as formidable as possible. Great care was taken in selecting those who were to go, or rather in rejecting those who were not to go, for as a rule every warrior was anxious to fight. A mounted party of several hundred warriors made a very imposing body, and if one was inclined to be nervous, their approach in fighting trim would not be likely to add to his comfort.

The time taken in preparing a war party varied. If there was no necessity for an immediate start, they were one, two, or three weeks making preparations. The entire time preceding the departure of one of these expeditions, all the tribes present devoted themselves to merry-making. During the day they engaged in horse-racing, gambling, or other amusements known to aboriginal life, and feasted almost constantly. When darkness came on they formed in circles in the open air, danced and sang, or rather howled, their weird chants.

Their dances consisted of jumping up and down on their toes, the men on one side of the circle and the women on the other; not joining hands, but each individual, covered with a skin or blanket, faces painted, hair decorated, acted independently, but all moved together to the time of their drums. All through the night they vigorously beat their tom-toms, or Indian drums. The noise they thus made could be heard in the rarified and still air a long distance. When the war party was ready to depart the females assembled, began weeping, wailing, and offering prayers at the same time to the Great Creator for the safe return of their braves, as well as for the success of the expedition.

It was necessary at all times to have a number of men in camp to do the hunting and keep the night watch, as every Indian camp always had its night watch to prevent surprises from hostile war parties, or unknown enemies, as well as to look after the animals. In military parlance this might properly be termed the camp guard.

When going into battle the warriors rarely, if ever, used saddles, and with the exception of the lariat around the animal's lower jaw in two half hitches, their horses were naked, the Indians hanging first on one side, then on the other, and using their animals as a shield to protect themselves from the fire of the enemy. When attacking whites they rode in a circle around and around them at the top speed of their mounts, yelling as only savages can; and as the fight progressed they became more daring and drew nearer, waving their hands and firing on the besieged, their object being to disconcert the enemy and stampede his animals. When this had been accomplished they withdrew and proceeded to round up and drive away the frightened herd.

But should the party attacked have other goods they coveted, a few of the warriors rounded up and secured the fleeing animals, while the main body continued the attack until successful or beaten off.

At that time the Indian's weapons were the bow and arrow, the lance or spear, the tomahawk, and occasionally an old-fashioned pistol or gun, consequently it was necessary for them to approach comparatively near the party attacked that they might use these primitive weapons effectively.

Notwithstanding the fact that the red men handled these arms from boyhood, and were expert in using them, they were not as deadly as generally described by writers of fiction, for the Indians had no idea of distance when firing, and made no allowance for the wind, which frequently diverted their arrows wide of the mark.

And further, their intellects being dull, they did not grasp the entire situation instantly, it rather having to grow to the rapidly changing moves and conditions of the conflict. This is the reason more whites were not killed by the red men in the many attacks they made upon them while crossing the great plains and mountains of the wild West, especially as a great many pilgrims were poorly equipped for defense against these sudden and fierce onslaughts.

One of the red men's methods of attacking trains, freighters, settlers and others was to surround them, and then by cunning draw the fire of the besieged, and when the latter had exhausted their ammunition, rush upon and destroy the entire party, or if any were spared, it was invariably the women and children, who were carried away captives to the Indians' far-off homes.

CHAPTER II.

THE COURAGE AND FIGHTING QUALITIES OF THE WILD INDIANS—FOES THAT ASKED AND GAVE NO QUARTER.

Going into Battle—How the Indians Planned a Massacre—Methods of Surprising their Enemies—How we Defended Ourselves against Sudden Attacks—Description of a Real Battle with Indians—Hardships of an Indian Campaign—Indian Courage and Ferocity in Battle—Personal Experiences—How we Felt in an Indian Battle— Nerved to Desperation—Mounted Indian Warriors—Their Personal Appearance and Peculiar Fighting Tactics—Fight to the Death—Giving and Asking no Quarter— Pursuing the Indians—Indian Wiles and Treachery—A Lurking Foe—Indian War Horses—How the Indians Scalped their Enemies on the Battlefield—Burial of the Bodies of Troopers—Burial of Indians who Fell in Battle—Mourning for the Slain— The Safest Place after a Massacre.

I HAVE been in many engagements with these red men, who always outnumbered us by two or three to one. When attacked, our plan of defense was to dismount, side line or hobble our animals, then tie them together to prevent their being stampeded. We then formed in a circle outside of our horses and mules, and waited for a warrior to approach sufficiently near to kill or wound him. We were careful to allow them to come near enough for our men to take deadly aim, for in reserving our fire in this way, we reserved our strength, and kept the enemy at a safe distance.

An Indian battle, as we usually see it portrayed pictorially, represents the warriors looking as though they had just feasted on a hearty meal at some hostelry; the Indians naked; their heads decorated with splendid war bonnets of eagle feathers; their faces and bodies gorgeously painted in all colors of the rainbow; their horses fine, fat and sleek; painted after Indian fashion in different-colored stripes on body, head, neck and legs; all decorated with jaunty eagle feathers in their tails and manes; the day perfect; the lay of the land just right; the troops in gay uniforms handsomely mounted on prancing steeds, and all indicating that everything had been prepared for an ideal battle.

Let me give a brief description of the usual conditions of a real battle with Indians. The trooper, more or less incapacitated by disease incident to long exposed camp life, was usually almost worn out by excessive fatigue;

his dress consisted of a pair of boots (no stockings), a pair of old military trousers (no drawers) full of holes and saturated with grease and dirt, a woolen army shirt, blouse and cap.   His rations consisted of hard bread (often filled with worms), rancid bacon, and sometimes pieces of fresh meat, frequently eaten without salt or pepper.   For weeks, and sometimes for months, he would be without shelter, sleeping on the ground under the broad canopy of heaven in all kinds of weather, often in rain or snow, sometimes with only a blanket crawling with vermin to cover him, half dead with repeated night watches and long daily marches over arid plains or rugged mountains.   Such was the trooper's physical condition. His horse, after subsisting on grass alone for a long time, and drinking stagnant water, would be much run down and weakened.   Such was his mount.   This is a true description of the actual trooper, in my time, as he usually engaged in battle with the Indians.

The engagement once open, neither men nor animals would get rest or food until it was over.   Sometimes the conflict lasted the entire day and per-haps late into the night.   Dur-ing the heat of the battle the

SPOTTED WOLF—TYPICAL CHIPPEWA.

hardships which the trooper had undergone for weeks past might be tempo-rarily forgotten; and as there was no rear to fall to in a fight with these red men, the safest place for him was at the front.

The night before the battle (and every old campaigner will bear me out in this assertion), while lying on the ground, probably in the rain or snow, trying to get a little sleep, the troops were more or less nervous and rest-less, being up and down the whole night.   When the battle opened there was great uneasiness even among the most hardened campaigners. We were always very anxious from the time the engagement opened until it was finished, for the Indians generally outnumbered us not less than two to one. Once wounded and left on the field, there was nothing in store for a white man but torture and death. The thought of such a fate added terror to distress, though, at the same time, it nerved us to desperation.

On the other hand, the Indian warrior when on the war path rarely, if ever, rode his war horse. He rode another horse, leading his war horse to mount when going into actual battle. This horse, which was the best owned by the brave, was a good one, and was generally fantastically decorated. When entering battle the warrior wore only his breech-cloth, with sometimes a pair of moccasins; as he was accustomed to living on meat only, he had probably fared plentifully on that and was in good fighting condition. When he thought the battle was likely to be a desperate one, or to the death, he would blacken his face with coals from the fire, or paint it in the most hideous manner, to make himself look as frightful as possible. A distinguished brave or chief might occasionally wear a war bonnet in battle, but this was rare, as it was a great incumbrance while fighting. Every warrior carried a round shield from two to two and a half feet in diameter, which covered his back or breast, and which by a dextrous movement of the body he kept between himself and the enemy. This shield was made of the thick hide of a buffalo bull, which when dried in the sun became very hard. The shield was slightly convex in shape and covered with soft buckskin. An arrow or lance would not penetrate it, but a bullet from any modern firearm would go through it and the wearer also.

The horse he rode was seldom incumbered with equipment, usually having nothing but the lariat rope by which he was guided, and carrying no weight but the rider and his weapons. The animal was thoroughly trained for this mode of fighting; being small and wiry, he was amazingly quick in his movements, as compared with the heavy and often jaded horse of the trooper. Both warrior and war horse seemed to enjoy the battle to the fullest degree, especially when they had the best of it. This is a true picture of the wild Indian as he usually entered battle.

A conflict with these red men was unlike an encounter between any other forces on earth. In reality it was a combination of a battle and a fight. There was little or no room for strategy on the part of the troops, as the Indian would attack at any point where he thought he could succeed by the force of numbers, and the troops had to attack the Indian wherever they could catch him. When the fight was in the open, it consisted of a series of charges and counter charges. The Indian was generally mounted, and the troops were necessarily so.   The Indians circled around and around the enemy with amazing, dazzling rapidity, necessitating constant movement and vigilance on the part of the troops in every direction, and at every point. Sometimes he charged close up to them; discharging his arrows or other weapons, and retired as quickly as he came. Again he sat erect on his horse for a moment, and then apparently fell as if dropped by a bullet.   But he was still there, clinging to the farther side of the horse, discharging his weapons at the enemy over or under the neck of the animal he rode, still circling around at full speed.   His courage was unquestioned, and he fought with the ferocity of a tiger.

He did not engage in a battle with the intention merely of defeating his foes; his only thought was to kill them, to exterminate them, if possible. Consequently, there was no quarter asked or given on either side, the Indian would not show any, and the trooper, in self-defense, could not give any.

When defeated, or fearing defeat, the warriors scattered into numerous small bodies and vanished in various directions.   Hence it was impossible for the troops to pursue them successfully.   Should they attempt to do so, they would lose their strong point of vantage, solid serried formation, and miss their object besides.   They might kill a few Indians here or there, but even this was next to impossible, as the latter went into battle on fresh horses, the best and fleetest they possessed.   Should the troops break in order to pursue the flying groups of Indians, they might be cut off, or surrounded by the Indians and killed in detail; for the warriors could return to the attack and reunite their forces as rapidly as they had broken up a short time before. By their method of signaling—which was understood by all Indians—they made it perilous for the pursuing party, which was liable to be ambushed or destroyed at an unexpected moment.

When an Indian's horse was shot in battle, he usually had another at a short but safe distance, tied or picketed, and was soon back again on his new mount. On the other hand, if the horse of one of the troops was shot or disabled, the soldier was compelled to fight and defend himself on foot as best he could.   If some of his comrades were killed, he might, perhaps, secure a remount, but even this was a matter of difficulty.   In short, the trooper was at a disadvantage in almost every respect, for he was compelled to fight the enemy after his own peculiar tactics and terms.

The officers rarely urged the troops during an engagement.   The troopers knew they were fighting not only for their country, but for their lives; and they soon learned the methods of Indian warfare, and the wiles and ways of the red man.   The only absolute requisite for the soldier was not to allow his wily foe to draw and waste his fire, or tire himself or his mount.

When, as frequently happened, troops attacked an Indian encampment, the manner of fighting was still more to the disadvantage of the troopers. It then became almost a hand-to-hand conflict, men, women, and children fighting with fiendish ferocity, using every accessible weapon, firing through peep-holes in their lodges, or from behind bushes, rocks, and every object that afforded concealment, with warriors on horseback charging from every quarter and assailing small bodies of troops whenever they could find them separated, or at a disadvantage. Should the encampment be a large one it was all the more difficult and dangerous for the troopers, for the Indians who had been caught in their lodges and unable to escape would remain where they were, preparing themselves for the approach of the troops, and shoot them down from their hiding-places.

Indian horses were usually small, and the Indian being an expert rider would mount and ride with lightning rapidity to a bush, rock, or other place of concealment, dismount, take aim, and fire a number of times with his rifle or his bow and arrow at his enemy, then bound on his horse and be off again like a flash. Should he be fortunate enough to kill an enemy in this way, he immediately rushed in and struck his prostrate victim, claiming a *coup*, (a brave deed or act, the killing of an enemy or securing his scalp); then proceeded to scalp him at once. The Indians scalped every person killed in battle whom they could reach. With the fresh scalp, dripping with blood and dangling from his hand, he would again spring on his horse and return to the fight, elated by his success and stimulated to further efforts by his bloody trophy.

The burial of the bodies of troopers who fell in battle in these lonely wilds was a saddening spectacle. The remains were thrown into a trench or large hole in the ground; these were generally dug up in a day or two and devoured by wolves or other carnivorous animals.

Should the Indians lose a number of their warriors in battle, the families and friends of the dead would repair to the spot for years after, where they bitterly wailed and mourned, and in accordance with their superstition " made medicine " on the scene of the battlefield. The Indians believed, and were taught from infancy, that death on the battlefield was the highest honor, the greatest glory that could be attained in life.

Should they perpetrate a massacre, destroy a wagon train, or commit a great outrage, the scene of their villainy was for some time afterward the safest place that a white man could select. The savages under such circumstances expected chastisement for the deed, and they immediately left the scene of villainy as far behind them as possible.

CHAPTER III.

THE INDIAN'S MENTAL FACULTIES—HIS PERFECT PHYSICAL SENSES AND BLUNTED MORAL NATURE—HIS GREAT CRUELTY—SCALPS AND SCALPING.

The Indian's Preternatural Cunning and Stunted Intelligence—His Highly Developed Physical Senses—His Perfect Vision and Acute Hearing—Vanishing like an Apparition—His Keenness in following a Trail—His Untiring Patience—His Intractable Nature—His Instinctive Cruelty—His Suspicious and Distrustful Nature—His Duplicity—Rarely to be Trusted—The Indian of Fiction, and the Indian of Fact—Indian Orators—Indian Languages—The Fate of Indian Female Captives—A Living Death—How Indians Computed Time—Mourning for their Dead—Return of a War Party—How the Indian Scalped his Foe—Customs in regard to Scalp-Taking—Jerking the Scalp from the Skull—Looking for Nits—How to tell an Indian's Scalp —Curing a Scalp—A Ghastly Spectacle.

THE Indian has been frequently, I may say generally, represented as having been endowed with great powers of observation and extraordinary gifts of natural cunning. This is only partly true. The Indian's mental faculties were sharpened by the necessities of his existence; but, like all other savage people, his intellectual gifts were limited. From his mode of life his physical senses were highly developed. His vision was usually perfect, and his sense of hearing was phenomenally acute. He could put his ear to the ground and detect the tramp of men, horses or other animals, at long distances. He could appear with the celerity of thought and vanish like an apparition. In following a trail he was as sure as fate. What to the ordinary observer was unnoticeable, was to him as plain as a well-beaten path, and his patience in following the trail was untiring. A broken twig, an upturned stone, or the appearance of the grass where trodden, had for him a significant meaning. He could find evidences of the presence of man or animal where the white man could not detect a sign. His intuitive perceptions enabled him to arrive quickly at a conclusion from the lay of the land or other material things. He depended upon his natural animal instinct more than on human judgment. Yet, granting his superiority in these and other ways, he could not compete with civilized man.

There was in the Indian nature a trait of intractability not found in any other portion of the human race. Unlike the negro, he could not be enslaved. The Spaniards in the early days of discovery endeavored to enslave the Indian; the result was that he died in his chains. He was the same when I first knew him as he was then—unamenable to law, and impatient of restraint. So far he had shown himself incapable of even a veneer of civilization. He might be brought up in the midst of civilized surroundings and educated, but at the first opportunity he invariably relapsed into his original barbarism.

Coupled with his barbarous instincts, or rather with a part of them, was

SPOTTED OWL—SIOUX.

his natural inclination to cruelty. It has been said that all savage races are like children, in that they have no adequate conception of suffering or pain endured by others. They were entirely devoid of sympathy. The controlling instinct of the Indian was to kill.

The Indian could hardly be said to have possessed any moral nature. In the first place, he had no abstract ideas. He could understand nothing unless it appeared to him in the concrete. There were no words in his language to express moral ideas. Virtue, vice, generosity, hospitality, magnanimity, and all cognate words were to him unknown. He only believed what he saw or felt.

He was naturally distrustful. This was one of the impediments encountered in the work of Indian civilization. He had been for ages the slave of heredity and environment, and he suspected an enemy everywhere. Of all the savage races the Indian was the only one who never tried to imitate the white man.

Any one knowing his character would not trust him in any way. He would not do right from moral impulse, for the reason, as already observed, that his moral perceptions were limited or undeveloped. To his mind everything was right that redounded to his own interest if he could successfully perform it; and anything was wrong (or bad, as he called it) if he failed.

His moral standard was measured by the difference between success and failure.

He was the very impersonation of duplicity. He might enter the cabin of a frontiersman, or a military fort, or an Indian agency, and listen to all that was said, without giving the slightest evidence that he understood what he heard, or that he was taking notice of his surroundings. In his attitude and facial expression, he might appear as taciturn as a Sphynx, and yet understand every word that was uttered and be planning a murderous raid at the same moment.

Occasionally, it is true, the Indian evinced some commendable traits of character. But these were the exception to the rule. Doubtless there are also instances of truthfulness and fidelity on his part. But granting this, it is still an indisputable fact that the Indian, of all uncivilized people, has offered the greatest degree of opposition to the influences of civilization.

Apropos of the intellectual qualities of the Indian, a prevailing idea is that he was a master of oratory. We read imaginary speeches of Indian chiefs in school books, and untrustworthy sources, then jump to the conclusion that the Red Man was a wonderfully eloquent though untutored child of nature. Nothing could be more foreign to the fact. The Indian vocabulary was extremely limited, and was confined to material ideas. All the poetic rhapsody and oratorical fireworks attributed to him are but the delusion of writers who have given free rein to their imagination. The alleged masterful speeches at council-fires, and pathetic appeals to the justice of the white man, protesting against intrusion on Indian hunting grounds, belong to fiction, not to fact.

It is difficult to place the Indian intellectually. Other savage races when brought within the environment of civilization have afforded brilliant instances of individual effort, but the Indian never. There is no instance in the four hundred years of American history of an Indian who attained greatness through the channels of civilization. The few Indians who stand out prominently in our history from King Philip down to Sitting Bull, achieved greatness not by adopting the ways of the white man, but by opposing them.

The Indian was proud by nature. He was animal in his instincts, and he neither knew nor cared about anything not connected with his material wants. He had an insatiable desire to excel. He wanted to be the bravest brave in his tribe. He resented injustice, even though he did not practice justice himself.

The Indian nations differed from most other savage people in that each had a different language. Except in a few instances there were no dialects among the different nations. The great Athabascan family, comprising as it did the Zunis, who attained the highest degree of civilization of any of its branches, the Mohaves, the Navajoes, and the Apaches, could communicate with each other through their somewhat varying dialects. But no distinct nation that I have ever known would communicate in the oral language of the other. Neither would they intermarry with one another, although sometimes it occurred that a female captive, especially if young and handsome, became the wife of the man who captured her. Even then her life was little more than a living death, as the women of the nation treated their captive sisters with great severity and contempt, although they might be the wives of prominent chiefs.

West of the Mississippi River there were many distinct languages spoken by the various Indian nations. This diversity of languages explains the existence of their sign language, which I shall describe in another chapter. This was the only common means of communication that they possessed; though it varied somewhat among the different nations they could nearly all understand it.

In conversation, both oral and by signs, all Indians were obscene to a degree unknown to any other people. They seemed to have no conception of vulgarity, obscenity, or decency. Frequently the most revolting and disgusting subjects formed the topic of their common conversation. They would sit in large numbers listening to stories told by different persons, some of which were obscene beyond description. The stories were not witty or of interest to the listeners, but idle, vulgar talk. Men, women and children listened to these stories with the utmost stoicism, their object being to retain as much of them as possible that they themselves might be able to repeat them to others.

The Indian was never demonstrative. He rarely manifested surprise. He was reticent by nature; what he could not understand did not trouble him in the least. A few things, however, excited his admiration beyond the power of silence. One of these was the mystery of how the white man could read. He imagined that the paper talked to the white man, and the reason it did not talk to an Indian was a puzzle he could not solve. I have seen Indians pore over an old newspaper by the hour, turn it upside down and inside out, manipulate it in every conceivable manner, then throw it away in disgust because it did not talk to them as to the white man.

The Indian had no regular method of computing time. He knew neither years, months, weeks, nor days. He counted days by the number of "sleeps," that is, nights; months by the number of moons; and longer intervals by the recurrence of winter and summer. To him every day was the same; he had neither Sundays nor week days.

He was very much surprised to see his civilized brother look at his watch to ascertain the time of day. I have seen Indians stare at a watch for hours, in utter amazement. We could not make them understand how, by looking at a watch, we could tell precisely where the sun was in the sky, although not visible at the time.

Some of the nations or tribes cut their hair, namely, the Osages, Otoes, Pawnees, Iowas, Sacs and Foxes. Some of them cut it off from both sides of the head, leaving only one stiff tuft, two or three inches in length and a couple of inches in width, on the top of the head from the forehead back to the scalp lock. All the Indians who did this lived along the Missouri River above the mouth of the Kansas River. How they acquired this custom I am unable to state. It probably originated among themselves. The cus-

YOUNG GIRL—FACIAL PAINTING—SIOUX.

tom of warriors cutting their hair as a sign of mourning differed from that which prevailed among those whom I have quoted. An Indian on losing a wife or child sometimes cut off all his hair except the scalp lock. In those days it was difficult for Indians to obtain scissors, as the trading posts were widely scattered. Accordingly, they cut their hair with a knife, or burned it, leaving it uneven and ragged. These are the only instances among North American Indians where the hair was cut short, it being the general cus-tom to let it grow in the most abundant profusion. An Indian woman sometimes mourned the loss of a near relative by cutting off one of her braids; then unbraiding the other she let it hang down her back, and over her shoulders in front.

The surest evidence that a scalp when taken was really that of an Indian was the fact that the hairs were covered with nits. Any person acquainted with Indians always looked for nits to be assured that it was the scalp lock of an Indian. Sometimes the hair of the scalp was coarse and a tuft of a horse's tail might be substituted for it; but the presence of nits on the hair was proof positive that the scalp lock was that of an Indian.

Tho manner of taking a scalp in battle was to cut with a knife, around the braid of the scalp lock, a circle two or three inches in diameter, and then with a jerk tear it from the skull. Occasionally, especially if not pressed by danger, and there was plenty of time, he would cut around the entire scalp, tearing it from the head. Such a scalp was often divided into numerous small locks, which were used in ornamenting his war shirt or other personal belongings. Half a dozen or more scalp locks often represented but a single victim. A few people who have been scalped by the savages, after they were supposed to be dead, have recovered, but were great sufferers ever after from headaches, earaches, nervous prostration, and constant colds. The cranium being without its natural protection, subjected the victim to great inconvenience with every climatic change.

The majority of Indians had a peculiar custom in relation to claiming the scalp. The one who first struck an enemy after he was down, and supposed to be dead, could claim the scalp, although the person killing him had made every effort to strike the prostrate body and demand the trophy. This custom I attribute to the warrior's desire to be the first to strike the enemy, so that he could claim to be in advance of all others in the battle, and therefore the foremost brave.

Scalps when taken in this way were the personal property of the individual who struck the dead body first; they were kept and exhibited by him and his family as a token of bravery. They would take a twig off a bush and make a hoop five or six inches in diameter; then thongs of rawhide were put through the scalp around the edges and fastened to the inside of the hoop, thus stretching the scalp tight, when it was left to dry. When a scalp dance took place, these scalps, stretched in their tiny hoops, and frequently ornamented with fur and other articles, were fastened to long poles, which the women carried in an upright position. Scalp dances were always held on the return of a victorious war party, especially if, in addition to scalps, it had secured a large amount of booty in the way of horses and mules.

When one Indian scalped another who had a feather in his scalp lock, this feather was fastened to the scalp, and dangled from the pole on which the trophy was carried. Such a scalp was the special admiration of the dancers, for the presence of the feather was supposed to be evidence of the superior bravery of the slain, and the still greater bravery of the captor.

Nearly every brave was the possessor of a number of these ghastly trophies, and he exhibited them conspicuously on all ceremonial occasions. They were his badges of distinction, as well as the evidence of his claims to greatness with his people.

CHAPTER IV.

INDIAN SMOKES AND SMOKERS—QUEER CUSTOMS AND SUPERSTITIONS—
HOW ANIMALS WERE AFFECTED BY THE UNSEEN PRESENCE OF
INDIANS.

Method of Dressing and Decorating the Hair—The Scalp Lock—Keeping It Greased,
Smooth, and Shiny—Combs made from Weeds—Curious Ornamentations—A Beard-
less Race—Manner of Smoking the Indian Pipe—Method of Lighting the Pipe—
Indian Surprise on First Seeing Matches—Smoking and Praying to Two Great
Spirits, the Good and the Bad God—Queer Superstitions—Killikinick, or Indian
Tobacco—Method of Preparing It for Smoking—Its Strong and Lasting Odor
—How Animals Detected the Approach of Indians in the Night—Olfactory Sensi-
tiveness of Horses and Mules—Smelling Indians at a Long Distance—Red Pipe-
Stone—Curious Legend as to its Origin—The Intermingling of the Blood of Whites
and Indians—Pipe Ornamentation—A Marvel of Beauty—A Neutral Ground for all
Indian Nations—Prehistoric Gatherings.

I HAVE never seen a North American Indian who was bald-headed.
Their hair was coarse, luxuriant, black, and straight. The men and
women plaited it in two plaits as a schoolgirl wears it, letting it hang over
both shoulders. These plaits were frequently covered with the fur of the
beaver or otter, cut in strips from one to two inches wide.

Men and women alike usually parted their hair in the middle, the end of
the part on the man's head reaching back to the scalp lock. This scalp lock
was two or three inches in diameter, and was formed of the hair drawn
together in a circle at the crown of the head. It was plaited in a braid by
itself, to which the men sometimes attached a strap ornamented with tin or
silver disks, a brass button being often fastened in the middle of each. The
disks were fastened on the strap as close together as possible without touching, the first disk next to the scalp lock being as large as an ordinary teacup
and diminishing in size until they reached the end of the strap, which frequently extended to the heels of the wearer, the last disk being not larger
than a twenty-five cent piece. Sometimes the disks were uniform in size.
Men did not cut their scalp locks, as it was considered an act of cowardice
to deprive themselves of this appendage. Indian women did not wear scalp
locks, but Indian male children had a scalp lock from the time they first
began to dress their hair. The more intelligent Indians, such as the Cheyennes, Sioux, Assiniboins, and Crows, took great care of their hair, oiling it

and keeping it smooth and shiny, though not clean.   When they had no combs a substitute was used.   The stem of a weed on which there were prickly points, often served the purpose of a comb.

With a pointed stick or bone they would sit for hours combing and separating the hair of themselves or each other, and as they only unbraided the hair at long intervals, it was not a great inconvenience to be without combs. After securing these articles from the whites, they were highly prized, and they were rarely without them.

The Indians did not have beards.   I have never seen an Indian with more

than a few straggling hairs, which sometimes appeared on the face, and these he immediately proceeded to pluck out with his thumb and forefinger; or if he could secure a pair of tweezers, he plucked at each hair as it made its appearance, and continued the operation for w e e k s and months until the beard was entirely eradicated.   The eyebrows and eyelashes of both sexes were sparse and thin, and it was rare to find hair on the body of either sex. They were, as a rule, a hairless people; but when hair made its appearance on any part of their bodies, except

MANY HORNS, GROS VENTRE INDIAN, WITH EAR PENDANTS OF IROQUOIS SHELLS TIPPED WITH LARGE SHELL.

the head, they at once proceeded to pluck it out and kept at it patiently and persistently until the roots were destroyed.

I have never seen or known of an Indian wearing a ring in his nose, as they are frequently represented in pictures.   The men generally sat crosslegged, like tailors, when in the lodges or tepees, or elsewhere on the ground. The females sat on their legs, with the feet together on one side or the other, seldom, if ever, resting on their haunches.   When a number of Indian men met and began a conversation, they first sat on their haunches or cross-legged in a circle, making the circle sufficiently large or small to be complete, and in this position they remained, talking and smoking for hours.   If there were sixty or seventy-five men in the circle, they had from fifteen to twenty-five pipes going at a time. After lighting a pipe each Indian, as the pipe was passed to him, took one, two, or three long whiffs, blowing the smoke up toward the sky; then holding the bowl in an inclined position with the end of the stem which enters the mouth toward the ground and lifting his face skyward, said a prayer. All of these prayers were about of the same trend, thus: "This smoke I hope will go to my Great Creator, who lives in the clouds, and who is very good to me. I hope he will take pity on me and my family, and send me something to eat and wear." With the other end pointed toward the earth, he would say: "This goes to the bad spirit, who I hope will not trouble me or make any disease." Indians were all superstitious. One might have a superstition,—his "medicine," as he termed it,—not to pass the pipe while smoking to more than one, two, three, or more men to his left. When his pipe was passed as far as his "medicine" demanded, it was returned by the last smoker to the man on his right, who handed it to the next man, and so on, until it reached the one who started it. Hence, there were many pipes going all the time. The pipe was never smoked when it was being passed from left to right. Each man had his own bag of "killikinick," or tobacco.

When the pipe came to the smoker with the contents gone, he immediately proceeded to clean, fill, and start it again. For cleaning these pipes every man carried a stick about the size of a lead pencil. The pipe was lit with a lighted ember, matches being rare among the Indians in those days. When they first saw a match and the manner in which it was lighted, by simply scratching it, their surprise was beyond expression.

Killikinick was the inner bark or pulp of the red willow. It lies next to the wood and immediately under the bark. The bark was first removed, then the pulp was scraped off with a knife and laid on the green stick from which it had been taken, and held over the fire and dried. It was then cut up fine and was ready for use. When the Indians had tobacco, killikinick was mixed with it for smoking. The flavor as well as the odor of this red willow pulp was pleasant, and it had none of the injurious qualities of tobacco.

Among the Northern Indians the women did not smoke. Some of those living along the Rio Grande, in Texas and in Arizona, made cigarettes of coarse tobacco rolled in brown paper or in the inner leaf of the corn husk. They acquired this habit from their Mexican neighbors.

The smoke of mixed tobacco and killikinick made a sweet and pleasant odor. The Indian's person and all his belongings were completely saturated with it, and it lasted for a long time. Horses, and particularly mules, whose sense of smell is very acute, could scent Indians by this odor at a long distance. It caused them to become uneasy and constantly look in the direction from whence the odor came. Animals, at the approach of Indians, would always get up and become restless at unusual times in the night, when the command was immediately put in fighting condition. In the morning we were sure to discover signs of Indians.

Animals when on the march and rather tired, if picketed or sidelined, or tied to the picket rope, would usually lie down when the camp grew quiet, about ten o'clock at night, and sleep for a half or three-quarters of an hour; then all would awake, rise, and remain in that position until about two o'clock, when they laid down again and slept for probably an hour. Every company of cavalry carried a picket rope. It was about one and a half inches in diameter, and two hundred, or two hundred and fifty feet long. A sufficient length of it was stretched to hold all the animals, which were tied to it on both sides, for safety by day or night. Should they get up at any other time in the night this unusual movement would attract our attention, and we knew that Indians were near.

The Indian pipe was a marvel of beauty. There is only one known quarry in the world where the red pipestone clay can be had, and it is located in Minnesota. The clay when first found is soft and can be cut with a knife. The Indians living in that locality were expert in carving and making pipes which were highly prized by them. I have in my possession the most beautiful specimen I have ever seen. It was smoked at the treaty of peace at Fort Laramie, between Colonel W. E. Maynadier and Red Cloud, and cost forty-five horses. The clay stem of this magnificent pipe is ten inches in length; the bowl, which stands upright, is four inches in height; the hole in the bowl for the tobacco is half an inch in diameter, and the hole in the clay part of the stem a little more than three-eighths of an inch in diameter. The pipe throughout its entire length is formed of two different colors of the stone, one side of it being a deep red, the other a pale red, the colors intermingling, and forming a beautiful mottle, after the style of a meerschaum pipe when just commencing to color. Those accustomed to Indian paraphernalia, who have examined this pipe, pronounce it the finest specimen they have ever seen. The Indians had a tradition that where the red pipestone quarry is located a fierce battle was fought between the whites and Indians a long time ago, in which a great many red men were killed, and that their blood soaked into the ground, thus forming the red pipestone. But of the piece of stone in this pipe, the legend recites that the blood of some whites who were killed in this battle sank into the ground and intermingled with the blood of the red men, thus giving the two colors,

RED CLOUD, THE NOTED SIOUX CHIEF.

the pale red and the very dark red. This legend gives an idea of Indian tradition.

Pipes made from this stone are susceptible of a very high polish, and after having been smoked for a time, become much darker, and rich in color like the meerschaum. The wooden stem to such pipes, made of hard wood, was generally from one and one-half to two feet in length, about one-half to three-quarters of an inch in thickness, one and one-half inches in width the whole length, and oval or flat in shape. On either end was a nipple, one for insertion in the pipe, the other for the smoker's mouth. An Indian never wet the nipple on the end of his pipe stem when smoking, as he only held it between the lips. Each smoker inhaled the smoke into his lungs, and blew it out of his nostrils and mouth in clouds, leaving the nipple as dry as if it had come out of an oven. Many of these pipe stems were artistically decorated with buckskin covers, upon which were handsomely worked ornamental designs in beads of many colors, or variegated porcupine quills. Some of the stems were carved into the figures of animals, birds, and other original devices. They would hardly be called artistic by a modern carver, but for Indians the carving was quite well done.

On the site of the quarry, according to Indian tradition, the Great Spirit once assembled all the Indian nations, and breaking a piece from the rock fashioned a huge pipe by rolling it in his hands. He then smoked it over them to the north, south, east and west, told them that the red stone was composed of their flesh and blood, and that the quarry belonged to all of them and was to be used for pipes of peace, and that all, even the bitterest enemies, must meet as brothers on its ground. Giving a final whiff, the Spirit's head disappeared in a great cloud of smoke and the stone for several miles around was melted and glazed. Two women, the guardian spirits of the place, then descended into the large ovens that opened beneath, and they ever afterward answered the prayers and invocations of the "medicine men" who visited this spot.

This and other legends connected with the place were spread throughout nearly all the Indian nations, and numerous excavations in the rock, marks, hieroglyphics, and other signs, testify that this spot was frequented by many Indian people from a very remote period. Here they met in peace and held their savage instincts in check, in their fear of the wrath of the Great Spirit.

The pipes made from this material were found among nearly all the Indian nations of the North American continent, and were highly prized by them. Parties from many nations made annual pilgrimages to this quarry to procure material for pipes. It differs from any other substance known to science, and is capable of receiving a lustre superior to and unlike that of any other material. Component parts of this material, as given by Government experts, are as follows:

Silicia	46	Carbonate of Lime	3
Alumina	28	Copper	2
Moisture	9	Magnesia	7
Peroxide of Iron	5		

The Indians procured this stone by digging through the soil and slate to the sub-stratum in front of the wall for a depth of four or five feet. Here they broke off the stone in such quantities as they required for making their pipes.

THE ONE WHO HITS THE BEAR—WITH RED STONE
PIPE AND PIPE STEM—DECORATED WITH
SCALPS—BLACK-FOOT INDIAN.

CHAPTER V.

INDIAN INQUISITIVENESS AND CUNNING—CRUEL TREATMENT OF PRISON-
ERS—THE FATE OF WHITE CAPTIVE WOMEN.

Indian Habits and Customs—Marvelous Instinct of the Indian—His Inquisitiveness—No
Idea of Morality, or of Right and Wrong—Power of the Chief—The Medicine Man
—Making Medicine—Medicine Horses and Medicine Dogs—How the Women made
Medicine—The Medicines of Different Nations and Tribes—How and why they
were selected—Women standing in Cold Water while making Medicine—Cutting
their Arms and Legs with a Knife—The Greater the Scar, the Greater the Medicine—Striking the Water with their Hands and Feet—Broken Medicine—Treatment
of Prisoners—Captive Indian Women—A Living Death—An Incident on Green
River—Indian Treatment of White Captive Women.

SOME of the faculties of the wild Indians were much developed and sharpened. They did not jump to conclusions, but arrived at them by a keen
process of reasoning after their own fashion. Their mental resources were
naturally limited, but in those practices which their mode of life compelled
them to adopt and on which their existence depended, they became very proficient. In traveling over the trackless plains and rugged mountains they
never lost their way; as they had no compass or means of guiding themselves, except by extinct, they went by the shortest route from place to
place with remarkable precision and never missed their objective point.

Another peculiarity was their inquisitiveness. They desired to know at
all times what was going on about them; although they would sit apparently
unconcerned, yet all their faculties were strained to the utmost to learn what
was going on and what was being said.

Morality, as we understand it, was unknown among them. Having no
conception of right and wrong, murder was not considered a crime. Theft
from strangers was considered an act of cunning. The more adroit the thief
the more he was respected. Among their own people, however, theft was
rare, for their individual possessions were small, and every one knew what
his neighbor owned. Furthermore, it was almost impossible for the thief
to conceal any article stolen from one of his own tribe. From their earliest

childhood they were brought up to understand that theft, or other crime, committed against a person outside of their own tribe was legitimate; consequently such a thing as conscience in an Indian was entirely unknown.

In some of the nations or tribes the chief was a despot in relation to the return of stolen property. He had authority to cause the return of such articles, and redress the wrong in any way he might see fit, except by taking life. When this was deemed necessary some member of the injured family was depended upon to take the life of the offender. Some of the penalties imposed upon members of the tribe were severe; this had much to do in keeping them honest. The power of the chiefs as civilization pushed westward was greatly diminished, until it was reduced almost to abstract influence over the tribe. The large nations were divided into many small tribes, each under its own chief; the latter used every effort to keep his tribe together and prevent its members from leaving and joining another tribe, or forming a new one. There was no penalty for this, but it was considered a disgrace to a chief for members of his tribe to desert him. Each chief looked after the unprotected members of his tribe, such as the women and children of dead warriors, and saw that they were cared

WIFE OF MANUETO—COMANCHE.

for. This was one of the redeeming features of the red man.

Nearly all had their "medicine chief," "medicine man," and their peculiar manner of "making medicine." This was not, as one would naturally suppose, the medical treatment of the sick and afflicted with herbs or drugs, but was a deep-rooted superstition peculiar to themselves. The medicine chief of some of the nations and tribes was a man who by bold-faced conjuring had induced his people to believe that he was possessed of super-natural powers, or some mysterious art. To maintain himself in this posi-tion he habitually went through all sorts of wild gesticulations, bodily contortions, and mysterious movements, both day and night, in order to con-vince those who noticed him of his superior ability and supernatural gifts. He made speeches and described in much detail his ability to perform cer-tain wonderful things. Occasionally, in endeavoring to convince those about him of his occult powers, he sacrificed his life in attempting rash deeds in battle, or in vain efforts to perform miracles. This excited other Indians, both male and female, to do many foolish things. The medicine man was not looked upon as a chief in any sense of the word, but was regarded as one possessing the power to perform wonderful feats and cures. The members of his tribe, both male and female, constantly applied to him for assistance to prevent disease, cure the sick, bring good luck in battle, in the chase, and particularly in all family affairs. The truth is, the medicine man was a base impostor, an unmitigated fraud.

The individual making of medicine was practiced by nearly all of the wild Indians, and was a purely superstitious rite. Each had his or her own medicine. An Indian would silently leave camp, sit alone in the sun on a hilltop or in a ravine for hours, hoping thereby to induce the power of "med-icine" to come and adhere to him. So with the women. Medicine-making consisted of peculiar forms among different Indians. With most of them it meant to do certain things only in a particular way. With others the med-icine consisted mainly in some peculiar manner of handling the pipe; or the manner of turning the face to the sun or the moon, when they first saw it. Others, after a long journey, would strike the water of a stream or pond with their hands, or with a bow, tomahawk, or other weapon, uttering a prayer to the Great Spirit at the same time.

They had their medicine horses; these were painted fantastically when they could obtain paints to do so. The tail, mane, and foretop were cut, and oddly decorated with feathers. Such a horse was supposed to be proof against all enemies, and was ridden or used on important occasions. They also had medicine dogs, which were supposed to possess extraordinary powers. These dogs were brought into requisition when they started on the chase, or were about to perform some particular feat. When they were used against the influence of spirits to cure, or prevent disease, they were brought inside the lodge and kept there for the purpose of warding off trouble. They were not killed and eaten so long as their medicine was effective, but woe to them when the Indian supposed their supernatural powers had departed or failed to attract their credulity.

The medicine-making of the Sioux was interesting. They would sit for hours in a certain position, with their faces directly to the sun, inviting the medicine to come to them. A woman made medicine by standing in the water and hacking her arm or leg with a knife, on the principle that the greater the scar the more powerful the medicine.

There were numerous other ways of making medicine. One of these was, when they first approached a body of water to strike it with the hand or foot, and if they had a vessel with them, to dip up and pour some water on the ground where grass was growing, before drinking, no matter how thirsty they might be. Another was to stand naked in the rain when it began to fall, until their hair was thoroughly wet. This was considered particularly good medicine; but should the rain be of short duration, they considered their medicine had been "broken." When an Indian had ill luck he would insist that his medicine had been broken, when he at once sought to discover the cause and invariably found a satisfactory explanation, and if he charged it to one of his wives she was sure to pay the penalty in some way. He might ignore her entirely until his luck changed for the better.

Different nations and tribes had different symbols and medicines. The Cheyennes had a medicine arrow, and the Arapahoes used the root of a tree or bush, which represented in form an image of man or beast. This they hung up when alone and made their medicine to it. They sometimes held medicine dances, although they were tame affairs. The medicine of the Utes was a stone figure, or the skeleton of a bird. The loss of this emblem was considered an evil omen.

The only medicine that was anything like universal among the wild Indians was the manner of treating the females of the lodge, in relation to their exclusion once every month. All the females of the family, be they wives, daughters, relatives, or visitors, when the monthly period arrived, be it day or night, no matter how inclement the weather, immediately left the great lodge and took up their abode in a small lodge, which was erected by the side of the larger one. Should there be no small lodge they must shift for themselves as best they could. The small lodge was their home until the period passed; there they were compelled to eat, sleep, and abide until recovered, when they might again enter the family lodge. But during this entire period they were not permitted to enter the great lodge. To do so was sure to "break the medicine" of the entire family, of which offense no Indian woman would be guilty.

Sickness was supposed to be the work of the bad spirit; it was to nullify the power of this spirit that the services of the medicine man were called into requisition. He might, or might not, believe in the efficacy of his medicine, but he was shrewd enough to exploit his special powers, and among the savages his pretensions naturally found easy credence. He occupied an influential position among his tribe, and frequently used this power with evil effects. He opposed any change that might tend to enlighten his people and diminish his own standing; hence his power was usually exercised in keeping the Indian in his primitve ignorance and barbarism.

It was difficult to eradicate from the Indian mind his belief in the efficacy of the medicine man. Even those who claimed to be civilized frequently reverted to the incantations and rites of these conjurors, in whom they placed implicit confidence as to their powers. Indians who had been taken away from their heathenish surroundings, brought under the influence of civilization and educational privileges, and who had given up their belief in the medicine man and his superstitious rites, no sooner returned to their tribe than they resumed their savage mode of life, and relapsed into their native barbarism. Such persons might speak English; conform outwardly to the requirements of the Christian religion; dress and act like the white man, and invest themselves with all the externals of civilization, but instinctively they remained at heart the innate savage.

The manner of treating prisoners differed among the various nations. Among some, women captives were invariably outraged by all the men of the party. Among others, a woman captive was subject to the caprice of all the party, until they returned to their own camps, when she became the slave of her captor. With others, the captor claimed the woman and kept her for the revenues derived from immorality. Among those who practiced this custom it was not considered degrading.

White women captives were highly prized by all Indians for the purpose of ransom. To hold white captives as hostages was a strong argument for peace. Cases have been known where they forced a white woman to write a letter on a tanned skin, a piece of bark, or other smooth substance, which was sent to the commanding officer of the nearest troops, as an appeal for peace, in order that her own life might be spared. But the Indians never allowed a captive white woman to fall into the hands of white soldiers until a treaty had been made, well knowing that should she inform the soldiers of the manner in which she had been treated, the troops would make no agreement with them.

I knew of a case where three women had been captured from a wagon train on Green River, and retained by the Indians without being violated. Knowing that they were closely pursued, the Indians voluntarily surrendered these women to the troops at South Pass, for which they received rewards in the way of supplies, and were treated as good Indians, because

they had not outraged the captives.   This was the most injudicious step
that the authorities could have taken, as it was a premium for these treacherous wretches to capture women and children from other overland wagon
trains for the purpose of getting a reward for their return.

When having women captives, and closely pursued by the troops, the
Indians placed them in such position, that in case the soldiers opened
fire, the captives must be seen and killed by them.   When a treaty was
made under these circumstances, it was always to the Indians' advantage.
Some of the captive white women who had been returned to the troops for
ransom told revolting stories of the brutal manner in which they had been
treated.

In dealing with the Indians under these conditions, the troops were more
or less hampered in doing their duty.   They knew there were influential
people in the East whose intentions were good enough, but who were misguided by ignorance of Indian character, who would condemn any action
the military might take in their efforts to punish these miscreants, no matter
how outrageously they treated innocent children and defenseless women
captives.

Warriors captured in battles between themselves were guarded with much
vigilance, for among some of the nations they were valuable as slaves;
others compelled them to inform of the numbers and whereabouts of their
tribe.   Information of this nature could only be forced from the unfortunate
by extreme cruelty, if at all.

The usual method of wringing such from the prisoner was to tie the hands
together in front; then just above the elbows of both arms two strong rawhide thongs were securely bound; to these a stout pole about six feet long
was fastened near the center, one end resting on the back of the head; then
some of the women seized the lower end, forcing the head of the person
downward on the breast, where it was firmly held until existence became
so unendurable that the sufferer either confessed or died in great agony.

During any and all cruelties inflicted, the unfortunate was allowed no
sleep, water, or food, and his sufferings were increased by constant shouts
of his torturers.

The red men derived so much pleasure from cruelty to both man and beast
that they were constantly devising new, and improving on the old methods of
torture; and the nearer they were to the tropics the more ingenious and
severe their practices.   The Comanches built fires on the bodies of captives,
and the Apaches bound naked prisoners to the giant cactus and left them to
perish of hunger and thirst.

CHAPTER VI.

THE INDIANS' STRANGE IDEAS OF THE HEAVENS—INDIAN CAMPS—SIGNIFI-
CANCE OF SIGNS—WONDERFUL SKILL IN TRAILING—THE INDIAN AS
A PLAINSMAN.

The Milky Way—Composed of the Shadows of Departed Spirits.—The Road of Departed
Spirits—Their Ideas of Thunder and Lightning—The Aurora Borealis—Lighting
the Road of the Spirits to the Happy Hunting Ground—Reverence for the Dead—
Placing the Dead in Trees—Providing Food for the Spirits to eat—Final Departure
of the Spirits from the Corpse—Indian Camps—Surrounded by Filth—Broken Bones
—Care of Wounds—Indian Fortitude—No Regular Time for Eating or Sleeping—
How they set their Lodges and made their Camps—Drinking Dirty Water—Signs—
Everything a Sign to an Indian—The most important Thing to all Indians—Skill in
Trailing—Punishment for Crimes—Lack of Muscular Strength—No Match for the
White Man in Personal Encounter.

THE wild Indians had peculiar ideas regarding the heavens, and what they
believed is contained therein. Nearly all attempted to explain the Milky
Way. Some said that it was composed of the shadows of departed spirits,
others that it was the road traveled by these spirits on the way to their
future abode, and others that it was the true happy hunting ground, where
all Indians would arrive after death, there to spend an eternity of bliss.
They did not arrive at this conclusion through a process of reasoning, but
accepted it as an indisputable fact. None of them had any theory concerning the constant change in the appearance of the heavens caused by the
movement of the planets; they could not explain the rising and setting of
the sun; the only thing they knew about the heavens was that the moon
changed at regular intervals. They also had strange ideas about thunder
and lightning. The Sioux believed that it was the direct manifestation of
the Great Spirit's anger. After the thunder was over they believed that
the anger of the Great Spirit had been appeased, and that no harm would
come from him for some time.

Many Indians believed that the Aurora Borealis, or Northern Lights,
was produced by departed spirits in the happy hunting ground, for the purpose of lighting the way for spirits which were then hovering around the
dead, and those which were still groping in the dark in their effort to find

the road to the Spirit Land. After this light had been sh:ning for some time, they believed that all the spirits which had lost their way would arrive safe in the Spirit Land.

All savage Indians showed great respect and reverence for the dead. No matter how bitter the feeling between two nations or tribes, when they came upon the burial places of the dead, whether of their own people or of their enemies, they conducted themselves with much solemnity.

They would not disturb the resting place of the dead, or remove anything that had been placed at or near it by the relatives or friends of the departed, no matter how much they might have been in need of it or how recently it had been left there.

The Sioux and some others, who placed their dead in

COMANCHE WARRIOR—GAP IN THE SALT.

trees or on scaffolds, would, after the poles had rotted away and the bones had fallen to the ground, gather up the bones, place them in a pile, and cover them with stones, to prevent wild animals from dragging them away. Even these piles of stones were respected by every red man.

Some Indians who placed their dead on scaffolds left a hole in the skins in which the corpse was wrapped for the purpose of allowing the spirit to look at the remains during the time it was hovering about; should food left for the spirit be eaten by carnivorous animals, nothing could make them believe that it was not consumed by the departed spirit. They believed that the spirit hovered around the body of the dead and returned at irregular intervals to witness the rites paid to the body before the spirit took its final leave.

There was no regularity in setting the lodges of an Indian camp. No one, not even the chief, had supervision over the manner or place where the lodges were to be set. They were erected in such places as best suited each individual owner. There were no streets or walks, neither did the owner of a lodge claim the space around it which he kept clean, and no sanitary precautions whatever were taken. Dirt, bones, and filth of every description were strewn everywhere, and the stench was frequently unendurable to any one but an Indian. The camps were located near a stream, and were generally set in such position that when a rain storm came, all the filth that had accumulated was drained into the watercourse. In tanning hides the women fastened them in the stream to soak for days, and the watercourse along the entire length of the camp would be filled with these filthy skins, polluting the water with the hair and dirt that soaked off from them. This polluted water was used for cooking and drinking purposes indiscriminately, yet it seemed to have no evil effect on those using it.

Being too lazy to go to a point above where the hides had been placed, for the purpose of securing good fresh water, and having no medical skill in treating ordinary diseases, it is surprising that the mortality was not greater among them. None of them knew anything about treating a broken bone. A bone once broken was liable to leave the owner a cripple for life. Neither had they any skill in dressing or healing a wound. A wound once inflicted was left to heal itself; yet it was rare for an Indian to die of a wound that did not strike a vital part. I have seen Indians with wounds that were sufficient to kill a white man, bear them with the greatest fortitude and recover from their effects.

They had no regular meal time. They ate when they had food and were hungry, that was all. This would seem to disprove the theory advanced by physicians that regularity in eating is essential to good health, as the Indians were a remarkably healthy race, and rarely, if ever, suffered from indigestion. Neither had they any regular time for sleeping. They slept when they felt like it, and arose in the same way.

One thing that all Indians were expert in was the reading of signs, and they were constantly on the alert to discover them. From their earliest childhood they were taught to look at all times for signs that betrayed the presence, recent or remote, of human beings and all animal life. No matter where they were they were constantly looking at the ground for footprints of human beings, animals, and birds, instinctively and persistently examining the grass, weeds, bushes, trees, and even the water, in their efforts to discover signs left by any living thing. These tell-tale signs were the Indian's trusted guide. To him the trail or footprint of man, beast, or bird, could be as plainly read as if printed in an open book. He knew, moreover, that by his own trail his enemies could fathom his intentions, and learn about his movements, hence he employed every art and devise to conceal his trail and mislead his enemies.

When a war or other party was on the move it had no advance or flank guard, but invariably had a rear guard, or body of watchers, which consisted of a small number of braves well-mounted, who kept to the rear of the moving party, at a distance of from a mile to two miles, scouting through the hills in every direction to discover if they were being followed. The rear guard of the moving body was rarely seen, but they were in a position at all times to know whether they were pursued, and if so, they instantly notified the main body, which at once scattered and broke the trail in every direction and reunited for defense as quickly as possible.

As hunters they could not compare with a mountaineer or frontiersman; but when on the hunt they were wonderfully patient and would work for hours to approach near enough to an animal in order to have a dead shot before firing. They gained this habit in their early days, when they had only the bow and arrow with which to procure food. After they secured modern firearms they continued to approach close to an animal before firing in order not to waste their ammunition, which was not easily obtained by them.

Trial by judge, jury, or council of the tribe was unknown. All such representations in works of fiction and tales of frontier life are purely imaginary. Neither was there a formal punishment for crime, or offenses committed by members of the nation or tribe. The only approach to such a rule was the penalty inflicted on women for marital infidelity, and this was general among nearly all the Indians of the West.

The only punishment inflicted upon the male members of the various tribes was administered by the injured party, or by his friends or relatives, if he had been killed. This partook rather of the nature of retaliation or vengeance than of justice or punishment, in our sense of these terms.

Neither did the Indians keep any record of the history or interesting events pertaining to their nation or tribe. Indeed, such a thing would have been impossible. In the first place they had no written language. Secondly, if they possessed such records, it would have been impossible for them to preserve them. They were continually on the move, and kept and carried with them only such articles as were indispensable to their wants and necessities. All attempts at picture writing, or efforts to perpetuate events by symbols were made only by individuals; these were the property of the author. As such pictures were generally executed on tanned hides, they might be disposed of by the owner at the first opportunity to exchange for some article he desired. Personally, he attached no great importance or value to them. Again, Indian habitations were frequently flooded during heavy rains, and such rude records would on these occasions be irreparably ruined. Add to these reasons the facts that the Indians had no accurate conception of time; cared nothing whatever about dates; that births, marriages, and deaths were regarded as common occurrences of which not even a mental record was made; finally, that the Indian lived only in the present, for the most part heedless of the future, wholly heedless of the past, and it will readily be seen that to expect him to keep chronicles of his nation or tribe was to expect the impossible.

The only past events that were worthy of an Indian's attention were his own deeds of prowess; these he could describe from memory, or if that failed, he did not hesitate to draw on his imagination, which could always be depended upon to make a glowing picture. As they held no traffic with other Indian nations—all trading they did among themselves was only an exchange of articles on the spot—they had no occasion to keep accounts, or records of any kind. They did not even tax their memories to retain an account of a mercantile transaction that occurred among themselves. Once an incident of this character was finished, the Indian dismissed it from his mind. While his faculties were preternaturally keen in all things pertaining to his everyday necessities, they were stunted and undeveloped in many things that were not essential to his existence.

The same may be said of his physical development. It will be noticed, by reference to the photographs in this book, that the Indians are lacking in muscular development. They possessed great endurance, but were destitute of bodily strength. This was largely owing to the fact that they lived almost exclusively on meat, a diet that does not seem to create flesh or increase muscular strength as do many kinds of cereal and vegetable foods. Furthermore, as the Indian never deigned to work, the upper portions of his body were not developed by exercise, and his outdoor life tended to make him lithe and active rather than stout or strong. Hence, in personal encounter, without weapons, the Indian was no match for the white man, and a fistic combat was unknown to Indian life and custom; whenever they fought, whether among themselves or with their enemies, it was with weapons, and to the death.

The females seldom engaged in loud or boisterous wordy controversies among themselves, and a fight was rare between women. Most all were mild-mannered and even-tempered; if otherwise, anger was seldom shown. This may be attributable to the fact that from infancy they were reared in menial and subservient conditions and accepted anything, however unpleasant with submission.

Indian women were universally kind to children, and no instance ever came to my knowledge of a woman striking a child, whether her own or that of another.

CHAPTER VII.

HOW INDIANS COOKED AND ATE—THEIR LOVE OF FINERY AND PERSONAL
ADORNMENT—PAINTING THEIR FACES AND BODIES—MAKING A WILL
—PLAINSCRAFT.

Cooking Pots made of Fresh Hides—Eating Raw Meat from newly-slain Animals—
     A Meal twenty-four hours long—A Daily Gorge—Insatiable Appetites—First-class
     Gluttons—Eating Skins and Moccasins—Their first Coffee—Indian Improvidence—
     A Chief's Powers and Limitations—The Chief in Camp and on the War-path—
     Forming a new Tribe—The Survival of the Fittest—Love of Ornament—Fondness
     for Soldiers' cast-off Uniforms and High Hats—Aversion to wearing Trousers—Fash_
     ion of Painting the Face and Body—Indian Dandies—Indian Artists—How an Indian
     made his Will—Distribution of Property before Death—Reading the Signs of an
     Abandoned Camp—Plainscraft.

WHEN the Indian first came into intercourse with the white man, his
most eager desire was to secure knives, hatchets, and kettles. He usually
cooked his food by broiling it, or by semi-boiling it in a pot made of fresh
hides, or in hollowed wooden receptacles which answered the purpose of kettles. In these water was poured, and heated by hot stones which were
constantly thrown in. When on the chase, and hungry, he often ate his
meat raw and bloody just as it was cut from the newly-slain animal.
    As to taste, it did not figure at all in the Indian's manner of preparing
his food. His only thought was to appease his hunger, not to gratify his
palate. Everything was cooked in miscellaneous fashion, a pot-pourri, or
mess, of which everybody partook while it lasted. Though the Indians ate
only once a day, it must not be supposed that they had only one meal during
every twenty-four hours. The meal, if there was enough of it, and the
diners were hungry, lasted the whole twenty-four hours through. They sat
around the kettle, or the roasted animal, and ate until satisfied, eating again
when sufficient appetite returned. The Indian meal was simply a daily
gorge—the white man's three meals in one. If another member of the
tribe chanced to enter the lodge while food remained he was at liberty to
help himself.
    When food was scarce—for the Indian was the impersonation of improvi-

dence—they would endure hunger uncomplainingly. When in desperate straits, they would eat skins, their moccasins; roots, buds, and the bark of trees were not despised. In times of want, as long as their ponies and dogs lasted, they did not fast long at a time. They didn't use salt with their food or as a condiment; they did not have it and were not accustomed to its use.

In eating jerked meat, they rarely cooked it at all. It was left until thoroughly cured, when the entire family could munch it all day. None of the fruits or berries that grew wild in their country were cooked, but were eaten just as they were gathered, or in dried form.

They sometimes put the *Pomme blanche*—a species of wild carrot—in their pots to boil with meat, but as they kept the pots boiling for a long time, the contents were eventually reduced to pulp, and the mess became a thick mass of nameless soup. Their manner of cooking fish was to boil them, sometimes putting in the *Pomme blanche*, which, when boiled with the fish, made a disgusting dish.

WHITE THUNDER IN MOURNING—IROQUOIS SHELL EAR PENDANTS.

They also cooked fish by digging holes in the ground, in which they made a fire, and, placing the uncleaned fish in the hot ashes and coals, left them to bake. Fish cooked in this way, with the help of a sharp appetite, could be eaten, although I must say that I did not relish it. They also broiled fish over hot coals, first placing a stick in the fish's mouth, and holding it over the fire, turning it until done.

The first coffee they had was taken from some emigrants crossing the plains, whom they killed. They boiled the green coffee for a long time, and, not being able to make anything palatable out of it, they wondered what the white people did with it. This they afterward learned, and became very fond of coffee, especially when well sweetened.

Their manner of selecting chiefs varied somewhat with different nations; there was no gradation, as a rule, between the chiefs of tribes of the same nation. In some of the nations they became chiefs by heredity. The honor was handed down from father to son, though it was necessary in all cases that the son should have the ability and courage to maintain his position after he had once secured it. Merit and personal attractions had their weight. In other nations a man was made chief by common consent, usually by the warriors of the tribe. There were many jealousies between chiefs and those who aspired to the office. Occasionally these jealousies resulted in the death of the chief or the aspirant, or both.

An Indian who was once made chief of his tribe would almost rather lose his life than the position. He would fight for it to the death. This is one reason why there were so many tribes of the same nation. Those who desired to follow a certain man or chief would secede from the original tribe and form themselves into a new one, taking some name by which they might be distinguished from their old tribe. This was particularly true of the Utes. It was regarded as necessary that a chief should be able to make a logical speech to his tribe. It was not so essential that he should show great bravery in battle.

A chief did not exercise supreme control over his entire people, nor were his counsels always taken. In the majority of instances he was simply a leading man, to whom the others looked for advice and instruction. When in camp he was little more than any other Indian, and had usually about as much control over the actions of individual members of his tribe as the mayor of a city would have over one of its citizens. When in battle, however, there must be one in command, and it was generally a noted chief, whose ability in this direction had been tested on many previous occasions. Even then he did not have anything like the control over his warriors that an army officer has over his troops. The warriors in battle usually fought independently, and could not therefore be subject to the command of any one, though the chief might from time to time give orders which were obeyed with promptness.

The chiefs of tribes were sometimes deposed, although this was rare. This was accomplished by a leader who, aspiring to be a chief, would create dissension in a tribe, and take as many followers with him as possible. Should the new leader, in setting up for himself an independent tribe, be able to reduce the adherents of the old chief to such an insignificant number as to be unable to defend themselves against their enemies, they either followed the new leader or abandoned the old chief and joined another tribe of their nation, thus leaving the deserted chief to seek some tribe to which he could adhere for protection.

Should the position of chief become vacant, and there be two or more aspirants for the office, a struggle followed. The bitterest passions of the rivals were aroused to such a degree that they became engaged in personal deadly conflict, and fought to the death with tomahawks or knives. To become a chief it was sometimes necessary for one of the braves to be the hero of two or three bloody personal combats. When this was the case he asserted himself as chief, and all recognized him as such. Should any one demur to his authority the person so objecting was bound to enter into a personal combat with him. In all such cases the chieftainship was determined by the survival of the fittest.

The office of chief had no compensation or emolument attached to it. It was honorary, laborious, and its duties were performed without thanks. There was no insignia of rank, except the head dress of eagle feathers worn by distinguished chiefs on ceremonial occasions and occasionally in battle; a chief did not dress better than the majority of the members of his tribe. Indians all wished to rule; this created a great deal of jealousy and ill-feeling. A chief had to secure his living in the same manner as the others, neither did he possess the great power usually attributed to him in fiction.

The photographs we see to-day of Indians generally represent them as wearing shirts, hats, coats, woolen leggings, and other articles of civilized apparel. During my time among them no wild Indian wore shirts or any wearing apparel whatever after the fashion of the white man. His dress usually consisted of a pair of moccasins, buckskin leggings reaching up to the thigh, a breech-cloth and a buffalo robe. Occasionally one would have a buckskin shirt or jacket elaborately decorated with beads, porcupine quills, and Iroquois shells; it was fringed at the bottom and on the lower part of the sleeves. In their hair they wore a few feathers, usually those of the eagle, wild turkey, or hawk. At a later period the men wore woolen shirts, and red or blue flannel for their breech-cloths and leggings.

They were fond of personal finery, and would decorate and adorn themselves with all sorts of trinkets. Brass and copper wire for wristlets and armlets were favorite decorations with both sexes. The brass ornaments of a soldier's hat or cap were much prized by them. Broken cross sabres, cross guns, old epaulettes, tassels, letters and figures of regiments were placed in their head gear in almost every conceivable manner. If they could procure a soldier's discarded hat or cap with the ornaments on, to which they would add feathers and trinkets, they considered that they were dressed in the

PAINTING ON BODIES—PECULIAR MANNER OF CUTTING THE HAIR—PIPE TOMAHAWK.

Twenty Years Among Our Hostile Indians.   Page 83

height of fashion.   Any and all decoration, no matter how ridiculous, was proudly worn, and in the most conspicuous manner.   I once saw some Sioux Indians on the South Platte, decked out in the most fantastic style.   Some of them had old discarded white and black plug hats, decorated with the soldiers' ornaments I have mentioned.   In many cases the hats were much too large for the wearers, resting on the top of the ears; others were much too small, sitting only on the top of the head.   Another wore an old vest many sizes too large, but buttoned up to the last button.   Several had large flam-

BUCKSKIN SHIRT WITH INDIAN DRAWING.

ing red ties around their necks, with no shirt, collar, or other article of civilization on them.   As they moved about in the most dignified manner in this peculiar uniform, several of the men who wore tall hats suddenly dropped the buffalo robes from their bodies, leaving as the only wearing apparel in view, the tall hats and breech-cloth, presenting a laughable spectacle.

No Indian would wear trousers.   He drew the line at this article of apparel.   If he secured a pair he immediately cut the legs off halfway between the knee and the hip, rip open the outer seam and have his wife sew them skin tight down the leg, leaving the surplus cloth on the outside of the seam. Some of them decorated the surplus strips of cloth with beads, deer and antelope hoofs, and frequently with scalps cut up for the purpose, so that, when walking or riding rapidly, they presented a striking appearance.

The women's dress consisted of a pair of moccasins, leggings reaching to the thigh, a low-necked, short-sleeved, buckskin skirt extending below the knee, the lower edge ornamented with fringed buckskin, a buffalo robe or blanket, and around the waist a belt made of hide and decorated with brass buttors, beads or porcupine quills when they could procure them. Though from long usage such articles of dress were dirty and greasy beyond description, nevertheless, they were highly prized, for they were the only ones the Indian woman had.

Every Indian, big, little, old or young, wore a belt. To the male's belt was attached a sheath knife, tobacco pouch, and other paraphernalia; to the woman's a sheath knife, small pouches containing bone awls and needles, and other feminine notions.

Painting their faces and bodies was also a favorite way of decorating themselves. When they could procure the colors they painted their faces in stripes and spots, in any style to please individual fancy. A common style was to paint stripes from an eighth to a quarter of an inch in width, starting at the nose, then running horizontally across to the ear, using red, yellow, blue, green, and as many other tints as they could procure. The forehead was striped in the same manner, with the lines running up and down. Sometimes the face was painted in spots, the pigments being daubed on without reference to any particular design, the sole intent seeming to be to make themselves as hideously ugly as possible. Their bodies were painted in much the same manner and colors, except that the lines were larger and sometimes wavy. The paints being originally mixed with grease remained on the body for a long time, for the wild Indian never under any circumstances washed himself.

I have heard of Indian dandies, but have never seen one. When a young man arrived at the age when he would naturally be a dandy his thoughts were taken up with securing a livelihood, or sufficient of this world's goods by plunder, or the hunt, to enable him to start in life and obtain for himself a lodge and family. That there were different characters among these people as to dress and ornament, must be admitted, but these were merely matters of personal characteristics, one being more cleanly than another and arranging his scanty wardrobe with more taste and effect.

At that time the Indian had no use for money. If he procured any it was usually in silver. He pounded the silver pieces into disks to ornament his scalp lock, as I have elsewhere described. Other favorite articles of ornamentation were brass buttons, particularly the old-fashioned smooth

THREE BOYS AND GIRL—UTES.

kind, about as large as a twenty-five-cent piece. These they fastened on their belts in various fantastic ways—sometimes artistically, but more frequently the reverse.

Some of the drawings on their buffalo robes, lodges, and skins, were, for Indians, well done, the artists being both men and women. Many of the drawings were pictorial efforts to tell the story of some event in family life, in battle, or on the chase. Some of them were so obscene as to be unfit for reproduction.

When an Indian who had several wives and a number of children was very ill, and thought he was about to die, he called around him as many members of his family as could be gotten together, then he proceeded to make his will orally, by distributing such of his worldly belongings as were not to accompany him on his journey to the Spirit land. He presented to each member of the family various articles, saying, "I give you this," until he had divided his entire possessions among them. It was the custom to make as nearly as possible an equitable distribution of his property among his family.

COMANCHE WOMAN AND CHILD.

Oral wills were always respected and no effort was ever made to break or contest them. Should his effects be limited and the number of family be large, they would continue to live together as before, using the possessions of each for the benefit of the entire household. Should one of his wives, however, become the wife of another man, she was at liberty to take her share of the goods and her children to her new home. The tepee of the Indian family being one of their most valuable possessions, one would naturally suppose that an Indian widow becoming the wife of another man would want her share of it, if not the article itself, or its value as represented by something else; yet such was not the case. She was satisfied to take such of his worldly goods as she was entitled to, and could carry away, leaving the tepee, with its good will, to the remaining members of the family. When it came to the last widow, she was then the sole owner of this habitation and could do with it as she chose. Should the woman, however, be taken by another Indian for his wife, he was supposed, if he had sufficient wealth, to pay a reasonable price for the lodge to its former owners, or return it to them.

As the Indian's worldly possessions were few, so his standards of value were limited. Horses and mules were the chief portions of his wealth; these were the general standard of value among all tribes owning them. Among some of the tribes where horses were plentiful and easily procured, their value was not rated so high as where the contrary conditions prevailed. One good horse was usually considered worth two poor ones.

Next to their horses, the principal standard of value was the buffalo robe. One good horse was usually considered worth twenty buffalo skins. But where the buffalo was abundant and easily killed, a lesser value was placed on the animal's hide.

Again a tepee was rated as worth from two to twenty horses according to its size and condition. In many places, especially on the barren plains, the poles of the lodge over which the skins were stretched were more difficult to procure than the robes, and were accordingly more highly valued.

The dressed skins of the deer and antelope, bear skins and other animals, also had a general value among most of the tribes. The bow and arrow, pipes, knives, and trinkets of various kinds, especially if procured from the whites, were all rated by the excellence of the article or by the difficulty in obtaining it.

All Indians, from the Atlantic to the Pacific Ocean, and from the central portion of Mexico to the country occupied by the Esquimaux in the British possessions, in whatever respects they differed, or whether one nation was more intelligent than another, or more advanced in the arts of civilization, or in war, had the distinguishing marks of the North American Indian indelibly imprinted upon them.

Their personal appearance, their mode of life, their innate cruelty, the treatment of their women, animals, and captives, were distinctly and purely Indian, and nothing else. Their amusements and pastimes; their inability to remain long in one place; their resistance to the advance of civilization; their tenacity of life in its primeval state, all were so distinctly Indian as to be very noticeable, no matter how far they might have been removed from savage life. The traits, habits, characteristics, and customs might differ widely in different Indian nations, yet all unmistakably showed their common origin; it is probably for this reason that some one once made the silly and often-quoted remark, "See one Indian and you have seen all."

No more untruthful statement could be made. A person who by personal intercourse, had become familiar with the different nations, could pick out the members of different nations wherever he found them, without hearing them speak a word. He could do this as readily as any one can make the distinction between a white person and a black one. By looking at their implements of war, their handiwork and personal effects, an experienced person could tell at sight which nation had made them. When coming upon places where Indians had camped, or in following their trails, an old mountaineer, or an experienced Indian fighter, could tell almost at a glance what nation had been there. So distinctly had each Indian nation its own way of making its camps that the trappers and plainsmen who had been among them for any length of time, voluntarily, or involuntarily, fell into the habit of making their own camps precisely like the Indians in whose country they were. To the ordinary person these abandoned camps indicated nothing; but to the experienced eye they not only told with surprising accuracy who the former occupants were, but at a glance told their number, how long they had been there, how long they had been gone, the direction in which they went, whether they were a war or hunting party, and other important information.

Their manner of hunting, butchering, traveling, and in fact everything they attempted, was so uniform that they practically and unconsciously left photographs of themselves which could be read at sight by the experienced observer. Suspecting, as he did, an enemy on every hand, the red man could not, or did not, change from that he learned in his youth; a habit once acquired was ever after retained, and it became a part of his nature. Originality or invention, even for self-protection, was entirely unknown to the most intelligent of our aborigines in their wild state.

Neither were they given to great flights of imagination, building wonderful air castles, seeing phantoms, and day dreaming, being optimistic one minute and pessimistic the next; but the red men were very earnest matter-of-fact beings, who required time to digest whatever was new or strange and of interest to them, otherwise it was dismissed unnoticed. In their homes they were cheerful, but of serious, sordid natures, and few saw the humorous or ridiculous in anything; loud and boisterous laughter, either individually or collectively, was seldom heard: a smile or snicker was about all the evidence ever given in appreciation of the humorous.

The Indian is a peculiar being; when anything foreign to his nature is to be met he becomes more intractable, and all the more confirmed in his savagery.

CHAPTER VIII.

INDIAN WOOING AND MARRIAGE CUSTOMS—BIRTH OF AN INDIAN BABY—
INDIAN WIDOWS AND WIDOWHOOD—NIGHT IN AN INDIAN LODGE.

How an Indian Secured a Wife—Price of an Indian Maiden—Daily Occupations in the
Lodge—Life in the Cámp—The Birth of a Child—Indian Babies—How they were
cared for—Endurance of Indian Women—On Hand for the Promised Present—How
Indian Babies were Cradled—Indian Widows—Weeping and Wailing at the Burial
Place—Genuine Grief—Married Women Slaves—Female Occupations—How the
Family Lived—Punishments for Infidelity—Mourning for the Dead—A Widow's
Weeds—Care and Affection for the Aged—Choosing a Name—How Names were
Selected—Life in the Lodge—No Privacy, and little Decency Observed—The In-
dian's Affection for his Wife and Children—Dying of Homesickness—An Indian
Elopement.

WHEN an Indian desired a woman of his tribe for a wife the custom
among many of the nations was to send one of his friends to the girl's
father, or to one of her nearest male relatives, to ascertain the price at
which she was valued. An Indian's wealth in those days was usually
counted by the number of horses he had, and these were the common
standard of value in negotiating for a wife. The friend then returned and
informed the wooing Indian of the price demanded,—that is, the number of
horses required to buy the girl,—when the barter began. A certain number of horses (always less than the number asked) were led to the tepee and
tied to the pole of the lodge where the girl slept; means would then be used
to induce some member of the family to come out. The latter, seeing the
horses so tied, knowing well the significance of the act, immediately informed the head of the family, or natural protector of the girl. The barter
then began in earnest, and was continued until the proposal was rejected
or accepted. If accepted, the horses were at once taken away to the herd
of those belonging to the girl's protector. Should the bid not be acceptable
the horses were left tied where they were, when more could be added by the
wooer, or the lot taken away; the latter meant that the price demanded was
refused.

The price of an Indian maiden was from one to forty horses, but on rare
occasions more were given, the number usually depending on the wealth and

ardor of the suitor.   I have known fifty horses to be paid for a girl.   If the bid was accepted the girl became the property of the man making the offer. She had nothing whatever to say about it, or about who her future husband was to be.   Should he be the most distasteful person on earth to her, she was his the moment her parents accepted the price they had placed upon her, and that ended it.   The husband was free to do with her as he pleased, even to the extent of taking her life.   If she died and the parents had another eligible daughter, they were supposed to make good his loss.

After an Indian woman entered the married state she was simply a slave. The domestic life of the females of the wild tribes was peculiar.   They had but few amusements with which to entertain themselves, and no light by which to see at night, except the light of the camp or lodge fire.   They generally retired early, and rose early.   During the day the old women usually occupied themselves in tanning hides, jerking meat (cutting it up in strips and hanging it on poles to dry in the open air), making moccasins, leggings, and other clothing from skins, making and repairing lodge covers, taking care of the animals, attending to general family duties, and doing the family cooking.   As they had no dishes or kitchen utensils, the labor imposed by cooking was very limited.   When they had a pot, everything was cooked in and eaten from it.   When they had none the meats were roasted over the fire.

One would naturally suppose that women whose natural functions had never been impaired by the restraints of dress, who had been reared from infancy in their natural condition, and enjoyed perfect health, would be prolific, yet such was not the case.   Indian wives rarely had more than two or three children, more frequently only one child, and often none.

In extremely warm climates Indian girls became wives and mothers at the age of twelve or fourteen years, and in middle life appeared old and wrinkled.   The women were extremely hardy and their endurance and fortitude were equal to that of the men.   I have known an Indian camp while on the move to stop, and a woman to have a lariat placed under her arms, the end thrown over the limb of a tree or lodge pole, and in a few minutes, while partly suspended in a sitting or squatting position, give birth to a child. In a very few minutes, without assistance, she would be astride of her horse, her child on her back, resuming her journey as if nothing unusual had happened.   At the first opportunity after the birth of a child an Indian woman would enter the water, no matter how cold, and bathe herself.   The child was usually laid on a robe or skin that was covered with a thick layer of the dried contents of the paunch of the buffalo.   This was as fine and soft as down.   The youngster was covered with this downy stuff, its arms placed

TYPICAL PUEBLO INDIAN.

alongside its body, the robe drawn over and around it and tied with a thong. The head was supported by the untanned skin of a buffalo calf or deer, and so placed that the child's face alone was visible, presenting the appearance of a diminutive mummy. In traveling, the mother would either carry it on her back, place it on a travois, or hang it by a noose over the pommel of the saddle. Infants were often left wrapped up in this manner for days without being taken out of their nest. When opportunity offered they were removed, washed and replaced in the same manner. The Indians had no infantile food, and mothers nursed their young until they were four or five years old. I have seen them run to their mothers and take their dinner, in a standing position, from the maternal fountain.

An instance characteristic of Indian childbirth occurred on Chugwater Creek, under my immediate observation, which is worth recording. One or two army officers and a few civilians were engaged in a game of cards in an Indian camp. We were in the lodge of a white man who had an Indian woman for his wife; in this lodge were several other women. About two o'clock in the morning one of the women on the other side of the tepee groaned as if suffering great pain. Some one asked her what was the matter; we soon discovered without her answering, for in a few minutes she was strapped to the poles of the lodge with a rawhide rope placed under her arms and in this position gave birth to a child. I asked the interpreter to tell her to be quiet, promising that if she did so, I would make her a present for herself and child whenever she came to my quarters at the Fort. Long before I was up next morning she was there with her child on her back, waiting for me.

Indian children were spoiled by being permitted to have their own way. They were allowed to grow up like young animals, with no other training than the force of example. Hence every generation was precisely like its predecessor. The child was inured to hardship and endurance from infancy. As the youngster emerged into boyhood or girlhood, it did as it pleased, rarely being corrected, taught, or restrained in any way. Though the Indians were fond of their children they were not given to manifesting their affection towards them. They seemed rather to regard them with total indifference until such time as the youth was old enough to enter the list of warriors, and the girl was old enough to be salable as a wife.

Children usually ran naked until they were from ten to fifteen years of age, though they commonly wore moccasins to protect their feet. After free access to the family dinner pot, their stomachs were very much distended and out of shape; and when a belt was fastened tightly around their waists, they presented a most peculiar and grotesque appearance. As a rule Indian children were healthy and there was but little disease among them; they were not subject to the diseases of children of the white people, such as measles, whooping cough, etc.

Indian mothers showed considerable ingenuity in making toys for their children. Toy dolls, often grotesque in dress and appearance, were common enough. Some of them were made to represent warriors and were adorned with miniature bows and arrows, and shields, thus early instilling the spirit of war into the minds of the young. Toy canoes, miniature horses with mounted warriors on them, and various other kinds of toys could be found in almost every Indian camp.

Infidelity on the part of the women was almost unknown among the majority of the wild Indians, as the punishment for that offense was so severe that no woman cared to incur it. She was even liable to lose her life for the offense, as the unwritten law of the Indians was an eye for an eye, and a tooth for a tooth. The punishment liable to be inflicted on an Indian who had killed one of his wives was that some relative of the woman might kill him at the first opportunity. The punishment for infidelity among several of the wild nations, especially the Sioux, was called "passing on the prairie." The offending woman was inveigled out of the lodge when she was immediately seized by a number of Indians in waiting, taken a distance from the camp, thrown upon her back upon the ground, a man holding each hand and foot, when each member of the party one by one violated her person. She was thenceforth an outcast of the tribe, and the lawful prey of any man. She could not enter the lodge of a medicine man, or other Indian whose medicine or superstition was against this class. The Apaches and Navajoes cut off the nose of the offending female as pun-

ishment for infidelity. The Comanches slit the nose from the point to its connection with the forehead, and prevented the wound from uniting. The Cheyennes were at liberty to inflict such punishment as they pleased, but their usual mode was to return the guilty woman to her parents, compelling them to restore the property, or its value, which was originally paid for her.

There was, aside from the question of morals, a special reason why the men were polygamous. They were almost constantly engaged in war and their number was depleted in consequence. Hence the women usually outnumbered the men two or three to one. When an Indian died, his wives were at liberty to become the wives of

WAR COSTUME AND SHIELD—SIOUX.

another member of the nation. He was not compelled to buy a wife after her widowhood, as when she was a maiden, unless she returned to her family and refused to become the wife of another without again being bought. When a woman lost her husband she went into mourning, and evinced her grief and proclaimed her widowhood at the same time by cutting off her long hair. As long as she remained a widow she would visit the burial place of her husband, remaining there for hours weeping and wailing bitterly. If the actions of the women at the burial places were a true index of their feelings, their grief was both genuine and poignant.

When an Indian lost a favorite wife or child, he too exhibited his mourning by cutting off one or both of the long plaits of his hair. Some of them cut off the braids of their long hair and blackened their faces with coals from the fire; others cut off the tails and manes of their horses and mules, which effected a strange transformation in their appearances.

The affection of the Indian for the aged of their families was very marked, and was one of the few redeeming features of their vicious nature. Many of them lived to a good old age, if their appearance was an indication.

APACHE WOMEN.

These were as tenderly cared for in their helplessness as were the young babies. In going from place to place they were given an animal to ride, if they were able to use it. When too infirm to mount a horse they were placed on the Indian travois, and were transported in the same manner as were the young children and the sick or wounded. It was the special delight and duty of one of their grown-up children, or if there were none, then of their friends, to care for them; so that the aged and infirm were rarely neglected. These persons looked after their every want, served them with food, saw that they had a good place to sleep, and afforded them every Indian comfort. There was, of course, no choice for either sex as to what they should do in life. When the male arrived at man's estate he had only one line of endeavor open to him—to hunt and fight; and the female had only one also—to bear children and to work for her lord and master.

Among them the question of "Woman's rights" was settled absolutely. She had the undisputed right to labor, and she was not expected to complain about it. Slave as she was by heredity and environment, she accepted her lot uncomplainingly. The women did not question the right of their lords not to do a stroke of work, and the latter did not question their women's right to do all the camp drudgery, and endure without a murmur the hardships of their menial position.

The manner of selecting names varied with different nations, although they were all of about the same character. They had no surnames. The male children were generally named after some animal, or given a name indicating some personal peculiarity, or commemorating some event or matter of note, as I shall hereafter describe. The names of the females were always in the diminutive; a woman retained the name that was given to her when she was a baby throughout her natural life, unless she changed it for some good and substantial reason. There was no prefix as Mrs. or Miss; when a woman became a wife she did not take her husband's name, but remained the same plain Yellow Chin, Sweet Grass, Yellow Leaf, Small Tree, or Running Water, as before.

A child might have a pet or diminutive name given it while very young, but with the privilege of exchanging it for another of its own selection when it arrived at the age of puberty. A change of name was to gratify their own wishes until the boy was grown to be a warrior and had counted a *coup.* So it was in naming their animals and favorite camping-places. Nearly all rivers and streams known to them were given permanent names. The large mountains also had names by which they were known, and so had notable places in their country. These supplied names for children born near them.

Nearly all the wild Indians were polygamists. The number of wives that an Indian could maintain varied with different nations, but the number usually depended upon his means to buy them. Sometimes he would have from one to twenty. Strange as it may seem, there was rarely jealousy among them. Their home life was generally congenial, and a married man was usually kind to his entire household. Ill-feeling rarely existed, much less was it ever shown in an Indian family. Should the husband show marked attention to one of his wives it was taken as a matter of course, and the favored one was not slighted or abused by the others. All the wives, be they few or many, lived in the same lodge, and there was little or no privacy. Each wife had her own particular place in the lodge; if she had children they slept with her. The only division between the sleeping places, which were always on the ground, was at the one next to the opening. Two sticks might be stuck in the ground and a skin or blanket hung on them. This was the only screen in the entire lodge.

The treatment of the female in the civilized world is usually considered the standard by which man's moral qualities can be estimated. This rule could scarcely be applied to the Indians, for the males of every Indian nation, with one or two minor exceptions, compelled the women to do all the labor and menial drudgery. One would naturally conclude that there could be little or no affection between a man and wives so treated. Such was not the case, however, for the affection of an Indian for his family and children was particularly marked, although rarely demonstrative. His love of home, not as a locality, but as a place where his family and friends were, was intense. To be separated from kith and kin was a hardship. Therefore it is not strange that nostalgia was common among captives; they have been known to die of homesickness, and not unfrequently went crazy from the refusal of their captors to allow them to return to their kindred and friends.

Among the far Northwestern nations the unwritten law was that a man should select his wives from different families. In some of them divorce— if such it could be called—was easily obtained. A woman could leave her husband at will and return to her parents, taking her children with her. This was considered a great disgrace to the husband. It sometimes happened that an Indian eloped with or stole the wife of another. When this occurred the girl's family were expected to make good the amount originally paid for her. This done, the man and abducted woman went to another tribe and became a part of it.

Different tribes had different ways of settling the value of a runaway wife. Among some of them, the new husband was compelled to pay the former husband for his loss a number of horses, skins, or other articles of value.

Captive women and children, especially when the captives were superior in intelligence and cleanliness, became the prisoners or wives of their captors. This custom was followed for various reasons. First, it did not cost anything to possess these women. Second, it was the desire of the captors to induce their prisoners to become part of their own people. Again, it prevented an effort on the part of the females to escape. Among some of the nations a female thus married was sometimes treated with kindness, not only by the man whose wife she became but by the people in general, though this was rare.

Polyandry was not practiced by any Indians living east of the Rocky Mountains, but among some of the Columbian group and those known as California Indians the custom prevailed and is referred to in the chapters on these people.

CHAPTER IX.

INDIAN AMUSEMENTS AND PASTIMES—THEIR THIRST FOR GAMBLING—THEIR
GAMES OF SKILL AND CHANCE—EXPERTNESS IN THROWING A KNIFE.

The Indian's Limited Amusements—Horse-racing the Favorite Pastime—Betting on
the Results—Women Gamblers—Ball Playing—Skill of the Players—How the
Game was Played—Proficiency in Running and Jumping—Skill in Throwing the
Knife—Indian Music and Musical Instruments—Serenading Dusky Maidens—The
Romance of Indian Youth—Admiring Himself in Nature's Looking-glass—Lack of
Amusements and Pastimes in Winter.

ALL Indians had amusements and pastimes of their own, though the more
ignorant the Indian the fewer were his pleasures. When the white man introduced playing cards among them, they soon learned to use them after
their own fashion, and this enabled them to gratify their thirst for gambling.

The Indian did not learn the vice of gambling from the white man. It
was universal among the savage tribes when the white man first came in
contact with them. This penchant for gambling was the natural result of
being compelled to pass long periods in a state almost approaching torpidity.
They indulged in it to break the monotony of their long winter days, when
frosts and deep snows shut them off from the chase and all active outdoor
life. Their sports were few, but their quickness of eye and agility of movement lent a peculiar interest to their simple games.

Horse racing was a favorite sport, and they raced their best horses at all
times, using the lash unmercifully, driving them to their utmost speed. At
races they usually bet on the result, but as their worldly possessions were
limited, and some of them absolutely indispensable, notably their weapons,
horses, horse equipments and articles of daily use, these were not usually
risked, although they were always ready to wager such articles as they
could spare. The women also bet on races among themselves, wagering all
sorts of feminine articles, and occasionally acting as jockeys, and handling
their mounts with skill. At times children also rode, and the whole population of the camp turned out at a horse race, all taking great interest in it; and
as they had no way of timing horses, their races consisted of matching two
or more, usually two, and the fleeter one was declared the winner. Another

favorite amusement was ball playing.   In this they used a ball stuffed with hair, the players having two bats shaped something like a lawn tennis racquet.   They used one in each hand, and were expert in playing the game. They sometimes batted the ball, but the favorite mode of putting it over the goal was to carry it over on their racquets.

When a ball game was to be played, the Indians were organized on two sides, a captain over each was selected, and a referee chosen.   Two posts were set up at each end of the field; the game consisted of passing the ball between these two posts or goals, each side having its own end of the field. A game would last one or two hours.   It was very exciting, and the only surprise to me was that they did not fight or squabble among themselves, for they were rough players, and would hit each other unmercifully with their racquet when striking at the ball.   To me these terrific whacks at one another seemed intentional, although they appeared to take them good naturedly.   The players looked decidedly picturesque, having nothing on but their breech-cloths and a pair of moccasins, their tall, lean, erect forms making them appear like athletes.   They were good runners, and played the game with skill.

Running was another favorite amusement.   A match between two Indians, with the judges appointed and everything in readiness, was sure to be interesting.   Sometimes the race was for a short distance, probably an eighth of a mile.   Another amusement was jumping.   In this some of them attained great proficiency.   The standing and running jump was practiced as well as the hop, skip, and jump.   The game of jackstones was a favorite pastime.   They amused themselves, too, by target practice with bow and arrow.

Throwing the knife at an object was a sport at which the majority of Indians were particularly expert.   Taking the knife in the palm of the hand with the handle toward the end of the fingers, and standing at from ten to thirty feet from the target, they would, by a dexterous movement of the forearm, throw the knife at an object often not larger than a saucer, and with such precision that the point of the knife struck within this small circle at almost every throw.   I have seen them stand at a distance of twenty-five feet from the target and hit it twenty-five or thirty times consecutively.

A buffalo chase or a hunt was not regarded as an amusement.   It was more like work forced upon them by the necessity of securing their food and clothing, for upon their success their existence depended.   They did not seem to recognize it as a pastime, but often went reluctantly about it as one doing hard work.   Neither was the killing of small game sport; it was hard work with them for they were frequently compelled to dismount and crawl a long distance to get within shooting range. Few, if any, of the wild Indians exhibited any musical talent.

What little musical efforts they attempted were confined to rude lutes, and consisted of a few notes without change or expression.

All noises or sounds being in the same key, neither were they played harmoniously.

In beating tom toms and flint hides at ceremonies and dances, perfect time was observed by each musician.

One of their musical instruments was a whistle or lute made of the bone of an animal or bird, or from a hollowed twig of the red willow or birch.

An Indian who could play a few notes on such an instrument considered himself an accomplished musician, and, dressing himself in his most gorgeous attire, would stand near some picturesque place—a spring if there was one in the vicinity—where the young girls came for water, and, admiring the reflection of himself in the water, blow his lute for hours for the entertainment of the dusky maidens.

Some of them made a banjo-like instrument, with two or three twisted sinew strings, which were tightened over the drum-like head. The strings were picked with the fingers, or struck with a hard substance held between the thumb and first finger.

The noise made on such an instrument was anything but grateful to the ear of one at all musical.

Their tambourines, made of flint hides, were the most perfect musical instrument they possessed, and nearly every family had one or two, which were in use almost every clear night; for among all the savages, night was the time for merrymaking, and at these times music was indispensable.

Vocal music, if such it can be called, consisted of three or four unpleasant sounding guttural notes. When singing in chorus they all sang together, but at the conclusion of each song all joined in a common yell.

None of their songs were poetical, but a repetition of a few sentences in relation to the subject in which they were engaged. If in merrymaking, the words related to the charms of both sexes, and were the same that had been used by them for generations.

The amusements I have mentioned were nearly all out-of-door sports, and were indulged in during the warm or summer months. The majority of Indians had few or no winter amusements, especially those living in a cold or inhospitable climate. Their principal occupation during the cold weather was to keep themselves warm and secure their food.

CHAPTER X.

INDIAN WOMEN TANNERS—THE MAKING OF AN INDIAN LODGE—INDIAN
ART AND ARTISTS—AN INDIAN VILLAGE ON THE MOVE.

Indian Tepees and Camps—How Lodge Covers were made—Lodge Poles—Erecting Lodges
    —The Entrance—Suffering from Cold—Going Barefoot in the Snow—Decorating
    the Lodge Cover—Deeds of Valor recorded in Picture Writing—Some well
    Executed Drawings—Going to bed with their Clothes on—Interior Arrangement of
    a Lodge—Expert Horsewomen—Dexterity in throwing the Lasso—Packing the
    Animals—The Travois—Adjusting the Pack—How the Old, Infirm, and Children
    were Transported—A Village on the Move—A Strange Sight—Crossing Streams—
    Clothing that was never Cleansed—A Filthy Race—The Art of Packing Animals—
    How Pack Animals were prevented from lying down.

INDIAN women did all the tanning for the family requirements, and the
work was done in various ways. When it was intended that a skin should
be very soft and pliable, only the brain of the animal and clear fresh water
were used. Skins tanned in this way were made into dresses, leggings,
moccasins, and other articles of personal and wearing apparel.

The skins used for lodge covers, and hides used for horse equipments and
coarser articles of home and camp life were tanned in a different way and
with much less care. They were simply thrown into the water and allowed
to remain until the hair fell off, when they were stretched tight on the
ground by driving sticks through holes cut in the edges while the hide was
wet and soft. Scraping knives made from the horn of the elk were generally used. The women would get down on their hands and knees on the
hide and scrape off all the flesh and pulpy matter. After the hide had dried
it was put through a process of softening before it was in condition to be
used as a lodge cover. The hide used for this purpose was usually that of a
buffalo bull, as it was much thicker and more serviceable than that of a
buffalo cow. Lodge covers were made by the women, who sewed them together with thongs. From ten to twenty hides were required for the coverings of each lodge according to its size.

Poles for the lodges were difficult to obtain by the Indians of the plains,
where wood was scarce and good straight poles hard to find, and they were

accordingly highly valued. They were procured and finished by the women, and were necessarily of sound, straight young trees, generally of pine, birch, or other light but strong wood. They were from one and one-half to three inches in diameter, and from fifteen to twenty-five feet in length. The bark and every small knot or growth was carefully removed from them and they were made perfectly smooth. In putting up a lodge from fifteen to twenty-five of these poles were used. The covering was drawn over them and fastened with skewers or sticks where the edges of the covering met. At the top of the lodge was a large flap in the corner of which the end of a pole

WHISTLING BEAR—BRULE SIOUX.

was inserted. When this flap was closed it kept the heat in and the cold out, and unless opened when the fire was built the interior would soon be filled with smoke. The lower edge of the lodge covering was fastened to the ground by long pegs driven deep into the earth. The pegs prevented the lodge from being blown over by high winds. The entrance was the only hole of any size, except the top, in the entire covering. This entrance was covered by a hide, drawn over a hoop made from a small branch and hung over the hole. The opening was rarely closed, except in cold weather, or to keep the dogs out.

Even the best of these lodges afforded but slight protection against severe storms or bitter cold. Rain found its way into them and the snow blew through the holes underneath the covering, half-filling the interior, making it exceedingly uncomfortable. During severe rainstorms the beds and sometimes the lodges were flooded, and the occupants were compelled to flee to higher ground with such effects as they could carry.

Lodge fires were necessarily built on the ground and around them the women and children huddled to keep warm. During winter storms when the Indians were compelled to go about their camps in the performance of necessary duties they frequently did so barefoot, as their moccasins and leggings became saturated with water or snow in a short time, and when

KIOWA LODGE.

in that condition were cold and disagreeable to the wearer. They preferred to keep their footwear dry even at the expense of temporary discomfort. Both men and women frequently carried their moccasins and leggings in their hands after having been caught in a cold rain or snow storm. Sometimes during cold weather they wore sandals made from the flint hides of some animal as a protection to the soles of the feet. During a prolonged cold storm or blizzard, which was frequent in the far north, the Indians and their animals, including their dogs, were great sufferers.

Lodges of this description were probably the best habitations that could be used by these nomads; for, being continually on the move, it was necessary to transport their entire camp equipment from place to place. They were easily and quickly put up and taken down, and it was a rare thing, even in the severest wind storm, for one of them to be blown down, although it sometimes occurred.

Frequently the coverings were fantastically painted with figures outlined in different colors, red and blue being the favorite. These figures represented different scenes, some depicting a warrior seated on his horse in deadly combat with a hostile brave; an Indian fighting a bear with his spear; an Indian on foot killing a man with his bow and arrow, tomahawk, knife, or lance; or some other prodigious deed of valor. Sometimes the entire lodge covering was decorated with these rude drawings. They generally commemorated some great event in the career of the occupant of the lodge, or hairbreadth escape of himself or some of the male members of his family. These drawings were usually made by the men, some of them showing considerable artistic ability. Some of the women also possessed no little skill. Nearly all Indians were fond of decorating their lodge covers in this manner, using the brightest colors they could obtain, and some of their imaginary or real deeds of valor were portrayed in the most picturesque style, though they were often more glaring than artistic.

When the wild Indians retired to sleep they wrapped themselves in the robes or blankets they had worn during the day. The beds were more a name than a reality; these consisted of the dried hides of buffalo, horses, or other animals, laid upon the ground to keep out the dampness. Occasionally they placed an additional buffalo robe or two on top. For pillows they used skins, or any bulky soft stuff which they might have at hand. The interior arrangement of an Indian lodge was a series of such beds arranged in a circle, leaving a space in the center for the fire on which the cooking was done, and it also served to some extent to warm the lodge in winter.

Some of the women were expert at drawing designs on buckskin for bead and porcupine quill work. In ornamenting their clothing they would first draw the outlines of the figure, then sew bead or porcupine ornaments on them, using an awl made of bone; and the end of a small sinew for a needle.

All Indian women were expert riders and rode astride on the animal's bare back, or on a man's saddle. Like the men they were expert in throwing the lasso, and were fearless of any animal, no matter how vicious. Children, both boys and girls, were tied on the backs of horses almost as soon as they were able to walk, and taught to ride, to manage animals, and to throw the lasso or the lariat rope.

When Indians moved their camp, which they were frequently compelled to do, the women did all the packing. Their belongings and the whole camp outfit was put in condition by them for transportation and fastened on travois, or packed on their horses, mules, and dogs.

Travois were made by lashing the ends of lodge poles together, then throwing the lashed ends over the saddle of an animal, leaving the other end of the poles dragging on the ground in the rear. Immediately behind the animal was a large oval frame made from the limbs of a young tree, with rawhide thongs woven in and out across it, so that it somewhat resembled a lawn tennis racquet, only that it was much larger and coarser. This frame was lashed to the poles on each side, forming the bottom of a rude basket on which their effects were to be transported. It also served to keep the poles a sufficient distance apart while traveling.

When the children, and the sick, infirm, or aged were to be transported on a travois, a cage-like covering of the same material was placed over this platform and lashed to it; over this lodge covers were thrown as a protection against the sun, rain, or snow, as well as to keep the inmates from falling out. In traveling, each animal had its travois. Even the dogs were not exempt from this service; most of them were required to drag a travois made of small poles. Children not old enough to care for themselves, but too old to be carried by their mothers, were placed in them. Drawing the travois was very severe on the animals. After a short time in this service their backs became a mass of raw sores. Horses and mules which had been in possession of the Indians for any length of time were rarely seen without such sores or scars upon them, which were sure evidences of the severe labor and punishment in drawing the travois.

To one not accustomed to it, it was a novel sight to see an Indian village on the move. Some of the horses carried one, two, and three children on their backs while dragging the travois, and others had two or three women astride in addition to dragging the load. The travois and pack animals were scattered in every direction along the route, but all moved together toward one general point. In dry weather the dust made by one of these

moving villages could be seen for miles.   When crossing swollen streams
the work of the women was very laborious.   Everything had to be removed
from the travois and packed on the backs of the animals to prevent the goods
from getting wet.   Once across they were replaced on the travois, and the
village proceeded until camp was reached, where they erected the lodges.

The packing of animals was an art in itself.   The pack saddle was made,
both at the pommel and cantle, like the figure "X."   The bottom, where it
rested on the back of the animal, was shaped something like the bottom of a

INDIAN TRAVOIS—BLACKFOOT.

wooden saddle.   The Indians used strong rawhide cinches to fasten the saddle to the animal.   The load was added gradually, and when the pack was
complete, a rawhide or hair lariat rope was placed around and over the
goods and over and under the animal many times, being fastened on the
crosses at the top of the pommel and cantle.   The pack of an animal should
be so placed on its back as to have the weight equal on both sides, and in
such manner that it would not slip or move, or any portion of it fall out or
get in such position as to cause repeated stoppages to adjust it.   Pack animals sometimes carried a load of five or six hundred pounds each, and
when packed it was necessary to lead them around in a circle constantly to

prevent them from lying down, for should they lie down with the pack they would be unable to rise again unless the pack was removed. Of all expert packers in the mountains and on the plains, none could compare with Indian women.

People of to-day little realize how long it took the Indians to acquire or accumulate the small amount of stuff they had in their keeping. Beads, porcupine work, Iroquois shells, claws and teeth of bears and mountain lions, arrowheads, lances, shields, pipes and stems, bows and arrows, and horse equipments largely made up their possessions. These were handed down from generation to generation, and were much prized as having been the property of their forefathers. As they never cleaned or washed their effects, their dirty condition can be readily imagined. All their habitations were foul-smelling from the unutterably filthy condition of their entire belongings.

All Indians were fond of trinkets, particularly of the Iroquois shell. The Iroquois is a shell-fish caught off the coast of British Columbia, in the waters of the Pacific Ocean. The method of catching it was to attach a piece of fresh meat to a rope and sink it to the bottom of the sea, when the Iroquois settled upon it as thick as the quills on the back of a porcupine. The meat was then drawn to the surface, the shell fish laid in the sun, and the animal life soon passed out. When cleaned and polished the shells were a beautiful white, like ivory, and slightly carved like a bear's claw. They were from one to three inches in length, tapering from the size of a rye straw at the larger end nearly to a point. The Indians passed sinews through the shells, and made necklaces and breastplates of them for the women and children. Ear pendants of Iroquois shells were also worn, and some were three feet in length and weighed from one to two pounds each.

Breastplates were also common. These were made of the small bones of the deer or antelope, worked round and belly shaped, then highly polished and bound together in two or three rows by thongs passed through the center lengthwise. Some of these were large, covered the entire chest and reached to the waist; these were heavy and in winter were cold and disagreeable to the wearer; but the intense vanity and love of display of the red men did not deter them from exhibiting their ornaments at all times, even at the expense of discomfort or suffering. White men made imitations of these bone beads of porcelain and traded them to the Indians for making breastplates.

CHAPTER XI.

THE SIGN LANGUAGE—ITS MYSTERIOUS ORIGIN AND SIGNIFICANCE—COMMUNICATION BY SIGNALS.

Indian Languages—Their Strange Diversity—No two Indian Nations known to Converse in the Language of the Other—The Sign Language—Its Mysterious Origin—The Arapaho, Sioux, Cheyenne, and Navajo Languages—Significance of the Sign Language—Sign Language by Horse Riding—The Sign Language of the Hands—Difficult Sentence in the Sign Language—An Incident in my own Experience—Sign Language by Movements of the Horse—Sign Language by the Mirror—Sign Language by Smoke—Communicating at Long Distance—How an Indian Wrote a Letter—Hieroglyphics on the Faces of Rocks in Texas—Rude Drawing in Caves—Difficulty of Interpreting Them.

ALL Indian nations spoke a different language, and this diversity has given rise to much discussion among philologists. It must be conceded that the Indian nations had a very ancient history, as they lived in comparatively close proximity to each other and yet spoke wholly different tongues.

The sign language of the Indians was nearly universal among all Indian nations, and was handed down from a remote period. Neither the learned nor the unlearned can throw any light on its origin. The Indians themselves did not know how they acquired it. It descended from their ancestors, and that is all they knew about it. The hieroglyphs of the Aztecs are not more mysterious in their origin than the sign languages of the Indian races of the West.

The wild Indian had the faculty of adapting himself to his surroundings, so long as they were congenial, and found means at all times to utilize everything suited to his needs.

Nothing in his entire existence was more useful to him than the sign language; through this silent means of communication a member of any tribe located in Texas, could converse with a member of another living in the far north, or along the St. Lawrence river, although both were unconscious of the existence of the other.

In this, immediately on meeting, conversation began by one of these mysterious mediums; probably the first was by the movements of the horse or smoke, when a truce was declared; then, if satisfactory, a friendly conversation was held by the more complete, or comprehensive means of the signs by the hands.

So well were the signs understood by all, that no practice was necessary between the parties.

Among no other peoples in the world speaking different languages, is there a general means of communication of any kind that is understood at sight. These signs were exceedingly graceful, as well as significant.

The oral language of one nation might be pleasing to the ear; another might be harsh, coarse, and guttural; in another the words might be very few. It was difficult and sometimes almost impossible for an Indian nation to acquire or speak intelligently any language but its own. So it was even with tribes of the same nation. The Navajo, for instance, a tribe of the great Athabaskan nation, could scarcely understand the Apache, who belonged to the same family. The Arapaho language in particular was very poor, having but a few hundred words, yet it was extremely difficult to acquire sufficient knowledge of it to converse on the most ordinary subjects; whereas the Sioux language was rich in words, pleasant in sound, and was much more easily acquired. The Algonquin language was also pleasing to the ear and readily learned.

Yet nearly all Indians possessed a means of ready communication between themselves through the medium of the sign language, which somewhat resembled the method of communication between mutes. All Indians were extremely reticent, speaking but few words, yet they would sit for hours conversing with each other in the sign language. The sign language of the hands was highly significant, though it was necessary to follow closely the thread of conversation, for the wrong interpretation of a single sign was sufficient to break the whole chain of thought.

Another peculiarity was the rapidity with which Indians could communicate with each other by it. The Sioux could by its use express a great deal more in a shorter time than by word of mouth.

The sign language was very figurative. For instance, if an Indian desired to say that you were not truthful, he touched his tongue with one finger, and held up two fingers toward you, signifying that you were double-tongued, that is, untruthful. If he wished to say that a given place was distant two, three, or more days' journey, he twirled the fingers of both hands, one over the other, like a wheel rolling, then inclining the head as if asleep, and holding up as many fingers as there were "sleeps," meaning nights; thus indicating the number of days' travel necessary to reach the place in question. If he desired to refer to the past, he extended the right hand in front with the index finger pointed, and drawing his arm back with a screw motion, meaning a long time back. If he intended to refer to the future, he placed his hand with the index finger extended at his back, pushing it forward with a screw motion, thus signifying a distant time in the future. If he desired to speak of being on horseback he did so by putting the first and second fingers over the fingers of the left hand, representing a man on horseback. If he wished to state that he had a large quantity of anything, he made the sign of a heap with his two hands shaped like a funnel, then moving them upward from the ground to a point, in the form of the

WI-CHA-I-WE—SIOUX.

letter A. If he desired to say that he had nothing, he opened the palm of his right hand, and in a sweeping way, with a movement of the forearm to the right indicated that the hand was empty. If he desired to say that he had had a good meal, he extended the thumb and forefinger of his right hand over the region of his stomach and moving the hand up to his mouth, indicating that he was full. These are a few of the symbols of the sign language. The signs employed were innumerable, and every one of them illustrated the idea to be conveyed.

One of the most difficult sign sentences that I ever tried to comprehend was in conversation with some Indians in the South Park. We were expecting to go into battle the next day, and the night before one of our Indian allies came to me and conversed in the sign language. The first sign given was one sleep, after which the right hand was passed rapidly under the left, both palms being opened downward, which meant "going in." The next sign was opening and shutting the fingers of each hand toward each other rapidly, which meant to fight, then a downward catch of the forefinger, which meant good or true; and last, the most incomprehensible of all, the making of the figure 0 with the index finger and thumb of the right hand and turning the hand over as though emptying a bottle. After repeated efforts to interpret the last sign I gave it up in despair, but finally learned the translation of it.

It meant to pour something out.   The whole sentence translated verbatim was, "To-morrow I will go in and fight good, if I pour my life out."   Such was the brief but graphic description of his intentions as expressed by the sign language.

Mounted Indians often communicated in the sign language by the movements of their horses.   I never was able to translate many of these signs, but to the Indian they were all perfectly plain.   I have seen Indians converse in this manner as far as the eye could see, understanding each other perfectly.   The movements of the horses were made in rapid succession, and seemed to me in the long distance all about the same.

Another means of communication was by the flashing of a mirror in the sun.   This method of signaling was sometimes used for long distances.   At that time, however, it was rare for an Indian to have a mirror, and as they could only be used in the sunlight they were not of great service.

Still another means of communication was by fire and smoke.   The latter was of great service while in the mountains, and to the Indians was perfectly intelligible.   Although smoke seems uncontrollable, yet they made it serve their purpose well.

The sign language enabled each nation of Indians to converse with one another intelligently.   By it bands of warriors of different nations could communicate at long distances, making alliances among themselves for descent on their enemies and for attacks upon settlers, overland travelers, and others.

None of the wild Indians had any method of general communication by means of pen or pencil, although I once saw an Indian letter written under the following circumstances: Some traders had been sent to trade with Indians in the vicinity of Rawhide Peak.   The Indians had brought in a great many more pelts than the traders expected would be offered, and the stores they brought for exchange soon ran low.   An Indian took the dressed hide of a deer and pictured a letter on it with colored crayons.   It represented an Indian leading a mule with a pack saddle on it; a red roll, representing a bolt of red cloth; a black tin can such as powder is sold in, and a drawing representing a bar of lead, thus signifying that his party wanted a pack mule, a roll of scarlet cloth, some powder, lead, and ammunition to trade.   This letter was considered a great curiosity by all who saw it.

Along some of the streams in Texas, there is a limestone formation with perpendicular smooth walls, varying in height from fifty to a hundred and fifty feet.   On the rocks along some of these streams are petroglyphics, drawn and cut by the Indians.   They are found in various portions of that

State, and are the work of different Indian nations. Some of the Jesuit Fathers claimed to be able to translate this figure writing, but I have never known any two of them to give the same translation. My opinion is, that the Indians, being in camp near these places, drew and cut these figures for their own amusement, and without any serious intention of perpetuating historical or other events. Nearly all the figures on the rocks in that State are of about the same kind, representing horses mounted and unmounted, Indian men and women, deer, bears, and other animals.

One striking feature is the great age of some of these petroglyphics. In that State some of the Indian nations buried their dead in the ground, and put a stone over the grave to mark the spot as well as to keep wild animals from digging up the remains. If the Indians were able to write, they would no doubt mark the spot with hierolgyphics cut in stone in some way that would be intelligible to those who came after. If these petrographs were not for this purpose it may be that they are of no special significance, but were rather the work of vain Indians who desired to show their ability as artists.

In most of the drawings on clothing, the figure of the hand was common; but among the more intelligent, when worked in beads and variegated-colored porcupine quills, and worn on headgear, it was significant of a position of importance; when drawn on lodge covers in colors, it was emblematic of a deed of valor by the owner of the lodge or a sign of friendship, and when cut in stone it was usually in connection with other figures which may have had a significant meaning.

INDIAN BARK HOUSE.

CHAPTER XII.

THE INDIAN AS A FIGHTER—HIS BRAVERY AND CONTEMPT OF DEATH—A
CUNNING, STEALTHY, AND TREACHEROUS FOE.

Born Fighters—The Indian's Contempt of Death—His Great Courage—Fighting and Hunting His only Occupations—Not easily Surprised or Ambushed—Indian Method of
Preparing for Battle—Return of a War Party—Re-enacting the Warlike Scene—
Treatment of Captives—Prolonging the Torture—Effect of Firearms on the
Primeval Indian—How the Indian first secured Firearms—Horse-stealing considered a Virtue—Indian Lack of Inventiveness—Articles that have never been improved on—The Snowshoe, Moccasin, Tepee, and Bow and Arrow—Great Buoyancy
of their Canoes.

WHATEVER may be said of Indian ferocity, whether in conflict with his
own race or with the white man, his courage cannot be disputed. From his
first contact with the whites until his recent round-up on the reservations, he
always proved himself a born fighter.

He usually hesitated to attack until he was sure he had the advantage;
but that only proved that he was shrewd as well as brave. The white man
had the best of modern weapons, while the Indian for the most part had to
depend upon his bow and arrow, or a rusty old gun or pistol, with limited
ammunition. If he resorted to treachery in fighting, and was wily almost
to cowardice during battle, he was only making up for his disadvantages,
and could not reasonably be blamed for it. When fighting with other Indians, on equal terms as to equipments of war, he evinced the greatest courage and showed supreme contempt of death. Fighting was as natural to the
Indians as hunting. They were fighting among themselves when the white
man first met them; they had traditions of strife and warfare from immemorial periods; and kept up a chronic warfare with each other, as well as
with the whites, until the national government reduced them to submission.

When fighting among themselves they had rude military codes and regulations, held war councils, and planned campaigns or raids, after true Indian
fashion.

It was not often that one Indian tribe surprised another, for the Indian
instinctively feared an enemy on every side, and was on the alert. Before

going on the warpath, many of them worked themselves into diabolic frenzy by engaging in their so-called war dance, painting their faces and bodies, uttering fierce cries and war-whoops. The aged, the feeble, and the young who remained behind,, cheered them on, and eagerly awaited their return with booty or captives.

When the war party returned, its approach was first announced by scouts, and the result of the adventure related. If the expedition had met with disaster, the names of the dead or captured were made known, when the women indulged in wild wailings and other signs of grief. Should the unlucky party, however, bring with them captives, all the passion and fury of the tribe was sure to be wreaked on them.

Unless thoroughly crushed, the returning party did not admit defeat, but indulged in shouts of triumph, brandishing their weapons and waving the scalps or other trophies they might have taken. An imitation of the warlike scene was re-enacted, and the exploits of the braves rehearsed in mimicry. If successful, the captives were sometimes spared and adopted into the tribe.

Captive men were rarely permitted to accompany a war party against their own people, the warriors fearing that the prisoner might escape and rejoin his tribe; besides the Indians were suspicious of every one, and placed confidence in no one outside of their own people.

When condemned to torture and death, the sufferings of the captives were intensified by every method of barbarity the tormentor could devise. In ingenuity of cruelty, and in the exercise of it, the women were invariably the most fiendish. If the victim manifested any indication of weakness or cowardice he was treated with jeers and scorn, and his sufferings were prolonged and multiplied. If, on the contrary, he bore his torture with indomitable stoicism—as he usually did—he elicited the admiration of his tormentors, and sometimes his torturers rewarded his fortitude by killing him to end his sufferings.

When the Indian first encountered the white man's firearms he was stricken with superstitious awe. He knew not what to make of the artificial thunder and lightning. As civilization advanced to the West he gradually secured modern implements of war, and became more or less proficient in their use. The adventurer and trader did not hesitate to supply the savage with these instruments of destruction, although they might be turned against those who supplied them at any moment.

Next to taking the scalp of his enemy, the highest virtue in the Indian's catalogue was success in horse-stealing. When the merits of a brave were recounted by others, adeptness as a thief was considered by his tribe as almost equivalent to exploits in battle. Hence there was for the Indian a double incentive in horse-stealing—it gained for him admiration and wealth at the same time.   The more horses he had the richer he was, and the more influential he was with his people.

The North American Indian was not noted for his inventiveness.   Like the animals to which he so closely adapted himself, he was satisfied with his existence, and did not try to improve his condition, or to render life more agreeable.   But there are several things that he invented which all the ingenuity of the white man has never been able to improve.   These are the canoe, the moccasin, the snowshoe, the tepee, and the bow and arrow.

BOAT MADE OF ONE TREE.

Each of these is simply perfect in regard to the use for which it was intended.

The Indians roamed over the entire country in search of subsistence, and utilized the water highways in their rovings to the fullest extent possible. The birch-bark canoe was well adapted to the end for which it was designed. It was made sufficiently strong to carry themselves and their belongings over the lakes and streams; it was also light enough to be transported over portages from one waterway to another.   Over portages they first transported their goods, and then returned for the boat.   The birch-bark canoe was generally used on the waters of the North and Northwest.   In the far western plains, where no birch trees grew, they fashioned boats out of the hides of buffalo, making the so-called bull-boat.   This was shaped by stretching the green hides over a wooden frame.

It was extremely difficult to adapt one's self to those frail canoes without overturning them, but Indians manipulated them with consummate skill. It is, however, worthy of note that the French *voyageurs* handled bull-boats and canoes with more facility, and adapted them to a greater variety of uses than the Indian had ever done. The material of which the Indian canoe was made was easily procurable, and if damaged it was easy to repair. Some of the bark canoes were capable of carrying many tons of freight, besides paddlers and passengers, and were used by all the fur companies, traders, hunters, and pioneers in transporting their stores.

The moccasin, as a foot covering, was as admirably adapted to the Indian as was the canoe. It was made of tanned deer skin, and was sewed with the sinews of animals, the hole for the sinew being made with an awl of bone or other sharp instrument. The moccasin kept the foot warm, did not impede perspiration, was elastic and soft, allowing perfect use of the foot and toes in climbing rough places or treading rugged paths. It was easily made and easily mended.

The snowshoe was a necessity for the Indian in the more northerly regions, enabling him to travel in winter through deep snows, and to hunt game. With it he could go over the deepest snow drifts without sinking, and where he had level footing he could run with great speed. The snowshoe is to-day universally used in cold countries, and in the armies of northern Europe is a part of the military equipment. It is, in its make and in its use, the same as the Indian gave it to us. Neither science nor art has improved on it in the least.

SNOWSHOES OF THE BLACKFEET.

Of the tepee, and bow and arrow, nothing further need be said here, as they are elsewhere fully described. The tepee or skin-covered lodge is a thing of the past. The Indian has passed from his nomadic condition and no longer requires this kind of habitation. Furthermore, the animals upon which he depended for the covering of this movable dwelling have become almost extinct.

BUCKSKIN SHIRT FRINGED WITH MANY HUMAN SCALPS—SIOUX.

CHAPTER XIII.

THE INDIAN'S NATURAL WEAPONS AND HOW HE USED THEM—TEACHING YOUNG BRAVES INDIAN WARFARE.

Indian Weapons of War and of the Chase—The Indian War Club—The Tomahawk—The Scalping Knife—The Lance and Shield—The Bow and Arrow—How they were made —Dexterity of the Indian in the Use of the Bow—His Lack of Proficiency in the Use of Modern Firearms—His Limited Use of Tools—Boys Practicing with Bow and Arrow—Securing their first Firearms—The Indian not a Good Rifle Shot—Sham Battles—A Realistic and Exciting Exhibition—Their Decorations and Equipment— How the Young Brave Acquired a Knowledge of War—Dexterity in Rescuing their Wounded during Battle—His thorough Mastery of his Horse.

THE oft-repeated and commonly accepted statement that the wild Indians of this country used a stone war club as a weapon of offense or defense is largely fictitious. In the first place, it is unfitted for such a purpose. The person using a club must first come in close contact with his enemy before he could make use of such a weapon. Again, the stone club is heavy and unwieldy, and is not dangerous except when the enemy is lying prostrate. Clubs of the kind referred to were common in Indian camps, but were usually employed as mallets in driving stakes or lodge pins, and for general camp purposes. It is true, however, that after a battle the women would sometimes dispatch the wounded and mutilate the dead on the battlefield by smashing their skulls with these clubs.

Some of the men carried a peculiar-looking club, painted in gaudy colors, the handle thickly studded with brass-headed nails. On one side, near the top, was fastened one or more formidable looking blades of iron. Other kinds of clubs had a solid wooden head at the end, in which was fastened a long iron spike. The Indians did not, to my knowledge, use these clubs in battle with white men, or between themselves. They were carried upon ceremonial occasions for show. The Indian loved to see himself portrayed with this ugly-looking, but useless weapon, conspicuously displayed, and nothing would tickle his vanity more than to have his picture taken with his favorite club in his hand.

With the advent of firearms among the Indians, the tomahawk also ceased to be an important war weapon.   It was commonly carried, but generally used as a pipe, the back or head being hollow and used for a bowl, and the handle, which had a hole through it, was used for a stem.   The blade or axe was of iron or steel; this they procured from white traders.   The tomahawk has passed into history as a bloody weapon, and at one time might have been entitled to its reputation as such, but of late years it was rarely used.   If by chance an Indian met another in a hand-to-hand combat his weapon was the knife.   Some of the duels with knives were of the bloodiest kind; they would stab and slash each other so terribly that both contestants died locked in each other's arms.   When a fight of this kind occurred it was sure to end fatally for one or both.   I once saw the bodies of two Indians who died in this manner, and counted eight stabs and twenty-one slashes on one body, and eight stabs and fourteen slashes on the other; the bodies were lying close to each other just as they had died.

WAR CLUB ORNAMENTED WITH BRASS-HEADED NAILS—BEAR CLAW DECORATION ON END OF BUCKSKIN SHIRT SLEEVES—FACIAL PAINTING—MINNECONJOUX SIOUX.

All Indians, both men and women, carried a knife in a sheath attached to the belt, and were dexterous in its use.   The knife was their inseparable companion, and was used for slaughtering animals, scalping enemies, and for general purposes.   Knives were kept as sharp as possible, the handle being often elaborately ornamented in true Indian style.   In early days on the plains it was difficult for them to secure a sufficient supply of knives, but that difficulty ceased after white traders established trading posts throughout the Indian country.

The wild Indian was also armed with a lance, which he sometimes used with deadly effect in battle or on raiding expeditions; many of the nations and tribes carried this weapon until they were disarmed. The head of the lance was made of iron or steel procured from white traders.

The old tradition, so common in history and fiction, of Indians using poisoned arrows, is without foundation. In the first place, I am at loss to know where they could procure the poison. It is claimed, however, by some that they used the venom of the rattlesnake for this purpose. Admitting this to be a fact they could have but few poisoned arrows, for the owner would be apt to be the first to suffer from contact with them. If they ever did use poisoned arrows it must have been of rare occurrence. I never saw or heard of any, in my long experience among the Indians.

The bow and arrow was well made, and was often a work of art. The shaft of the arrow varied in length among different tribes, and was usually made from reeds, or carefully selected straight, slender branches of the red willow. The lower end was feathered along the sides from two or three inches to more than a foot. The point or head was ordinarily made of hoop iron, and was fastened to the shaft by sinews. Some of these were barbed on both sides like a fish-hook. Once a barbed arrow entered the body of a human being it was necessary to push it entirely through, or cut it out, in order to remove it, for should an attempt be made to draw it out the way it went in, the barbs would catch in the flesh, and pull off of the staff. Should an arrow remain in the flesh for a length of time the sinew used to fasten the head to the shaft became soft, and an effort made to withdraw the arrow at once disengaged the shaft and left the arrowhead in the wound.

LANCE AND BELT—SIOUX.
DOG SOLDIER INSIGNIA.

The bow was usually made of hickory, willow, mesquit, or Osage orange wood. Occasionally bows were reinforced or backed with the sinew of the elk or buffalo, which made them very strong and elastic. A person not accustomed to a bow of this kind might scarcely spring it two inches, while an Indian would spring it a foot or more, driving the arrow with tremendous velocity. With a strong bow he could drive the arrow half its length into the body of a buffalo. The bowstring was of twisted sinews and was very strong, lasting a long time. It would cut like a knife when used by unskilled hands. The Indian protected his arm at the wrist by a piece of rawhide, to prevent the relaxed bowstring from cutting and disabling him.

A bow and arrow outfit was usually carried in a bow case and quiver, attached to each other, made of skin, generally of the mountain lion, otter, or buffalo, and was slung over the Indian's back.

Indian boys frequently stood in a line when practicing with the bow, each having his hand full of arrows, and at a signal they fired them with such rapidity that the air was filled with them, and after they were through firing each ran and collected his own arrows where they had fallen. This seems incredible, as all the arrows looked alike, yet a mistake was rarely made.

At first the only firearms they had were the old-fashioned, flint-lock, muzzle-loading pistols and muskets. Later on, however, they managed to obtain the best modern arms, but they still clung to their natural weapon, the bow and arrow. With the advance of civilization the Indians experienced less difficulty in securing modern firearms and ammunition.

It is a notable fact that Indians did not acquire proficiency in the use of firearms. Even after the red man was employed in the United States military service, where he had every facility for improvement, he did not compare favorably with the white man in handling firearms. The common idea gained from Cooper's "Leather Stocking Tales," and more modern literature, that all Indian warriors were superior marksmen, is a romantic delusion. The best that can be said of them is that they made progress in the use of modern arms. They were not experts with the rifle, and rarely, if ever, practiced target shooting—which is absolutely necessary to make a fine marksman—principally for the reason that such practice meant a waste of ammunition; as it was difficult for them to obtain this they preferred to reserve it for fighting or procuring food. Not until about 1863 or 1864, when some benevolent people of the East took pity on these poor red men, did they obtain modern firearms, such as Winchester repeating rifles, Spencer carbines, and other magazine pieces. As it was necessary to have metallic cartridges for the use of these arms, they were particularly careful not to waste this kind of ammunition. Besides, the Indian did not acquire proficiency in the use of tools, nor did he have them, so when his modern firearms got out of order he was unable to repair them; therefore they remained useless weapons. Efforts were made to teach Indians in the employ of the government the principles of marksmanship, but according to a recent department report they did not reach much more than one-third of the average of the white man either in individual or collective firing with the rifle. At pistol firing they were somewhat better in mounted practice, showing some improvement over their degree of skill with the rifle. In spite of all efforts of the government the record made by them was far below that made by the troops.

Notwithstanding the Indian's constant use of his weapons and the fact that from earliest childhood he had but one ambition, proficiency in war, they did not organize themselves into bodies for drill with arms, or in manœuvring or instruction in the art of war. When a drill of any kind was attempted, a number of men came together and indulged in a sham battle. Generally a chief or leader was chosen to direct the movements of an imaginary fight, but the deafening yells of the flying warriors prevented but few orders being heard; besides each warrior was supposed to be proficient in the art of war and needed no commands. Sham battles were not for instruction but amusement, and each brave was at liberty to join in the fun and retire when he pleased.

Those participating were fantastically dressed with war bonnets and feathers; their faces, arms, legs and bodies hideously painted in all colors obtainable; and all naked as if entering the fiercest battle.

They mounted their best war horses, which were also painted in various colors on bodies, necks, heads and legs; and in their manes, tails and foretops were entwined feathers, grass, and strips of fur. All being in readiness, the warriors formed themselves in line facing the imaginary foe; suddenly a charge was made in the direction of the supposed enemy, and after that every warrior acted independently; throwing himself from one side of his mount to the other; charging and counter-charging; circling as though surrounding the enemy; throwing his lance, firing arrows, uttering fierce war cries and yells, and making all sorts of movements and gesticulations as though participating in the most desperate conflict.

On these occasions their shields were indispensable; these were suspended about their necks and over the shoulders by buckskin thongs, and by dexterous movements of the body—but without the use of the hands—they were constantly moved from one side to the other, to the back and front, and kept in every position possible to prevent the wearers being pierced by the weapons of the opposing party.

They presented a picturesque appearance when moving and circling rapidly with gaily colored war bonnets and feathers; especially if scalps dangled from the center of the shields, which was frequently the case.

During sham battles the yells of the flying warriors were deafening. These imaginary conflicts usually lasted but a short time, for it was hard work; to this, the red man was constitutionally opposed.

The Indian was so independent in his nature and so impatient of restraint, that it prevented his becoming a part of an organization for the purpose of instruction or drill. The young brave acquired much knowledge of war from listening to the old warriors as they told of their many battles, and the glorious part they had acted in them. After hearing these stories the young man at the first opportunity mounted one of the best horses belonging to himself or father, and went through an imaginary fight by himself. In this way he became a good horseman, as well as versed in the movements of Indian warfare.

One thing all Indian warriors practiced and became proficient in, was the manner of seizing and carrying off a wounded comrade from the field of battle to a place of safety. Owing to this practice the troops rarely captured a wounded Indian. They also practiced how to disperse in case of defeat; this to them was one of their important manœuvres in escaping from the enemy. They scattered in every direction, in ones, twos, and threes, to prevent pursuit. After going a short distance they returned and repeated the same manœuvre, each Indian selecting a different comrade and going in a different direction.

When mounted on a vicious or untrained war horse, it is surprising with what skill a warrior managed his mount, with nothing on the animal but a lariat rope around the lower jaw. He was perfect master of his horse, twisting and turning him within his own length, and in every direction without apparent injury to the animal.

When in actual battle these movements were rarely ever adhered to, but they served to teach the young warrior how to conduct himself during a real engagement, and made him an expert in handling his mount and weapons.

Indians did not use spurs. It would have been difficult to obtain them ; moreover, when riding they thumped the animals constantly with their heels, and spurs would have cut through their sides in a short time.

All Indians mounted and dismounted from the right, or off side with or without a saddle. When in battle they mounted from either side, when necessary. When mounted they were expert with the lasso, throwing it with great precision, catching an animal around the leg, neck or almost any part aimed at. This they could do when going at any speed. In throwing the lasso, men, women, and children were all experts.

CHAPTER XIV.

AN INDIAN DOG FEAST—FINGERS VERSUS FORKS—AN INDIAN DINNER PARTY—PERSONAL EXPERIENCES.

Why the Indians were Nomadic—A Dog Feast—Cooked in its Skin with the Hair on—
How the Favorite Dish Tastes—Its Peculiar Flavor—Giving a Dinner to a Famous
Chief—Astonished Indians—Eating all Night—Indians with "Good Hearts"—A
Perfect Gorge—Eating with their Fingers—Refusing to use Knives and Forks—A
Delicate Meal—Speech of a Great Chief—"Wacpominie"—What it consisted of—
Old-Man-Afraid-of-His-Horses—An Embarrassment of Riches—Some Valuable
Presents—Disagreeable Pests—Manner of Ridding Skins of Vermin—A Pertinent
Conversation with a Chief and his Significant Reply—The Grossest Insult known to
the Sioux.

In their wild state the savages were kept moving constantly from one place to another, for the reason that when the grass was consumed in and about their camps, they went elsewhere,—not to get away from the filth which had accumulated about them, but to supply forage for their animals and food for themselves.

Besides, the wild Indian was naturally of a roving disposition; he was not satisfied to remain long in one place, no matter how comfortable it might be. He had an insatiable desire for new scenes, to visit old and new acquaintances. Often he changed location to please one of his daughters, whose heart was attracted to another portion of the country, where she hoped to see some young man she fancied; again he moved for reasons known only to himself. I have seen them locate in beautiful places, that afforded protection from the rigors of the winter. In a few weeks the spot was deserted and they were occupying a barren, inhospitable place. The weather had no terrors for the red man when he desired a change of locality; they were constantly on the move during all seasons of the year.

On notable occasions they held a feast. Of these the greatest of all was a dog feast. Their dogs—every Indian village and camp was overrun with them—were a species more or less inbred with the coyote and gray wolf. For a feast of this kind some of the fattest dogs were killed. The Indians would sit all night eating the meat of a dog boiled in a pot, bones and all, cooked without salt, and eaten without accompaniments of any kind. The flesh of a dog, when boiled Indian style, has its own peculiar flavor. It is stringy and tough, though the fat of the animal when boiled is passably palatable. I have been to many of these feasts, and must confess that I do not relish dog meat.

A great feast was once held near Fort Laramie, pending negotiations between Colonel Wm. E. Maynadier and Red Cloud, at which many Indians were present, probably ten thousand, all Sioux. Old-Man-Afraid-cf-his-Horses was not present at the treaty, but arrived a few days afterwards, when I had a talk with him. This was after the massacre of August, 1863. As he called me his son, I gave him a banquet consisting of hard bread (a kind of cracker supplied by the government to the troops), bacon, salt pork, dried beans, peas, rice, hominy, sugar and coffee.

There were about two hundred and fifty Indians present at this feast, including Old-Man-Afraid-of-his-Horses, and other chiefs less notable. The cooking was done by the troops in kettles and pans belonging to the garrison, and was served by the soldiers on tin plates. Our Sioux guests sat in a large circle after their own fashion, and ate with their fingers, refusing to use the knives and forks with which we supplied them. This was not a meal, but as some of the troops aptly remarked, a perfect gorge. The Indians sat eating the entire night; when morning came there was not a vestige of what I had supposed was an abundant supply, besides something for each one to take to his lodge for his family. The amount of very much sweetened coffee they consumed was astounding. This feast would not commend itself to the ordinary white man on account of the tempting dishes provided, but as few, if any, of these Indians had ever tasted such a variety of food, they made many grunts and gesticulations testifying to their high appreciation of such a delicate repast. They licked their fingers and looked at each other in astonishment, their eyes following the men serving the food as if saying to them, "Give me some more."

After the feast was over and the Indians had "good hearts" for the time being, on account of the fullness of their stomachs, Old-Man-Afraid-of-his-Horses arose and made a speech, saying in substance, "For this feast and for all that we have received at the hands of our friend Possuscopie" (Roman Nose, for that was the name these people called me) "we will pour out the goodness of our hearts." Many of the Indians who partook of the feast made me presents afterwards, mainly consisting of buffalo robes, some of which were decorated in the most gorgeous style of aboriginal art. I also received some tanned deer and antelope skins, and other articles of small value. I must have received that day, in all, fully sixty or seventy skins. Many of them were handsomely decorated with porcupine quills, and were as soft and pliable as a piece of the finest cloth. The labor of tanning them on the fleshy side required great skill. In preparing them the roots of the hair were not injured; otherwise the hair and fur would constantly shed, which would diminish the value of the skin and annoy the wearer. Among these presents were a number of beaver skins, which were not only of intrinsic value but were rendered more so by the way the pelts had been prepared. These were tanned with the brains of the animal and had a pleasant smell. I had some of the beaver skins made into a robe that was much admired, and which often served to cover me while lying on the ground exposed to the rain or snow.

I returned some of the presents to the donors. It may be asked why I did so. In the first place it required a long time for Indians to make such accumulations; secondly, I could not use them all; and lastly, and the most important reason was, they were filled with vermin.

The manner of ridding buffalo robes of vermin was to lay the robes on the ground upon or near the hills of the large black ants which were numerous in that country, when the ants would seize the vermin and eat them. It took many days to rid a hide of the pests, as each hair had numerous nits or eggs upon it. These had to hatch out (which took some time) and be destroyed by the ants before the robe was entirely freed from the vermin.

On this occasion, there were present Red Cloud, Spotted Tail, Old Smoke, The Trunk, Dull Knife, Lone Dog, Ribs, Old-Man-Afraid-of-his-Horses, and many other Sioux notables. I asked Old-Man-Afraid-of-his-Horses to answer one question, insisting that he should do so frankly. Prefixing my question by saying, "You call me your son. What would you have done to me, had you met me in a defenseless position during the time of the massacre?" He hung his head for a moment as if in deep thought, and without raising his eyes or looking at me, said, "My son, I should have regretted meeting you. I would not have harmed you, myself, but I could not have been responsible for the acts of my young men." My reply was, "I understand fully what you mean; you would not have killed me yourself, but some of your young men would have had that pleasure." To this he made no answer.

The Washington Post of July, 1902, published a statement made by one of the oldest and most experienced employees of the Indian Office, which says in part:

"Notwithstanding all that has been said about the progress the government is making in civilizing the Indians, the full blooded Indian of to-day is right where he was one hundred years ago.

"There is something about the Indian, his singularly narrow, perverse and stubborn nature, that places him beyond all efforts at his regeneration. Our experience has been that the Indian never rises above the intellectual and mental status of a child of fourteen years. His ways are childish, curious and hard to understand, and his thoughts and manner of reasoning so utterly unlike that of a white man that it takes the latter long years of association with, and residence among the aborigines before he can understand their mental processes.

"They are naturally taciturn and reserved, and if they fail to understand a thing, the more you talk and try to explain, the more bewildered they become, and the less likely are they to grasp what you are trying to tell them.

"About twenty years ago several Wild West shows petitioned the Indian Office for permission to take a number of Indians from the different tribes to travel about with their shows. The propositions were granted, and they secured all the Indians they wanted.

"The results were just what a practical man might have expected from the start. The Indians who traveled about with these shows in this country and in Europe learned

ORNAMENTED CAP, SHIRT AND LEGGINGS.

all the manifold vices of the white man and not one of his virtues.

"From every reservation we receive letters from the agents begging us not to allow any more Indians to leave the reservations with Wild West shows. These Indians had seen civilization; they had been to London and Paris, but they had seen only that part of civilization which attracted their barbaric and childish fancy, and in consequence they returned home full of whiskey and disease, meaner than they were before they left, more perverse and stiff-necked."

CHAPTER XV.

BURIAL OF THE DEAD—STRANGE FUNERAL RITES AND CEREMONIES—THE
INDIAN'S IDEA OF THE FUTURE STATE—LIFE IN THE SPIRIT LAND.

Funeral Ceremonies—Burial of a Chief—Last Rites—Final Resting-Place of their Important Personages—Buried in a Sitting Posture—Scaffolds on which the Dead were
placed—How they were thrown down by Buffalo—Taken by the Whites for Fuel
—Killing Animals at the Funeral—Women and Female Children buried in various
ways—Dead Bodies eaten by Carnivorous Animals and Birds of Prey—Intolerable
Stench at an Indian Burial-Place—Journey of the Soul to the Spirit Land—The
Indian's Inability to Compute Time—Feeding the Soul during its Journey—Belief
that the Spirit left the Body through the Mouth—Why Indians Mutilated the Slain
Bodies of Enemies—Execution of Big Foot, Black Crow, and others by hanging in
Chains—Death in its most Dreaded Form.

THE burial ceremony among Indian nations varied. Among the majority

SCAFFOLD GRAVES ON THE PLAINS—SIOUX—PLATTE
RIVER.

of them the death and burial
of one of their chiefs was attended with great ceremony.
Large numbers of warriors
would assemble to attend the
last rites. The body of the
dead chief was always attired
in the best raiment he possessed during life. His war
equipments, bow and arrow,
lance, shield, saddle and horse
equipments, blankets, buffalo
robes, and other personal belongings were left with the
body when placed in its final
resting-place.

The body of one of these
distinguished personages was
sometimes deposited in a tree
particularly adapted to receive
the remains. Others were
placed on a platform, six to eight feet in width, and ten to twelve feet in

length, resting on upright poles set in the ground, and from ten to fifteen feet in height. On these platforms were frequently placed the bodies of several important chiefs. Scaffold graves were usually set on the summit of a hill or in a valley, selected because it was a favorite place of the deceased during life. On top of the platform was laid one or more bodies, over which buffalo robes, a lodge cover, or skins of different kinds, were tightly drawn, and securely fastened by thongs to prevent them falling to the ground. In this manner the corpses were left until they rotted and fell. The bodies of common warriors were frequently disposed of in the same manner, usually being dressed in the best clothing they possessed during life. Some of them were placed in a sitting posture, and presented a peculiar appearance; others were left lying on their backs, all being covered to prevent birds of prey from eating the flesh.

On the plains, the scaffolds on which the bodies of the dead were left did not remain standing for a great length of time unless carefully watched. The buffalos, when roaming over the prairie, their hair filled with buffalo gnats, which ate great sores into their tough hides, would, in trying to rid themselves of their tormentors, rub against the poles and throw them down. If the buffalo did not do so, the oxen and domestic cattle belonging to freighters crossing the plains, when turned loose to graze near these places, would rub against the scaffolds with the same result.

When the platforms were erected near the Overland road, the numerous emigrants, in crossing the plains, were usually vandals enough to cut them down for fuel for cooking purposes; consequently this was not so secure a method of disposing of the bodies as placing them in trees. The Indians, however, had an aversion to placing their dead in trees where members of the tribe were likely to make their camp, as the stench from the decomposing bodies remained for a long time; and as horses, mules and dogs belonging to the deceased were frequently killed and left at the funeral spot, the stench from the decomposing remains of warriors and animals was intolerable, especially when the sun came out very hot after a rain storm.

I recall the illness and burial of one of Spotted Tail's daughters. A very noted Indian was Spotted Tail. He fought the whites only when he could be benefited by increasing his number of horses, mules, and stores by pillage. He had his headquarters and that of his tribe in the neighborhood of Raw Hide Peak. When one of his daughters, to whom he was much attached, was taken seriously ill, he immediately repaired to Fort Laramie and asked assistance of one of the army surgeons. His daughter was kindly treated by the surgeon, but finally died, and was given the usual Indian funeral about twenty-five or thirty miles from that place. Her body was placed on a

BROTHER AND SISTER—SIOUX.

scaffold of poles set up after Indian fashion.   Afterwards her remains were interred in the hills just outside the fort.   I was present at this burial, and was particularly interested in the prayers said by each one of the friends of the family who spoke.   Charles E. Guerreu, who was the best interpreter of the Sioux language that I ever knew, stood near me and repeated the prayer that each one made.   The body was interred in the early evening. One of the Indians in his prayer said: "We bury your body as the sun goes down, and as the sun rises in the morning, so your spirit will go to our Great Creator with the rising of the sun, which will take you to the spirit land, and there keep you until all your family and friends shall join you. You will be in life again with them, and live for a long time without want or care."   Other prayers were equally expressive, and all of the same import.   The death of this young girl, and the kindness of the whites at the fort in caring for her during her illness, seemed to soften Spotted Tail's savage nature.   For a long time he was quite friendly, and made almost weekly visits to the grave of his daughter, after which he would visit the fort, where he was kindly treated.

The bodies of women and female children were frequently buried in caves, or in ravines or holes; as the Indians had no tools for digging the ground, the corpses were covered only with a little dirt, over which grass, leaves or branches were usually thrown.   Bodies buried in this manner did not remain long undisturbed.   Wolves and other carnivorous beasts in search of food would eat the flesh entirely from the bones in from one to two nights, and drag the remnants far away from the place where the corpses were left.

At nearly all funerals of warriors, and sometimes of their favorite sons, a sufficient amount of food was placed near the deceased to supply them during the journey to the new home.   No Indians I have ever conversed with could tell me how long it took the disembodied spirit to make the journey to their imaginary heaven.   The Sioux believed that the soul arrived at the spirit land at the adult age, ready and equipped for all the pleasures incident to adult life, and that their animals arrived with them in good condition. The Indians had no way of computing time; it was therefore exceedingly difficult for them to explain how long a time was required to make this journey, nor could they explain how it was made.   When it is considered that the most intelligent of them did not attempt to account for the change from day to night, or why the seasons varied, it can readily be understood how difficult it was for them to explain anything about the time required for the journey of the soul to its future home.

I once had a talk with Old-Man-Afraid-of-his-Horses in relation to the soul from the time of death to its arrival in the spirit land, and asked him if he believed that the soul would have in its new home the articles which were buried with the body here, and if, during its journey, the road would be a pleasant and safe one, or one in which all sorts of wild beasts and other

TREE GRAVE—BRULE SIOUX—REPUBLICAN RIVER.

dangers or obstacles might be encountered. I asked him if the soul made this journey alone, and whether it traveled during the light of day or the darkness of night; also to explain the flight of the soul from one point to another. He said he could not explain anything about it, but he knew well enough that the articles that were buried with the remains would not be with the person in his new home; that such a person would know how to make exact reproductions of what was buried with the body here, and that the souls of horses and dogs killed at the funeral were to accompany the soul of the deceased, and be the souls of those animals in the happy land. I asked, if that was true, why they placed meats on the scaffold for the journey of the spirit. He replied that it was necessary for the soul to have something to subsist upon during its journey, be it long or short.   I then inquired where he got all these theories.   He said, with some warmth, that they were not theories, but facts; that it was necessary for everything that lived to have something to feed upon, and, as the soul was alive, it was necessary that it should be fed in passing from one stage to another.

I then said to him: Suppose the soul had left the body for several days, during which time it had traveled a long distance, how could it feed upon the food which was left upon the scaffold and which still remained there? He replied that the soul was a spirit, and that it extracted the spirit food from the meat, which accompanied the soul on its journey.   I then asked him how he arrived at such conclusions.   He said he did not reach them at all; that this belief had been handed down to him by his forefathers, that he believed they knew, and he did not trouble himself to learn anything further about it.

He abruptly turned and asked me what my belief was—whether the white man expected, when he died, to go to a happy hunting-ground, or a spirit land.   My answer was in the affirmative.   He then inquired how our spirits reached that place.   Frankness compelled me to reply that I did not know. The questions he propounded as to the change from one life to another required more of a philosopher than I to answer.   Every one of his questions would be called, if asked by our children, "a poser," and I found it was much easier to ask questions of this nature than to answer them.

The Indian believed that the spirit left the body through the mouth, and that all Indians who were not scalped or hanged went to the spirit land, there to live forever after the manner they had lived here, but on a grander scale.   He needed there all the things he required here, or he could not be happy.   Hence the best weapons he possessed in life were buried with him, and his best animals were killed at his final resting-place.   As he expected his career in the future world to expand and be far superior to his earthly life, he must, therefore, all the more require all the means of securing a livelihood, and of defense against his enemies.

The Indian's idea of the future life was purely materialistic.   He had no spiritual conceptions, consequently it was impossible for him to imagine a condition of things in a future state different from what he knew in this. The other world or state of existence was to him only a magnification of the present one.   Anything that could be procured here he believed could be obtained there; hence, the only things that were buried with him were those that would be needful to him in procuring his subsistence in the spirit land.

If the warrior had not as complete an outfit as was deemed needful in this world at the time of his death, his friends endeavored to supply the deficiency before his burial. The final resting-places were never despoiled. A superstitious awe attached to them, and no Indian would dare draw on himself the wrath of the Great Spirit by touching any of the articles left for the use of the dead.

MANDAN BURIAL PLACE—DISH WITH FOOD FOR THE SPIRIT.

Another phase of Indian belief was that the body in the next life appeared in exactly the same form as it was when the earthly life departed from it. Young or old, whole or mutilated, it r e m a i n e d in the spirit land forever t h e s a m e. Hence the fiendish mutilations of the dead by the Indians. They endeavored after killing their enemy, to make his existence in the next life as miserable as possible.

The Indian's idea of a future life was based purely on tradition—he never reasoned on the subject. His fathers believed it and that was sufficient for him. He had no fear of death in its natural form, or in battle. He was a stoic and a fatalist.

When Colonel Moonlight decided to execute the Indian chiefs, Big Foot, Black Crow, and others, about the years 1864-65, they were told of their approaching fate, tied, put in a six-mule wagon, and driven to the place of execution. During the time they were being transported to the gallows, on which they were to be hanged in chains and left for the birds to prey upon, or to rot down (which they eventually did), they did not evince the slightest fear. They sang their weird death chant, and were driven under a scaffold made of two poles twenty feet high, with a pole across the top, with the chains hanging therefrom. The chains were adjusted around their necks, the wagon driven from under them, and they were left dangling in the air. Apparently the least concerned of all were those who were executed, and, as they were to be hung in chains, which, according to their belief, prevented the spirit from leaving the body through the mouth, the stoicism was all the more remarkable, as death came to them in its most dreaded form.

Some tribes of the great Athabaskan nation had different ways of disposing of the bodies of the dead.

The Zunis, another tribe of this nation, burned the bodies of the dead. First digging a shallow hole in the ground, in this the remains were placed; logs and branches were then laid over the spot and set on fire; after all had been consumed, the location was marked with a stone.

The Chippewas of the Algonquin family buried the corpses in the ground in a sitting posture, and the funerals were attended with great ceremony, often lasting for weeks. Among these people females and children received the same funeral as the males and adults.

Some of the California tribes had peculiar burial customs: these are fully described in the chapter on those Indians.

TREE GRAVE, SOUTH DAKOTA.
Photographed in 1884—Am. Mus. of Nat. Hist.

CHAPTER XVI.

THE GREAT SIOUX NATION—A FIERCE AND WARLIKE PEOPLE—LIFE AND SCENES AMONG THEM.

One of the Largest and Most Warlike of Indian Nations—Old-Man-Afraid-of-his-Horses—A Noted Chief—How he acquired his Name—How he became Famous—When and how a Brave could change his Name—A Nation of Meat Eaters—Their Manner of Cooking and Eating—The Universal Dirty Cooking Pot—A Voracious Sioux—Drinking Dish Water—Why Indians were constantly on the Move—Always at War with their Neighbors—Why they had no Intoxicating Liquors—Insulting an Indian by asking his Name—Indian Vulgarity—Indian Mothers-in-law—How they were regarded—An Indian Forlorn Hope—An Alliance that meant Death and Destruction—Splendid Horsemanship—The Stone Bath—Practice of Voodooism—Heroic Treatment—Wealthy Indians—Many Ceremonies—Demonstrative Love—No Social Castes—Dog Soldiers—Widely Separated Tribes—Superstitious fear of Hail-storms.

SLOW BULL—TYPICAL SIOUX.

THE name of the great Sioux nation as known among themselves was the Lakotas or Dakctas. The early French trappers gave them the name of Nadowesioux, or Nadcessi; this was afterward abbreviated to the word Sioux, by which name this nation has long been known.

During my life in the Far West, the Sioux were the largest and most warlike nation of North American Indians, numbering from sixty thousand to eighty thousand souls according to the best estimates, for no accurate census could be taken at that time. They occupied the entire country from the Mississippi River on the east to the eastern chain of the Rocky Mountains on the west, and almost from the boundary line between the British possessions and the United States on the north, as far south as the Republican River in Kansas and an imaginary line about due east and west from the mouth of that stream, crossing the South Platte River between Julesburg and Fremont's Orchard.

They were divided into many tribes, each with its own name and chief. Some very prominent Indians were chiefs of the different tribes. The most noted chief in the entire nation at that time was Old-Man-Afraid-of-his-Horses. All the other chiefs bore much the same relation to him that the Governors of the different States do to the President of the United States.

It may be asked how Old-Man-Afraid-of-his-Horses acquired such a peculiar and suggestive name. The story as I received it from his own lips was as follows: When he was a young man and an aspirant for Indian honors, a war party was made up of Minneconjou Sioux to attack the Pawnees and Pottawottomies in their hunting grounds in Kansas and Nebraska. During

INDIAN CAMP—BUFFALO SKIN-COVERED LODGES.

the battle that followed, this young warrior captured some very vicious horses and evinced great fear of them; for this the Indians dubbed him Old-Man-Afraid-of-his-Horses. Being thus ridiculed by his Indian comrades he determined to relieve himself of the stigma fastened upon him by his name, by performing deeds of valor at the first opportunity; and in subsequent battles he acquitted himself with such distinction that his people looked upon him with great favor.

For these acts of bravery, his sound advice, and personal magnetism, he was afterward made chief of the Minneconjoux. On many other occasions war parties were made up of his and other tribes of the Sioux, for the purpose of making war on the Crows, Snakes, Utes, Cheyennes and Arapahoes, as well as on their old and inveterate enemies, the Pawnees.

When war parties were organized, and he was one of them, the command by common consent was always given to him; and he showed such superior judgment and military ability that he was soon recognized as the most important chief of the entire Sioux nation.   He was a man of large stature, with a massive head denoting superior intelligence, mild in manner, and, if it can be said of an Indian, not without some generous impulses.

It was customary among the Sioux when a brave counted a *coup*, to change his name for any other that he preferred; but as Old-Man-Afraid-of-his-Horses had achieved great distinction under his old name he clung to it ever afterward.

After the death of this illustrious old warrior his name was handed down to his son, who was known as Young-Man-Afraid-of-his-Horses.   Both father and son were widely known, and for years retained great influence with the Sioux.   Both tried as far as lay in their power to keep the Sioux at paece with the white people.

The country occupied by the Sioux was the natural home of the buffalo, elk, moose, black, white-tailed, and mule deer, the antelope, mountain sheep, black, grizzly, and cinnamon bear, beaver, otter, foxes of various kinds, gray wolves, black wolves of the timber, and coyotes.   These animals, in addition to their dogs, horses, and mules, supplied them with an abundance of meat; for the Sioux ate the flesh of all the animals mentioned.   When they were fortunate in a hunt and secured more meat than they could eat at the time, the women jerked and cured the surplus by cutting it into long strips, which were hung over poles outside of the lodge, and out of the way of dogs and wolves, leaving them there until thoroughly dried.   The meat was then packed in bags made of hide, and kept for use during the winter months after the buffalo had migrated to a warmer climate.

The Sioux were carnivorous.   They did not eat cereals, or BARBED AR- vegetable food.   They often ate their meat raw while the blood ROW HEAD of the animal was still warm.   Commerce and trade were un- —SIOUX. known to them.   They fashioned their own implements of war, stole what they could from their neighbors, and later on from emigrants and freighters crossing the plains.

They were great gluttons and ate enormous quantities at a time, which did not seem to distress them in the least.   When they had a pot or other vessel suitable to cook in, the meat was put into it and boiled.   When they had no vessel the meat was thrown on the coals and broiled, or held over the fire and roasted. The cooking, when in camp, was done by the women. If they had a pot it was always on the fire, and the contents were kept constantly boiling. Each individual helped himself whenever he felt like it, everybody fishing out the food from the pot with their fingers; as Indians never washed their hands the pot and its contents after a time would become anything but clean. I have never been attracted by Indian cooking, unless when stimulated by excessive hunger; and then I preferred my meat broiled rather than have it cooked in the universal pot.

While many of the stories told of the Indian's insatiable appetite are grossly exaggerated, it is nevertheless true that he could consume at times an amount of food that would astonish the white man. This may be partly accounted for by the fact that the Indian passed most of his time in the open air, in a state of bodily activity, and did not take his meals with regularity.

An amusing illustration of the Indian's abnormal appetite came under my personal experience in the Rocky Mountains. My command encamped in the vicinity of Deer Creek, some miles below Fort Caspar. A body of troops were crossing to the Pacific slope and encamped within a few miles of us. I had been apprised in advance of their coming, and had secured for the officers a pleasant surprise in the way of an abundant supply of fresh meat of the antelope and mountain sheep, and other eatables usually acceptable to soldiers after a weary march over the arid and scorching plains. I rode down to the camp shortly before dinner and invited the commanding officer and his staff to dine with us. He replied by inviting me to dine with him and his mess, remarking that he had an abundance of bacon and hominy. I laughingly answered, as I urged my invitation, that I had an Indian in my camp, a Sioux brave, who alone could eat all he had. "If your Indian can do that," he replied, "I will accept your invitation with pleasure." I accordingly despatched one of my escort to our camp, with instructions to return with Short Ribs, which was the name of the voracious individual referred to. The mess was duly set, and the Indian invited to eat. He needed no pressing, but at once proceeded to clear the table. As the victuals continued to disappear, the astonishment of the officers was amusing to behold. Short Ribs soon devoured all the food that had been prepared. I asked if they had anything more left; the officer laughingly answered, "Nothing except a basin of dish-water." This was ordered to be brought in. Short Ribs placed the dish-pan to his lips and drank about a third of its contents, setting down the vessel with a grunt of satisfaction, which indicated that he considered it the proper beverage with which to

LITTLE WOUND—WAR BONNET DECORATED WITH SCALPS ON END OF FEATHERS—
BEADED LEGGINGS AND MOCCASINS—RED STONE PIPE AND ORNAMENTED STEM.

Twenty Years Among Our Hostile Indians.

wash down his enormous meal.   The amount of food consumed by him on this occasion had been prepared for four hungry army officers.

Large bodies of nomadic people cannot long remain in the same place, especially if, like the Indians, they have a great number of animals, as the struggle for food and fodder is ceaseless.   Owing to their numbers the Sioux were less stationary than other nations; as they lived exclusively by the chase, they had to be constantly on the move to maintain existence.   In summer they hunted the buffalo and other aniamls, and their horses lived

GROUP OF SIOUX—WOMAN ON RIGHT, SHOWING MANNER OF SITTING ON THE LEGS.

on the grass; in the winter they were compelled to secure food for their animals.   This was frequently supplied by the tender branches and the inner bark of the cottonwood tree.   As the Sioux had no axes or implements for felling trees, they often followed in the track of the beaver, which in some localities cut down with its teeth enough trees to give sufficient food for the Indian's animals.   This fact affords a striking illustration of the countless number of beavers that existed along the streams and rivers of the West in those days.

The Sioux roamed over so vast a territory that they were almost continually at war with some of their surrounding neighbors; owing to their superior numbers they were generally victorious.   Man to man they were not equal to the Cheyennes as warriors, but were more advanced in general knowledge than any other wild Indian nation.   They learned many things that were unknown to smaller tribes, as they were brought into contact with the white man more than any other tribe or nation, as civilization trended to the west.

The Fremont trail, or the Overland route, led through the heart of their territory.   They attacked emigrant and other wagon trains crossing the plains, and from these marauding expeditions secured arms, implements, and supplies of many kinds.   They sometimes captured muskets and ammunition, and were intelligent enough to use them.   After the ammunition had been exhausted these arms were practically useless until more could be obtained in a like manner; meantime they necessarily returned to the use of their own implements of war and destruction.

After the establishment of trading posts along the Overland road the Sioux began to trade with the white man, a few of them visiting the stations and bartering with the traders for articles which they carried to their far-off homes.   Trading posts were necessarily many miles apart, and all were thoroughly fortified.   Each post had a large corral for the protection of men and animals, and was well adapted for defense.   The corrals were made of trunks of trees a foot or more in diameter, sunk deep and firmly in the ground, standing close together and usually about ten feet high, having holes and interstices through which to fire in case of attack.   The Indians traded largely through middlemen.   They exchanged with the traders the tanned hides of the buffalo, antelope, elk, moose, deer, bear, mountain sheep, and the flint and tanned hides of the beaver, otter, wolf, fox, and other animals, receiving in return small round mirrors, red cloth, blankets, paints with which to paint their faces and bodies, and other coveted articles.

The trader in those days was careful to prevent the red man from obtaining intoxicating liquors, should they have any on hand, which was rare, as the government prohibited liquors being taken into the Indian country.   Most of the hackneyed stories of the Indian being ruined and demoralized by the firewater of the unprincipled white trader are baseless and absurd.   The trader, knowing Indian character too well, was anxious under all circumstances that they should not have liquor, well knowing that one or two drunken Indians would be liable to make trouble at his post, and that he might be the first to suffer by them.   For this reason the traders themselves were especially anxious to prevent any person supplying the Indians with liquor.

One of the most impolite things a Sioux could do was to ask another his name. The Indian to whom such an inquiry was addressed would not reply, but would haughtily turn to some one who knew him, and say in the loftiest manner, "Tell him my name." Every Indian considered himself so prominent and well known that he regarded the question an insult to his dignity. Sioux names, both male and female, were often obscene beyond expression. Generally the names referred to some personal peculiarity of those who bore them, or to some incident or exploit in their career. Thus: Crying Eagle, Lone Elk, Long Dog, Skulking Wolf, Kicking Horse, Bear Tamer, The-One-Who-Walks-under-the-Sun, The-One-Who-Walks-Before-Day, The-One-Who-Strikes-Twice, Crazy Horse, Eagle Eye, Bear Catcher, Blue Day, Rain Cloud, Snow Eater, and so on interminably. I mention these because they were the names of noted Indians of different tribes, all of whom I knew. The Sioux located their camps far away from military posts, frontier traders, and the Overland road. When braves of this class met on the warpath it meant an assault upon every living thing of flesh and blood with which they came in contact.

The only thing that was considered vulgar by a Sioux was to speak to his mother-in-law. This custom was carried to the farthest extreme. If any communication was to be made to a mother-in-law, it was invariably made through a third party, generally some member of the family; but it was their unwritten law that under no circumstances should an Indian speak to his mother-in-law. I tried, but unsuccessfully, to ascertain why the custom prevailed; but no one could or would tell me its origin or why it was so persistently adhered to. No one seemed to have sufficient courage to face the ridicule that would follow. I once asked an Indian,

GOOD HAWK, IN FULL CEREMONIAL
COSTUME—SIOUX.

"Suppose your wife was dangerously ill, and your mother-in-law was the only person present, and it should be necessary to give her instructions on the carrying out of which depended your wife's life, what would you do?"

"I'd let my wife die," he replied with a grunt, "before I would speak to my mother-in-law."

SIOUX CAMP—SHIELD ON TRIPOD WITH SCALP HANGING FROM THE CENTER.

When the shield of a warrior was fastened on a tripod outside of his lodge, with a scalp dangling from the center of the shield, it informed all comers that the scalp was captured by one of the male members of the lodge. It was a token of no little significance. A visitor could not tickle the vanity of an Indian more than to enter the lodge and make inquiries about this trophy. He would be told in the most graphic manner of the terrible battle with the owner of the scalp, of his desperate character, and of the hair-breadth escape the brave had in killing his victim and securing the prize. Indian ingenuity would be almost exhausted in describing the different stages of the fight, and the tremendous difficulty the warrior had in dis-patching so gallant a foe. Nothing pleased the braves more than to be asked all the minor details of the combat, and the imaginary or real battle would be described in glowing colors. I use the word imaginary, for should they by stealth manage to kill a person while asleep they would weave about it a picture of prowess and glory that could not be outdone by Cooper or Longfellow.

In treating the sick the Sioux used the stone bath. A large number of round boulders were placed in a pile, eight to ten feet in length, three to four feet in width, and one to two feet in height. On this a fire was kept burn-ing until the stones were thoroughly heated, after which the fire was re-moved, and sticks two or three feet high were bent over the entire pile. Over these sticks were thrown the coverings of lodges, three or four thick-nesses, making the hole thus enclosed almost air-tight. In this the person who was to receive a hot-air bath was placed, lying at full length on the heated stones over which was spread his blanket or buffalo robe. If a steam bath was required water was thrown on the stones while the patient occupied the bath.

The suffering of a patient in one of these baths was intense, although the sufferer would never display signs of discomfort. The patient was kept in them from twenty minutes to two hours; when the bath was over, he would sometimes take a plunge into the river or pond, near which the sweat houses were always built.

The appearance of the patient as he emerged from the sweat house, after a long bath, was pitiable. He was usually bleached to a deathly color, and presented the appearance of one who had undergone a trying ordeal.

Another manner of treating the sick was through the ministrations of the medicine man and his voodooism. He made wild gesticulations, and did many mysterious things which nobody could understand, under pretense of benefiting the afflicted person. When his conjury failed he endeavored to save his reputation by claiming that he had not called upon the right "med-icine" to effect the cure. The old women resorted to voodooism also, as well as to teas made from herbs, meats, berries, and barks; even portions of rare animals were often administered in efforts to relieve the afflicted.

One of the greatest feats known to the Sioux was termed by them "throwing himself away," or "pouring himself out," and would be with us called

SWEAT HOUSE OF THE SIOUX.

"a forlorn hope." When one nation determined to have a pow-wow or a talk with another with whom it was at war, a party of young warriors would carefully approach and signal the other party. If their signal was not respected, one or two of the warriors were selected to make a dash into the camp or a village of the enemy with whom a talk was desired. All being in readiness, the warriors would "throw themselves away." Mounted on their best horses, and riding at the top of their speed, they would dash into the camp of the enemy, gesticulating in the sign language that they wanted to talk. If the feeling was not too bitter between them they might be accorded a pow-wow. If the pow-wow was granted they would sit conversing for hours in the sign language. Should their desires not be granted, however, they paid the penalty of their rashness with their lives. If the interview terminated favorably, it portended disaster for some one, as it meant the alliance of the two peoples for the warpath. When Indians allied in this way, the warriors of one vied with those of the other in deeds of bravery and atrocity. A war party of this kind was always formidable, and left nothing undone to accomplish the object for which the alliance was formed. When the object of the expedition had been attained, the alliance which had been made with such great effort came to an abrupt end, and it would not be long before the parties were again at war with each other; though there are instances where such alliances were lasting, namely, between the Cheyennes and Arapahoes, Utes and Apaches, Comanches and Kiowas.

TURNING EAGLE—SIOUX.

The Sioux—and all Indians for that matter—were splendid horsemen, using saddles of wood made by themselves; these were covered with rawhide sewed with a thong of the same material. After this covering had shrunk and dried on the saddle it was very tight. The stirrups were also made of wood, covered with rawhide, the stirrup straps being short. The bridle consisted of a long lariat or rawhide rope, the noose of which was placed loosely around the animal's neck, thence to and around the lower jaw in two half hitches, and thence to the rider.   The long end was left trailing on the ground, the rider using it as a whip when driving the herd.   When he desired to strike one of the herd he could, by a dexterous movement of the forearm, hit an animal a severe blow on any part of the body he wished.

All men, women, and children, when riding, carried a quirt.   This was

BASKET WEAVER—PUEBLO.

a riding-whip, with a handle of wood from twelve to fifteen inches in length and of convenient size.   Through a hole in the end a rawhide thong was passed, in two strands, with a knot in the middle.   The lashes were from twelve to eighteen inches in length.   At the other end a thong of tanned skin was placed through a hole made in a loop, and passed over the wrist for carrying it.   A whip made after this fashion was a severe instrument;

with it, an Indian would take an animal which had been overridden and abandoned by a white man and get many more miles of travel out of it.

The Sioux wore moccasins of two kinds, one kind having soles of flint hide and uppers of buckskin sewed together with sinews; the other was made from one piece of buckskin, the soles and uppers being alike. Moccasins were generally ornamented with beadwork of various colors, or porcupine quills: moccasins were strong and durable, and well adapted for going over rough ground; they were also soft, pliable, and comfortable for the wearer in dry weather.

The Sioux—men, women and children—frequently wore large ornaments in their ears, which were slit open from the top to the bottom of the lobe, sometimes with an inner cut. From these slits hung pendants of various kinds, often of huge size and length. These consisted of Iroquois shells or beads, and to the end, which hung over the shoulders to the breast, was attached a huge shell, usually mussel or mother-of-pearl. From the inner slit hung rings of brass, copper, or iron. Wristlets and armlets of wire were commonly worn.

In the extent, variety, and quality of their handiwork the Sioux were far in advance of any other Indians of the West.

Their women were more comely than those of other Indians. This may be partly accounted for by their manner of living. Occupying an immense territory, abounding in all kinds of game, the women were not subjected to the privations and drudgery endured by the women of other nations.

A certain sort of communism prevailed among the Sioux. Sometimes several families occupied the same lodge, and the stock of food was common to all. But unlike some others, there was no tribal communism.

The Sioux were polygamous, securing their wives, few or many, by purchase after the usual Indian fashion. Infidelity was practicably unknown among them, and families lived in harmony in their homes. They possessed more wealth in horses, mules, lodges, robes, skins, arms and wearing apparel than any of the savage Indians in the entire West. Wild horses were numerous in their territory, from the herds of which they caught large numbers.

The Sioux had more ceremonies, dances, feasts and pastimes, than any other nation of wild people on this Continent.

Living in a good climate they were constantly engaged in some outdoor amusement. Their clothing was well made, and for Indians they were well dressed.

Their Indian weapons were of the best. Nearly all of them had the red stone pipe; groups of men would sit in circles in the open air smoking them in silence for hours. These people believed in, and worshiped the Great Creator, to whom they smoked. Originally they smoked the pulp of the red willow; when they could procure tobacco it was mixed with killikinick for smoking. Some of their pipe-stem ornamentation was handsome, *i.e.*, for Indians. The tribes of the Sioux living along the foot hills, or in the Rocky Mountains were the most ferocious of any Indians I have known—

being so far removed from civilization, they seldom saw or came in contact with the whites.

In those days it was perilous for the whites to enter their country. After our Powder River expedition opened their territory, they continually attacked and killed the troops, as well as others who had the temerity to enter their hunting grounds. These tribes were numerous, and well able to defend themselves against all comers.

The Sioux buried their dead warriors on scaffolds or in trees. The bodies of dead females and children were thrown into gullys or ravines, then covered with stones or branches of trees; wild beasts and birds soon left no trace of them.

SPOTTED TAIL.—CHIEF.

The only case of demonstrative love that came under my observation among the wild Indians was in the tribe of the Ogalalas of this nation. A short, stout, comely young girl caught the heart of a young man. They were so enamored with each other that they were constantly together. He would sit for hours by her side, combing her hair with a stick, oiling and braiding it, painting and patting her face, and paying her his most delicate attentions. If water was needed he would run for it, returning in the shortest time. He finally secured her for his wife without cost or ceremony. After this they seemed more cemented together than before. So strong was his affection that he could not be induced to go on a war party, or to any place she could not accompany him. The others ridiculed him, calling him "woman's heart." This made no difference; he was the same constant lover.

When I last saw them they had no children, and their love seemed as deep-rooted as ever. They lived with his parents, who, for Indians, were well-to-do. It was not necessary that he should go on the hunt, consequently they were not separated, and both seemed to take no other interest in life than to be together all the time. Their conduct was so unusual that the tribe could scarcely understand what to make of them. At first some of the Indians claimed both were crazy. After they learned what it meant they were the admiration of the tribe.

The oral language of the Sioux was rich in words, pleasant to the ear, and easily learned. Some of the tribes living along the Missouri River had a slight dialect. They acquired this from their surrounding neighbors.

There were no social castes among the Sioux. Every person seemed on the same level in this respect. There was a semimilitary organization known among themselves as the "Dog Soldiers." Each member of this fraternity had an insignia of some kind, usually a lance, spear, shield, or war implement, which he carried as a mark of distinction.

With this in full view, warriors would strut about in the most imperious manner. Each member considered it a great honor to belong to the "Dog Soldiers," and thought himself much better than those who were not members of this organization.

What the object of this clan was, I was never quite able to discover, as they had no drills or other war instruction.

This was the only society of any kind among the wild Indians in those days.

The Sioux differed from the majority of other nations in that the large tribes were not subdivided into numerous small ones. Each of the large tribes retained their district tribal cohesion.

Should necessity compel them to separate temporarily, the members remained

ZIN THA KIN-YAN (FLYING BIRD)— TYPICAL SIOUX—TOBACCO POUCH, LEGGINGS AND MOCCASINS ORNAMENTED WITH BEADS OF VARIOUS COLORS.

loyal to their original tribe; consequently each tribe of this nation was large and powerful. Some of the tribes were so widely scattered that their members rarely, if ever, met. This was notably true of the Assiniboins, Mandans and Yanktons, and the Ogalalas, Minneconjoux and Uncpapas.

The Sioux were very superstitious, and a severe hail storm during summer filled them with terror, as they believed it was the Great Spirit showing his

anger. After storms of this kind, both men and women claimed that their medicine had been broken, when they indulged in their mysterious rites to recover the broken charm.

They recited a legend that, in the autumn during Indian Summer, when the horizon was covered with thick haze, it was the Creator indulging in his annual smoke and blowing it in great clouds over them—his chosen people—from his great pipe in acknowledgment of his appreciation of their devotions during the year; but if the haze was light or of short duration they claimed that he was displeased. Then large numbers assembled and smoked almost constantly.

With the lighting of each pipe, the smoker filled his mouth and lungs with smoke and, blowing it skyward, said a prayer. This was repeated by each as the pipe reached him; on these occasions the bad god was never recognized, as they claimed that the Evil Spirit was then in the swamps, marshes, or damp places awaiting an opportunity to counteract their efforts in appeasing the offended deity.

They also claimed that by the density of the haze the coming winter could be foretold; that if it was to be mild the haze was dark and deep, but if the haze was light and of short duration the winter would be long and severe.

In trying to forecast the seasons, they observed closely the actions of animals and

STANDING BUFFALO.

birds, and the aged foretold with much accuracy the seasons by following the habits of all wild animal life.

CHAPTER XVII.

STILL AMONG THE SIOUX—THE MANDANS—INDIAN FREE MASONS—THE
ASSINIBOINS—THE GROS VENTRES, OR THE BIG BELLIES, CUISSES
BRULES OR BURNT THIGHS.

The Mandans—Their Interesting History—Nearly Exterminated by Small-Pox—Indian
Free Masons—A Great Mystery—How did they Acquire a Knowledge of the Order?—
Their Pastimes—The Buffalo Dance—Manner of Disposing of their Dead—How the
Skulls of their Dead were Used—Their Happy Domestic Life—The Assiniboins—
Their Hunting Ground—A Far Northern Tribe of Indians—Their Characteristics and
Customs—Scourged by Small-Pox—The Gros Ventres, or Big Bellies—Origin of the
Name—The Brules—Battle of Ash Hollow—The Ogalalas—Their Country—The Bad
Faces—The Yankton Sioux—Their Hunting Ground—The Minneconjoux—A Savage
Tribe—Their Hunting Ground—The Uncpapas—A Fierce Tribe—Where they Lived
—The Kaws or Kansas—The Winnebagoes—The Poncas—The Omahas—The Osages
—The Quapaws, or Arkansas—The Otoes—The Iowas.

MOURNING CUSTOMS.

THE Mandans were a portion of the great
Sioux family, and originally belonged to
the Yankton Sioux, from whom they separated at the time the Assiniboins left the
Sioux nation. Their home or principal
hunting ground was to the north of the
Missouri River, and about the mouth of
Wood River. They were first known by
the white man when Lieutenants Lewis
and Clark made their exploration of the
Missouri River; at that time they were
among the most intelligent Indians on this
continent.

They lived in huts which were superior
to anything of the kind built by Indians
north of New Mexico. Their dwellings
were circular in shape, and from twenty to
thirty feet in diameter. The framework
was made of poles and posts, the whole
covered by willow mats, and thatched with grass and covered with

earth. The roof was conical, a hole being left in the center to let out the smoke. The entrance was by a long passage, something like that of an Esquimaux snowhouse. Inside were curtains of willow matting, which divided the hut into rooms. Mats of this kind were also used to carpet the floor.

Their habitations were kept clean and neat, and the floors were swept daily. Their beds were usually on the ground; these were kept clean, being made of robes of the buffalo and other animals.

In the center was a large open space, within which a fire was built to keep the hut warm, as well as to do the family cooking. One of these huts would accommodate from twenty to thirty persons, though at times the number of the occupants was less, at other times much greater.

The Mandans at one time numbered about two thousand five hundred; but were reduced by the small-pox to less than twenty-five persons.

They had a rude kind of civilization. The sexes wore a different dress; had certain rules of decency and manners unknown to their surrounding neighbors. While polygamy may have been permissible among them, it was not generally practiced. They were a peaceable people, consequently the men were not killed off in battles between themselves and neighbors. I have never heard of their going on the warpath at any time, either before or since the small-pox epidemic.

It is claimed that they understood the principles of freemasonry. How they acquired this knowledge, if they had it, no one I have ever met has been able to satisfactorily explain. During the winter that Lieutenants Lewis and Clark passed near their villages, some member of this expedition may have taught the Mandans the secrets of this order.

Their sports and pastimes were more numerous than that of any other tribe of Indians in the great Northwest, and consisted of ball playing, at which they were experts, canoe racing, and many other pastimes. In none of these amusements did they indulge in rough horse play, so common to the Indians.

The Buffalo dance of the Mandans was sometimes continued for days uninterruptedly. The Mandans attributed the annual coming of buffalo to their observance of this ceremony, and would persist in it until the animals appeared. This dance was often grotesque. In the center of the village was a circular space of perhaps two hundred feet in diameter, in the center of which a lot of stout poles, about eight or ten feet in length, were firmly planted upright in the ground and bound together with thongs or young saplings. This sacred spot was the rallying point of the whole tribe.

CHIEF WITH BIG WAR BONNET—FULL DRESS—BEADED LEGGINGS AND MOCCASINS—
TOMAHAWK—SIOUX.

Twenty Years Among Our Hostile Indians.

During the dance two braves, with the skins of grizzly bears thrown over them, stood by the poles, while the principal dancers, clad in buffalo hides with the horns, hoofs and tails on them, wildly jumped and yelled, making ludicrous efforts to imitate the actions of the buffalo. The bodies of the dancers were nearly naked, and were painted in fantastic colors. Each dancer had a lock of buffalo's hair tied to his ankles, holding in one hand a rattle, in the other a small rod or staff, while a bundle of willow branches was tied to his back.

In this condition the dancers made all sorts of manœuvres, and bodily contortions, appealing to the Great Creator to send the buffalo. Both sexes, children and the aged, joined in the dance. This was the greatest, as well as the most important ceremony they had.

They were staunch believers in the efficacy of this dance, that without it the buffalo would not return. This is probably the reason why it was continued so long at a time.

In their religious belief the Mandans worshiped the Great Creator. They also believed that the soul of the departed went to a happy spirit land, that its path would be strewn with food, and everything in readiness for a comfortable journey. Neither did they kill their horses and animals under the trees or scaffolds where their dead were placed. Some of their legends relating to the journey of the spirit to its new home were poetic and beautiful.

The Mandans wrapped their dead in skins and placed them in trees or on scaffolds to dry, always being careful to have them at sufficient height to be out of the reach of carnivorous beasts. After the bodies crumbled to dust and the bones and skulls fell to the ground, they were gathered by members of the tribe. The skulls were placed in a circle around a hill or mound in which were also buffalo skulls, food was placed at night near the remains by relatives of the dead, or other members of the tribe. This food was supposed to be consumed by the spirits of the deceased after their departure for the spirit land.

Often food was left at the funeral place after there was nothing left but the skulls and bones.

Sometimes the skulls were collected and placed in a large circle, the face being outward; a receptacle was then placed in front of each skull and food was left on it for the spirit. In the center of the circle several poles were set in the ground, then buffalo skulls were fastened to them near the top. To these places relatives and friends went almost daily; here they sang weird chants for the spirits of the dead.

The Mandans had great reverence for the dead and burial places, more so than any other Indians in the West.

The Mandans were not nomadic, but lived in fixed habitations. Some of their villages were quite large. They were governed by selectmen. Neither did they have medicine men who claimed to cure by voodooism. The sick were treated by administering teas, made from herbs, roots, berries, leaves, etc. They were expert boatmen with the bull-boat and canoe.

In the division of the property of a dead Mandan an effort was made to dispose of it equitably by giving to each member of the family a fair share of his earthly possessions; it rarely occurred that a controversy arose about the distribution. There was less jealousy and more good feeling among the different members of the tribe than among any other Indian

WASH-ONA-KOORA—RUSHING WAR EAGLE—BEAR-CLAW NECKLACE—MANDAN SIOUX.

people in the entire West. Sometimes eight or ten families would occupy one habitation at the same time, yet all lived in peace and harmony.

THE ASSINIBOINS.

The Assiniboins were among the most northerly of any Indians on this continent, their hunting grounds extending as far into the British possessions as the Great Slave Lake, and about as far south as the Missouri River. They were a part of the great Sioux family, and originally belonged to the Yankton Sioux, from whom they separated in the early part of this century.

Why they left the Yankton has always been a mystery. They must have had some reason satisfactory to themselves for leaving and going so far north to such an inhospitable climate. The members of this tribe were much darker in color than the Sioux in general.

Their skins were rough and coarse, which was something unusual among the Sioux. Like the others of this nation they were polygamous until they joined the Mandans; after this, although permissible, it was not practiced.

SIOUX CAMP AT AGENCY.

At one time they were a cruel, vicious and treacherous people, murdering every white man who entered their country. After joining the Mandans they became more tractable.

They were called by the other tribes of the Sioux, "Hopa," or Rebels. For a long time they made their home near Lake Winnipeg, frequently going south far into the United States, but not with hostile intentions. They sometimes formed alliances with other tribes or quarreled among each other, but remained at peace with the whites. At one time the tribe was numerous, and next to the Mandans it was probably one of the most intelligent in this country. In the early part of this century they lived exclusively by the chase; as game was abundant at that time, they lived well. Inhabiting an extremely cold climate they made warm clothing for themselves from the skins of various animals.

They understood the making and handling of all kinds of boats. The bull-boats were of great service to them in crossing rivers with their stores during journeys to the south, when the rivers and streams were swollen by the melting snows from the mountains.

In habits, customs and personal appearance the Assiniboins resembled the Sioux closely. They spoke the same language, and their home life was nearly the same. They were a cleanly—and if such a thing can be said of Indians—a thrifty people. All their belongings were superior to, and better cared for than those of any other Indians in that country, except the Mandans. When the small-pox epidemic visited the northern country with such fatal results it nearly exterminated the Assiniboins. Those that were left immediately moved north to Lake Winnipeg, where they remained for a long time, believing that the Great Creator had sent this scourge among them for wrongs they had committed, or for having gone south to the vicinity of the Missouri River.

I have never been able to learn why they were called Assiniboins, as they did not themselves use this name, but were known to each other as the Assinpalik, or Stone Sioux. They greatly assisted Lieutenants Lewis and Clark while making their first expedition up the Missouri River, these explorers having passed a winter near one of their villages.

GROS VENTRES, OR BIG BELLIES.

The name Gros Ventres, or Big Bellies, as applied to the Indians of the prairie, is a misnomer. The term was applied to this tribe by French Canadian trappers and traders, because they claimed some of the members of the tribe had abdomens of aldermanic proportions.

So far from being a corpulent people, the so-called Gros Ventres were a lithe and well-formed race; in fact obesity was almost unknown among them. They were as comely and active as any tribe in the Northwest.

In characteristics, customs, habits, and general appearance little can be said of them that has not already been said of the Sioux in general.

Their hunting ground was near the northern limits of the United States, principally around the north fork of Milk River, and east of the eastern chain of the Rocky Mountains.

As their country was cold and inhospitable during winter they moved east to the regions of the Mandans and Assiniboins, and were there when the small-pox epidemic visited that region.

The entire tribe was nearly exterminated by this scourge.

After that event the Mandans, Assiniboins, and Gros Ventres lived in the immediate vicinity of each other, all three tribes living together in friendship and harmony. The Gros Ventres gave up polygamy and their savage ways, adopting the mode of life of the other two tribes.

BURNT THIGHS, OR BRULE SIOUX.

In early days one of the most powerful of the Sioux tribes was the Brules. At that time the French trappers gave them the name of the Cuisses Brules, meaning burnt thighs. They were distinctly a prairie people, and claimed as their hunting ground what is now Western Kansas and Nebraska.

BUCKSKIN COAT ORNAMENTED WITH VARIEGATED COLORED PORCUPINE QUILLS—BRULE SIOUX.

This territory was covered with tall, rank grass. In the fall or winter the grass became dry and very inflammable.

When it caught fire the heat was intense, and the spread of the flames so rapid that scarcely anything could get out of its way.

Prairie fires were often caused by lightning.

Many of this tribe were caught by prairie fires and burnt to the waist. It was for this reason the early French gave them this name. They have adopted the name into their own language, and have been known by it for a long time.

All other tribes or nations when speaking of them in the sign language called them "Burnt Thighs." In early days they were a very fierce and vicious lot, causing much trouble to all the whites and other Indians who entered their country.

During the time Singing Bear was their chief, they committed so many serious depredations on the whites, that the government finally sent an expedition to chastise them; the command was placed under Gen. William S. Harney, U. S. Army, familiarly known as "Old Harney." About 1856-7, he organized his troops at Fort Leavenworth, Kansas, which numbered about thirteen hundred men, and was composed of infantry and dragoons, and what is now the First and Second Cavalry was then the First and Second Dragoons. Harney with his command marched up the valley of the Platte River, where the Brules were committing many depredations, until he reached the valley of Ash Creek, a tributary of the Platte. Joe Tesson, an old plainsman and mountaineer, was the principal guide, who, after discovering signs of Indians made a reconnaissance, and reported to Harney that there were large numbers of Indians in the vicinity. Harney

GIRL WITH LONG EAR PENDANTS OF SHELLS.

prepared his troops for battle, and marching down the bed of a dry creek, he soon came in front of the Indian camps. Upon seeing the troops the Indians sent forward two of their number for a pow-wow, in order to gain time to enable them to retreat. Harney, knowing Indian character thoroughly, had sent a portion of the dragoons up the valley to cut off all chance of escape.

The two warriors who had been in conversation with Harney, seeing that their ruse had failed, immediately returned to their people. After delivering a volley, the dragoons charged, scattering the Indians in every direction. Harney promptly ordered the infantry to advance and fire. The latter soon put their opponents to flight. After this it was a running fight between the Indians and Dragoons. The Indian horses being fresh, soon carried their riders out of danger, although the flight extended a distance of about ten miles.

In this engagement the red men lost over one hundred killed, and left behind them twenty-five wounded.   The other wounded were carried off

MA-TO-SHI-SHA—WICKED BEAR—WAR BONNET
DECORATED WITH SCALPS ON TIPS OF
FEATHERS—SIOUX.

by the Indians.   About a hundred women and children were captured, besides a large number of animals.   All their camp equipage and provisions were destroyed by the troops.   A large quantity of clothing and other articles of civilization were found in their camps, which had formerly belonged to emigrants, and others, whom they had doubtless slain.   Among the animals taken in this fight were a number of horses that had formerly been attached to the artillery, and were captured by the Indians on the occasion of the Grattan massacre, thus showing that the Ogalala and Brule Sioux had been the chief actors in that bloody affair.   Among the Indians who lost their lives in this battle was the noted chief, Singing Bear.   It was he who led the Indians on this and former occasions.   After his death Little Thunder assumed command.   He reorganized his warriors and prepared for continued depredations, claiming that his people had not been defeated, but only demoralized by the death of Singing Bear

Little Thunder was chief when I knew this tribe, and was an Indian of superior

judgment.   He was a giant physically, weighing about two hundred and seventy-five pounds, and fully six feet six inches tall. After this battle the Brules recognized the power of the army, and were more inclined to peaceful ways toward the whites.

This tribe took part in the massacre of 1864, killing every person for some three hundred miles along the Overland road.

Immediately after the massacre I went over this road.

The scenes of destruction, death and desolation were appalling.

Travel ceased over this line for the whole season, and it was a long time before the country was again sufficiently quieted for settlers to enter that territory in safety.

THE OGALALAS.

The Ogalalas were also a numerous and warlike tribe. They claimed as their hunting ground all that territory west of the Brules, to the country of the Minneconjoux, and from about the northern boundary of Colorado as far north as the Yellowstone River. Practically they were plains Indians, as there was but little timber in the country they

GROUP OF DANCERS—SIOUX.

roamed over. Some of the members of this tribe who lived in the north were very savage. At the treaty at Fort Laramie, Wyoming, Red Cloud said to the officers present, that it was the first time that he and many of his warriors were ever under a roof made of shingles.

Red Cloud was chief of this tribe, and was very noted among all the Indians and whites of the West.

This tribe caused much trouble, and it was necessary for the Government to keep a strong military force in their country at all times to keep them quiet.

THE BAD FACES.

The Bad Face tribe lived within the hunting ground of, and were strong allies of the Ogalalas. Black Curling Smoke was chief of the Bad Faces. When the warriors of these two tribes went on the warpath together they were very formidable. When in battle they were very fierce, as both tried to out do each other.

These two tribes were so closely allied that they were practically one, there being a sort of communism among them, the warriors of both going on raids and the warpath together, without the ceremony of a big talk to decide on an agreement or understanding.

They selected wives and husbands from each other as though of the same tribe. Neither of these tribes knew anything about building or handling canoes or the bull-boats.

THE YANKTON SIOUX.

Originally the Yankton Sioux were a powerful tribe. For a long period

they occupied what is now portions of Iowa, Minnesota, Dakota and Nebraska as their hunting ground.

As their country became settled by whites, they grew less and less aggressive toward them.

It was a portion of this tribe who were the principal actors in the New Ulm massacre. After that bloody affair their warlike spirit was greatly reduced.

They have long been under civilizing influences, consequently are not troublesome. Some of the Yanktons left their tribe, forming themselves into new tribes, moving far

BLUE HAIR HORSE—SIOUX.

away from their original homes; adopting new names by which they were afterward known.

THE MINNECONJOUX TRIBE.

The Minneconjoux were another large tribe of the Sioux family. They claimed and occupied as their hunting ground all the territory east of the eastern chain of the Rocky Mountains, and as far east as the country of the Ogalalas, as far south to about the northern boundary of Utah, and as far north as the country of the Uncpapa.

Being so far removed from civilization they rarely came in contact with the whites.

Consequently they remained in ignorance of the ways of civilization longer than many other of their kindred tribes. The Minneconjoux were very fierce and savage, retaining all their innate savagery longer than any tribe of the Sioux.

When the Bozeman road was opened through their country, they became greatly alarmed, and the warriors of the whole tribe started on the warpath against the whites, attacking troops, travelers, and all who came within their hunting ground.

It was not until our Powder River expedition entered their country that they realized the strength of the Government

SPOTTED DOG—SIOUX.

and became reconciled to the advance of civilization.

Even after this they constantly attacked the troops, defeating them on several occasions.

Their chief, Man-Afraid-of-his-Horses, was the general who planned and carried out most of the attacks.

It was not until after the Civil War ended that sufficient troops were sent to subdue these savage people, that this country was safe for miners, pros-pectors, and wagon trains to enter.

THE UNCPAPA TRIBE.

Another very fierce, savage, numerous and warlike tribe of the Sioux was the Uncpapa.

They had their hunting ground immediately above the Minneconjoux and below that of the Crows. The chief of this tribe was Gall.

He was one of the ablest leaders of the entire Sioux nation.

The Uncpapa and Minne-conjoux Sioux united in their resistance to the entrance of the whites through their re-spective hunting grounds.

Under the leadership of such able men as Gall and the Man - Afraid - of - his - Horses, the savages of both tribes fought the advance of the whites with great vigor and ferocity, and it was not until after the battle of Little Big Horn that this country was safe for any one to enter who did not belong to either of the tribes mentioned.

Both these tribes were almost constantly at war

BLOODY MOUTH—UNCPAPA SIOUX.

with the Utes, their neighbors on the south; the Crows and Snakes, their northern and northwestern neighbors; their eastern neighbors, the Northern Cheyennes. These two tribes frequently joined in war parties going south to the country of the Cheyennes and Arapahoes to make war upon them. Being almost constantly in battle, they became skilful warriors, and were the dread of the surrounding tribes. They even defeated troops in battle for many years, and it was not until after the battle of Little Big Horn that they were finally subdued.

THE KAWS, OR KANSAS.

The Kaws, or Kansas, were a part of the Sioux family, and occupied the territory just west of the Missouri River, which is now embraced in the State of Kansas. In their wild state they lived wholly by the chase. The buffalo was plentiful, and they were able to secure their food without much difficulty. The country occupied was an excellent tract of land and if they had had the inclination could have raised by agriculture a sufficient amount of food for their wants. The Indian's natural aversion to labor prevented this, and they were on the verge of starvation nearly all the time, until the Government came to their relief. Even this furnished them with but scanty supplies of food.

They were of small numerical strength, but were treacherous to their weak neighbors, on whom they made war. In their habits and customs little can be said that does not apply to all Indians of that territory.

WINNEBAGOES.

The Winnebagoes originally lived in territory lying between Green Bay and Lake Winnebago, in the present State of Wisconsin. Though belonging to the great Dakota family they allied themselves with the Sacs and Foxes and Pottawattomies, against the Dakotas, and the fierce Huron-Iroquois. They were always a peace-loving people, and were never inclined to make trouble for red man or white, if let alone.

They had a fine country, the streams and lakes furnishing an abundance of fish. Game was plentiful, and they lived well for Indians; they remained on their lands until the pressure of the white population compelled them to cede them to the Government and move west of the Mississippi. They were again removed to a reservation in Minnesota, where they were assured a "permanent home." Here they made progress, although they became addicted to drunkenness and gambling, both of which vices they learned from the whites. Many of them became discontented and wandered back to their old home in Wisconsin, where they remained.

When the Sioux massacre broke out in 1863, the Winnebagoes refused to join the hostile Indians, and the Sioux threatened to exterminate them. After the massacre the people of Minnesota demanded that all Indians be removed from the State, and the Winnebagoes were again removed from

CHIEF HOLLOW HORN BEAR AND FAMILY—BRULE SIOUX.

their homes, at their own expense. They were located in a barren, alkali tract of country in Dakota near the Missouri River, where nothing grew, and they dared not go to hunt for fear of the surrounding hostile tribes. To escape starvation they built canoes, and the greater portion of them, about two thousand in number, made their way down the river to the Omahas in Nebraska.

THE PONCAS.

This tribe was a part of the Sioux nation. From the first time the Poncas came into contact with the white man they were looked upon as being among the most peaceable Indian peoples of the West. Their original home was near a branch of the Red River and Lake Winnipeg. They were afterward driven west of the Missouri River by their old enemy, the Chippeways. The latter again drove them from their new home, and the Poncas joined the Omahas, who became closely allied with them.

War was constantly made on these people by the Sioux, Pawnees, Osages, and the Kaws or Kansas. These wars greatly reduced them in numbers, and small-pox and the white man's vices destroyed most of the survivors. The remnant was placed on a reservation near the mouth of the Niobrara River in Nebraska.

The Government, failing to carry out the terms of its treaty with them, they were again compelled to go on the hunt, but were forced to return by their old enemies. After this they suffered severely from want of food. Afterward   they   were

OWNS THE DOG—SHIELD AND TOBACCO POUCH.

forcibly removed to the Indian Territory, where they suffered from unwholesome water. A great many of their animals died, and from one hundred and fifty to two hundred out of the total of seven hundred of the Poncas died in a short time. The remainder, after a three-months' journey, succeeded in reaching their old friends, the Omahas.

The treatment of these peaceable Indians by the Government aroused much discussion throughout the country, and they were afterward restored to their

YOUNG GIRL—SIOUX.

former reservation at the mouth of the Niobrara River in Nebraska.

South of the Omahas lived the Otoes, who also belong to the Lacotah family, and living near the borders of civilization they early fell into the habits of their white neighbors.

The Osages are of the same stock and are one of the most intelligent tribes of this family. Physically, they are one of the finest bodies of red men on this continent; man for man, they are equal to the Cheyennes. The men cut the hair off both sides of their heads, except a roach in the center about three inches wide and of the same height, from the front back to the scalp lock; this, with their tall, erect forms, gave them the appearance of ideal Indians. At that time their hunting grounds were in Kansas.

The Omahas were a large tribe of the Sioux nation, and when first found by white men they were living along St. Peter's River, but after the smallpox epidemic, they abandoned their homes and wandered to the Niobrara River in Nebraska, and after a succession of treaties, they were assigned a reservation in the eastern part of that state.

The Iowas when first known to the whites, occupied the territory near tne Mississippi River in the present State of Iowa, and their hunting grounds extended far east into Illinois; being constantly attacked by the Sacs and Foxes, they allied with the Winnebagoes for mutual resistance, but they were finally driven west to their present locality.

The Quapaws or Arkansas Indians, also of Sioux stock, when first known, were living along the Ohio River, but were driven to the mouth of the Arkansas River by surrounding tribes, where they lived until removed to the Indian Territory; here several other tribes amalgamated with them.

The early French trappers called all the Sioux whom they found about the headwaters of the Mississippi River and to the west, Tetons, as they believed the great numbers of Sioux there belonged to this tribe.

All tribes of the Sioux nation are fine specimens of red men and of a general uniform type; being tall, straight, and of athletic build; their faces are pleasing, eyes bright, and prominent Roman noses are common in both sexes. Their skins are thin, smooth, and of fine copper color, with their coal black, long straight hair neatly dressed, and having an elastic step they walked about with proud and haughty mien.

Although brave and fierce in battle, the Sioux have a superstitious dread of attacking at night, as they hold a tradition that when a warrior is slain in battle at night, his soul will forever remain in darkness, and can never find its way to friends in the spirit land.

HOLLOW HORN BEAR'S SON—SIOUX.

There have been cases where a number of Sioux crept close to the troops during the darkness and fired into them, then disappeared as stealthily as they came; but these can hardly be called attacks, as they were only efforts of some young braves taking desperate risks to exhibit their courage and fearlessness to their own people, with but little chance of being killed or wounded.

At long distance signaling all the Sioux are experts. By shading their eyes with the hands, they can see on clear days ten miles or more, when conversation is held by smoke, mirror, or the movement of their mounts.

On General Custer's last campaign, one of his Sioux scouts discovered with his naked eye as above, an Indian village twelve miles away; and after the Battle of Little Big Horn, the news was conveyed by signs, signals and orally, over seven hundred miles in a direct line overland in eight days.

They are also experts in concealing themselves; and when scouting through the mountains or over the great plains, they know every move of the party whose trail they follow without being discovered themselves. When General Crook's command left Fort Fetterman in 1876, it was known that there were ten thousand hostile Indians somewhere in front, yet, during

CHIEF OF THE OMAHAS.

Twenty Years Among Our Hostile Indians.

his march of some three hundred miles, not a sign was seen of an Indian, but all moves made by the troops were well known to the savages.

The Sioux, when scouting on the plains, usually do so on foot, and conceal themselves by binding tall grass to the upper portions of their bodies which extends above their heads; when thus masked, they appear to the casual observer bunches of grass, or, if in brush, the latter is used in like manner. If there is an elevation, the scouts crawl snake-like to near the top and remain there for hours making a complete survey of the surrounding country in every direction, or if there is no elevation, any slight depression in the land is used for the same purpose; in either case, they patiently watch for any disturbance of the grass or the appearance of dust, which is immediately communicated to the main body, when they prepare for battle.

The Sioux are probably the best of our Indians in fighting mounted, for their lines are often thin and long, which causes the enemy to fire divergently while his is convergent. If their lines are pierced at any point, they immediately ride to a number of others and form again, charging with great fury from every direction, thus making it very difficult for the enemy to withstand their onslaughts.   To the Sioux and Apaches, the military are greatly indebted for the present manner of throwing out the advance guard in the shape of an open fan.

When anticipating attacks, their camps are located with a view to the greatest security and sentinels are sent in every direction around the locality, but at night if near an elevated spot, the watchers descend to just below the brow of the hill, so that everything is plainly visible against the horizon. It was not until red men were used as scouts by the troops against the hostile Indians that the military learned this mode of scouting and posting pickets, which finally resulted in the capture of the last of the Sioux and Apaches. After Custer's defeat, the Sioux compelled the Government to abandon many military posts in their country along the Bozeman Road, and before that time they held up the completion of the Northern Pacific Railroad at Bismarck for a long time.   In June, 1876, Crazy Horse at the head of a large body of Sioux and Northern Cheyennes defeated the troops advancing toward the Yellowstone River, and it was not until a fresh body of soldiers was sent to give this wily chief battle, that they were finally captured; their country wrested from them and they were placed on reservations.   In 1877, the remainder were in the hands of the Government.   Thus ended the wild life of the last of a people as brave and cunning as ever were created. The great chief, Crazy Horse, the hero of innumerable battles, in attempting to gain his freedom was mortally wounded, and died September 7, 1877.

CHAPTER XVIII.

THE COMANCHES—FIERCE TRIBES OF THE SHOSHONEE NATION—GUARDING
AGAINST AMBUSH AND SURPRISE—THRILLING INCIDENTS.

Where the Comanches Lived—A Fierce and Implacable Foe—A Terror to all Settlers—
    Alliance with the Apaches—Bloody Raids—A Mexican Bandit Leader and his Fol-
    lowers—A Lot of Murderous Renegades—The Comanches Receive their First
    Chastisement—Attack on Fort Lancaster—Soldiers Lassoed while Guarding their
    Herds—Carried Away and Murdered—Carrying the Mail through a Hostile Coun-
    try in a Concord Buggy—Cruel Fate of the Driver and Guard—The Wagon Train—
    Vast Sums in Gold and Silver Carried through a Hostile Country—How the Trains
    Were Waylaid—Horrible Fate of a Wounded Trainman—Guarding against Sur-
    prise.

COMANCHE WOMAN.

THE Comanches were the most southerly
branch of the Shoshonee nation. Their
original language was Shoshone, but living so long near the Mexicans, they acquired a mongrel sort of dialect. Some
of them understood the Spanish language,
but would not converse in it unless they
were engaged in some nefarious expedition,
and desired it charged to the Mexicans.

The name Comanche, by which these
people were known, is supposed to have
been given to them in early days by the
Spaniards. The name they originally had
and by which they called themselves,
was Naiini, which meant in their tongue,
"Those that live," or, "We are alive."
Years ago they were numerous but became much reduced by war, disease,
and other causes. At one time cholera
and yellow fever threatened them with
extermination, for, like all other Indians, they had no effectual means of
combating disease.

The principal rendezvous of the Comanches for a great many years was in the Hueco Mountains, Texas, and in the passes of the Chihuahua Mountains, in Mexico.   They were divided into four or five different tribes each under its own chief.

The names of the largest or principal tribes were the Yamparack, and the Tenawa.   The former roamed over the country east of the Lipans, and were the fiercest as well as the most numerous tribe of the Comanches.

The Comanches were among the fiercest Indians on this continent.   For years they committed depredations in Texas, on the settlers, traders, and others, killing hundreds of men, women and children.

During the time the present state of Texas was a Republic the Comanche committed so many depredations against its inhabitants that they organized the Texas Rangers to repel and drive them out of that country. When attacked by these troops they fled across the Rio Grande River into Mexico, knowing that the troops could not enter that country to give them battle.

Here they recuperated until ready for another dash into Texas.   These raids continued until as late as 1875 or 1876.

When committing depredations on the citizens of that Republic, and pursued by Mexican troops, they would recross the Rio Grande into Texas, where they felt secure for a time with their plunder.   They terrorized the entire country along the Rio Grande from its mouth to its source, and on both sides of it, roving north into the United States for hundreds of miles, and south into Mexico for probably the same distance.   To them belongs the discredit of keeping that portion of Texas entirely unsettled until about 1866 or 1867.

It was not until after our Civil War that the Government sent troops to Texas, who prevented to a certain extent, these marauding Indians from continuing their frequent expeditions.   The entire country for probably a hundred to a hundred and fifty miles in Texas, parallel with the Rio Grande River, was without grazing herds of domestic animals, solely on account of these depredations.   Even after the troops were sent there the Comanches continued their destructive and frequent raids, and for a time effectually prevented the country from being settled.   The Comanches, Apaches and Kiowas—stealing as they did so many horses and mules from both Mexicans and Texans—were always well mounted, and consequently in prime fighting condition.   Knowing that international law would not permit United States troops to pursue them into Mexico, or Mexican troops to enter the United States, they hovered about the border line and fled across whenever they committed depredations on either side.

For more than a century the Comanches were at war with the Spaniards living in Mexico.

They came near annihilating De Soto's army.

The feeling between the two people was so bitter that there was constant warfare between them, the Comanches making expeditions far into Mexico to engage the Spaniards, as well as for booty.

The Comanches were at home everywhere, either on the plains, in the mountains, or the timbers, thus having great advantage over their adversaries.

Furthermore, the supposed boundary line between the United States and Mexico was the Rio Grande River. This river is wide, and in a great many places runs through a low country with sandy soil. When there was a great freshet—this usually occurred every year—the river would suddenly cut a new channel for a long distance, sometimes taking two or three miles of territory that had formerly been in the State of Texas, transferring it to the Republic of Mexico, on the other hand, sometimes transferring portions of Mexico to the United States. This did not tend to weld the bond of friendship between the Mexicans living along the river in Mexico, and the Texans living on the other side in Texas. For this reason an intensely bitter feeling existed between the two peoples; many depredations were committed by the Texans on the Mexicans, by which the former grew rich in horses, mules, and other animals, the Mexicans returning the compliment at every opportunity.

To add to the disturbance the Mexicans had a daring leader of banditti, in the person of Juan Nipomecina Cortina. This leader held some kind of commission in the Mexican army; although freqeuently ordered to the City of Mexico by the authorities of that Republic, he persistently refused to go, consequently he was not brought to justice. He had a large following, composed of the worst vagabonds and cutthroats that could be found in that country. Cortina himself grew to be very wealthy from thieving, numerous raids, and the natural increase of his animals. He was never seen alone, always having with him an armed escort of his renegades. To him and his party must be credited the killing of a great many people, the destruction of much property, as well as the loss of many animals along the Rio Grande at that time. Nearly everybody in the northern portion of Mexico was either in his employ, or terrorized by him or his band.

All raids and depredations committed by them were laid at the door of the Comanche and Apache Indians. Consequently they were sometimes charged with outrages of which they were innocent. Still, they were bad enough, and if not guilty of all the crimes attributed to them it was only because they lacked the opportunity.

It was not until about 1871 or 1872 that Colonel Randall S. McKenzie, of the 4th U. S. Cavalry, organized a body of troops at Fort Clark, and followed these Indians across the Rio Grande into Mexico, where he gave them their first chastisement. After some hard marching he reached their headquarters, surprised and defeated them, securing a large number of stolen animals, and returned to Fort Clark with them.

Before this the government of Mexico had been pressed by the authorities at Washington, who demanded that measures be taken to stop the raids of the Comanches, and their whilom allies, the Apaches. The governor of the State of Chihuahua at that time was Don Louis Tarasas. He directed a body of about a hundred cavalry to be made up from volunteer Mexican rancheros, to show the United States authorities that an effort was being made to check these raids. Captain Tarasas, a brother of the governor, was placed in command. The troops crossed the Rio Grande, between El Paso and Los Crucas, trailing the Indians to the Sierra Blanca Mountains, where a battle was fought, the Indians defeating the Mexicans, who returned to their homes. This was the last effort made on the part of the Mexican Government toward suppressing these Indians.

In the summer of 1867, the allied bands of Comanches and Apaches attacked the garrison at Fort Lancaster, situated on Live Oak Creek, near its confluence with the Pecos River. This fort consisted of corrals, officers' quarters, storehouses, barracks for the troops, etc.; all were built of sun-dried bricks called adobé. The troops and civilians garrisoned at this point numbered from a hundred to a hundred and twenty-five. The troops belonged to the regular army, and were well armed and equipped. The Indians captured the animals belonging to the garrison, and actually lassoed and carried away some of the troops who were guarding the herds. The bodies of the men were found where they had been left after having been killed and mutilated by the Indians.

About this time Ben Ficklin established the first mail line from San Antonio to El Paso, a distance of about seven hundred miles. The Indians gave this line a great deal of trouble. When it was first established the mail was carried across the country in a Concord buggy, drawn by two horses or mules; a driver and guard made up the outfit. Once when one of the buggies was traveling between El Muerto and Eagle Springs, a Comanche jumped from behind some rocks after the buggy had passed, ran after the vehicle, and thrust his lance through the bodies of the unsuspecting driver and guard. I mention this instance to show the audacity of this

treacherous people. They were responsible for more loss of life and property, were more ferocious and cruel to the inhabitants of Texas than any
Indians within its borders. It was by no means uncommon for them to attack travelers and wagon trains of freight while making the overland journey, and destroy them.

In those days freight trains consisted of prairie schooners (wagons), each
capable of transporting seven
or eight tons of freight. Two
mules were hitched to the pole
of the wagon, and then four
abreast until the entire team
was made up, which some-
times consisted of fourteen,
eighteen, and occasionally
twenty - two animals. The
number of wagons that made
up a train varied from eight
to twenty-five. It can readily
be seen what a rich haul the
Indians made in capturing
one of these large overland
outfits, as well as the great loss
the owners sustained by its
destruction.

At this time the only means
of transporting gold and silver
coin and bullion from Mexico
into the United States was by
wagon trains. The gold and
silver was placed in boxes of
convenient size, and shipped
from Chihuahua, Mexico, to

COMANCHE WOMAN.
Leslie's Weekly.

San Antonio, Texas, a distance, probably, of one thousand miles,
requiring from thirty-five to sixty days to make the journey. The
route was through a country almost uninhabited except by the Indians.
The trains carried great quantities of coin, sometimes amounting to several
hundred thousand dollars, and it is but natural to suppose that such a large
sum of money, with the animals and equipment belonging to the train,
would be a tempting prize for the Comanches, for the wagon trains passed
directly through their country. Strange to say, they did not, to my knowl-

edge, attack a train that carried a large amount of money. Whether this was the result of accident or design I do not know.

At Howard's Wells the Comanches and their allies attacked a wagon train loaded with stores, while in corral there, killing all the trainmen and securing the animals. After taking what stores they could carry away, they burned the rest, including the wagons. One of the men, who was badly wounded and left for dead, fell under a wagon which was loaded with salt. The hot salt fell upon, and burned him in a frightful manner, adding intense agony to his sufferings until death relieved him. I arrived there shortly afterward, and was much impressed by the destruction of this ill-fated train and the massacre of the entire party.

I mention the fact of the Indians attacking this train while in corral, because it was unusual for them to attack a wagon train while in this fortified position, the trainmen having a better opportunity to protect themselves by using the wagons for breastworks. The usual manner of attacking a wagon train was to do so when it was on the move; then it was extended over the road for a long distance, each wagon with its team measuring probably a hundred feet, and a train of twenty-five wagons extending over the road not less than half a mile. The wily savages would conceal themselves behind bushes and rocks along the route-in advance of the slowly moving train; at a given signal they would attack each wagon separately, making the whole train an easy prey.

When a train was in corral and was attacked by Indians, the assault was usually made to secure the animals. When these were quietly grazing at a distance from the train the Indians would suddenly rush upon them with frightful yells, flaping their blankets, stampeding the terrified animals. To prevent this, when a train was in corral the mules were usually side-lined or hobbled. Side-lining is the fastening of the hind and forefoot on the same side of the animal together; side-lines had a chain between the feet to prevent the Indians from cutting them and releasing the animals.

In addition to this a bell-mare usually accompanied the train. This mare was gray or white, with a bell around her neck. She was securely held by one of the herdsmen, and it was difficult to separate mules from a bell-mare. In this manner the animals were sent from the train in a herd for food and water, being guarded by a number of armed herders. Sometimes, when the Indians were particularly anxious to secure animals, they attacked the herds, killed the herdsmen, removed the side-lines and hobbles, then seizing the bell-mare and as many animals as possible, rapidly made off with them.

Hobbling of animals is fastening the two forefeet together by the same means as the side lines, except that the chain between the feet is shorter.

CHAPTER XIX.

THE COMANCHES CONTINUED—PUNISHMENT INFLICTED ON THEIR WOMEN—
STEALING CONSIDERED A FINE ART.

Comanche Home Life—A Nation of Thieves—Polygamy common among them—Miserable Women—Never known to Marry outside of their own People—What made them unusually Virtuous—Severe Penalty for Unfaithfulness—Slitting the Nose—Self-inflicted Wounds—Mourning for the Dead—Superstitious Healing of the Sick—Their Medicines—Curing the Bite of a Rattlesnake—Capturing Wild Horses—Killing Wild Turkeys—Their Scanty Clothing—A Filthy and Repulsive People—Feats of Horsemanship—Cutting the Hamstring of a Running Animal—Mothers at Twelve Years of Age—Making up a Party for Plunder and Pillage—Living in Rocks and Caves—Expert Thieves—Stealing considered a Mark of Honor.

MOUNTED COMANCHE WOMAN.

WHAT little home life the Comanches had was congenial. Like the majority of Indians, they were kind to each other. They were polygamous, each family living in a separate habitation. Their lodges were miserable affairs made of poles, over which tanned skins or cloth were drawn. They were not advanced in the ruder arts beyond other Indians. For supplies they depended more largely on their ability to steal, than on honest efforts of their own. Their camp effects were few; even these were generally secured by theft.

A Comanche woman did not become the wife of a Mexican, a white man, or an Indian of another nation, except after capture. Although miserable, dirty and ignorant, the women were chaste, possibly from fear of punishment; for the penalty for infidelity was terribly severe. For unfaithfulness the offending woman, while being securely held, had a knife inserted in the cartilage at the end of the nose, which was then split to the eyes. The husband forced this wound to be kept open until healed, to prevent its uniting. A woman so marked presented a horrible appearance.

They had no religion or worship above a rude superstition. They believed in the Great Spirit, but seemed to take no interest whatever in learning how they came here, or in speculating about the future state. They lived only for the present.

When mourning for the dead, the Comanches were very demonstrative. The period of mourning lasted from three to fifteen days. During this time the family and friends of the dead visited the burial place of the deceased and showed their grief in various ways. The principal manifestation of sorrow was by slashing their arms, legs and bodies with knives. Sometimes the blood ran down their bodies in streams from head to foot from these self-inflicted wounds. With them the severest wounds indicated the greatest intensity of grief. On the persons of old Comanche women could often be seen great scars of wounds made on these occasions. At mournings the men smoked to the Great Spirit, to whom they also offered a prayer. The first puff of smoke was to the Great Spirit, the second to the sun, and the third to the earth. During the period of mourning, whenever they ate the first bite was offered to the Great Spirit for the benefit of the dead. Then some of the women buried a portion of the remaining food in the earth, that it might be eaten by the spirit of the departed.

They had no medicine men, but performed all the rites of this class themselves. In addition to their superstitious faith in their ability to heal the sick, they made medicine from roots and herbs for the treatment of bites of venomous insects and reptiles, which were very numerous in their country. They claimed to be able to cure the bite of a rattlesnake, but aside from cutting out the injured part at once, either by the person bitten or by some one else, then sucking the wound, their medicines were of little avail.

They resorted to conjuring, singing weird chants, making all sorts of noises and hideous displays to drive away disease. Childbirth with them, even when the mother was only twelve to fourteen years of age, was a matter of little moment. Sometimes within three or four hours after the first pains of labor the child was born, and the woman was going about as though nothing unusual had occurred.

The country inhabited by the Comanches was, after that of the Sioux, the largest, and more abundantly supplied with game, wild horses, fruits, berries, and nuts than that of any other nation of Indians. Their hunting

MAN AND WIFE IN NATIVE DRESS—UTES.

ground covered the northern portions of the States of Tamaulipas, Nuevo Leon, Coahuila, and Chihuahua in Mexico, and Texas from the Brazos River on the north to the Rio Grande on the south. Within this vast area wild horses were abundant. Here, also, the buffalo roamed in vast numbers in winter, besides several kinds of deer, bear, and wild turkeys in great abundance. The latter lived principally on the pecan nut, and were the finest turkeys I have ever seen.

The Indians' mode of killing wild turkeys was simple and effective, though it could hardly be called sportsmanlike. The birds roost night after night in the same tree. After discovering a roost the Indians visited the tree at night, and, with bow and arrow, drop the birds one by one, always shooting the one nearest the ground. The turkeys looking up for the trouble, would not fly so long as they were not disturbed from above.

The climate of their territory was warm, and they wore but little clothing. A blanket or robe, belt, and breechcloth were indispensable parts of a man's dress; these they usually had. The portions of their bodies requiring the most protection were the feet and legs, as the ground in this region becomes hot in summer; in many places it is covered with sharp stones, and overgrown with thorny plants and prickly undergrowth. The dress of the women consisted of a blanket or skin, hanging to the knees, from a belt around the waist. This, with the foot covering and leggings, made up their apparel.

Comanche men or women took but little care of their hair, letting it grow long and hang over the shoulders and backs, never washing it, and it was in consequence filled with vermin. On the whole, the Comanches presented a repulsive and disgusting appearance. Both sexes tattooed their faces after the style of Indian art. They were fond of painting their bodies, and frequently used mud of various colors in this ornamentation, striping their faces, foreheads and cheeks. When paint was abundant, and the Comanche was enabled to indulge his fancy for personal decoration of this kind, he could make himself disgustingly hideous-looking.

In cold weather, or during a norther (a cold wind and snowstorm from the north), they wore a buffalo robe or blanket over what little clothing they had, squatting around the fire in vain efforts to keep warm. During these cold blasts they were extremely miserable and suffered greatly.

The Comanches differed largely from other Indians in characteristics, customs and sports. They were expert and daring horsemen; and practiced riding and racing almost daily when not on the hunt or warpath. Horses were abundant in their locality, and they were almost a race of Centaurs. The feats of horsemanship performed by them were equal to, if they did not excel, anything achieved in this line by any other Indian tribe or nation. On foot they were slow in their movements, but when mounted, they seemed to have undergone a complete transformation. The Comanche off his horse seemed out of his element.

When on a buffalo hunt the Comanches would ride close to the hind legs of the fleeing animal, and with a knife, cut its hamstring, compelling the helpless animal to fall. The women and children then attacked the prostrate beast, cutting it up, almost alive. When butchering animals, they drank the warm blood, and when hungry, ate the liver and entrails raw. At best they ate their meat only partly cooked. The meat secured on one of these hunts was cut into strips, dried in the sun for use as occasion required.

It was not an uncommon thing for them to eat their horses and mules, or the meat of an animal which had been dead for days.

Notwithstanding their low order of intelligence, the men were brave, and were expert in handling their weapons. During battle the horses were kept in continual motion. When in large numbers, they formed themselves into subdivisions, charging the enemy almost simultaneously from every direction, running away with lightning rapidity, and re-forming, charging again and again in the same manner. It required courage and vigilance to withstand their attacks. Their arms consisted of bow and arrow, lance, shield, and modern firearms.

When an important subject was to be considered, every person was invited to the talk, the warriors doing the talking. At these talks the affairs of the tribe were discussed to a conclusion.

Comanche females became wives at an early age, and mothers of twelve and fourteen years were common. The women were compelled to do all the drudgery of the camp, and treated cruelly. They looked old and haggard at thirty-five and forty years. A Comanche could have as many wives as he could buy. He could also repudiate them at any time, and take back the property he had paid for them. Should a wife abandon her husband, the latter was considered disgraced, and the stain could be wiped out only by his killing some of her relatives.

On reaching the age of puberty the names of the children were changed, the diminutive or pet name was dropped, and a name more dignified or suitable to the age of the person adopted.

Drunkenness was rare, although they made a strong intoxicating liquor from the mescal, a plant which grows wild in that country and is plentiful.

The Comanches were nomadic, rarely remaining more than a week or two in the same place. They frequently lived in caves when in a mountainous or rocky region. The women gathered the mesquit bean, piñon nut, the agave and other fruits that grew wild in that country; these they used for food.

During the winter when the buffalo migrated into their country, everybody, men, women and children, joined in the chase. They were skillful buffalo hunters, and rode fearlessly into a herd, killing the animals in large numbers with bows and arrows and lances. When in Mexico, they readily supplied themselves with an abundance of fresh meat by raiding the flocks of sheep and goats owned by Mexicans, or by stealing cattle.

Among them the acquisition of other people's property by theft was considered a mark of distinguished honor. The warrior who returned from a raiding expedition with the greatest amount of plunder was not only regarded as the most courageous and skillful brave, but was highly respected for his success as a thief. An old Comanche warrior, in speaking of the good qualities of his two sons, capped the climax of praise, by declaring that they understood horse stealing better than any other two young men of the tribe. In their predatory expeditions they feared only one disgrace, that of returning without plunder.

From infancy they were trained to war. Each warrior kept a war horse, which was chosen for its swiftness. When raiding a settlement they descended upon it with surprising suddenness, vanishing as quickly as they came. At this time the Comanches had more arms than any wild Indians in the Southwest. Their territory was so vast and adjoined that of so many people having modern firearms that they easily secured a liberal supply from their neighbors, both Texans and Mexicans. Their principal difficulty was in securing ammunition.

They were governed by a chief whose term of authority depended on general consent. He was their leader in war, and presided over their councils in peace; but if proven guilty of cowardice or incapacity was at once deposed.

The Comanches counted by their fingers, ten being the highest number they were able to grasp; this was used in the same manner that we use our hundred; thus, two tens, three tens, four tens, and so on.

The Comanches were nearly always in friendly relations with the Kiowas on the north, as well as the Lipans and Apaches on the west. All these Indians held the Mexicans in contempt, frequently allying to enter their country and make war on them. When a body of any of these Indians entered Mexico, they raided everything in their path, seizing what they could carry away, and destroying what they could not.

CHAPTER XX.

THE APACHES—APPALLING RECORD—THEIR STEALTH AND CUNNING.

In the Country of the Apaches—Shaving off the Nose of a Woman—Horrible Mutila-
tions—Apache Depredations—The Ishmaelites of all Men—Their Repulsive and
Hideous Appearance—Their Small and Peculiar Feet—Painting Themselves with
Mud—An Unspeakably Dirty People—Swarming with Vermin—Murderous War-
riors—Art of Concealing their Persons—How they Made Themselves Resemble a
Rock—Looking like a Bunch of Grass—Mistaken for a Bush or Shrub—Their
Stealth and Cunning—On the War Path—Return of a War Party—Thievish and
Cruel Propensities—An Appalling Record—Driving Out Ten Thousand Settlers—
Hiding in the Dense Jungles.

LOCO, CHIEF OF THE WARM SPRING
APACHES.

THE Apaches were the most southerly
tribe of the Athabaska nation.

It is more than probable that at one time
they lived among the other tribes of this
family in the far north, and that they were
driven by other Indians whose territory
they entered, further south to their present
locality.

They have been so long in their present
territory that neither they nor any one else
can give reliable accounts of having been
elsewhere. Their headquarters were in
Arizona, anywhere between the Gila Range
and the Mogollon Mountains. They were
an itinerant people, and in habits, appearance and characteristics closely
resembled the Comanches. Their depredations extended as far north as the
Wasatch Mountains, and they frequently made raids as far as the Brazos
River in Texas.

The Apaches, with the Comanches, were responsible for the southern portions of Texas, New Mexico, and Arizona having been so long closed to
white settlers. In their raids they destroyed everything in their path,

secured all the booty they could, attacked villages, settlements, and wagon trains, killing hunters, miners and settlers, capturing their entire belongings. If the booty was more than they could carry away the excess was burned.

Their habits and home life were of the lowest order. Though polygamous they were very rigorous in regard to the fidelity of their wives. Any infraction of this law was punished by shaving off the nose of the offending woman close to the face. A woman thus mutilated presented a revolting appearance. But happily, there were few of them who had undergone such a severe mutilation; this affords convincing evidence that the Apache women were generally faithful.

The Apache was distinguished from all other Indians by his thievish propensities. The Comanche was bad enough in this respect, but the Apache could outdo him. He was a born thief, and his education in this respect was never neglected. The Apache would undergo toil and danger to secure, by stealing or raiding, the articles he could have more easily obtained by hunting or working like his northern brothers, the Pueblos. They were the Ishmaelites of Indians, the inveterate enemy of all men, red or white, except when they allied with the Comanches against a common foe.

It was rare to see a pleasing countenance even among their women. They had thick, rusty, black hair, and a mongrel cast of features. Their eyes were sharp and piercing.

A notable peculiarity was their remarkably small feet, and the fact that the great toe was widely separated from the others. This was the result of the children wearing sandals made of thick hide, which were fastened to the feet by strong rawhide thongs, the larger thong passing between the great toe and the next.

They painted themselves more profusely and hideously than any other Indians, using a great variety of colors in doing this. They sometimes plastered their heads and bodies with mud, both as a protection against the heat of the sun, and as a preventative against vermin. They often ornamented their headdresses with deer hoofs, fishbones, shells, beads, and porcupine quills. They were good horsemen, and experts in the use of the lasso. At the time I was among them their arms consisted of the bow and arrow, lance, tomahawk, and old-fashioned guns and pistols.

When hunting, they covered themselves with skins of various animals, and by imitating their movements, managed to approach the game within shooting distance. They ate every portion of the animal, the entrails being considered the daintiest part. Usually they half-cooked their meat, but sometimes it was eaten raw. Although they were gluttons of the most pronounced type, and could consume an enormous quantity of food at a time, they could also, if occasion required, go without eating for an incredibly long time.

They were unspeakably dirty, both in person and habit. They had a natural antipathy to water as a means of cleansing themselves; their lodges reeked with filth and swarmed with vermin. Offal, as well as the remains of dead animals, was allowed to remain in and about their camps until the odors became almost unbearable.

Their fighting was invariably of a murderous character. They rarely attacked an enemy unless success seemed certain. They would lie patiently in ambush for days to surprise an enemy, and at the first opportunity sneak upon him under the cover of night. They were trained from youth to theft, murder, and cruelty, and practiced these at every opportunity.

The Apache was an adept in the art of concealing his person. He sometimes covered himself with a blanket, or sprinkled earth on his body, then placing himself among the rocks and boulders, remain as silent and immovable as his surroundings, so that an inexperienced person often passed within a few yards of him without detecting his presence. Again, he covered himself with grass, and lying on the ground, would so closely resemble a shrub or bush as to be easily mistaken for either.

When once they entered on the warpath they fought with deadly ferocity. They traversed a large extent of territory, knew every portion of it, and utilized all the strategical advantages of the situation. When approaching a settlement, village, or intended victims, they swept upon them with the fury of a cyclone, securing all the animals and plunder they could carry away, after deliberately killing all who were so unfortunate as to be within their reach, then mutilating the bodies of the victims in every fiendish manner, leaving them in the heat of the almost tropical sun to rot, or be eaten by wild animals. I have seen the bodies of women and children who had been killed by these diabolical wretches, mangled in the most horrible manner; and have taken as many as fifteen arrows from the body of one of the victims. These bloodthirsty wretches killed people merely for the sake of killing. This did not, as a rule, extend to their captives from Mexico; but the latter would have preferred death rather than suffer what they did at the hands of these miscreants.

Before entering on a marauding expedition the families of the warriors were concealed in some of the most inaccessible of the mountain fastnesses, the paths to which were known only to themselves. When they returned laden with booty and elated by victory, a period of feasting and rejoicing followed; but if they returned empty-handed they were met by the women with reproaches and jeers. When pursued too closely they killed the captives, and even the horses and cattle that they had stolen rather than allow them to fall into other hands.

If one Apache killed another he was not punished for it by the tribe, but the nearest relatives of the dead man might kill the murderer.

When a girl arrived at a marriageable age the event was celebrated with feasting and dancing, during which time the girl was isolated in a lodge; at the conclusion of the ceremony she was divested of her eyebrows. A marriage was sometimes celebrated with a feast of horseflesh.

WOMAN WITH NOSE CUT OFF FOR INFIDELITY.

The warriors considered it beneath their dignity to do anything but hunt and fight. The women were even compelled to saddle the horses for the braves when going on a chase or raid.

As far back as 1762 the Mexican Government Reports state that the Apaches alone had destroyed and depopulated one hundred and seventy-four towns and stations. It has been estimated that the Apaches killed or drove out of the country in recent years, more than ten thousand settlers. The Jesuits in the early days built missions all through the northern and central portions of Texas as well as New Mexico and the northern portion of Arizona, some of which are at present standing, although in a dilapidated condition. The Jesuits were never able to establish a mission successfully among the Apaches, nor did their teachings have any effect upon them.

After the acquisition of the territory they roamed over the government of the United States with its handful of troops undertook to exercise supervision over them; but the Indians were so refractory that nothing could be done. While the government did not abandon its project or efforts, it made no progress in subduing them. Some portions of their country were over-grown with chaparral as well as various kinds of undergrowth, such as cat-claw bushes and other thorny plants.

These grew so dense in places that not a blade of grass grew under them. These spots were the hiding places of the Apaches after their raids. It was impossible to penetrate these jungles without the aid of a sharp instrument, on account of the interminable entanglement of the undergrowth.

The Apaches wore shoes made of flint hide that successfully resisted the sharpest thorns or cat-claws, and served also as a protection against the bite of the black ant, the scorpion, the centipede, the wingless bumblebee, the chigoe, popularly called "chigger" or "*jigger*," the rattlesnake, and other venomous reptiles and bugs that infest that region. Their legs were also protected by a thick pair of leggings made from flint hide, with the hairy side out; for in walking, and especially riding rapidly through cat-claw bushes and thorny chaparral, without this protection the legs of the rider would in a short time be a mass of raw flesh. Horses when ridden rapidly through this country instinctively jumped cat-claw bushes whenever possi-ble, otherwise fifteen minutes of travel through this undergrowth would tear the skin of their legs into shreds.

Living in a hot climate, under an almost tropical sun, the Apaches re-quired, and had but little clothing. The dress of the men consisted of a visor or shade for the eyes, made of flint hide and fitted over the head to afford protection against the sun, and a Navajo or other blanket, which they had no doubt stolen on some thieving expedition. The women wore a piece of blanket around their waists extending to the knee, and had the same kind of protection for the feet and legs as the men. They have implicit con-fidence in both medicine men and women—of which there are many—and they control all ceremonial dances, and feasts, as well as preparations for the war path. All diseases are believed to be the work of the spirits of witches, and the medicine people must either expel or placate them, other-wise death ensues. In their efforts to cure the afflicted, fires are kindled, and singing in chorus, with dancing, accompanied by deafening noises, is resorted to. Every person carries about him medicine charms which have been blessed; these consist of hats, idols, arms and other paraphernalia.

The spirits of the dead are supposed to remain in the vicinity where they left the body for four days and nights, and that communication is held with living friends during the time they are hovering about through the voices of owls or cuckoos; that when relatives hear these sounds at night they believe that it is the voice of the deceased, when they rush to the medicine men and inform them of the fact, then means are used to cheer the spirit to under-take its journey to its future abode.

CHAPTER XXI.

THE APACHES CONTINUED—ELUSIVE, CUNNING AND DARING INDIANS—EX
PERT TRAIL FOLLOWERS—INDIAN LIFE IN TEXAS, NEW MEXICO, AND
ARIZONA.

Expert Trailers—Detecting Signs—Concealing their own Trail—Their Cunning in eluding
Pursuit—Apache Cruelty to Captives—Fate of Captive White Boys and Girls—
How the Apaches Lived—Great Aversion to Telling their Names—Queer Super-
stitions—Burying their Dead at Night—Their Fear of a Dead Body—Traveling One
Hundred Miles a Day on Foot—Marvelous Endurance—Victorious in Capturing
Trains—Raiding Settlers—Bones of Victims—An Able but Vicious Chief—The
Deadly Fear He Inspired—Attacking Ranch and Cattle Men—Dreadful Fate of a
Mexican Captive—Stripped, and Staked out on the Ground over an Ant Hill—A
Horrible Death—Midnight Groans and Screams—The Story of a Noted Chief's First
Raid as Told by Himself.

WARM SPRING APACHE.

FOR many years after the acquisition
of Texas by the United States the
Apaches had their headquarters and
chief hunting ground in the San Carlos
Mountains in Arizona and New Mexico,
and it was impossible either for the
United States or Mexico to chastise them
successfully. They were as elusive when
pursued as they were daring when attacking.

In following a trail an Apache could
detect signs which, to an expert white
man were invisible, and in endeavoring
to escape he covered and broke his trail
so that it was almost impossible to fol-
low him. He doubled on his track, twisted, turned, and circled around in
the most inexplicable and cunning manner. Sometimes the party dispersed
or scattered only to meet miles away at a point previously agreed upon.
In this respect they surpassed all other Indians. They were endowed

with great physical endurance, could travel on foot surprising distances in an incredibly short time, and penetrate into almost inaccessible recesses. When broken up into parties each band left signs for the information of others which their pursuers could not read, or, as a usual thing, could not notice. When on the warpath they carried with them the least possible quantity of impedimenta. They depended for subsistence on what the country afforded, or on what they could steal.

After capturing their enemies they usually dispatched them; if they had time and opportunity, they frequently did so with the most fiendish cruelty, though when white boys and girls were captured who were old and strong enough to endure the hardships of Indian life, they were sometimes adopted into the tribes.

The Apaches had a great advantage over other Indians in resisting the white man,—they could procure food far more easily than they. The Indians of more northern latitudes lived almost exclusively on animal food, and could, when driven to places where this kind of food was not easily obtainable, be starved into submission.

Not so with the Apaches. When driven to the mountains they found an abundance of deer and other animals to supply them with food; when on the southern plains, on either side of the border line, they subsisted on the vegetables, fruits, and esculent roots which grew abundantly there. The mescal, or agave, the fruit of the Spanish bayonet, the mesquit bean, the giant cactus fruit, acorns, nuts, and wild potatoes were all eaten by them. They could live on cacti if need be, and accustomed themselves to go from forty-eight to seventy-two hours without water. This they did by placing pebbles in the mouth under the tongue to promote the flow of saliva, also by sucking moisture from pieces of cactus. They always found some means of subsistence and were at home anywhere.

An Apache would not tell his name, but he would permit any one else to tell it for him. They usually buried their dead at night; they had a superstitious fear of a dead body, never going near one when it could be avoided. They did not like to speak on the subject of death, and rarely mentioned the names of the dead; though the name of a warrior who had achieved distinction or performed some special act cf bravery, might, if sufficient time had elapsed since his death, be conferred on a near relative. They were very superstitious, hence the medicine men exercised great influence among them.

There was less uniformity of type among the Apaches than in many other Indian nations. Some were tall, sinewy, and athletic-looking, while others were short and broad-chested. But all possessed wonderful physical endurance, as every old cavalry officer who has had occasion to pursue them can

testify.   Their animals also had great endurance.   Having an almost unlimited territory to roam over, and each warrior having from three to five
well-trained horses or mules that lived on the grass and underbrush, and
carried nothing but the riders, their arms and ammunition, consequently
they could travel long distances each day.   Knowing every water hole and
every foot of ground of the vast country over which they committed depredations, they traveled the most direct route from place to place.

They also knew about the location of almost every wagon
train, or bodies of men or animals in their country; often
waiting for their intended victims to reach a certain locality
before attacking them.

At the first indication of pursuit they dispersed in every
direction, each party riding in Indian file, one after another,
leaving but one path, so that it was impossible for those in
pursuit to estimate the number of Indians in each broken
party.

Occasionally, when they desired to make a raid and feared
that troops were near at hand, they did so on foot.   After a
raid of this kind it was almost impossible to find an Apache
anywhere, as they scattered and vanished in every direction.
The distance they could cover in a day on foot or mounted,
sometimes without water or food, save what little they could
pick up on the way, made it almost impossible for the troops,
no matter how well mounted, to overtake them.   They have
been known to travel on foot one hundred miles in twenty-
four hours.   This they did in a dog-trot, which was kept up
incessantly for long intervals, going from five to six miles
an hour while in motion.

They could lie on the ground and by ingeniously making
use of materials near at hand, earth, grass, bushes, etc., could,
chameleon-like, appear the exact color of their environments.

WOOD ARROW-   They would haunt the road and lie in ambush for a day or
HEAD.   more to attack a wagon train, which they knew was *en route*
through the country and which they were in readiness to attack at a favorable
point they had previously selected.

I do not recollect a single instance of a party of Apaches that had arranged
to attack a wagon train that did not successfully carry out their plans.   The
many graves, the countless bones of men and animals left to bleach under
the almost tropical sun, bear sufficient testimony to the number and murderous character of attacks made by them throughout their country.   Once when

scouting through their territory with an old and experienced guide, many times each day he called my attention to the bones of animals and men, or to small mounds, saying: "Here the Apaches murdered such an expedition," or "Here they killed so many men." Upon questioning him I failed to find that any Indians had been killed, though he declared that if such a thing happened the remains of the dead would not fall into the hands of the white men.

Their country was in every way adapted to attract white settlers, possessing a fertile soil, fine timber lands, as well as minerals of almost every description. Game was also plentiful. Buffalo in winter, wild turkey, deer, bear, and wild horses abounded. These and many other inducements would long before have attracted settlers to this region were it not for fear of these people.

GERONIMO, CHIEF OF THE APACHES.

The Apaches sometimes, in company with their allies, the Comanches, made raids into the northern portion of Mexico through Sonora and Chihuahua. The raids were made for booty, and were always accompanied by disastrous results to the Mexicans. Men, women, and children were frequently carried off in captivity to their captors' mountain fastnesses, where they were usually treated with great severity.

The raids, however, into Mexico were not as frequent as they were elsewhere for the reason that the limited possessions of the people in the northern part of the Mexican States were not of great value to the Indians.

The Apaches had some able leaders, Cochise, Geronimo, and Mangus Colorado being especially notable. Mangus Colorado was a chief of great ability, relentless, treacherous, and possessed of much low cunning. He, more than any other one man, was responsible for keeping white settlers out of that country; he caused more devastation than any other Indian chief of his nation. He frequently led the allied bands of Comanches, Apaches, and Kiowas on the path of plunder and pillage. It was he who commanded the Indians in their attack on Fort Lancaster. When a party once started on a warpath under his direction they swept the country clean of everything within their reach. They attacked settlers, herds, and wagon trains at sight, without waiting for the usual position of advantage. During my long experience I cannot recall a single instance where a party under the leadership of Mangus Colorado was ever overtaken and chastised by government troops.

Whenever settlers made their appearance over what Mangus Colorado considered his hunting ground, he immediately organized a party and proceeded to destroy them. When a daring rancher or cattle man located his herds on what the Apaches considered their territory, they were seized or driven off by them. Mangus Colorado levied a constant tribute on the small Mexican settlements all through the lower portion of Texas near El Paso and northern Mexico. The inhabitants and villagers of that whole section lived in deadly fear of this miscreant and his followers.

Cochise was the hereditary war chief of the Chiricahua Apaches, and was one of the ablest leaders they ever had. His operations extended through Arizona and New Mexico into Old Mexico.

An officer* who was speaking with Cochise one day asked him if he was sorry for anything he had ever done while on his numerous raids. He replied that one day he "roped" a Mexican and his women stripped and staked him on the ground in the hot sun over an ant hill. When the ants began to work up the nostrils, into the mouth and ears of the helpless man, Cochise said his cries were terrible, and the poor man died a lingering death in great agony. Cochise said that every dark night, when everything was quiet, he could hear the groans and screams of the dying Mexican. For that reason he said he was sorry he had tortured him and wished he had shot him instead.

Geronimo was at one time a medicine man of the Chiricahua Apaches, but became chief because of his success in raiding the Mexicans. He related to Lieutenant Capron the following story of his first raid:

"When I was a little boy my people made many raids into Mexico. I always noticed that many Apaches were killed and that sometimes a whole war party would be lost. No one could account for this. Not even the

---

* Lieutenant Allyn K. Capron, Seventh Cavalry.

medicine men.   The first war party I went with made a raid into Mexico, and one day we came to a little Mexican village.   All the Mexicans came out and gave the Indians mescal.   Most of the Indians got drunk.   I did not take any, as I thought it was bad medicine.   When the drunken Indians were lying and rolling on the ground the Mexicans came around and killed every one of them with knives.   I jumped on my horse and went back to my people.   Pretty soon I took a war party down to the same place.   The Mexicans came out with the mescal, just like the first time, and my men made believe to be very drunk.   Then I gave the signal and we killed every Mexican that came out.   This made me a big man, and a chief; when I went home all the people called me a big chief.''

Geronimo, and Natchez, son of Cochise, war chief of the Chiricahuas, with twenty-two men, fourteen women and three children, were on the warpath in Arizona and Mexico for more than a year; over two thousand troops were called into the field to capture them, and it was not until September, 1888, that these people surrendered.   The Lipans are of the same stock and have lived on both sides of the Rio Grande in New and Old Mexico, in a state of semi-civilization for a long

MANGUS COLORADO.

time.   Many of them speak the Spanish language and have adopted the Catholic religion, as some of their marriages, births and funerals are solemnized by that order.   There are also several other Athabaska tribes in Arizona; there are the Papagos, Maricopas, Yumas, etc.   Each has its own tribal organization and chief, cacique or selectmen, who make such rude laws as are requisite for their simple needs, and whose duty it is to care for the interests of their respective tribes.   They are filled with many absurd superstitions and engage almost constantly in ridiculous ceremonies; recounting legends of which there are an unlimited number.

All paint their faces in stripes and pigments, and some tattoo themselves in various colors and designs. This latter is done in accordance with their legend in relation to the journey of their souls, as they believe that their souls when traveling to their future abode, must cross swift running water on a bridge of the body of a great snake; that when the spirit reaches the water the serpent appears and asks the soul for its tattooing, then the spirit covers the snake with its original tattooed skin; the latter recognizes the former owner and forms itself into a flat bridge on which the soul passes over the water in safety; but if the spirit is without tattooing, the serpent forms a bridge as before, and when the soul is crossing, the snake suddenly draws itself into a thin body and throws the spirit into the swift running water when it is carried away and lost.

Grain is ground on metates, and some of the meal is blessed by the caciques; this is their sacred meal. At funerals the corpse is sprinkled with the meal, and it is the food of the soul during the time the remains are in their habitations, but on the day of the funeral, meal is strewn over the ground in a trail leading direct to the west, as this is the direction the soul travels on its way to the spirit land and is its food during its journey.

They make pottery which is decorated with various figures, but that which is to contain sacred meal is embellished with snakes around the vessel on the outside near the top; the serpents are usually colored black. Baskets are also woven and decorated with figures of men, deer, and reptiles of various kinds; some are woven so close that after becoming damp, water will not percolate through them.

The most remarkable fact in connection with these people is that there are many Albinos among them who are full-blooded Indians; these freaks are the result of inbreeding for centuries. Albinos have straight straw-colored hair, very weak pink eyes which constantly squint through the nearly closed eyelids; white tissue-like skins on which great blisters burn if exposed for any length of time to the midday sun, and their bodies are as weak and delicate as their eyes.

Albinos seldom leave their habitations on bright sunny days, as exposure to the heat causes them intense pain; but in the evening they appear, walk and stare about as though the scene was a wonderland. They are interesting and uninteresting at the same time, for they seldom speak or otherwise interest a stranger, whose natural impulses compel him to ask, how can these white red men be induced to wash the accumulations of dirt from themselves, comb their beautiful long golden hair, heal the sore eyes, parched lips, blistered noses and skins, and then become attractive.

CHARLIE—LE FOYA—AND SANCHES—APACHE CHIEFS.

CHAPTER XXII.

THE MYSTERIOUS UTES—THEIR SECRET CUSTOMS AND QUEER DOINGS.

The Mysterious Utes—A Part of the Great Shoshonee Nation—Their Fierce Encounters
with their Neighbors—A Wandering Tribe—Rarely Defeated—Small, Black, Strong
and Vicious—Constantly on the Warpath—Their Home Life—Their Poverty—
Filthy Indians and Dirty Lodges—A Lazy People—The Most Secretive of all
Indians—Their One Great Peculiarity—Profound Secrecy—Secret Burial--The
Mysterious Grave of a Ute—Where Did they Bury their Dead?—Death of the Head
of the Family—Destruction of his Property—Birth of a Child—Treating the Sick—
Their Food, Clothing, and Arms—Eating Rats, Mice, Crickets and Snakes—The
Pah-Utes and the Pi-Utes—A Miserable Lot of Red Men.

BLACK SPOTTED HORSE.

THE Utes were a part of the great Shoshonee nation and were divided into many
small tribes, each under its own chief.
There was no grand chief, neither was
there any gradation among the chiefs of
the different tribes. Warriors chose one
of their number for a chief who was fitted
for the position both mentally and physically, and who possessed personal attraction as well as popularity. The chieftainship was not hereditary; when the office
became vacant from any cause another
chief was selected in the same manner as
his predecessor. A chief could also be
deposed by the same power that elected
him, though such an occurrence was rare.
The Utes covered the large territory em-
bracing the greater part of Utah, western Colorado, northern New
Mexico, the northern part of Arizona, and the southern part of Wyoming and Nevada. The different tribes of Utes were never at war
with each other. When a hunting party from one tribe came upon
a village of another tribe of Utes they were always welcome, and some

of the warriors of the latter tribe might join the expedition. In their hunts and raids, which were frequent, the Utes often wandered into the country of the Cheyennes and Arapahoes in Colorado, the Kiowas, in the Indian Territory, and the Apaches in Arizona.

They have been known to go as far east through the territory of their enemies, Cheyennes and Arapahoes and Sioux, as the States of Missouri and Kansas. They were bold and fearless in all their raids and hunting parties, and had many fierce encounters with the Indians whose territory they invaded, in which they were generally victorious. One of their favorite hunting grounds was the South Park. Here they had many battles with the allied Cheyennes and Arapahoes; as this part of the country was filled with game, the right to it was contested by several Indian nations. It was seldom that the Utes were defeated in conflicts that took place west of the Snowy Range of the Rocky Mountains. They also had frequent encounters with the Crows, their neighbors on the north.

The Utes were small in stature, very dark in color, strong, wiry, and vicious; in battle it was an even chance that they could hold their own against their most warlike neighbors. When they went on the warpath it meant war in earnest; there was no extreme to which they would not go to conquer, especially when they were searching for new hunting grounds or in need of game or wanted a fresh supply of horses and mules.

When the Overland road was established across the plains it passed directly through their country. The Utes, seeing the large number of wagons and white people going West over this road each year, believed that nearly all the white people in the East traveled through their country during the summer; that they returned to the East by another route and passed through their territory again the next year. After the Mormons occupied Salt Lake City the Utes began to realize the great number of the whites, and treated them with much more consideration. It was in the territory of the Utes that the famous scout, Jim Bridger, established one of the first trading posts in the West, which is still known as Fort Bridger.

The Utes were a nomadic people, living in skin-covered lodges, which were made after the typical Indian fashion. Their possessions were few, and almost everything they had or made was for utility and not for ornament. Like all Indians, they were lazy, and dirty both in person as well as in their habitations; both they and their belongings were generally covered with vermin, which they caught and ate.

They worshiped stone and wooden images. Why they did so I was never able to learn, for they believed in the Great Creator and were sun worshipers after their own fashion.

Of all the Indians in the great West none were more difficult to understand. Everything they did, or attempted to do, of a personal nature was kept a secret among themselves. They would not permit an outsider to learn anything about their personal characteristics if they could prevent it.

A Ute would not even tell his name or that of any member of his family, neither would he permit any one else to do so, nor would he mention the price put on one of his daughters when she was to become the wife of one of the tribe. It was known to the father and intended husband only. Everything a Ute did seemed to be obscured in mystery; for that reason less was known of them than of any other Indians in the West.

They had one peculiarity which was unlike any other nation or tribe, namely, the great secrecy they observed in their funeral ceremonies; for no white person, so far as I know, has ever seen the funeral of a Ute, or the grave or burial of one of their dead. When one of them died the corpse vanished. Whether they themselves generally knew the resting place of the dead is difficult to decide.

It was generally believed by those who knew most about them, and closely observed their ways, that the bodies of the dead were removed during the night and secretly buried in a cave or in the ground, though this is merely surmise. At any rate, they secretly got rid of the bodies in some way. It is my opinion that they buried them deep in holes in the earth during the night, and so carefully covered them after interment as to leave no trace of the burial spot. There was no mourning after the body was removed from the family lodge. They would neither talk of the dead or mention their names, and, unlike other Indians, if they knew the burial place would not go near it. Secrecy and a desire to obliterate all remembrance of the departed as quickly as possible were marked characteristics.

UTE STONE
KNIFE.

At the death of the head of a family, the survivors destroyed almost everything belonging to the deceased. This is one reason why they were so miserably poor. The lodge covering was cut into shreds, and every article owned by the dead was so distributed as to scarcely leave a vestige of its former owner. They would burn articles of great value to them, that had once belonged to the deceased, and sometimes the entire camp moved.

The Utes were never visited by small-pox, cholera, or other dread diseases. Had an epidemic made an appearance in one of their camps it would have

MOUNTED WARRIOR, LANCE AND SHIELD.

annihilated them, owing to their filthy habits as well as lack of means or knowledge of combating disease.

In the treatment of the sick and afflicted they had little if any skill. They administered a few herbs and teas, and their medicine men, in their efforts to perform a cure, went through the usual mystifying process, the meaning of which was known only to themselves.   They did not even have the sweat-baths so common to the Sioux.

The women, in giving birth to children, did so in their characteristically stealthy manner; frequently nothing was known among the tribe of the new arrival until after the child was some weeks old.

Like all other nomadic people, they were compelled to move frequently to obtain subsistence for their animals and themselves.   When camp was to be moved the women, after usual Indian fashion, did all the work, taking down the lodges and packing the effects on the animals; when the latter were in-sufficient, the women themselves became beasts of burden.

The women were homely and repulsive in appearance, and wore only the scantiest clothing, consisting of a covering hung over a belt around the waist extending to the knees.   They made winter clothing from skins of dogs and wolves, as well as the rabbit and other small animals.   Children of both sexes were almost always naked during the warm months.

The men wore their hair long and sometimes braided in queues; the women cut theirs just above the shoulders.   Neither sex took much care of it.   Nor did they paint themselves like other Indians.   The men wore the customary breechcloth and a pair of moccasins, which, with a robe of buffalo or of some other animal, constituted their dress for winter.

The Utes at this time lived wholly by the chase, although large game was not abundant in their territory.   They were frequently compelled to live on rabbits and such other small game as they could secure in their im-mediate vicinity.   The scarcity of large game in their country compelled the absence of the men almost constantly on hunting or war parties.   If small game was lacking, they ate their horses and dogs.   In times of great scarcity, rats, mice, crickets, snakes, roots and buds served them as food.

Their arms consisted of the bow and arrow, lance, and modern firearms. At an early day they had a few flint-lock guns and pistols; these they ob-tained from white people, and were greatly prized by them.   But when sur-prised, or compelled to abandon any portion of their equipment, they always discarded the firearms, clinging to their primitive weapons.

Unlike the Indians east of the Rocky Mountains, the Utes did not all have the large red pipe.   When smoking became more common among them they used large cigarettes, made by rolling their smoking material in paper, the leaf of a tree, or the inner bark of the red willow.   They were too miserably poor to indulge in smoking except at long intervals, or upon special occa-sions.

They usually avoided war with the whites, but occasionally some of their bands plundered emigrant trains and killed overland travelers passing over the route in the vicinity. As they were divided into so many tribes, which were constantly breaking up and intermingling with others, it was almost impossible to enter into treaties with them. They would so change and shift from one to another that no sooner would a treaty be concluded with one tribe than one-half of it joined with others that were hostile.

The Pah-Ute tribe numbered about six hundred, and inhabited the country which is now the northern portion of Nevada. They were nomadic in summer, and lived in houses made of rushes, during the winter.

UTE FAMILY—MAN AND THREE WIVES.
(From a very old photograph.)

Some of the tribes refused to join the Mormons fighting against the Government during the Mormon war. This created bad feeling between the two peoples. There was also considerable trouble and fighting between the Utes and miners in that region. Winnemuca defeated Major Ormsby on Truckee River in a well-contested battle. Subsequently some of the tribes ceded their lands to the Government, agreeing to go on reservations, but a bad spirit soon manifested itself among the Indians. The Pah-Utes, under their chief, Black Hawk, committed many depredations, and for several years kept his people in constant war. The chief of the Sampiche tribe was accused of aiding Black Hawk; after his arrest by the troops he attempted escape, but was killed.

Some time after this, Colonel Alexander defeated Onkotash, chief of the Mohache, killing many of his warriors. A treaty was then concluded between the Government and the chiefs of a number of Ute tribes, whereby a tract of territory was set apart for the Indians.

It was stipulated by the treaty that no outsiders should be permitted to

settle upon the lands. For ten years succeeding the treaty, the tribe increased in numbers and wealth, and were as peaceable as could be expected. But the invasion of the territory followed, when hostilities again broke out between the red and white men. The agent and a number of his employees were killed at White River Agency; the buildings burned, the women and children seized and carried off.

Troops were called out and the war that followed was very costly, as well as sanguinary, as the Utes in all its many branches joined, making common cause against the whites.

PI UTE HABITATION.

The Pi-Utes tribe inhabited the southeastern portion of what is now Nevada. They had their habitations far away from the Overland road, and did not come in contact with or molest the whites. They were miserable beings, and of about the same standard as their cousins, the Bannocks.

All of the Ute tribes bore the indelible mark, and spoke the language of the Shoshonee nation; the Utes were probably the best specimens of any tribe of this family. The Utes in all their branches constituted one group, but was made up of confederated tribes; of their characteristics and customs all that applies to the Utes in general cover the other tribes.

CHAPTER XXIII.

THE SNAKES AND ROOT DIGGERS—INTERESTING AND PECULIAR TRIBE— LOAFERS AND GAMBLERS.

The Snakes a Part of the Shoshonee Nation—An Interesting Tribe—Their Hunting Ground—Afflicted with Goitre—Necks Larger than their Heads—Their Great Enmity with the Cheyennes, Blackfeet and Sioux—A Crafty, Treacherous Tribe —Their Fiendish Cruelty to Prisoners—How they Secured Firearms—Manner of Wearing their Hair—Their Poverty—Securing Wild Horses—Their Expertness as Boatmen—Description of a Bull-Boat—Ingenuity of the Snakes—Manner of Catching Fish—Lazy Fishermen—Their Expertness in the Use of the Sign Language— Communication by Means of Horses, Fire, and Smoke—The Bannocks, or Root Diggers—A Miserable People—Loafers and Gamblers.

THE Snakes were a tribe of the great Shoshonee nation. There being no other tribe of that family in the immediate vicinity, the early trappers and frontiersmen called them Shoshonees, believing them to be all there were of this peculiar people. Lieutenants Lewis and Clark also labored under the same mistake. The Snakes occupied the territory in and around the Snake River Valley, and their hunting ground extended eastward to the foot of the Bitter Root Mountains, and as far south as the Ute country. Living so far north they were subject to the rigors of severe winters, and knew how to fortify themselves against bitter cold.

It was among this tribe that Jim Baker, a famous scout and frontiersman, lived the Indian life for many years, married into the tribe, and had many children by his numerous Snake wives. Whether his influence, which was great among them, modified their wild life, is an open question, though I am strongly inclined to believe that it did to some extent.

The water in the country occupied by the Snakes was supplied by mountain gorges which were filled with snow and ice. Many of the men suffered from goitre—an enlargement of the neck—from drinking snow water. It was not uncommon to see a Snake Indian with his neck as large around as his head.

Their country was well wooded with various kinds of trees which furnished ample fuel and afforded some protection against storms. To protect themselves against the cold the Snakes often camped near a beaver dam where these little animals had cut down trees, and from the fallen timber they made corrals for their animals, and fortifications to protect themselves against the wintry blasts and severe storms so common in their country.

TYPICAL SNAKE INDIAN.

Physically, the Snakes are a wonderful people, with fine deep chests, slender sinewy limbs, hands and feet of delicate size and shape, massive jaws, high cheek bones, small piercing eyes and dark skins as tough as that of a buffalo. They are fleet runners and can run for miles at great speed, and make a practice of running down deer, rabbits and other small game on foot; when on a chase of this kind they run through thick thorny brush without having their skins torn to shreds. They can go at long intervals without food, water or rest, and their fortitude in enduring pain is as remarkable as their fleetness of foot.

On one occasion wolves with rabies entered a camp of Snakes, and biting a number of them, hydrophobia was contracted; a short time after the disease developed and some were in convulsions. The medicine men, having no knowledge of a disease of this kind, were overawed and the services of a white doctor were called; when he informed them the nature of the trouble, they calmly awaited the return of the paroxysms again and again, until death ended their agony.

The doctor told me that he had never witnessed greater contempt for suffering and death, than was shown on this occasion by the unfortunates of both sexes.

The Snakes did not differ materially from other Shoshonee tribes. They were cruel, treacherous, crafty, thievish, and were continually at war with all their neighbors, but were particularly aggressive toward the Crows, northern Cheyennes, Sioux, and Blackfeet. As warriors, they were exceedingly brave. They treated captives with great brutality, often killing male prisoners after subjecting them to pitiless and prolonged torture. Female captives were turned over to the women, who took delight in torturing them with fiendish ingenuity. Children captives were frequently adopted into the tribe, the girls eventually becoming the wives of a Snake, and the boys were brought up as warriors.

The more scalps a Snake warrior had to his credit the greater was he honored by his people. They often ate the flesh of a brave enemy, in the belief that the valor of the slain would be imparted to them.

They were skillful in evading pursuit, both when mounted and on foot; and would scatter in all directions, making it impossible to follow so many trails; or if near a shallow stream they would travel in it for miles; in this way leave no trail to follow.

A favorite method of attacking was at night. When approaching by stealth, under cover of darkness, they always endeavored to take the party by surprise, causing a stampede of their animals and creating a panic. Their weapons were few, consisting of the usual bow and arrow, lance, and tomahawk. Later they obtained firearms from the traders; but were generally too poor to secure effective weapons, as they had nothing to exchange for them. Their principal means of supply was from their greatest enemy, the Blackfeet. When victorious in battle with them they secured the arms belonging to the beaten tribe. Their great difficulty however, was in procuring ammunition, for this was not plentiful in their country; consequently they were nearly always compelled to use their primitive equipment.

The Snakes wore their hair long and allowed it to flow loosely over the shoulders. They sometimes cut it straight across the forehead, giving the face the appearance of being in a black frame. In habits they were filthy, taking no care whatever of their person, and their hair and bodies swarmed with vermin. They were fond of ornament, adorning themselves in fantastic ways, when they could get material for the purpose; but being miserably poor they had little indulgence in this direction. With them it was an open fight for existence at all times; they were more concerned in securing a livelihood than in ornamenting their clothing and bodies. They lived in lodges, were nomadic, and constantly on the move to secure game for themselves and food for their animals.

They secured horses from the many wild herds that ranged over their territory. These animals were small and when put to the hard work imposed by the Indians proved of little value.

Both men and women were expert workers in making the birch-bark canoe, as well as the bull-boat. A bull-boat was made by fastening together boat knees made of young, tough trees. The framework was made very strong, and braced throughout in the center. Over this was stretched a sufficient number of raw hides of buffalo bulls to cover the entire frame. The hides were sewed together with thongs, and when thoroughly wet were stretched on the frames as taut as possible and left in the sun to dry. The seams and holes were covered with strips of rawhide, sewed on with sinew and fastened by glue made from the hoofs, horns, and hides of the animal. They made a very tight, snug, and serviceable craft. Bull-boats were of invaluable service in crossing the many rivers that traverse that country. It is my belief that the Snakes showed Lieutenants Lewis and Clark how to make bull-boats, for they were afterwards in common use by the troops and others in crossing swollen and large rivers. Bull-boats can be made almost any size. Some of them were large enough to carry a team of horses or mules, with a loaded army wagon, across a river in safety. They were very buoyant, but it required a good boatman to handle them.

The Snakes were a hardy and healthy race, and associated or allied themselves with no other Indians. They, unlike the majority of Indians, made some provision for future needs. During the summer they killed a sufficient amount of buffalo and smaller game, and jerked the meat for use during the winter. They also made jackets for themselves from the hides of the elk, moose, or bear, to protect them against the extreme cold.

Their handiwork was not so ornamental as useful, although they made pretty work with Iroquois shells. The men were expert in the management of horses, treating them and other animals with more kindness than some of the Indians farther south.

A favorite method of catching fish was to wait for the water of swollen rivers to recede, when the Indians threw out with their hands fish that had become land-locked. The majority of Indians in the West did not eat fish. The Indian so often represented floating down a stream in his canoe, with spear in hand, spearing fish, may look well in a picture, but such scenes were never witnessed among the wild Indians of the West.

In their home life the Snakes were kind. The male was master of his entire household, but universally considerate to all. Women were not required to do all the work, there being a tacit agreement that the men should assist in work of a heavy nature, and caring for the live stock was a part of their daily labor.

The Snakes were surrounded on every side by Indians of other nations speaking different languages; when they wished to converse with them it was necessary to do so in the sign language. Consequently, they were more expert in the use of this language than any other Indians in the far north. They were not only skilled in the sign language of the hands, but could readily communicate by the movements of the horse, or by means of fire and smoke. Their oral language was identical with that of the Shoshonee family, but they had a dialect of their own, which differed materially from that of many other tribes of this nation; so much so, that they could not converse orally with many of their kindred tribes, but were compelled to use the sign language.

The Snakes were polygamous; they had little or no religious belief, but few ceremonies or pastimes, and were contented to live a miserable life with the least possible exertion.

The Bannocks were a part of the Shoshonee nation, and their original language was Shoshonee, but they spoke a dialect of their own. Their principal hunting grounds were west of the Bitter Root Mountains and south of the Cœur d'Alene River. They acquired the name of Root Diggers from the fact that a large portion of their food consisted of roots, of which wild potatoes were the most plentiful. For gathering roots, the women went to the mountains armed with pointed sticks or other sharp instruments, and dug sufficient for the family needs; in addition to these, various kinds of fruits, berries, seeds and nuts grew wild; these were gathered and dried for winter use. Acorns were plentiful; these with other nuts were cracked and the kernels dried, then pulverized and made into bread. As the acorn contains much tannin, it was necessary to subject them to many washings to filter out this substance before the meal could be eaten.

For cracking nuts, stones with shallow pits on the upper surface held the nuts set on end, then with other stones blows were struck until the shells were broken; the dried kernels were mealed by stone mortars and pestles or between two stones; nut meal makes nutritious, sweet bread, and if properly baked, it can be kept for a long time. They caught rabbits and other small game with traps and snares, which supplied them with a limited amount of meats, and skins for clothing, bedding and horse equipments.

Although of a low order of intelligence, the women were imitative and made beautiful baskets of varied forms and designs from rushes, grass and fibrous barks. These were embellished with figures of birds, animals, and other objects in colors. For holding nuts and dried fruits, baskets were woven of willow splints; some of these were three feet high and two feet in diameter at the largest bulge; these were of great service as storehouses.

In stature they were short but strongly formed, with dark, rough skins, coarse black dirty hair—which was seldom or never combed—and being indolent were miserably poor in consequence.

They were filled with many absurd superstitions, and resorted to sweat baths to drive away evil spirits, disease and nightmares; being firm believers in dreams, they were constantly trying to counteract imaginary ills.

They believed their ancestors came from coyotes or prairie wolves and

MAN AND THREE WIVES; SUMMER ABODE—BANNOCKS.

worshiped this animal; when they were eating, a goodly supply of food was given to the wolves as an offering to the spirits of their forefathers.

When an important person dies, the body is bound with rushes and tied in a standing position to a tree, then fences are built around the place to prevent carnivorous animals from eating the remains; women, children and common men are dragged to a cave or hole and left there, without being covered by anything but a few brush.

CHAPTER XXIV.

THE DIGGER INDIANS—OUTCASTS OF OTHER TRIBES—THE LOWEST OF THE
LOW.

How the Diggers Acquired their Name—A Conglomerate Lot—Living on Roots and Burrowing in Holes—The Lowest in Intelligence and most Degraded of all Indians—Only one
Remove from Apes—Their Repulsive Appearance—Extraordinary Voracity—Surrounding the Carcass of a Horse—Leaving Nothing but its Bones—Selling their
Children to Obtain Food—Living together in Herds—Below the Level of Beasts—
Going Entirely Naked in Summer—Living on Insects and Reptiles—The Personification of all that is Low and Vile—Their Filthy Lodges—Living in Caves—A Tribe
of Vermin Eaters—Their Gaunt, Half-Famished Dogs—Ignorance of the Sign Language—Marriage Unknown among Them—Eating Raw Fish—Ostracized by Every
One—How a Sick Digger was Taken Care of—His Fate after Death.

In stature and bearing the Digger Indians strongly resembled members of
the great Shoshonee family. The name Digger was applied to them from
their habit of digging in the ground for edible roots, and burrowing in holes
for their habitations. The term has been somewhat indiscriminately used
in describing the Indians of California, Nevada, Utah, and the contiguous
country. The true Digger Indians lived in the northeastern part of what is
now the State of Nevada.

It is my opinion that the Diggers were not tribes at all, but were the outcasts of different tribes of the Shoshonees; that when individual Snakes,
Utes, Bannocks, and others became so low as to be unfit to remain in their
respective tribes they were forced out, finally coming together as a conglomerate band formed from the outcasts of various tribes.

At best their life was but little above that of the ape family, and it is
therefore very difficult to establish for them an individuality at all satisfactory.

The Diggers were divided into two parts, which, for want of a better
name, I shall call tribes. One of these tribes, numbering about five hundred, occupied the country about the confluence of the north and south forks
of the Humboldt River. The other tribe, numbering about six hundred,
lived farther west along this river.

In personal appearance the Diggers were the most repulsive of all Indians.

Their hair was long, reaching to the waist, and in coarseness resembled the tail of a horse or mule. Their faces were as devoid of intellectual expression as if they were the lower animals; indeed, one could not but notice a strong similarity to wild beasts in their appearance and actions.

Their voracity when they could procure a supply of food was almost incredible. Five or six of them would sit around the carcass of a horse or mule and remain there until nothing but the bones were left. Unlike their Indian neighbors, they stole horses and mules, not to ride but to slaughter for food, and they have even been known to sell their children in order to increase their scanty food supplies.

Of their home life nothing can be said, for they had no home life, even in the lowest sense. In some respects they seemed below the level of beasts. They sometimes went entirely naked, and their clothing at all times was of the scantiest. They lived or rather herded together without distinction of sex or regard to family relations; decency being wholly unknown to them. They were as low morally as they were poor in worldly goods.

Marriage was practically unknown among them; they lived together promiscuously. At times some of them lived together as families, but there was nothing binding in the arrangement, and members of the family could leave when they chose.

In winter they suffered greatly from the bitter cold of their climate, and they lived, the Great Creator only knows how. They had no arms, or horses, and were too lazy or too ignorant to hunt. They lived on what little meat they could procure, and on anything that grew wild in the territory they roamed over. Sometimes hunger compelled them to eat grasshoppers and crickets in order to save themselves from starving. They were also clay-eaters. Altogether they were the most miserable people I have ever seen.

There was not an article in all their belongings that another Indian, no matter how poor, would have. They were never engaged in war either among themselves, the white, or red men. It has been said that there is not a thing on earth that has not been placed here by the wisdom of our Great Creator, for some beneficent purpose, yet I could never understand why Digger Indians were placed on earth, nor what they were good for.

One of the greatest insults that could be offered to a white man or to an Indian of another tribe or nation, was to compare him to a Digger Indian, as they were acknowledged by all, to be the personification of everything that was ignorant and vile. Their lodges, when they had any, were small, dirty, open affairs, and the stench coming from them was enough to cause the strongest stomach to revolt.

In summer, when lying indolently on the ground, naked, or almost so, the men compelled the women to draw the bushes over them for shelter, or, if there were no bushes, to pile up stones or sticks in such a manner that a skin or blanket could be thrown over the top to protect the lazy occupants from the heat of the sun. In winter they lived in caves, or in holes in the ground, in which numbers dwelt at a time without the slightest regard for decency. These habitations were rarely visited by white men. They reeked with filth and swarmed with vermin which the Diggers picked from each other's bodies and heads and ate with avidity.

They would surround the carcass of an animal which had been dead long enough to putrefy, and eat it, sometimes raw. The small amount of food that these miserable, half-starved creatures subsisted upon was surprising. Notwithstanding all this, their bodies did not show evil effects from lack of food, or the poor quality of the little they had.

Their dogs, which were few, were half-coyote or gray wolf, and, like their owners, were half-famished, their bones almost sticking through their hides. Their gaunt bodies and fierce eyes presented a horrible appearance.

The Diggers were about the only people of Indian origin who did not understand the use of the sign language. They had a dialect which was understood by all bearing their name. It was difficult for a white man to acquire it.

In summer they lived principally on what fish they could catch in the streams. These were secured by the women, in small quantities, with a scoop net, made from grasses, fastened to a hoop, attached to a pole. The fish were eaten raw, or if they attempted to cook them they were not more than half done. They also ate frogs, toads, snakes, and insects of all kinds.

The Diggers were so low that none of their surrounding neighbors ever went to war, or had any dealings with them. So repulsive were their women that no person other than their own people ever went near them.

In comparison to other Indians, the Diggers were as low as the commonest tramp is to decent, well-ordered society among civilized people. It is impossible to conceive of anything in the semblance of humanity presenting a more degraded appearance.

A tramp will migrate from place to place, while a Digger would lie stretched at full length on the ground, in all kinds of weather, too lazy to stir, and scarcely traveled a mile in a week. The Digger was too ignorant and lazy to be vicious, which was the only redeeming quality about him. He did not molest anybody, and no one molested him. When one of them was taken sick some of the old women might possibly take compassion on the sufferer and attempt to relieve, or make him more comfortable. Generally, however, the patient was left to shift for himself as best he could until he recovered or died.   After death the body was dragged a short distance away and left to be devoured by their half-starved dogs or wild animals.

Their amusements or pastimes were very limited, for their possessions were so few they had nothing to gamble with or stake on a game of chance. They did not indulge in any of the usual Indian dances or outdoor sports, such as running, jumping, ball-playing, or kindred amusements.

At one time they had a head man or chief, Yellow Hand.   He exercised some little control over them, but as they were so indolent his power was merely in name; though when they stole from the whites, he often caused the return of stolen articles.

WINTER HABITATIONS.

CHAPTER XXV.

THE BLACKFEET—THE SMALL-POX EPIDEMIC—APPALLING SCENES OF DEATH
AND DESOLATION—A CAMP OF HUMAN BONES AND DESERTED LODGES.

The Blackfeet Indians—How they got their Name—Their Country—The Neighbors with
whom they were at War—The Piegans, Bloods, and Gros Ventres of the Prairie
—Their Standing Grudge against the American Fur Companies—Trapping
under Difficulties—How Trappers Protected themselves against the Indians—
Unwritten Laws of the Blackfeet—Their Superstition against Fish—Their Religious
Beliefs and Burial Ceremonies—Flight of the Spirit—Manner of Feeding the Spirit—
The Dual Spirit—Carrying out Dreams—The Small-Pox Epidemic—How it Gained
a Foothold—Fearful Ravages—How they Treated this Dread Disease—Fifteen Hun-
dred Lodges and their Dead Abandoned—Appalling Scenes of Death and Desolation
—Small-Pox Corpses Eaten by Wolves.

BLACKFOOT CHIEF—HEADDRESS OF EAGLE FEATHERS.

THE Blackfeet were the
largest, most fierce, proud
and haughty tribe of the
Algonquin nation. Their
language was that of their
mother tongue. They wore
moccasins and leggings in
winter made from the skins
of black animals tanned
with the hair on; the moccasins and leggings made
for summer use were also
blackened, and the tribe
w a s　i n　consequence in-
variably k n o w n as the
Blackfeet. They were one
of the great Indian peoples
of the Northwest. Their
home, or principal hunting
g r o u n d, was about the
headwaters of the Missouri and Milk Rivers.

The Blackfeet claimed the country as far south as the Yellowstone River,
and far north into the British possessions. They were an intelligent, and,

when aroused, an extremely warlike people. Though living in a cold climate, were healthy, hardy, and long-lived.

They were constantly at war with the Sioux, Crows, Snakes, and all their Indian neighbors to the west. The battles between them were of the fiercest kind, for all were warlike and determined fighters; when either of them encroached on the hunting grounds of the other there was sure to be a bloody and desperate contest.

In summer their country teemed with buffalo and other game, of which they killed large numbers, laying by a good store of meat for winter use. Wild horses were also numerous, and the Blackfeet always had good mounts.

The women made warm clothing from the skins of bear, buffalo, buffalo calves, elk and deer. This usually consisted of a jacket and leggings tanned with the hair on. The entire family dressed in this manner during cold weather. In winter they made their camps in well-wooded valleys of streams, where forage for their animals and fuel for themselves were easily procured. These valleys also afforded considerable protection from cold winds and storms.

Their number was estimated in early days at from twenty-five to thirty thousand souls, but they were divided into many small tribes, the principal ones being the Surches, the Piegans, and the Gros Ventres of the Prairies.

Trappers generally spoke of the Blackfeet as being among the most peaceable and well-disposed Indians of any in the Northwest. From the earliest recollection they were friendly toward the whites, though they had a standing grudge against the American Fur Company for some real or imaginary cause; I am inclined to think that it was more real than imaginary, for the Fur Companies were very unfair and arbitrary in their dealings with all Indians. The Blackfeet claimed that the Fur Companies had killed several of their members without provocation. When the Fur Companies made expeditions into the Blackfeet country, it was necessary for them to have from seventy-five to one hundred well-armed and equipped men in each party; even then they were not safe, for they were often attacked, robbed of their stores, and killed by the implacable Blackfeet. Their hunting ground supplied a large number of beaver, otter and other valuable pelts, and the Fur Companies were not disposed to abandon this region.

Being surrounded by so many tribes speaking different tongues, compelled them to use all the different sign languages almost constantly. In consequence of this they were experts in the use of the sign language in all its branches.

Their home life was very simple. In dealing with each other they were more honest than any other Indians in that wild country. The unwritten laws of the nation were few, but they protected the rights of each person about as common sense dictated. They were nomadic, living in skin-covered lodges during summer. They subsisted entirely by the chase. None of them ate any kind of water fowl, amphibious animal, or fish. They had a superstition against the use of this kind of food.

They believed in and worshiped the Great Spirit, and offered their prayers only to him. Their ideas of the immortality of the soul were beautiful. They believed that after death the soul went to the Spirit Land. When it arrived there it was in the same condition as when it left the earth. During the journey it suffered want and privations; that the road traveled was filled with many obstacles, which it must overcome or avoid. They believed in the soul's duality; that one soul remained in the body while the other was groping through darkness in its effort to discover the road which led to its new home. They also believed there was another spirit which was sent by the Great Creator to accompany the soul until its safe arrival in the Spirit Land.

The Blackfeet buried their dead in the ground, then placed the implements of war and ornaments belonging to the deceased on the grave. They did not kill animals at the grave, like some other Indians. The corpse, dressed in its best attire and ready for burial, sometimes sitting and sometimes lying, presented a strange appearance. After burial the friends and family of the deceased visited the burial place every night for a long time. They kindled fires on the grave that the spirit of the departed might find its way back to the burial place, to observe the respect and affection paid by relatives and friends to the remains of the dead. During the time these fires were burning, food was left for the sustenance of the spirit.

To a Blackfoot there was no such thing as hell or the Bad Spirit. To him all things were the work of the Good Spirit. When evil came he claimed it was the anger of the Good Spirit visited upon him, which he made an effort to appease. They were firm believers in dreams. After the death of one of the family all dreams the living had concerning the dead were carried out literally, if possible; though many of them were ludicrous to every one except a Blackfoot.

About the year 1837 occurred a memorable epoch in the history of the Indians of the Northwest. The small-pox epidemic, having gained a foothold among the Indians along the Missouri River, was carried from tribe to tribe until it reached the Blackfeet in the far north, destroying fully one-half of their numbers. The Arickarees were so terribly depleted by the scourge that they subsequently migrated north and united with some of the neighboring tribes. The Crows also suffered fearful ravages, but were not so unfortunate as their neighbors, for they fled to the mountains as soon as the disease made its appearance among them. The havoc made by the epidemic was largely due to the cold climate and ignorance of a remedy or proper treatment for the afflicted. This was especially true of the Black-feet.

TYPICAL WARRIOR.

When this epidemic first made its appearance among them they attempted to combat it. Their first effort to cure it was through the conjury of the medicine man. Finding this of no avail, they resorted to heroic treatment. When the patients complained of burning with fever they were taken from the lodges and rolled in the snow, which meant almost instant death. Another remedy was the steam bath. The patients were placed on heated stones, over which water was poured, and after being thoroughly steamed they were thrown into the river. It is needless to say that they entered the river and the happy hunting ground at about the same time. They also tried other remedies, but without effect; as the disease spread rapidly, attacking a great many, they finally gave up in despair, declaring that the anger of the Great Spirit had been visited on them and threatened to annihilate them. Those who survived were disfigured by great pits in their faces and bodies; being excessively proud of their personal appearance, they were so humiliated at sight of these blemishes and scars that some of them committed suicide. As suicide was almost unknown among the North American Indians, one may obtain from this some idea of the distress of the Blackfeet over their disfigured appearance.

Some of the survivors of this dreaded disease became insane; as insanity was something new to them, they believed that the anger of the Great Spirit was specially directed to those who had had the disease. As the epidemic visited them during the winter, they could not very well remove their camps. They longed for the return of spring, and as soon as the weather permitted, left their camps, leaving the sick and dead in the lodges. Up to the time I last saw them, I do not believe that one of them had returned to it. For years after the visitation of this scourge, the mere mention of small-pox almost created a panic among them.

The Blackfeet, Piegans, and Gros Ventres of the Prairie suffered so fearfully from this dreadful scourge that, according to their own story, more than fifteen hundred lodges were abandoned by them. The lodges were left standing with the bodies of the dead in them just as they died. The Indians who had not been attacked by the scourge fled in every direction, leaving the wolves and other wild animals to feed on the remains of the dead and occupy the habitations of this once proud and haughty people.

The scene of desolation in these abandoned villages where the disease had destroyed so many Indians was heartrending. The bodies of the dead were stripped of their flesh by carnivorous animals, and their white bones were strewn everywhere. The deserted lodges, the deathlike silence, and the absence of almost every kind of life presented a never-to-be-forgotten scene, and one that was almost indescribable.

Edward Umfreville maintains* that the Blackfeet had a peculiar manner of mutilating themselves by cutting off several joints of their fingers. Beginning at the first joint of the little finger on the right hand, they would take it off; then, after a short time, the first joint of the next finger; and so on until all the first joints of the fingers on that hand were removed. They then did the same with the left hand. Again returning to the right hand, they removed the next joint of the little finger, and so on until they had removed all the joints of the fingers on that hand, and then proceeded with the left as before. According to him it required a long time to complete this operation, as the stump of each finger had to heal before the next joint was removed.

I do not believe that this mutilation was done for the purpose of beautify-

*In " The Present State of Hudson's Bay," published in London, 1790.

ing themselves, as the author referred to states, but was rather an exhibition of their fortitude in enduring pain. I have seen Indians have a white surgeon extract some of their large teeth, which were perfectly sound, for no other purpose than to show their fearlessness of pain; and other Indians presented themselves for the same operation, and for the same purpose, until the doctors refused to extract more sound teeth to gratify their foolish whims.

CHOPPED UP—PIEGAN.

PIEGANS, BLOODS, GROS VENTRES OF THE PRAIRIE.

The Piegans, Bloods, and Gros Ventres of the Prairie were three tribes that lived to the west of the Blackfeet, and were a part of the same people. Each one of them had its own tribal organization, spoke the same language, had the same manners and customs, abided by the same general laws, and were known among themselves by their respective names and no other. None of these tribes were at war with each other, but all lived in harmony. The Blackfeet proper, with the three tribes just named, constituted one of the most powerful Indian peoples in the Northwest.

When starting on the warpath warriors of all the four tribes often joined against a common enemy.

During winter these people wore a warm head covering reaching to the shoulders and covering the entire head except the face. Head coverings were made of skins with the fur on, or of blankets, and warm mittens made of the same material were also worn by both sexes.

Their winter coats were fashioned after the manner of civilization, but with a hood attached to the garment to cover the head. A strong belt bound the cloak close to the body at the waist, and as they were made of blankets or hairy skins they were very comfortable.

Nearly all this group wore caps with visors. Caps were made of the finest furs, and gaudily decorated with feathers, tails of foxes, wolves, otter, and ermine cut in strips, as well as shells, beads and variegated porcupine quills. These and a few of their surrounding neighbors were the only red men in that country who wore this kind of head gear. Their handiwork was skillfully, and some of it beautifully done, and the bows and arrows made by them were superior to those of any other Indians in the Northwest.

Some of the birch bark canoes and dug-outs fashioned by these people were models of beauty and grace, and it was from this source that so many beautiful canoes were obtained.

The bull boats constructed by them were the lightest, most buoyant, and largest as well as the staunchest of any made throughout the West, and they were experts in handling all kinds of water craft.

Snow shoes made by them—or in fact by almost all of the Algonquin tribes—were the best, lightest, and most durable as well as the handsomest of any manufactured by civilized or savage man.

From infancy they were taught to walk, run and dance on snow shoes, and it was by this means that they traveled on foot over the snow during a large portion of the winter.

All of this group were intelligent and fine specimens of manhood; were good hunters and warriors, and while there was nothing in common between the tribes, in times of scarcity the men joined in a general hunt for the benefit of all.

Polygamy was common, and this tended to unite the tribes more closely.

They were not given to painting themselves in the homely and hideous manner of some of their neighbors on the south and west; being somewhat cleanly and careful of their personal appearance they were more attractive to the white men who visited that country than any other Indians in the Northwest, as the many half-breeds in their territory testify.

CHAPTER XXVI.

THE CROWS, OR UPSORUKA AS THEY CALLED THEMSELVES—JAMES BECK-
WOURTH, THE FAMOUS MULATTO FRONTIERSMAN—LIFE AMONG THE
CROWS.

The Crows—Driven out by the Sioux—A Skulking, Thievish Race—A Tall and Athletic
  People—Their Flowing Hair—The Crow Women—How the Crows Attacked Trap-
  pers and Traders—Murdering Entire Expeditions—Night Attacks—The Home of
  the Beaver, Otter, and other Fur-Bearing Animals—The Famous Mulatto Trapper,
  Jim Beckwourth—His Alliance with the Crows—His Great Influence among Them
  —His Return to St. Louis and Supposed Death—Effect of the Rumor on the Crows—
  A Bloody Tragedy Averted—Reappearance of Beckwourth—A Brave and Sagacious
  Man—A Warrior Race—Bitterness between the Crows and Sioux—What Happens
  after Death.

THE Crows were originally a part of the great Sioux nation, but were ex-
pelled from their original hunting ground by the Sioux. After having been
driven out they made their home in the country of the Flatheads, Blackfeet,
and other mountain Indians, and subsequently wrested it from them.

The Crows were divided into three tribes, Absoruka, the name applied
to the Crows proper, the Annahways, and the Allakaweah. The Crows
were the next in intelligence and physical stature to the Sioux. They were
tall, athletic, and strong of build, far surpassing in this regard most of their
neighbors. Being originally a part of the great Sioux family, their habits
closely resembled those of their ancestors, although they tried to establish
manners and customs of their own, owing to their intensely bitter hatred of
the Sioux. Occupying a country farther removed from civilization than
almost any other Indians in the Northwest, they were among the last of the
red men to come in contact with the whites. When I knew them they were
wilder than any other Indians living in that country. For a long time it
was almost an impossibility for a white man to have intercourse with them.

While nearly all Indians of the far West were opposed to the white man,
none were more dreaded by adventurous traders and trappers than the Crows,
or, as they called themselves, the Upsoruka or Absoruka. They lived near
the eastern chain of the Rocky Mountains, and their hunting grounds embraced the basins of the Yellowstone, Big Horn, and Tongue Rivers. Their
territory extended to the south as far as the Sioux would permit them to go,

which was near the headwaters of the Yellowstone.   On the east they roamed to the vicinity of the Big Horn River.

They were skulking, thievish, and after becoming known to the white man, they were noted as marauders, murderers and horse thieves; although they were crafty and avoided becoming embroiled in open war with the whites, they robbed and killed them at every opportunity, and they were dreaded by all the trappers and traders in that region.

They were almost always at war with their neighbors, especially the

CROW LODGES.

Blackfeet, who greatly outnumbered them.   The result of this constant warfare was that the proportion of women to the men was greater among the Crows than among any of their neighbors.

A peculiar characteristic of these Indians was the length and profusion of their hair, which they cultivated with much care, and regarded it as the greatest ornament of their person.   It was not unusual to see a Crow Indian with hair reaching to, and sweeping the ground.   Some of their neighbors tried to imitate this peculiarity by binding false hair to the natural growth.

In the construction of their lodges the Crows did not differ materially from their neighbors. For winter use they built houses of logs or birch bark, about half-hut and half-cabin. These habitations were located in some low and timbered spot, where they were protected against the severe storms so prevalent in the mountains. They were also used as breastworks against attacks from their enemies. In summer the Crows were constantly on the move, impelled by their natural love of roving and the necessity of procuring food.

In their wanderings the women were compelled to do the work of putting up and taking down the lodges, packing the camp belongings on the horses and mules, carrying wood, water, and doing the cooking.

The Crow women were among the best tanners of any Indian women in the entire West. In dressing skins they made them very soft and pliable and almost pure white. Their clothing was made of these neatly prepared skins, which were decorated and ornamented with porcupine quills and beadwork. Though the men were among the finest specimens of Indian manhood, the women did not appear to be physically superior to those of neighboring nations.

The Crows were exceedingly troublesome in early days to the fur traders and trappers. They were well acquainted with all the routes and resorts of the trappers, and knew where to find them in the trapping season, as well as where they were stationed in winter; they often made raids on them, killing all the men in the expeditions, securing their entire equipments and outfits.

The various Fur Companies were justly apprehensive of the safety of every expedition they sent into the Crow hunting ground. Every party of trappers that entered this country had a larger number of men and a better outfit than was considered necessary for any other territory. The Crow country was the natural home of fur-bearing animals, and more valuable pelts could be secured there than in other regions. At times the trappers were compelled to abandon it for a long period, through fear of these Indians, for the Crows were nearly always on the warpath, and if a war party came up on a trapping expedition, if they did not kill the entire party, they were liable to take their belongings, and let the trappers subsist, or escape, as best they could. Sometimes war parties went on foot the better to skulk through the mountains, where they could surprise and ambush trappers.

The Crows frequently attacked their enemies at night, hoping to precipitate a panic by making a sudden and furious dash. Should the attacked make a determined stand, the Crows skulked off to a safe place and made another attempt later on.

For the privilege of trapping in their country the Hudson Bay Fur Company supplied the Crows with arms and ammunition. When they had plenty of ammunition they were aggressive, and made war on all people they could reach.

The rivalry between the different Fur Companies finally became so fierce that they would take almost any hazard to trap in the country of the Crows. The result was, that it was overrun by numerous expeditions, which were themselves victimized by individual white trappers and traders, who led the Crows into many excesses.

James Beckwourth, a mulatto—popularly known as "Jim" Beckwourth —was a trapper who went from St. Louis into this country in the employ of a fur company. He and others of the party suffered great privations on their first expedition, and would perhaps have perished but for the aid of some Indians. Having returned to St. Louis, he was prevailed upon to make another trip to the headquarters of the fur company in the Rocky Mountains. He traded for a time with the Blackfeet, among whom he had many alleged adventures, finally making his way into the Crow country. He soon acquired considerable fame among the hunters for his skill, and among the Indians, he was regarded as a brave. It is said that one of his companions persuaded the Crows that Beckwourth was a Crow who had been captured in one of their wars with the northern Cheyennes, some twenty years before, and sold by the latter to the whites. At any rate, he was adopted into the Crow tribe. It has been claimed that he became chief of the tribe, but there is no evidence of the truth of this statement. It is, however, certain that Beckwourth acquired considerable influence among the Crows. He was brave, adventurous, sagacious, and was therefore greatly admired by them. He accompanied them in their raids, wars and hunts, and impressed them by his courage and skill.

Beckwourth returned to St. Louis some years afterward. A party of trappers who had heard of his departure told the Crows that he had been killed by the great white chief, because he had lived among the Indians.

This story created much excitement among the Crows, who, after a council, determined to kill all the white men at the trading post, and then send out parties to kill all the whites in that section of country. The director of the trading post prevailed on the Indians to wait until he should send to St. Louis and bring Beckwourth back. This was reluctantly agreed to by the Crows, and after several months, Beckwourth again made his appearance, having traveled the distance of two thousand seven hundred miles in fifty-three days, a great feat at that time. After his return the Crows were much more friendly toward the whites.

Since I left that country I have read and heard much of the adventures and daring exploits of Jim Beckwourth. I knew him well. The greater part of these stories belong to fiction; for, at that time the entire country north of the Platte River as far as the British possessions did not contain more than a few hundred white men. The character and doings of these were well known to each other, and to all the people throughout this vast territory. Among them Beckwourth did not have the credit of being anything more than an ordinary trapper and mountaineer, who had become by marriage a member of the Crow people, and lived the life of the Indian.

As warriors the Crows were equal to any Indians in that part of the country. Being trespassers on the hunting grounds of their neighbors, they incurred the hatred of tribes on the east, north, and west of them. As the Crows were renegade Sioux, and their neighbors on the south were also Sioux, the feeling between them was intensely bitter. Hence, they were entirely surrounded by enemies. They had frequent and bloody battles in which they held their own; but if any of their neighbors had allied, and made war on them it would have been disastrous for the Crows.

Some of the battles fought between the Sioux, Blackfeet, and Snakes against the Crows were of the fiercest, and had the latter not been warriors of superior ability, their numbers would have been greatly reduced.

A-ra-poo-ash was a noted chief among them. He was the hero of scores of battles and encounters, principally with the Blackfeet, the hereditary and inveterate enemies of the Crows. On one occasion a large party of Blackfeet made a raid into the Crow territory, killing a number of them, capturing nearly all their animals, carrying off many of their women and children, and committing the usual Indian depredations.

A-ra-poo-ash, smarting under the effects of this unexpected raid, called his warriors together. He then harangued them, exciting them to wild frenzy by his talk on the humiliation of their surprise and loss. A war party was at once formed to pursue the Blackfeet for the purpose of rescuing their women and children and recovering their animals. The Crows had but few animals left; these were used for packing purposes only, the warriors going on foot. After traveling almost incessantly for several days and nights, they overtook the Blackfeet.

A bloody battle ensued. The Blackfeet greatly outnumbered the Crows, and being well mounted, the latter were at a disadvantage from the first. The Crows, led by A-ra-poo-ash, formed themselves in a circle, keeping the Blackfeet at a distance for a short time. A-ra-poo-ash then called upon the warriors to charge the enemy in full force and rescue the captives. The charge was so impetuous that the Blackfeet were thrown back in confusion, and a number of captives were rescued. The Blackfeet at once sent the remaining captives, under a strong guard of dismounted warriors, up a ravine thick with underbrush. A-ra-poo-ash on discovering this move directed the main body of his warriors to continue the battle, then taking with him some twenty braves started for the place where the captives were concealed. Here a fierce and bloody encounter took place, and, what was unusual in Indian warfare, both parties fought on foot. Under the direction of their great leader the Crows fought with the ferocity of tigers.

A-ra-poo-ash, seeing that his party had exhausted nearly all their ammunition, now drew his knife, brandished it above his head, shouting to his warriors to follow him, and cut the enemy to pieces. A-ra-poo-ash led the attack and disemboweled the first Blackfoot he met with a stroke of his knife. He then rushed upon another, and nearly severed his head from his body. He then attacked the third, but before he could strike, a lance in the hand of a Blackfoot was plunged through his body, inflicting a mortal wound. Thus died the great A-ra-poo-ash, the hero of scores of battles, the Napoleon of his people.

As soon as their chief fell the Crows returned to the main body. Being without a leader they ceased to be aggressive and sought places of safety among the rocks, where they remained until dark, when they started for their own hunting ground.

In this battle many warriors on both sides were killed. Many of the captives were also killed, not only by the enemy but by their own people, for they were intentionally placed by their captors in an exposed position. This battle was a great blow to the Crows, and it was a long time before they recovered from its effects.

This is the true story of this bloody fight as given both by the Blackfeet and the Crows themselves, at the time. I heard it translated by Jim Beckwourth, just as it was narrated to him by the Crows. Jim was then living with the Crows, and had at least one of their women for a wife.

The Crows had little religious belief. Unlike the Sioux, they believed only in the Good Spirit. When evil befell them they believed that it was the work of the Good Spirit who was punishing them for some wrong they had committed. When one of their number recovered from sickness or grievous affliction, they believed that the anger of the Good Spirit was appeased and that they had gained his favor, after which they indulged in feasting, rejoicing and dancing.

The one portion of the Sioux belief which they tried hard to change to suit themselves was in relation to the Great Spirit and the soul. They believed that the soul left the body through the mouth; that it was a shadow which hovered about the corpse until it began to decay; and that the smell from the putrefying remains drove it farther and farther away until it started on its journey to the Spirit Land. They believed that the road which the soul traveled was the same by which all souls had gone before. This road was broad and well beaten by numerous spirit travelers. It crossed many swift-running waters, tall mountains, and dense forests, and led direct to the west, where the setting sun lighted the soul into paradise. When the soul finally arrived in the Spirit Land the souls of all members of the tribe that had gone before were in readiness to meet it. The new arrival was welcomed by dances and merry-making. The Crows believed that it took the soul a long time to make this journey, but they had no idea of the condition it arrived in, whether in the form it left the earth, or as a child or adult, mutilated or whole. They believed, however, that the soul arrived in perfect condition to enjoy life forever after in its new home.

INDIAN ENCAMPMENT—BUFFALO SKIN-COVERED LODGES.

The Minitari, or Hidatsa, were an offshoot of the Crows, from whom they separated a long time ago. They held friendly intercourse with the Mandans, but were particularly hostile towards the Snakes and Flatheads. From the time they were first visited by white men they were peaceably inclined toward them. Trappers and traders secured from them more valuable pelts than from any other nation or tribe of Indians, per capita, in the Northwest.

For transporting hides in winter, bobsleds were made from the ribs of the larger animals; one entire side of ribs was in the front and the other in the rear; light, but strong poles were then bound to the top, forming the sleds, on which heavy loads were drawn over the snow.

From the ribs of the smaller animals they fashioned a sort of snow shoe for the feet, and it was interesting to watch them sliding down steep hills over smooth snow and ice, as they fell over one another in the most laughable manner.

CHAPTER XXVII.

THE FLATHEADS—WHY SO NAMED—PECULIAR CUSTOMS—FLAT HEADS A MARK OF BEAUTY — SUN WORSHIPERS — BURIAL CUSTOMS — THE KOOTENAI.

The Flatheads—Their Peculiar Language—Manner of Flattening the Heads of Their Children—The Camas, how Gathered—Peculiar Manner of Cooking It—Boat Building by Fire—Personal Appearance—Commendable Rules or Laws—Murder Settled for in Valuables—Sun Worshipers—Peculiar Superstitions—How Disease Reached Them—Mortuary Customs—Burials in Sitting Posture—Friends Visiting Burial Places—Widowhood—Keeping the Husband's Spirit Away—The Kootenai—Their Hunting Grounds—Filthy Habits—Treatment of Captives.

THE Flatheads were a part of the Selish nation, and their original homes were in the vicinity of Flathead Lake, which lies east of the Bitter Root Mountains, and their hunting grounds extended to the eastern side of this chain.

At that time all the Indians in this locality were known as Flatheads. They were segregated into many tribes; the principal ones were the Flatheads proper, or Teetwees, the Pen d'Oreilles, or as they called themselves Kalspel, and the. Cœur d'Alene or Skitsuish; there was no central authority, but each tribe was governed by its own chief.

Many of the tribes spoke distinct dialects, but all sprung from the same mother tongue. Their language and dialects were so inflexible and difficult of pronunciation, that the early pioneers and trappers could not acquire it, and therefore it was not reduced to any form of writing.

All the tribes intermarried, were fond of home life, and strange as it may seem, they were almost monogamous. This may be partly accounted for from the fact that they were not aggressive and warlike, and the sexes were in about equal numbers.

Wives were secured by purchase and kindly treated, and while there was little or no modesty as civilization understands the term, there was no immorality.

The name Flathead was given them from their peculiar custom of flattening the heads of the children. This deformity was produced by pressure upon the forehead of the young child, while the skull was soft. The infant was placed on its back on a slab of bark or wood, and at the end of this was fastened a shorter piece, which was pressed over the forehead of the baby, the two pieces somewhat resembling the letter V. The end of the wood above the face was bound downward with thongs to the under board, and as the skull receded or yielded to the pressure brought upon it, the thongs were tightened more and more, until the head assumed the desired shape. Some heads became so flattened by this process, that there was a straight line from the end of the nose to the apex of the deformed skull. Not more than a few months were required for the operation, after which the head did not resume its normal shape. The custom produced no noticeable change in the intellect of the person. A flat head was considered a mark of beauty, and the flatter it was the more they admired it. They dressed their hair with great care, parting it in the middle, and allowing it to hang loose on both sides; the hair commencing near the eyebrows and running to the apex gave the person a peculiar appearance, and when riding rapidly, it streamed from the flattened heads and appeared to be a flag of hair.

In no other nation or tribe of North American Indians was this custom practiced, except among their neighbors, the Chinnooks.

Many kinds of natural fruits and vegetables grew wild all over their hunting grounds; of these the camas was the most important. It is a small onion, white and insipid when first taken from the earth, but black and sweet when prepared for food. The women provided themselves with long sticks when going in search of the camas, and having procured a quantity after long and painful labor, they dug holes in the ground from twelve to fifteen inches deep. The bottoms were then plastered with a kind of cement, made red hot; these were covered with fresh grass or wet hay, on which was placed a layer of camas, then another layer of wet hay and a third of bark; the latter was then overlaid with mold, on which fires were kept burning for fifty, sixty, and sometimes seventy hours; the camas thus acquired the consistency of thick paste; this was then made into loaves and was ready for use. It was excellent food, especially when boiled with meat, and if kept dry it could be preserved almost indefinitely.

The mountain streams were filled with many varieties of fine fish; for catching these, the women wove nets of silk grass and the fibrous bark of the white cedar; they also twisted fishing lines of the same materials, and fashioned hooks from bones and wood for catching fish with hook and line; although not very serviceable, a few fish were caught in this manner.

For cooking fish and food in general, troughs were made of wood or fresh skins; in these heated stones were thrown and when cool, they were taken out and replaced by hot ones, until the water boiled and cooked the food.

They fashioned canoes from the trunks of white cedar, birch and fir trees; some were from forty to fifty feet in length and capable of carrying from twenty to thirty persons. They were good boatmen and drove these large boats rapidly with paddles. When they had but few tools of civilization, boats were hollowed out and shaped by fire. The process was tedious, laborious, and required patience and skill; but the heat seasoned the timber and made the craft buoyant and light. Their primitive weapons were very inferior, and some of their spear and arrow heads were made of roots hardened at the points by fire, or pointed with bones.

In personal appearance they were coarse, and a pleasing countenance was seldom seen in either sex; they were much darker in complexion than the typical red men; their eyes were small but piercing, and it was seldom that they looked strangers in the face.

From appearances there seemed an entire absence of affection in their compositions; yet orphan children were readily adopted and treated kindly until old enough to provide for themselves.

A few commendable rules or laws were observed: if murder was committed, the offender was compelled to compromise with the relatives of the victim by a satisfactory payment of horses or other articles of value; for a common warrior twenty-five horses were sufficient; the life of a female was about one-half the value of a male, and it was rare for them to wreak vengeance by killing the murderer, as was the custom among other Indians.

They were sun worshipers, and made their devotions to that great luminary for giving them light, heat, causing the grass and trees to grow, and bringing the buffaloes back to their country. They believed the sun gave them shadows which were their souls, and as the shadows were without voice, they must also be likewise when making their prayers.

Disease they believed was inflicted upon them by the sorcery of their enemies during the night, and as a protection they carried about them bones and the dust of owls, that by so doing the power of vision of these birds was imparted to them that they might see better the approach of, and prevent sickness reaching them during the darkness.

They claimed that the echo was the voice of the spirit then hovering about of some recently departed friend.

When an important person was ill, another member of the tribe was compelled to assume the name of the afflicted and retire to the forest, as they believed the disease followed the name.

They were very superstitious in relation to a lingering or wasting illness, as they claimed that the body arrived in its new home in the same form it left the earth, and they feared to arrive there in an emaciated or enfeebled condition.

Some of their mortuary customs were peculiar to themselves. When the remains of a chief or leading man was interred, it was placed in the grave in a sitting posture with the face to the west; this they believed was the direction the spirit traveled 'on its way to its new home, and that the body could see the spirit daily with the setting of the sun, until the corpse rotted and became a part of the earth.

Friends visited the burial places in death-like silence; offered mental prayers and left as stealthily as they came. Upon returning to their homes there were no loud lamentations or other noisy demonstrations of grief, neither were animals killed at the grave nor articles of personal effects left there.

After the death of a husband, the widow used all devices known to her to drive away the spirit of the departed, that she might be free to marry again. She blackened her face and body, dressed in her poorest attire, and built fires around her sleeping place to prevent the former husband coming near; after a sufficient time had elapsed, she believed this had been accomplished and that she was free to again enter the matrimonial contest.

The Kootenai were the neighbors of the Flatheads on the west and northwest, and their hunting grounds extended far north into the British possessions.

Of all the red men in that vicinity they were the most filthy; their habitations reeked with dirt and the smell coming from them was enough to cause the strongest stomach to revolt, while their persons and belongings were covered with vermin. It was disgusting to see them with one end of the raw entrails of a recently slain animal in their mouths chewing at it as though famished, and when eating cooked meat one end was chewed in the mouth until it was full, then with a knife they sawed off the piece and swallowed it half masticated.

Winter habitations were built of logs and the spaces between the timbers closed with mud; all houses contained but one room in which many families lived. Each family occupied its own place, and made holes in the ground floor in which their food was cooked.

In summer when roaming and shelter was needed, the tops of bushes were drawn together and skins thrown over them; in these large numbers sought refuge from the elements.

They were exceedingly cruel to prisoners or captives, and resorted to every device known to them, such as pulling out the nails, eyes and teeth; and when retaliating on captives of other Indians with whom they were at war, they bound them to trees, then scalped and left the victim to die an agonizing death from flies, which settled in countless numbers on the bare cranium of the helpless man.

CHAPTER XXVIII.

THE KIOWAS—A PART OF THE SHOSHONEE NATION—BRAVE, TREACHEROUS
AND CUNNING—SOME FAMOUS CHIEFS—RAIDS AND WARS.

The Kiowas—Part of the Shoshonee Family—Originally from the Far North—Hunting
Ground in the Black Hills—Driven Out by the Sioux—Their Last Home—Charac-
teristics of the Kiowas—A Murderous People—Treacherous, Cunning and Vicious—
Stealing from each other—How Stolen Property was Returned—Medicine Men—
Death of Santanta—Raids into Mexico—Their Alliances—Their Personal Appearance.

LARGE EAR
PENDANTS.

THE Kiowas were the most cleanly, intelligent, and best warriors of the Shoshonee nation.

Coming in contact with so many different Indian tribes, as well as the whites, they had better opportunities to inform themselves than any other portion of this family. They did not keep to themselves like many others, but allied at times with their neighbors, and observing the characteristics and customs of others improved themselves accordingly.

The Kiowas have long been known as southern plains Indians; but originally they came from the far north, and because of their vicious disposition and thieving propensities, their neighbors drove them south to the headwaters of the Missouri River and its tributaries.

Here the Sioux attacked them, driving them farther to the south. Again they made an effort to locate in the Black Hills, in what is now Wyoming. From here the Sioux drove them farther south along the foothills of the mountains through Colorado.

Finally reaching the Arkansas River, where they met the Comanches, who resisted their farther advance. A long and bloody war ensued, which was finally ended through a Spanish trader. A treaty and alliance of the two people was made, and the Kiowas were permitted to occupy that territory until their final round-up. The country claimed by them as their hunting ground embraced the territory as far north as somewhere about what is now the southern portion of Colorado, and Kansas, and on the west to the Rocky Mountains, and on the south far into Texas.

At one time they roamed over the country on the east to the Mississippi River.

The Kiowas were restless, roving and constantly on the move, and knew every portion of the country for hundreds of miles in every direction, and also knew of every wagon train, or settler, within their territory. These they raided at every opportunity.

They were constantly on raiding and marauding expeditions, and killed more people per capita than any Indians of the entire West.

After an expedition in which they had killed many people, and captured much property, they immediately sought refuge in the cañons of the mountains, where they remained until they could reconnoiter and learn if it was again safe to return to the open country.

About 1868 or 1869 they raided the settlers in the northern part of Texas, killing many of them, securing the animals and effects and carrying many women and children into captivity. It was not until after this raid that the Government determined to chastise them for this and former misdeeds, and after a sustained effort succeeded in capturing a party of them. Among the number taken were two Comanche chiefs, Santanta and Big Tree, and two Kiowa chiefs. All four were sent to Jacksboro, Texas, where they were tried for their crimes; having been found guilty were sentenced to death. This was commuted to life imprisonment, the United States Government interfering with the State authorities; they were not only not executed but liberated. After being set free each went to his own people, and was as hostile and turbulent as ever, though their raids on settlers were less frequent.

Some time afterward the Kiowas, Comanches, and some others went on the warpath for nearly a year. It was not long before Santanta was rearrested and sent to Texas to serve out his life sentence. After vainly waiting for some time expecting release, he committed suicide by jumping from a second-story window with shackles on his limbs, dashing his brains out on the pavement below.

The Kiowas often made alliances with the Comanches and Apaches. When these allied nations went on the warpath they made a strong party, and swept the entire country over which they roamed. When alliances were thus made and a raid was determined upon, they laid out one route only at a time. This route might be a raid on the Arapahoes and Cheyennes, their neighbors to the north, or the Sioux along the Platte River.

If they were successful each party returned to its own people with its share of the plunder. Arrangements having been previously made they met again to make similar raids on the people to the east, and in this way succeeded in doing an immense amount of damage.

The feeling between the Kiowas and the Sioux was extremely bitter, and

PRIMITIVE TRANSPORTATION—WOMAN WITH PONY TRAVOIS.

war parties from each nation were constantly making raids into the territory of the other. As the Kiowas always had a good supply of horses and mules, the raids by the Sioux were frequent, the chance of securing a large number of animals being a great temptation to them.

As they were not numerically strong, it was necessary for them to have allies, that they might make successful raids, as well as resist the encroachments of their neighbors and enemies from the north.

In the use of the sign language by their hands, the horse, fire, smoke, and the mirror they were the most proficient of any wild Indians in the southern portion of this country. They were also one of the most expert body of Indians in following the trail, as well as in eluding pursuit.

As warriors the Kiowas were brave, artful and cunning. They did not go to war as frequently as many other Indians, but when they did they killed and captured everything they could reach. They were among the first Indians in the southern country to come in contact with the white man, as the Santa Fé trail passed directly through their country. They were also among the first to acquire modern firearms and articles of civilization, as well as many of its vices. This added to their Indian cunning, made them the terror of all trainsmen and travelers, whom they constantly harassed and kept in a continual state of anxiety.

The country which they occupied had a fine climate, rarely being very cold in winter or hot in summer; therefore they did not require much clothing or shelter, and could go from place to place with ease. Game of all kinds was in abundance, and for Indians, they lived well. In their home life they were more cleanly, and less brutal to the women and animals than any other portion of the Shoshonee nation.

They had peculiar ideas concerning property. Among most Indians theft outside of the nation was permitted and looked upon as honorable; but among the Kiowas, stealing from each other was not only permissible but considered and practiced as an art. Despite this constant stealing among themselves, they rarely came into personal combat; when they did so, one Indian killed the other, and that ended it. They seemed to consider theft from each other as a matter of course, and in endeavoring to secure the return of stolen property they usually tried to do so without appealing to the chiefs or head men, but by compromise between each other. With their limited amount of worldly possessions it was not difficult for an Indian to trace the articles which had been taken from him. When the stolen property was discovered, the barter commenced. The thief, considering possession a strong argument, made an effort to secure from the owner the best terms possible before giving up the property. When the interested parties could not agree they appealed to some head man, who settled the difficulty.

The Kiowas were more unreasonable, unreliable, and intractable than any of the surrounding neighbors, except the Comanches, with whom they have been allied for a very long time.

Polygamy was practiced, but not to such a great extent as among many other Indians. Like most Indians the women were not prolific, and they did not increase in numbers rapidly.

The medicine men had great influence with them, and many of their superstitious rites were attended with much ceremony.

They had little religious belief outside of the medicine men.

In treating the sick the medicine men were depended upon almost entirely.

The burial of dead bodies of the Kiowas was the same as that of the Sho-shonee family in general.

This group was divided into five or six tribes, each under its own chief, and each tribe was known among themselves by its own name; but to the whites they were all known as Kiowas.

At one time they had three very prominent, daring and dangerous chiefs. Santanta, "styled the orator of Indians," Big Tree, and Black Eagle. These three Indians were responsible for more loss of life and property, as well as carrying into captivity more women and children, than any other three men known to American history.

War parties of Kiowas often went through Texas to the country of their friends and allies, the Comanches. When warriors of the latter joined them, they frequently swept the country as far as the present States of Durango, Zacatecas and Chihuahua, killing many people, capturing many animals, and carrying away much property. For years the Mexicans and Texans suffered severely from the raids of these two peoples. There were no wild men on this continent who roamed over so vast a territory as the Kiowas.

In personal appearance these people were short and strongly formed, hav-ing much more muscular development than any of their surrounding neigh-bors. Being also very dark in color, it was therefore easy to distinguish them at sight.

Their hair was parted in the middle, and braided in one braid on the left side. This was only unbraided once a year. The hair on the right side was worn loose and cut off a few inches below the ear.

They made a sort of visor of flint hide as a protection for the eyes against the sun during summer. This was generally worn by the men. The women wore but little clothing, a skin shirt, leggings and moccasins, with a blanket or buffalo robe in winter constituted their dress. None of them were skilled in handiwork for ornamenting their clothing. Some of them painted their faces, but this was not common among them.

For killing large game they made long lances of strong poles; one end was split about one foot, and shaped like a large Y. In the jaws of this was set diagonally across a sharp blade of steel; then mounting fleet horses they rode close to the quarry, and with a thrust drove the open end with its knife over the hamstring of the animal, severing it with one blow. This process was continued until a sufficient number of animals were lying helpless, when they were killed. The Kiowas were the only Indians who used lances of this kind, and practiced this method of slaughter.

CHAPTER XXIX.

THE BRAVE AND WARLIKE CHEYENNES—THE FINEST BODY OF SAVAGES IN
THE WORLD—THEIR SINGULAR FRIENDSHIP FOR THE ARAPAHOES—
BLOODY AND COSTLY WARS WITH THE WHITES.

A Brave and Intelligent People—Manner of Caring for their Hair—A Nation of Warriors
—Expertness of Cheyenne Women in Handiwork—Religious Belief of the Cheyennes
—Their Dances and Ceremonies—Their Language—Their Alliance with the Sioux
and Arapahoes—Their Attacks on Emigrant Trains—Treaties with the Government
—Broken Faith followed by Fierce and Bloody Battles—The Chivington Massacre—
A Bloody and Costly War—Nearly Forty Million Dollars Spent in Fighting the
Cheyennes—Their Home Life—Peculiar Marriage Customs—Treatment of their
Wives and Children—Their Singular Friendship with the Arapahoes—A Friendship
that has never been Explained—Burial of the Dead—Their Lodges—Primitive
Weapons—Symbols used by Them—The Northern Cheyennes.

THE Cheyennes were of Algonquin stock, and were the most intelligent
tribe of this nation. I consider them the finest specimen of wild man in the
world. They had none of the low skulking ways so common to the ordinary
savage, but seemed above this type in almost every respect. Their language
was that of their original family. Both sexes were comely, healthy and
seemed contented. In one trait they showed a marked difference to most
other savages; this was in punishing each other by flagellation. Should one
of their number commit an offence against the customs of the tribe he was
soundly beaten, the culprit rarely taking revenge by killing or injuring any
one who joined in the chastisement. Wives and children were often beaten
severely by the husband or father. The Cheyennes were the only Indians
who used this mode of punishment.

They were divided into two parts, the Northern and Southern Cheyennes,
the latter being the more numerous of the two. Their principal hunting
ground was south of the Republican River in Kansas, and south of an imaginary line running east and west from the mouth of that river to the Rocky
Mountains. This territory embraced a portion of what is now western
Missouri, southern Nebraska, Kansas, and eastern Colorado. Having been
friendly with the Arapahoes for upwards of a century, the Cheyennes
roamed over the entire country south of the line mentioned and east of the
Rocky Mountains to what is now the dividing line between the Indian Ter-

FEATHER WOLF—TYPICAL CHEYENNE WARRIOR.

Twenty Years Among Our Hostile Indians. Page 241.

ritory, Colorado and Kansas. A portion of this territory belonged to the Arapahoes, but by common consent each roamed over the country of the other.

Physically the Cheyennes were among the best developed of all North American Indians, and were also the most cleanly of any that lived by the chase. The men were the best and bravest warriors of any Indian nation on this continent. Man for man they could defeat any other Indian, and no body of Indians with whom they came in contact were ever ready to give them battle on equal footing. They were the best riders and marksmen, and had the best horses, mules, and dogs that could be found among any Indians in that wild country.

The Cheyennes were driven out of the Eastern States by the advance of civilization, and forced their way west through hostile tribes across the Missouri River to the Black Hills country of South Dakota, and afterward settled near the Cheyenne River, from whence a large portion of them were subsequently driven by the Sioux. This body retreated to the south, and have long been known as Southern Cheyennes. Those that remained were known as Northern Cheyennes, and allied themselves with the Blackfeet and others, retaining possession of their original home.

CRAZY HEAD AND SPOTTED WOLF—CHEYENNES.

The Southern Cheyennes raided their neighbors to the south and west, frequently going as far south as the Arkansas River. The eastern portion of their territory was near the borders of civilization, and the settlers living there suffered greatly by their depredations. They made good use of their observations among the whites, and were far in advance of their red brothers who were more remote from civilization.

The territory they occupied was well watered, wooded, and covered with nutritious grass.   It was the natural home of the buffalo, deer, antelope, and other game, which furnished them at all times ample food, as well as an abundance of skins for clothing, lodges and other requirements.   Beaver and otter also abounded in the streams, and their pelts were traded for articles of civilization.

They took particular care of their hair, greasing, combing, and dressing it every day.   Both men and women parted their hair in the middle; the parting line on the scalp was painted a deep carmine.   Their brown faces, smooth skins, coal-black hair, well-oiled and kept, and their tall, erect forms, wrapped in robes, made them look much more imposing than any other Indians of the plains.

Their women were expert in fancy work requiring the use of awls, sinews and porcupine quills.   Their bead and paint work was beautifully done, far better than that of any other Indian nation.   I have often seen specimens of their beadwork that could hardly be excelled by white women.

The religion of the Cheyennes was much the same as that of a majority of Indians.   They believed in two Spirits—the Good and the Bad.   They believed that there was a happy hunting ground to which all spirits went after death.   They did not attempt to explain where the Spirit Land was nor how the soul of the departed reached it.   Their Sun Dance in honor of the Great Spirit resembled the Sun Dance of the Sioux.   They had other ceremonies, but the Sun Dance was the most important rite of their religious worship.

They allied themselves at times with the Sioux; when they made an alliance of this kind, the party committed many depredations, killing everybody they met, and carrying away everything they could lay their hands on.   I have known of war parties, made up of Sioux, Cheyennes and Arapahoes, to go far north, along the foothills of the eastern chain of the Rocky Mountains, into the country of the Crows, for the purpose of making war on them.

It was among the Southern Cheyennes that Kit Carson became prominent. He had his headquarters, most of the time, at Bent's Fort; this was near the southern portion of their territory.   Other traders also had trading posts in their country.   The Santa Fé trail passed through a portion of their hunting ground, and created a bitter feeling on the part of the Cheyennes toward the whites.   They made numerous attacks upon travelers over this road, and on the outposts of civilization within their reach.   Many treaties were made between them and government agents.   But as soon as a treaty was made it

NECKLACE OF HUMAN FINGERS.

This necklace of human fingers is made of a round collar of buckskin, incrusted with blue and white beads; these are arranged in alternate spaces an inch or more in length; there are also a number of shell beads made by Indians. Pendant from the collar are five medicine arrowheads of stone. The fingers, eight in number, are the left hand middle fingers of hostile warriors killed by High Wolf. The four medicine bags were examined by Dr. Yarrow, U. S. A., under a powerful glass and pronounced by him the most delicate portions of a man's anatomy.

was broken by one side or the other, the Government regarding its obligations as lightly as did the Indians. The Indian soon learned to look upon these treaties as little better than a means of securing from the Government the usual stores and presents which accompanied these formal talks; and the Government itself, therefore, educated the Indians in the arts of lying and dishonesty. Owing to the constant failure of one or both parties to keep the treaties, hostilities at length broke out, and the Cheyennes were, for the first time, engaged in regular warfare with the Government and white settlers.

Shortly afterward, however, negotiations were begun on the part of the Government to restore peace. While these negotiations were pending, Colonel Chivington, of the First Colorado Cavalry, attacked the Sand Creek village of Cheyennes and killed more than a hundred men, women and children. At the time of its occurrence the Indians were formally at peace with the United States and under the protection of its flag, which protection they had been promised and induced to seek by the Government. On the approach of Colonel Chivington's soldiers the great chief, White Antelope, ran forward holding up his hands, pointing to the United States flag, indicating that he and his people were under its protection. His appeal was disregarded. Seeing that the attack was deliberate, he made no resistance, but folded his arms and remained standing quietly until shot down. The United States flag floated over the lodge of Black Kettle, the head chief, as an additional precaution against attack, he having been advised by United States officers to keep the national colors constantly in sight.

As may be naturally supposed, a desperate war was the result. The Indians believed that it was the purpose of the Government to exterminate them, and they fought with the ferocity of despair. The Cheyennes, as already mentioned, were among the bravest Indian warriors, and superior to their neighbors in intelligence and cunning, and the war that followed was bloody while it lasted; it is said to have cost the Government from thirty to forty millions of dollars. Even after the conclusion of peace there was constant trouble with the Cheyennes. Treaties were made as before, but as usual, were violated or ignored.

Some time afterward, General Hancock burned a Cheyenne village on Pawnee Fork; this precipitated another outbreak, in which General Custer defeated the Indians, killing their chief, Black Kettle and thirty-seven others, two-thirds of them being women and children. In this war more than three hundred soldiers and settlers lost their lives. Treaties were again made with the Cheyennes, who from that time forth manifested a desire to live at peace with the whites. They subsequently divided into three bodies, in each case mixing up with the Arapahoes—one body settling on Milk

STARVING ELK—TYPICAL CHEYENNE WARRIOR.
Twenty Years Among Our Hostile Indians. Page 246.

River, Montana, another on the North Fork of the Canadian River, and one remaining in their old territory.

The Cheyennes were polygamous, each male having as many wives as he was able to buy. A man sometimes secured all the daughters of one family for his wives. Having bought the eldest daughter of a family, he in turn became the possessor of each of the others, as they became old enough to marry. Instances were also common where a mother and her daughters became the wives of the same man.

For nearly one hundred years the Cheyennes and Arapahoes were the warmest friends and most devoted allies, living together in the same villages, going together on hunts, and fighting in the same battles against common foes. The singular friendship existing between the two peoples was very striking, for the Cheyennes were a cleanly and intelligent people, their lodges were large, and, for Indians, they were rich in this world's goods. The Arapahoes, on the other hand, were ignorant, filthy and miserably poor. Their lodges were small, dirty, and swarmed with vermin. Their clothing was scanty and of the poorest kind. They took no care of their persons whatever. Their hair was never combed, and hung in matted locks, and they were in every respect repulsive beyond description. Yet, with characteristics so directly opposite, these two peoples lived together in the closest friendship for nearly a century, during which time each preserved its individuality. No instance was ever known where they intermarried, or where a member of either tribe learned the language of the other. Their children grew up together from infancy to old age, yet could not converse with each other, except through the medium of the sign language. This is the only instance of a lasting friendship between savage Indian nations that was known of on this continent.

The Cheyennes placed the bodies of their dead in trees. All through the country they roamed over where there was timber could be seen tree graves. These were well built, and often several bodies were placed on the wide platforms; females and children were given the same burial the warriors received. They did not place the articles owned by the person during life on the graves, nor were they superstitious about the dead.

The Cheyennes were very proud and dignified. They dressed well, and all their personal belongings were well cared for. Their lodges were the best of any Indians using this kind of habitation. The interior was nicely arranged, and the beds were the most comfortable of any used by the wild Indians. They were made of robes and blankets, and cleaned daily. They were arranged around the lodge in a circle next to the lodge poles; each person had his or her own sleeping place.

CHEYENNE WARRIOR IN FULL WAR COSTUME.

Twenty Years Among Our Hostile Indians.   Page 248.

They had an abundance of good horses; these were treated kindly. Their horse equipments were also well made; they used bridle bits after the fashion of the white man. Their primitive weapons were the best made by any Indians. Some of their bows were from five to six feet in length, and backed with sinews glued to them the entire length. With a bow of this kind a man could drive an arrow two-thirds of its length into the body of a buffalo.

Their arrowheads were made of iron; these were largely secured from white traders. They also had a few tools made by the white man; with these they made many articles for themselves, such as bows, arrows, saddles, bridles, pipe stems, lances, and lodge poles. The females used needles, awls, scissors, and bodkins in making clothing and various family articles.

The Cheyenne symbols were medicine arrows, and staffs. They did not worship these, but carried them as charms which brought good luck. Their ''Dog

MEDICINE STAFF AND MEDICINE ARROWS—CHEYENNE.

Soldiers'' also carried any war implement they fancied for the same purpose.

After their separation the Northern Cheyennes remained in their original territory, which is now Wyoming and Montana, following the natural impulses of wild men. The Indian Bureau, after the battle of Little Big Horn, requested the War Department to capture and place on reservations all Indians in that territory; the news of this move soon reached the Cheyennes, when they prepared to resist giving up their free life at any cost. Alliances were made with many Sioux tribes in that locality, and all determined to defy the Government in removing them.

In the autumn of 1876 a formidable military expedition was fitted out for a winter campaign to execute the orders. A large number of Indians from some of the various nations were enlisted to accompany the command as scouts; these were under army officers, and when on the march they were miles away on the flanks and in advance of the troops looking for signs. After many days' travel in polar cold the expedition reached Crazy Woman's Fork, of the Powder River, when the Indian scouts returned and reported a Cheyenne village three miles long, located in a deep, narrow canon of the Big Horn mountains. The cavalry and scouts marched all night, and at dawn the Indian scouts fell upon the village with great fury, the troops coming up rapidly, when a terrific battle ensued, but after desperate resistance the Cheyennes were driven from their encampment and, taking refuge among the precipitous rocks of mountains, poured a galling fire on the troops, who were burning the village and everything inflammable therein. After the destruction of the village, an officer, when going over its former site, found two necklaces of human fingers, one of which is shown in a photograph on page 244. The commanding officer, not liking such gruesome objects in possession of the military, ordered the other buried; this one was preserved and sent to West Point for scientific purposes.

Both necklaces belonged to the foremost medicine man of the tribe, but in his surprise and precipitate flight, they were left in the village.

Probably the severest property loss suffered by the Indians on this occasion were these objects, as they believed them to be so charmed that no harm could befall the tribe as long as they were in their possession.

That night the cold was so intense that eleven children froze to death in the arms of their mothers, and the next, two more suffered a like fate.

With nothing left but a few horses and dogs, the Cheyennes, with brave, but broken hearts, wandered about over the mountains in deep snows until their discomforts became unbearable, and receiving no assistance from their former friends and allies, the Sioux, under the renowned Crazy Horse, in March, 1877, Dull Knife, Two Moons, and Hump, their principal chiefs, induced them to surrender.

CHAPTER XXX.

THE DIRTY AND POVERTY-STRICKEN ARAPAHOES—A SHIFTLESS AND LAZY
PEOPLE—HOW THEY LIVED—BEGGARS, MENIALS, AND THIEVES.

Where did the Arapahoes come from ?—Obscurity of their Origin—A Lazy People—Their
Habits, Characteristics, Customs, and Language—A Filthy Lot—Their Strange
Friendship for the Cheyennes—Brutal Treatment of their Wives—Menials and
Thieves for the Cheyennes—The Vilest of Beggars—Begging and Stealing for a Liv-
ing—Unable to Speak their own Language—A Language rarely Acquired by a
White Man—Their Poor Weapons for War and the Chase—Too Lazy to Fish—How
they Made their Clothing—Swarming with Vermin—Disgusting Habits—A Wretched
Existence.

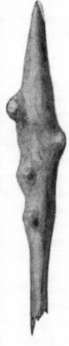

ARROWHEAD
MADE FROM
A ROOT.

FROM whence the Arapahoes came or what their origin was,
I will not hazard an opinion. They were unlike all other
Indians east of the Rocky Mountains, and must be regarded as
a distinct nation or tribe. Their habits, characteristics, customs, and language were distinctly Arapahoe and nothing else;
in these respects they bore no resemblance to any other red
men of the West. If their looks or actions suggested any
nation of Indians it was the Shoshonees. In stature, color,
and shape of their heads, they bore more resemblance to
the Comanches or the Snakes than to any other Indians.

They were the most filthy, poverty-stricken, and shiftless
Indians east of the Rocky Mountains. They took no more
care of their persons, surroundings, or belongings than they
were actually compelled to by necessity. They had scarcely
enough energy to secure their food, and would live on anything rather than exert themselves to procure a decent living.
Although game was abundant at the time I knew them, they
were too lazy to secure more than enough to last from day to
day, and were content to live in small, dirty lodges. Wild
horses were plentiful in their territory, these they could have
easily captured, yet they had only a few, even these were miserable and dejected specimens. The burdens put upon the poor
animals when moving the camp would make a heavy load for
a strong sound horse, but their brutal women masters forced
them along with extreme cruelty by beating them unmercifully.

It was a rare thing for a party of Arapahoes to go on the warpath by themselves, for the reason that they had not enough horses and mules to enable them to make a strong expedition. When they accompanied their old-time friends, the Cheyennes, on the warpath, they were compelled to do the camp drudgery and the stealing for the whole camp; when in battle they were forced from necessity and the instinct of self-preservation to arouse themselves and fight for existence.

Of all Indian peoples they were among the meanest to their wives. Their women were degraded and extremely repulsive, and were forced to do all the hard drudgery and dirty work of the camp while the men sat in the lodges or in a comfortable place, loafing and taking their ease. The men believed that the women were placed on earth to be slaves, and compelled them to act as such. They had little idea of morality, and a husband was at all times ready to barter the honor of his wives or daughters to a stranger.

The one remarkable trait among them, which has often been commented upon, was their singular affection and great friendship for the Cheyennes. This I can account for only from the fact that the Cheyennes were infinitely superior to them in intelligence, enterprise and appearance, and the Arapahoes looked upon them with admiration, and were willing to act as menials to them.

The Arapahoes did not claim any particular hunting ground of their own, but roamed over the country to the south of the Sioux, all along the base of the Rocky Mountains, under Pike's and Long's Peak, as far south as the Spanish Peaks, and as far east as the country occupied by their friends, the Cheyennes. After the Overland road was established, many of them went down the South Platte along this road to beg and steal for a living. The women were the vilest beggars in that country.

Their language was so poor in words that the Arapahoes themselves could scarcely converse with one another upon the most ordinary topics without the use of the sign language. Their oral language consisted of harsh guttural sounds, unpleasant to the ear. As they seldom smiled their faces looked rigid and drawn when speaking, as though it required an effort to talk.

The worldly possessions of the Arapahoes were of such small value that when the Utes, who held them in great contempt, crossed the mountains in war parties they seldom attacked them, and the Sioux, when passing south through their country to that of the Kiowas, rarely disturbed or molested them, because they did not consider the Arapahoes worthy of notice. Their bodies, clothes, and lodge belongings swarmed with unmentionable pests.

They had only the poorest of weapons for war and the chase. A miserable bow, a few arrows, an old-fashioned, discarded firearm, and a heavy lance usually made up their entire equipment.   Had they possessed energy enough to secure good arms for themselves they could have lived as well as any other Indians on the plains and mountains, for the country which they occupied was filled with choice game of every kind.   Fish were abundant in the streams, yet the Arapahoes were so indolent that they would almost starve rather than exert themselves to catch them.

They had but little intercourse with the whites after the latter entered that country.   What they did have was with dissolute persons, and proved of lasting injury to the Indians.   The better class of whites avoided them, and the abject poverty of the Indians did not permit them to have much communication with the traders.

They continued to degenerate in every way, and decreased in numbers, from the time they were first visited by white men.

The famous Indian pipe, from the red pipestone quarry, was owned by only a few, although all the men smoked when they could procure the necessary material without much effort.

Still they were satisfied with the few things necessary to their wretched existence. They did not trouble themselves about their origin, nor with religious beliefs, or what became of the spirit after death. They had no medicine men, in the

ARAPAHOE LODGE—DRYING MEAT.

Indian sense. In treating the sick, the old women performed a few mysterious rites in addition to administering to the patients teas made from roots and herbs. This was the extent of their efforts to relieve or cure the afflicted.

The Arapahoes generally were physically weak, a strictly healthy or sound one being the exception and not the rule.   The fact most to be regretted in connection with this statement is, that their physical condition, which, primarily, was the result of their filthy habits and immoral lives, was greatly intensified by their intercourse with dissolute white people with whom they came in contact at an early period.   Previous to this time they were more or less troubled with scrofula, and worse diseases soon followed the advent of the whites.

At a subsequent period their condition was somewhat improved under the influence of civilization, but children who, after a critical examination, had been pronounced sound by medical examiners, developed disease as soon as they were subjected to a change of diet and habits, many of them dying at the reservation schools. In some cases children who were returned in time to their homes or camps regained their former health. This was due to freedom from all restraint, and a return to their original outdoor life. Indian nature was so incapable of restraint, even among a people as indolent as the Arapahoes, that any attempt to confine them in the least caused sufficient mental anxiety to develop an insidious disease lurking in the system. A malady once started usually proved serious, and as no effort was made to check it, they were soon in a pitiable condition.

The Arapahoes were not divided into small tribes, but all lived together in one group, having but one chief, and two or three sub-chiefs. The whites captured an Arapahoe boy when very young, taking him to St. Louis, where he was educated. After he had grown to man's estate he returned to his people, again adopting their customs. He spoke English, but preferred the life of the Indians. As he was captured on a Friday, the whites gave him that name. Almost everybody in that country at the time knew Friday.

He had great influence among the Arapahoes, as well as the Cheyennes, the Ogalala, and Brule Sioux, and did much to keep these people quiet. He prevented many wagon trains from being attacked and destroyed by the Indians mentioned.

The clothing of the Arapahoes was made from the skins of wolves, dogs, rabbits and such animals as they happened to kill on the chase. With the hair hanging in mats over the face, and dressed in dirty clothing of this kind, they presented a disgusting appearance.

Among them there was no buying of wives; a woman consented to live with a man; that constituted the marriage ceremony. Should she leave and go to another, it ended the former and began the new nuptial agreement.

They were too lazy to quarrel among themselves over anything, much less about a woman.

It was rare for one Arapahoe to injure or kill another; if it occurred nothing was done about the matter, for they had no method of redressing wrongs.

Sometimes the dead bodies of prominent chiefs were placed in trees. The common way of disposing of the corpses was to place them in holes or caves, then cover them with stones.

CHAPTER XXXI.

CLIFF DWELLERS—THE NAVAJOES AND THEIR COUNTRY—THE TONKAWAYS
—THEIR WARS AND WANDERINGS—CANNIBALISM AMONG THE INDIANS.

How the Navajoes Resembled White Men in their Habits—A Tribe of Cliff Dwellers—
Their Famous Blankets—Their Handiwork and Skill—Horsehair Lariats—Beautiful
Earthen Ware—How they Purified and Cooled Water—How the Cactus was used
for Clearing Water—Peculiarity of the Cactus Leaf—Personal Appearance of the
Navajoes—Children Adepts in throwing the Lasso—An Expert Indian Lad of Ten
—His Feats with the Lasso—Catching a Dog by either Leg—The Navajoe in his
Family—A Model Indian—Deserted Dwellings—The Tonkaways—A Remnant of a
once Powerful People—Their Vague Traditions—Their Wars and Wanderings—A
Cannibal Race—Killing and Eating their Prisoners.

TYPICAL NAVAJOE.

THE Navajoes were a portion of
the Athabaskan nation, and in
their wild state resembled the
white man in his habits more than
any other Indians of the far West.
They were cliff dwellers. In the
arid country occupied by them,
with its high temperature, they
lived far up the mountain sides,
pasturing their animals in the valleys and to the summits of the
mountains. Their horses, mules
and burros (a small species of the
donkey) thrived on the nutritious
grass in the valleys, and their
cattle were generally in good condition for slaughter.

From the wool of sheep and
hair of goats they made blankets,
wraps, and other articles of wearing apparel which were very serviceable, and some of them were
very handsome. The fabrics were
woven by the women by hand; a
long time was often required to
complete them, especially if the
article was a blanket, and intended to be ornamental as well as useful. It

often took them more than a year to complete one of these blankets. They were generally woven so close, and the material twisted so hard that they were impervious to water. One of them could be taken by its four corners and filled with water, which it would hold without leaking; the water seemed to swell the threads and make the fabric closer and firmer.

They were also expert in making lariat ropes from the hair of horse tails, by braiding the hair over a round stick. Some of these lariats were made smooth and in various colors. Others were made very rough with the ends

NAVAJOE WOMAN WEAVING.

of the hair sticking out all over them. These rough lariats were used for general purposes, as well as a protection from reptiles while the owner was asleep on the ground. When used for this purpose the lariat was carefully laid in a circle around the sleeping place, and it was claimed by teamsters, herders and others living in that country that neither rattlesnakes, scorpions, centipedes, nor any of the reptiles which are so numerous there would cross this hairy rope; the stiff and prickly hairs of the rough lariats protruded in every direction and in many instances may have served as a sufficient barrier against unwelcome, crawling intruders, as it is a fact that lariat ropes of this kind were carried by almost every one in that country, and were always used in the manner described while sleeping on the ground.

The Navajoes also made a ware from clay which they decorated and glazed after the style of the Guadalajara Indians of Mexico, which was of great service to every one living in the Navajoe country. When used for cooling and purifying drinking water the ware was left unglazed and was porous. Such a vessel, filled with water, was covered with two or three thicknesses of a wet blanket, and suspended in the open air. Filtration went on rapidly;

after passing through this vessel the water was distilled into another vessel below. This simple process made the water clear, sweet, cool, and thoroughly purified it.

All through Texas, Arizona, and northern Mexico is found a species of cactus, the thick leaves of which when sliced in two and thrown into a vessel of water will in a short time precipitate the sediment to the bottom.

Two or three leaves of this plant, after having been cut in two and thrown into a pail of dirty water drawn from the Pecos River, would in a short time precipitate the sand and sediment to the bottom, leaving the water on the top clear and drinkable.

The ware made by the Navajoes was also used largely throughout that country for cooking purposes, for they as well as the Mexicans ate large quantities of *frijoles* (a black bean), and earthen pots were of much service in cooking them.

The Navajoes were a friendly race, and were never known to make war on the whites. They lived on the meat and vegetables they raised, including *frijoles*, or, as the Mexicans called them, "nationalies." Game was scarce in their country, and they did not follow the chase.

NAVAJOE IN WAR COSTUME.

Nor did they go on marauding expeditions, although parties of their young men have been known to seek revenge in this way for wrongs committed on them by other Indians.

The Navajoes were black and swarthy, and did not paint or tattoo their faces, as they are sometimes represented. Their clothing resembled that of the white man, or Mexican Greaser, more than that of

NAVAJOE WARRIOR.

the Indian. They were expert horsemen, and were kind to their animals.

As soon as their children could walk, boys and girls were taught the use of the lasso. They began practicing with a string, or a small rope with a noose at one end, catching cats, dogs, chickens, or each other; every living thing being used as a subject. I have seen a Navajoe boy, ten years of age, lasso a running dog, on any foot he was told to catch. He could take a rope with a heavy substance on one end, but with-out a noose, and throw it in such a manner that it would wind two or three times around the neck of an animal and fasten itself tight enough to allow the victim to be seized by the hands before the rope became disentangled.

The Navajoes were a healthy and hardy race, some of them living to very old age. Their home life was congenial; cruelty or harsh words rarely disturbed the harmony of the family circle, as they were by nature more gentle than most other Indians. The men were considerate to their women, did not compel them to do all the work of the family, but shared the labor of raising the crops with them, also attending to the animals, as well as doing outdoor work.

Though living near white men, they preserved their individuality scrupulously. It was a rare thing for a white man or Mexican to marry a Navajoe woman, or for a Navajoe to go outside of his own people for a wife. Polygamy may have been permissible, but was not practiced.

They were governed by a chief and a few select men of the villages, who made a few crude laws or regulations which were respected by all.

They had their own religion, which was a kind of idolatry, as they worshiped both stone and wooden images.

Both men and women smoked, usually a cigarette made after the style of the Mexicans.

They cared but little for intoxicating liquors, although they manufactured a very strong alcoholic beverage from the maguay plant and from bear grass, a species of Spanish bayonet. It had a burnt flavor, and produced intoxication quickly, although the effects soon passed away.

The Navajoes rapidly decreased in numbers, as the numerous unoccupied dwellings scattered throughout their country testify. They made no marked progress during the long period they were known to white men, were singularly conservative

CEBRA NEGRA—NAVAJOE.

in their mode of living, and did not differ materially from their ancestors of generations ago.

THE TONKAWAYS.

In northern Texas, between Salt and Clear Forks of the Brazos River, lived the remnant of the Tonkaways, a once powerful people. Of their origin nothing is known beyond vague traditions sometimes recounted by the old men. According to them, a long time ago the Tonkaways lived near the shores of "the great ocean," supposed to be the Gulf of Mexico. In many bloody wars with their neighbors they became greatly reduced in numbers, and at length were driven north to the vicinity of the Arkansas River. Here again they were surrounded by hostile neighbors, and were finally driven into northwestern Texas.

When living in their original home on the shores of the sea, their neighbors claimed that they were cannibals; that their chief object in battle was to secure prisoners rather than to kill the enemy; and that these prisoners were subsequently killed and eaten.   After they were driven to the Arkansas River all the surrounding tribes made war upon them for the same cause. The Kiowas and Pawnees claimed that the Tonkaways captured children for the purpose of eating them.   The Pawnee tribes were especially embittered against the Tonkaways, for they declared that they had at one time killed and devoured a favorite child of a chief of the Pawnee nation.   This eventually caused an alliance of the Kiowas, Pawnees, and other tribes against the Tonkaways, who were finally driven into northwestern Texas, where they made their last stand.   Some of their old men admitted that, long before, when living near the coast, the Tonkaways captured the crews of ships that came ashore, killed them, and ate portions of their bodies.   They also admitted having eaten portions of the bodies of their enemies, captured in battle, but claimed that they only ate the heart, and for the purpose of acquiring the courage of the slain.   The Tonkaways were the only Indians against whom the charge of cannibalism was openly made.

When I last saw any of these strange people they were living in skin-covered lodges, thus showing that they were nomadic, and although having been surrounded somewhat by civilization for some time, they kept to themselves and retained their aboriginal habits and customs, painting their faces in bright colors and decorating themselves in the usual manner.

They held a superstition that the spirits of their ancestors were originally contained in wolves, and that these animals being rovers, they must forever be likewise; that after death their spirits returned from whence they came to again rove continually.

Once a year a ceremony was held, at which a few concealed themselves in the tall grass or brush, then others sought them, and when found they were brought together and presented with bows and arrows and commanded to be rovers forever.   After this a feast was held in commemoration of the spirits of the dead, and a goodly supply of food was left for the wolves, which animal they worshipped.   They never killed or molested wolves, as they feared to injure or kill some of their forefathers.

It was claimed that the Karankawas and others who lived along the shores of Matagorda Bay, and in the older States bordering on the Gulf of Mexico, were also cannibals, but this was a charge only; although both Lafitte's and La Salle's men claimed to have witnessed many feasts of human flesh by the red men, while held prisoners by them.   The Attakappa tribe were also accused of being cannibals, as that name was supposed to have meant man eaters.

CHAPTER XXXII.

THE PUEBLOS AND ZUNIS—HIDEOUSLY UGLY GODS AND IDOLS—CUSTOMS OF A STRANGE PEOPLE.

Where did they come from?—Why did they keep to themselves?—Supposed to be Christians, but in reality Heathen—Their Ugly Idols—A Mooted Question—Why they were made so Ugly—Smashing them to Pieces—Putting an Idol to a Queer Use—Using a God for a Liquor Flask—Homliness an Antidote for Pain—Where have the Pueblos Gone?—An Unsolved Mystery—Walled Caves and Ruins of Stone Dwellings—A Lost Art—How did they make Cement?—The Zunis—How they Lived—Their Numerous Flocks and Herds—A Strange People—Praying to the Spirits of Ocean—The Pimas or Papagoes—Buried in a sitting Posture—Feasting at the Grave—Praying for a New Husband—Tar as a Cosmetic.

ETHNOLOGICALLY, it is difficult to place the Pueblos. They seemed to be a distinct people. In some of their characteristics and customs they somewhat resembled the Navajoes, but in general, all their peculiarities were distinctly their own. They were scattered through New Mexico and Arizona, where they lived in villages, and followed the manners and customs of their ancestors. They received their name from their custom of living in fixed places, the word pueblo being Spanish for village or town. They raised a small quantity of vegetables and grain for their own use, and made excellent pottery, which they exchanged for the necessaries of life; they were gentle in their nature, treated their animals with kindness, and did not use horses or dogs for food. They were courteous to strangers who entered their villages, and did not make trouble unless interfered with.

They were supposed to be Christians, but in reality were heathen, if the number of their gods and goddesses was an indication of idolatry. It was difficult to obtain any account of their religion, and it is therefore a question whether they worshiped idols or not. They made and kept them in their dwellings, and did not appear to respect or fear them; they would sell them for a few cents, or barter them for liquor or other articles. These gods were frequently made hollow, and the Indians sometimes put them to the ignoble use of holding liquor. It was not uncommon to see a Pueblo enter a place where liquor was sold and present one of his hollow gods to be filled. At the first opportunity he substituted himself for his little god and speedily became the liquor holder. The gods were made as hideously ugly as possible, in order to ward off pain or disease; if they failed in this the Indian did not hesitate to smash them to pieces if he could not sell them.

The ruins and relics scattered throughout this region indicate a population of great numbers in the past. Fragments of pottery are found in many localities in all this section, which embraces upwards of ten thousand square miles. Stone foundations and walls of cities show that at some remote period thousands of people dwelt within them.

The Pueblos had no written language, nor were there traditions current among them as to the cause of their depleted numbers, or if there were they would not impart them to others. There is no record of any branch of the Pueblos having settled elsewhere, so that large numbers of them must have perished near their present location.

Pueblo stone foundations are usually found along the streams tributary to the Rio Gila, but occasionally at a long distance from the water. In these cases, however, the topography of the country shows the beds of streams which have long since run dry, or have changed their courses at some remote period. Walled caves are also found in large numbers in this region, the history of which the present inhabitants have no knowledge or tradition. In proximity to these caves appear also the ruins of stone dwellings built without cement, and numerous traces of irrigating canals and ditches, which show that the Pueblos were once engaged in agriculture.

There are a number of Indian languages spoken among the Pueblos, but the majority speak Spanish from necessity as they are surrounded by, and trade with the Mexicans.

When a child is born, it is the duty of the father to keep sacred fires burning for eight days—the fires are kindled and blessed by caciques— but if the parent permits the fires to go out, he runs to a priest and informs him of the fact, when he is handed a firebrand by the latter; the father then runs home and relights the fire, for if started in any other manner, it portends evil to both mother and child.

They are very strict with young girls and maidens and never permit them to walk or converse with young men before marriage, except in presence of their parents. When a maiden wishes to wed, she selects the man and tells her father, who calls on the parents of the young man and informs them of his daughter's desires, then if satisfactory, the match is consummated; but it is obligatory on the parents of the bridegroom to compensate the family of the bride for the loss of their daughter, by making presents in proportion to their wealth and station. Matches are never made against the wishes of the parents of either party.

The Zunis were at one time a powerful people, as the early Spaniards could not enslave them. Even when first known to the white man they were engaged in industrial pursuits, and while scientists have been theorizing in vain over their hieroglyphics and picture writings cut in walls of the cañons, they have been unable to translate any messages left by them and their meanings have been lost in the mists of antiquity.

When one dies, four-days' food is provided for the soul's journey, as it is supposed to travel that length of time before it reaches its final home; during this time many ludicrous ceremonies are performed to prevent witches following the spirit.

The personal effects of the deceased are "killed" at the "killing place," by breaking and burning, that they may be again with the departed in the spirit land; killing places are covered with broken pottery and all kinds of personal effects which have been destroyed. When the corpse is interred in the consecrated graveyard it is wrapped in blankets or skins, but the Mojaves cremated their dead and claim to know the future abode of the soul which travels to its new home through its own smoke, during incineration.

Both sexes make cigarettes by rolling tobacco in corn husks: this has been their smoke from time immemorial. Nude children roll and smoke cigarettes made of their native tobacco

MAN AND WIFE—PUEBLOS.

which is very strong, and blow the smoke in great clouds skyward, making supplications to the sun, moon and stars.

The Moquis make and use a boomerang of wood for killing rabbits and are dexterous in throwing them; even boys are adepts in their use and throw them with great precision.

When hunting rabbits they form on foot in long lines around the field, then all converge toward a common center, and as rabbits make their appearance, the boys kill them with boomerangs. The Pueblos make pottery, which they ornament with grotesque figures of snakes, frogs, men and animals; the colors are made from milkweed, sumac which gives the red, and the roots when boiled down and mixed with juniper, the black.

The burning is done by laying the vessels around in circles and covering the pottery with refuse from the corrals, which makes a very hot fire. None of their pottery is glazed with silica or other material.

Like the Aztecs, they had numerous festival and fête days, which, clad in rich and varied costumes, they celebrated with processions and dances. They were reticent in speaking of their religious beliefs, but admitted that they worshiped the sun.

The government of the Zunis consisted of a Governor, an Alcalde or Mayor, a number of caiques or councilors, eleven of whom were elected annually, and a chief councilor, who was elected to serve for life. They had also an officer known as the War Chief, but he had no influence in their councils, unless the tribe was threatened with danger.

In their domestic habits the Zunis were more cleanly than any other tribe in that vicinity. They had but little household furniture, nor was much required for their simple wants; they worked, cooked, and slept on their well-kept floors. Their women were usually busy weaving clothing, grinding grain, baking bread, and in other household occupations.

The traditional type of Indian seemed wanting among these people. All, including the women, smoked. They usually smoked cigarettes made from tobacco and rolled in the thin husks of the corn. Their pipes were crude, looking as though they were made of the coarsest clay.

Many of the Indians in that section lived close together, had common interests, traditions, customs, dress, yet spoke a language unintelligible to any of the others; none of them bearing any resemblance to the Aztecs of ancient Mexico, or to the nomadic tribes throughout that region.

The Zunis had a tradition that their gods brought them to an arid and sterile plain for a home, far removed from the ocean, and that their forefathers taught them the prayers whereby water could be obtained. These prayers were addressed to the spirits dwelling in the ocean, the home of all water, and the source from which the blessing must come. They believed that in answer to these prayers rain clouds were brought from the ocean by the spirits of their ancestors.

PIMA, OR PAPAGOS.

The Pima Indians, or Papagos, as they were sometimes called, confined themselves to a restricted territory on the Gila River in Arizona, were peaceful and semi-civilized. Their civilization was their own, for in no way had it been acquired from the white man. Originally they lived in the northwestern part of Sonora, Mexico, and had in a certain way accepted the Christian faith as taught by the Spaniards; this, however, continued to be mixed up with their own heathenish belief.

Intolerant of Mexican rule, a large portion of them migrated north to the territory called Pimerica Alta, and adopted the name of Pimas. This portion of the tribe numbered about fifteen thousand. After their arrival in Arizona they did not trouble either the white man or their Indian neighbors, but lived in a half-civilized way, apart from all other tribes, though they held friendly intercourse with white men, as well as with the Opata Indians. They were a stationary race, both before their migration from Sonora, and after their arrival in Arizona.

Notwithstanding their peaceful inclinations and semi-civilized mode of life they were, when occasion required, as brave warriors as any on the continent. This they proved many times by repelling successfully the attacks and incursions of the Apaches. They lived almost exclusively by agriculture, and in this, as well as in many other characteristics, they seemed to be related to the Pueblos.

The Pima Indian was a stoic, and lived and died a fatalist. When the head of a family died a council was called, and all of the property of the deceased was equitably allotted to members of the tribe. When a chief died the body was borne to the grave, where it was placed in a sitting posture, and the entire tribe participated in the funeral ceremonies. On such an occasion instead of signs of mourning, there was rejoicing, and a great feast was prepared. A sufficient number of cattle were slaughtered at the grave to afford every one a full meal, and a goodly portion of meat was carried home to each family. A division of the property of the dead chief was made and distributed equally among the various members or families of the tribe.

On the death of the husband, the widow invested herself with the usual signs of mourning and painted her face with tar. This she continued to do for a stated period, in the meantime praying for a new husband. A young and good-looking woman sometimes married a few days after the burial of her husband, although it was her privilege to mourn for a conventional period, if she so desired. In that case custom required that the husband also should besmear his face with tar, until his wife ceased to mourn for his predecessor.

Among the Pima Indians there were no marriage ceremonies; the man and woman elected to live together, and that constituted them husband and wife. Divorce was as simple as marriage. Whenever a husband or wife felt inclined to dissolve the matrimonial contract they separated and that was the end of it. It was not necessary for the abandoning party to assign cause for separation, and no stigma or disgrace attached to either on account of the dissolution of the marriage tie. For this reason divorces among them were frequent.

The Pimas believed in a Good God and a Bad God, attributing to the intervention of each respectively all the benefits and evils they experienced during life. Although they had some of the traditions of Christian teaching inherited from the time of their subjection to the Spaniards, they had no particular form of worship.

PIMA HABITATION—WOMAN GRINDING GRAIN ON METAT.

They live in the most primitive manner, and their brush-mud huts are the same as the Spanish explorers found, when they first came in contact with these Indians in their present territory about the middle of the sixteenth century.

The women grind grain on *metates* with rubbing stones for making bread; all their food is highly seasoned with *chili*—pepper—and some edibles contain so much of this vegetable, either green, red or dry, that those unaccustomed to its use after taking one bite, feel as though their mouths were aflame. It is a fact, that corpses of Mexicans who during life, consumed large quantities of chili, laid on the ground under a tropical sun, dried to dust and blew away with little or no smell, while those of persons who did not use this pepper became so offensive under the same circumstances, that in one day the effluvia is so strong it is almost impossible to go near, and in less than three days, the corpses were putrid crawling masses of worms.

In making pottery, basketry, and other articles, each village of Pueblos has its own distinctive quality, shape and designs, but most are more glaring than refined.

CHAPTER XXXIII.

THE PAWNEES—A NATION WHOSE ORIGIN IS UNKNOWN—FEUDS AND
FIERCE BATTLES—SKINNING A MAN ALIVE—TRIBES CONSTITUTING
THE NATION.

Once a Numerous and Warlike People—Peculiar Manner of Cutting their Hair—Their
Hunting Ground—Natural Home of the Buffalo—Jealousies and Feuds Created in
Hunting Them—Hated by all their Neighbors—Hatred of the Sioux—Ambition of
the Sioux to be Known as a Pawnee Killer—Vicious Tribes traveling a long way to
Fight the Pawnees—Vindictiveness—Skinning a Man Alive—Pawnee Religion—
Priests and Doctors—Medicine Bags—Widows of the Pawnees—The Wichitas.

BEYOND vague traditions little or nothing is known of the origin of the
Pawnees, and they must therefore be classed as a distinct nation. They had
their own language, and called themselves Pani, or Panna; their characteristics and customs were peculiar to themselves, and in these they differed from
all their neighbors in many interesting ways. When left undisturbed they
were inclined to be peaceful, but when aroused they were very fierce and warlike. At one time they numbered not less than thirty thousand, but constant and bloody battles with all their neighbors, as well as fierce tribes from
afar, reduced them greatly.

Their hunting ground embraced what is now Nebraska, Kansas and
northern Missouri. Their entire country was covered with nutritious
grasses; a large portion of their territory was covered with a thick carpet of
buffalo grass. This was the natural home of the buffalo.

Millions of these huge beasts roamed all over the country claimed by
them. These animals drew hunting and war parties from all Indian nations
and tribes north, south and west of them. This resulted in jealousies and
feuds, which brought the Pawnees in deadly conflict almost constantly.

One day it was with a party of Sioux, the next with a band of Cheyennes
and Kiowas, the next a war party of Osages and so on.

The Sioux in particular bitterly hated the Pawnees, and the battles between them were very bloody.

So strong was the hatred of the Sioux that they would go to almost any
extreme to kill a Pawnee, and the highest ambition of a Sioux warrior was
to call himself "Pawnee killer." I knew several Sioux warriors who
claimed this title; upon making inquiry as to why so many had this same

name, each gave a most vivid description of a bloody and desperate hand-to-hand conflict with a Pawnee.

Nearly all Indians who went to war with the Pawnees would give graphic descriptions of battles in which they had been engaged with them, and nothing seemed to delight them more than to recount how they had fought so valiant a foe, each narrator claiming to be the victor.

Two fierce tribes of the Sioux—the Minneconjoux and Uncpapa—who had their hunting ground in the foothills of, and in the Rocky Mountains often traveled the long distance from their country to that of the Pawnees, for

PAWNEE VILLAGE.

the express purpose of engaging in battle with them, that they might return to their own people and recount their battles in glowing colors.

The Pawnees were originally composed of three tribes, the principal being the Pawnees proper.

The French trappers and traders called them the Loup or Wolf, after their principal symbol. Another tribe was the Arickarees, afterwards nicknamed the Rees. These people separated from the Pawnees in the early part of the century. Originally their hunting ground was the same as the others, but after their separation they moved to the country of the Mandans, with whom they became fast friends, and have remained in that vicinity ever since. The third tribe of the Pawnees was the Wichitas, sometimes called the Pictured Pawnees, or Pawnee Picts.

PAWNEE WARRIORS—MANNER OF WEARING THE HAIR.

This name was applied to them from their custom of tattooing themselves in various colors, blue and red being the most prominent. Some of their facial and body ornamentation in this manner was, for Indians, well done.

All the tribes of the Pawnees had a peculiar manner of cutting the hair, cutting it as close as possible all over the skull, except a roach about two or three inches wide, from about the center of the head back to the scalplock, leaving a stiff tuft standing erect in the center, and inclining back to the height of the scalplock. With hair cut in this fashion, large rings in the slits in their ears, faces and bodies tattooed or painted on their dark skins, made them a strange-appearing people.

PAWNEE HABITATIONS—MUD HOUSES.

All of the Pawnees were good hunters; as many kinds of game were plentiful in their country they had an abundance of meat, especially that of the buffalo. They also had plenty of horses; these were kept in good condition for war purposes.

After civilization made inroads into their territory, they ceased to be nomadic, and lived in fixed habitations. Some of these were made of logs, others were a sort of mud house, none of them having more than one room; this was kitchen, dining room, parlor, sleeping room and all. After they became stationary they cultivated the soil after Indian fashion, raising corn, pumpkins and the coarser vegetables.

Although the Pawnees early came in contact with white settlers and adopted some of their ways, they could not divest themselves of the vindictiveness and ferocity of Indian nature.

For example, a party of emigrants passing through their country, had a

PAWNEE WARRIOR—FULL WAR COSTUME.

Twenty Years Among Our Hostile Indians.

braggart among their number, who boasted that he would kill the first Indian he saw. In his endeavor to make good his threat, he fired upon and killed a Pawnee. The Indians assembled in large numbers, surrounded the train, and demanded that the offending man be delivered to them. The trainmen being greatly outnumbered, and knowing that a refusal meant death to all of them delivered the man to the Indians.

GROUP OF PAWNEE BRAVES.

He was at once stripped of all his clothing and literally skinned alive. The Pawnees cut his skin into strips from a half to three-quarters of an inch in width, commencing at the shoulders and neck, and cutting down the back and legs to the heels; they then cut the skin at the top and pulled it off strip by strip, until death came to the wretched man's relief. The story of this horrible act was scattered broadcast throughout the western country, and thereafter the Pawnees were treated in a deferential manner by people passing through their country.

The nation originally was governed by one chief, the position being hereditary, but the ruler could be deposed should he not have the necessary qualifications for the office.

Each of the tribes had its own chief. Tribal chiefs had sub-chiefs for their staffs as advisers. These ruled the affairs of the tribe, but they were all subservient to the grand chief. When there was to be discussed an important matter affecting the whole nation, the head chief called the chiefs of the tribes with their staffs together, when the matter was debated by all present; but should the decision of the majority be against the opinion or desire of the head chief, he was compelled to submit.

Constant warfare reduced the number of men greatly, consequently there were many more females than males. This may account for the numerous wives each man had; all the wives and children of the man lived together in seeming contentment, and the articles a woman used during the life of the husband were supposed to belong to her. After his death she could live with the family as long as she did not become the wife of another man; if she did so, she carried her belongings with her. Should a widow have considerable property, she was much sought after, as she cost nothing and brought wealth besides.

They had a crude religion, and priests who were supposed to be the medium of communication between them and the Great Spirit.

Priests did not exercise the functions of medicine as known by the more westerly nations, and were not supposed to heal the sick.

For this purpose they had doctors whose duty was to look after and care for the afflicted, whom they treated with teas, roots, and herbs.

The Pawnees were exceedingly superstitious in relation to their "medicine bag"; every habitation had its family medicine bag, which was about the size of a child's head. It was supposed to contain the "medicine" necessary to bring them all the good luck desired; they also believed it to be efficacious in keeping away disease, as well as in assisting them in all their undertakings. This bag was scrupulously guarded, and no member of a family could be induced to speak of its contents.

Each individual also carried a small medicine bag on his person. This was considered a great charm, and no warrior ever went into battle without it.

The men were the most expert hunters of any Indians in the West, and were constantly on the chase for all kinds of game. They had a great many good dogs which accompanied them, assisting them in bringing down a wounded animal.

The Wichitas sacrificed prisoners of war as an offering to the sun until about 1825, when the Pani compelled them to desist; this brought on fierce battles between the two tribes, and at length the Wichitas were defeated and driven away, when they located near a stream which bears their name.

After this they often joined with the Kiowas and others and made war on the Pani, and when hunting, they covered themselves with skins of animals and, imitating the actions of the animals whose skins they wore, approached game and killed it with arrows.

All the tribes of the Pawnees were virile, dark in color and clever in their undertakings.

GRASS HOUSE OF THE WICHITAS.

The Wichitas constructed dome-shaped habitations of the sod of buffalo grass, as it was the only turf that answered their purpose for building houses of this kind. Grass houses were from fifteen to twenty feet in diameter at the base and ten to fifteen feet high, and contained but one room, the door being the only opening in the house. In building them, the sods were bound together by cords passed through the center lengthwise; the binding continued through the entire row around the structure. It required no little ingenuity and patience to build these strong and water tight.

The Wichitas were the only red men who constructed this kind of dwelling. They were unhealthy and the authorities are compelling their destruction, and, like everything else aboriginal, they will soon disappear and live only in history.

CHAPTER XXXIV.

THE CHIPPEWAS, OCHIPPWAS, OR, AS THEY CALLED THEMSELVES, OJIBWAS —ALGONQUIN STOCK.

The Chippewas—Who They Were—Treatment of the Sick—Curious Customs—Widows— Snowshoe Dance—Striking the Post—Story Telling Season—Large Scars—Strange Burial Customs—The Crees Practiced Sun Dancing to a Recent Date—Sacs and Foxes —Ottawas—Pottawattomies—Miamis—Kaskasias—Seminoles—Caddoes—Wacoes.

GOOD VOICE EAGLE—BOY.

THE Chippewas, or as they called themselves, Ojibwas, were a part of the Algonquin nation. Their language was that of the Algonquin, although more or less dialectic. It is from this group of Indians that many words have been accepted, and generally believed by English-speaking people to be applicable to all Indians, for instance: Calumet, squaw, mocassin, pappoose, as well as many other words are generally understood by civilization to mean the same among all Indians. These words are Algonquin, and are not understood by other nations.

The different Indian languages have supplied names for many States, counties, towns, villages, rivers and localities. None have been more largely used than the Algonquin, as the tribes of this group were scattered throughout the country from the mouth of the St. Lawrence River west to the Rocky Mountains; and all early came into contact with white men.

The hunting ground of the Chippewas extended from the Great Lakes as far west as the Blackfoot country. At one time they were estimated to number from fifteen thousand to twenty thousand, and were divided into

many small tribes, which were scattered over the large territory they
claimed as their hunting ground. They lived principally by hunting and
fishing, and were expert in both. They also gathered wild rice, which grew
in abundance in the lakes and marshes; it was threshed
by digging holes in the ground into which the dried
heads of the plant, inclosed in a skin, were placed.
The men then treaded on the bags until the grain
separated from the stalk.

The Chippewas resolutely resisted encroachments on
their hunting grounds; often proving their courage and
ability as warriors. They were the first of the Indians
to come into contact with the white man; securing
muskets, knives, and steel tomahawks long before the
tribes farther west. They made the best snowshoes of
any Indians, and could travel with them as rapidly
over the deep, soft snow, as over bare ground in
summer when lightly shod. They also made the best
birch canoes of any of the tribes of all this region; not
even the white man could make an improvement on
them.

In habits the Chippewas were filthy, and they did not
hesitate to eat any kind of animal; whether it was freshly
killed, or a half-putrid carcass, made no difference with
them. They were exceedingly superstitious. In the
treatment of the sick the medicine men were at all
times ready to go through mysterious performances for
the recovery of the patient, by placating the spirit that
had inflicted disease. When a Chippewa was ill it was
the custom to erect in front of his lodge a pole stripped
of its bark, with various ornaments and trinkets attached
to the top. This pole was painted in various colors,
and made as gaudy as possible, in order to please the
Great Spirit, believing that in so doing it would induce
him to withdraw his displeasure. These poles were
regarded with great reverence, and no Chippewa disturbed them until the patient either recovered or died.

INDIAN RUNNER.
Am. Mus. Nat. Hist.

A peculiar custom prevailed among them in relation to the burial of the
dead. Fires were built on the grave in the early evening, and kept burning
far into the night. This was continued invariably for four successive nights,
and often longer when the deceased was a favorite relative, or a noted war-

rior. On the death of an infant, the mother carried about with her for months a rude wooden image in the same cradle or frame in which she had carried her child. When a husband died it was the custom for the widow to select her best wearing apparel, wrap it in a skin or blanket, attach to it the ornaments her husband had worn during life, and then lay the bundle away until after the period of mourning; she appearing for a time, generally two or three months, clad in her poorest garb. When a sufficient period had elapsed, the nearest relatives of the deceased presented her with articles of apparel as a mark of regard for her fidelity to the memory of her husband. This was an intimation to the widow that she was at liberty to dress as she chose, and free to become the wife of another member of the tribe.

They believed in a multitude of minor deities or spirits, some of which exercised good, others evil influences. Superstitious rites were performed in the worship of both. They believed that spirits lived in the vicinity of water and watercourses, that they could hear every word spoken, and were cognizant of the doings of every individual of the tribe; but in winter when the streams were frozen the spirits lapsed into a torpid state like the frogs and snakes, and were unconscious of existence. During this period the Indians would sit around the fires in camp or lodge at night, relating the tales and legends of the tribe, as they could then speak with the fullest freedom with no spirit near to overhear them. But at the earliest return of spring, which in this particular relation was supposed to be indicated by the croak of a frog, all story telling of this nature abruptly ceased until the spirits had again gone to sleep with the coming of winter.

A widow was sometimes regarded as a seer or prophetess, exercising greater influence with the tribe than the medicine men. When answering questions propounded to her the prophetess occupied a peculiarly constructed lodge, where she was supposed to be under the direct influence of the spirits.

WOODEN AR-
ROWHEAD.

The Chippewas enjoyed the distinction of being able to compute numbers, something which the average Indian was generally incapable of doing. They counted as many as a thousand, doing so by the decimal process; taking ten, the number of fingers, as the basis or unit, then counting ten for each finger, which made a hundred, repeating the process until they had counted a thousand. The value of a dollar was at first a puzzle to them when trading, but by taking the exchange standard of a dollar in skins they could by their method of computation deal with the white man without giving him much opportunity to swindle them.   Thus, if a dollar was worth so many raccoon skins, they computed from that basis how much they should receive for so many beaver, otter, wolf or other skins.

The Chippewas did not practice polygamy to any great extent.   They rarely had more than two wives, and frequently only one.   This may be accounted for partly by the fact that they were not constantly at war like many other Indians, consequently the women did not greatly outnumber the men.   The men had some regard for their wives; in this respect, they frequently excelled the white man with whom they were brought in contact. When traders arrived among them, the Chippewas often secreted their women until the white men had departed—a proceeding that was not very complimentary to the white men in that country at the time.

Every year, at the approach of winter, when the first heavy snow fell, they celebrated the event with a snowshoe dance, a practice peculiar to the Chippewas alone.   Its object was to manifest their gratitude to the Great Creator for sending the snow, which enabled them to chase and secure game with greater facility.   The ceremony did not differ from the ordinary Indian dance, save that it lacked the savagery and ferocity that characterized Indian dances in general.   The men jumped around in a circle, dancing, uttering whoops and yells, and waving their weapons of the chase to the rattle of their tom-toms.

A custom commonly practiced by them was that known as striking the post.   On these occasions a large number of the tribe, both men and women, assembled.   The warriors circled around the pole, uttering fierce cries, dancing to the unceasing beat of the tom-toms, and wildly brandishing their war weapons.   Then all suddenly stopped, when one, usually a chief or noted warrior, rushed madly at the post, striking it with his tomahawk.   Amid the silence that followed, the brave recounted one or more of his exploits to the multitude.   His story generally described some desperate encounter in battle, how he met his foe in single combat and scalped him; or perhaps a successful contest with an infuriated bear, wolf, or other fierce animal.   These stories were very graphically told, and invariably highly exaggerated in the Indian's usual manner; although it was not uncommon to see a brave bearing on his body unmistakable scars of encounters with both man and beast. Most of the warriors present took their turn at story telling; at times some of the old men, carried away by the enthusiasm of the moment, would suddenly rise from the circle, where they sat apart, and rushing to the pole narrated wonderful exploits they had performed in their youth, quite outdoing in boastfulness all who had preceded them.

The Crees were another tribe of Algonquins, speaking that language. Originally they claimed as their hunting ground the immense territory lying between Lakes Athabaska and Winnipeg, and from Hudson's Bay to the Rocky Mountains. In early days they were a warlike people, repeatedly driving their neighbors, the Athabaskas, far away to the north. They early acquired firearms and were fairly proficient in their use. They were not of large stature, but were well built, having a smooth skin of a light copper color.

At this time they numbered from three to five thousand, but small-pox reduced them greatly. After the visitation of this scourge they allied with the Assiniboins; being unlike the latter in many respects, they refused to conform to the customs of the Assiniboins, then moving farther north made their homes between them and the Blackfoot country.

Nearly all Algonquin tribes were intelligent, readily adopting the customs of civilization, but the Crees retained their ways more persistently than any other tribe of this family, and were very fierce toward many of their Indian neighbors. Coming in contact with the French trappers and *voyageurs*, as well as the employees of the various Fur Companies, the French Canadians took many of their women as wives; the half-breeds and their numerous descendants in that region to-day are largely of Cree blood.

The Crees were firm believers in the Sun Dance, practicing this cruel ceremony after the manner of the Sioux.

They held this dance up to a recent date, persistently refusing to discontinue it, claiming that it was a religious ceremony which they had a right to perform. After the whites settled in the Cree country both the local authorities and the United States Government used their best efforts to prevent it, but without success.

The Kaskasias, Cahokias, Tamaronas, Peorias and the Michigamis were a number of Algonquin tribes that formed themselves into a confederacy for mutual protection, and were known under the name of Illinois. The Ottawas were of the same stock and occupied the country contiguous to the river which bears their name, and they compelled the Hurons and others to pay them tribute for the privilege of passing up or down any of the rivers in, or traveling through their country. After the defeat of the English under Braddock, by the Indians and French, their great chief, Pontiac, organized the Miamis, Shawnees, Ottawas, and such other Algonquin tribes as cared to join into a vast army to drive the whites from their hunting grounds. Runners were sent to inform other tribes of this move, and when the Illinois learned of it, they also took the warpath; this was the beginning of the so-called seven-years' war. The horrors and cruelties practiced by the red men during this time have no parallel in any other Indian war on this continent. The massacre at Michilmacinac, and the siege of Detroit, together with atrocities perpetrated elsewhere, so inflamed the whites, that the commanding officer of the British troops ordered the savages inoculated with small-pox, by sending them infected clothing, or to use any means to destroy them as so many mad dogs.

During this war, the Miamis and Shawnees were the most bloodthirsty, and could always be found at the front where the battles raged with the greatest fury; and after the war they were the last to surrender. The Shawnees, broken in spirit, fled south to the mouth of the Wabash River; from here a portion traveled to Missouri, and located near the mouth of the Kansas River; others went to Florida, but receiving no welcome from the Indians or whites there, they again wandered north, and joined their kindred in Ohio.

Of all the tribes of their nation, the fate of these two was the saddest; first being attacked by the fierce Huron Iroquois, and a portion of them held in vassalage; and like others who followed Pontiac, the male members of both tribes were reduced to mere skeletons of these once powerful peoples.

It may be of interest to note, that some tribes of this family living in the East, fashioned shell beads—which they called *wampum*—these were used as money by the Colonists until 1640. Beads were made of three colors, white, blue and pink, the white having the least,

BLACKFOOT INDIAN, WITH STONE HAMMER.

blue the next, and pink the greatest value according to size and condition. Discs and half moons from one to four inches in diameter, also served as money, and were valued at from one to five dollars each; these were cut from Conch shells, and worn by chiefs as ornaments on the hair and clothing.

The Wampumnaogs derived their name because of their ability as wampum makers, and it was this tribe of which Massasoit was chief who, during his time assisted the early settlers greatly, but upon his death, his son, Metacomet, assumed the chief-tainship and followed the policy of his illustrious father for more than ten years; when he was persuaded by his restless young warriors to declare war upon the settlers, and because of his cruelties during this time, he was given the name of King Philip; hostilities finally ceased, and a treaty was signed by him and the Massachusetts Bay Colony in the old church at Taunton in 1671.

The Pottawattomies were another tribe of this family and originally occupied the country around Green Bay, Wisconsin, but subsequently pushed to the territory on the southern end of Lake Michigan, driving out the former occupants and seizing their country; subsequently they were removed to Kansas, where they lived for a long time and increased in numbers, but were again moved to the Indian Territory.

The Outagamis or Sacs, and Foxes are of the same stock; the two tribes have been so long living together that they are practically one, and, al-

BABY CARRIER AND BABY.

though living far to the East among the whites, they have persistently refused to conform to the customs of civilization.

The Sacs and Foxes adopted warriors of other tribes whom they made chiefs. One of them, Black Hawk, was a Pottawattomie by birth; Keokuk was also a noted chief and led his tribe during the Black Hawk war, when they allied with the Winnebagoes.

VARIOUS INDIAN PEOPLES IN TEXAS.

On the headwaters of the Brazos River, lived the Huecos or Wacoes. Little is known of their origin, but they spoke their own language; they were few in numbers and are now semi-civilized. The Keechies were another small body of Indians having their own distinct language; and have their homes

in northwestern Texas, where they lead pastoral lives, and remain stationary. The Tawaconies spoke their own language and at one time were quite numerous and nomadic, but as civilization surrounded them, they were compelled to remain stationary. The Iones were of distinct linguistic stock, and originally roamed over a large portion of northwestern Texas, and lived by the chase. Many of these people held friendly intercourse and lived at peace with each other; but the characteristics and customs of some were very different; among others there was a strong resemblance in customs and language.

The Caddoes constituted one linguistic stock and have lived in the country contiguous to the creek which bears their name, since known to the white man. They were without doubt at one time a powerful people, for at the time Texas was admitted into the Union, they numbered more than two thousand warriors; when I last saw them, about 1870, they were partly civilized and living at peace

BUCKSKIN DRESS—UTE WOMAN.   with the whites and their Indian neighbors.

Near Fort Duncan, or the town of Eagle Pass on the Rio Grande River, live a tribe of Seminoles who originally belonged to the Appalache nation and had their homes in Florida, but upon the breaking out of the civil war, Coacoochee, their chief, led them to Mexico. Becoming intolerant of Mexican rule, they wandered north and located where they now are. It is difficult to conceive a more radical change in numbers and personal appearance than has taken place in the Seminoles, since their wars against the Government, when led by their great chief, Osceolo. That they married and intermarried with negroes, is evidenced by the fact that a large number of them are less than half-blood negro; their hair is curly, noses flat, and their language is guttural and sounds much like the ignorant negro of slavery days.

CHAPTER XXXV.

THE NEZ PERCÉS, OR PIERCED-NOSED INDIANS—ON THE WARPATH—SUR-
RENDER OF CHIEF JOSEPH—THE CAYUSES.

A Part of the Shahaptin Family—How the Nez Percés were first Discovered—Their
Pierced Noses—An Intelligent Tribe—White Squatters—First Outbreak against
the Whites—Going on the Warpath—Organizing a Bloody Campaign—A Fierce
Battle—Indian Tactics—Troops in Pursuit—Peculiar Incident of the Battle—Birth
of a Child during the Engagement—Chief Joseph—His Daughter Lost in the Confu-
sion of Battle—Devoured by Wild Animals—The Chief's only Heir—His Wonderful
Retreat of Two Thousand Miles—His Military Ability—Indians Fighting with their
Clothes On—Rare Instance of Indian Magnanimity—Surrender of Chief Joseph—
Asking no Favors—His Patriotic Speech—The Cayuses—Low, Cunning—Great
Thieves.

THE Nez Percés, or Pierced Noses, were the most numerous tribe of the
Shahaptin nation, and spoke the language of that family. The name was
given them by French Canadian trappers and traders, for the reason that at
one time they pierced the cartilage at the end of the nose; in this a polished
bone, stick, or feather was worn.

They have been erroneously called by many other names, such as Shahaptin, Numepo, Shopomish, etc.

This can readily be accounted for from the fact that they were divided
into many small tribes, each of which had its own name. Sometimes the
whole tribe was called by the name of one or another of the small ones.

When first discovered by Lieutenants Lewis and Clark at the headwaters of the Columbia River, they were peaceable and hospitable, and
aided the party greatly in making explorations in that region. In their
report to the War Department these officers stated that the Nez Percés occupied almost the entire Northwestern Territory, that they were the richest
tribe of Indians in that country and that they numbered from twenty thousand to twenty-five thousand.

How they arrived at this conclusion I cannot understand, for the Nez
Percés, with even their superior intelligence, had no means of making or
keeping records; and as they were scattered all over their territory, it was simply impossible for Lieutenants Lewis and Clark, during their short stay
among them, to have seen more than a small portion of them. I never knew
any one to make an estimate of their numbers to exceed five thousand to ten
thousand.

INDIAN DANCER—PAWNEE.

The Nez Percés were one of the most peaceful and intelligent of Indian peoples, although they sometimes engaged in hostilities with the Blackfeet, on which occasions they generally proved themselves superior warriors. There were two divisions of this tribe, designated as the Upper and Lower Nez Percés.

At one time the Nez Percés and some other tribes of their kindred stock were the richest Indians in the West.

Wherever there was one of their camps, all the valleys and plains were covered with large herds of good horses. The owners often had so many that it was necessary to mark them; this was usually done by cutting the ears in different ways, often a large slit was taken out in the shape of the letter V, another cut off the top of both ears. A handsome horse was often changed to a homely one by these large marks.

These Indians made for themselves warm clothing for winter use from the skins of various animals. Sometimes coats were made double, with fur or hair inside and out.

They took much care of their effects, persons and habitations, and laid away large quantities of dried meat, wild fruits, as well as the camas for winter use.

Not being constantly engaged in war, the women did not outnumber the men; consequently polygamy was not general among them.

It was among these people that some of the first missionaries from Canada located. They did much good teaching some of the Indians the Christian religion, and also did much to soften their savage instincts, as well as to teach them the ways of civilization by which they could better their condition. After this the Indians progressed, were contented, and had they been properly treated, would not have caused the loss of life and treasure from the unjust acts of the Government and whites in their country.

With the advance of civilization is always accompanied desperate characters, whose only aim is to secure lands or property without much effort or exertion. So it was in this case; as white squatters became more numerous the hunting grounds of the Indians grew less. This so incensed them, that their savage instincts were aroused to such an extent that they could bear it no longer.

They were brought into prominence by their first outbreak against the whites, having entered into several treaties with the Government, which had scarcely been made before they were broken by one side or the other. As the Indian lands were valuable, as fast as the whites invaded the country they settled upon them. After many whites had taken possession the Government made an effort to secure another treaty, but their chief said,

THUNDER-ROLLING-IN-THE-MOUNTAINS, OTHERWISE CHIEF JOSEPH—NEZ PERCE.

Twenty Years Among Our Hostile Indians.   Page 286

"No, we have kept our faith with you, now keep yours with my people."
The old chief died and his son took his place; both he and his people refused
to submit to the decision of the Government, although the Indians had agreed
to live on the reservation.   Knowing the futility of going to war, the chief
reluctantly consented to make concessions; but many of the Indians resented
this, and organized themselves into war parties, taking the warpath against
the whites.   This occurred during the absence of the head men, who were
away on a hunting expedition.   After their return they upheld the acts of
the others, and organized all the warriors of the tribe into a fighting body.

One of the fiercest battles that followed took place in a deep basaltic
walled cañon on White Bird Creek.   The troops which had been sent in pursuit entered the cañon thinking that they could approach the Indians and
lead them away, as they had always been peaceful.   In this they were mistaken, for the latter threw out a herd of horses to cover their movements.
They then deployed as skirmishers, and with some fine manœuvres closed
on the troops, and in a short time turned their flank.   Among the troops
were a number of volunteers from the settlers, who, observing the success of
the Indians, became panic-stricken and broke from the lines; the Indians
then made fierce and sudden dashes on the soldiers, demoralizing the whole
body.   The first dash was so quick that the troops had no time to get into
position; but for the coolness and courage of the regular forces the whole
body of whites might have been annihilated.   The army officers forced the
fighting, compelling the Indians to retreat.

During this retreat, which lasted more than four months, the Indians
fought many pitched battles with the United States troops, in which the
former were usually victorious.

A very unusual thing occurred during this retreat.   When passing
through a village of Indians who wished to join him in his fight against the
whites, Chief Joseph rejected their proposition, saying, "Remain where you
are, and let me fight this out my own way."   He also requested them to do
what he recommended, and not to commit any outrage that might embitter
the feeling then existing.   His orders to his warriors to spare all white prisoners taken in battle and not to kill a white woman or child, was something
unknown among the North American Indians in time of war.   Such magnanimity is entirely foreign to Indian character.   During the many battles
with the troops the Indian warriors did not strip off their clothing, as was
their usual custom, but wore their breechcloths and moccasins, and did not
look so hideous while engaged in conflict.

A peculiar incident of this battle was that Chief Joseph's wife gave birth
to a child during the heat of the fight.   This infant daughter was the only

MOUNTED WARRIOR—PAINTED WAR HORSE—NEZ PERCE.

Twenty Years Among Our Hostile Indians.

child left to him when he finally surrendered; his other child, a girl about ten years, ran away on the day of the final engagement, and being lost, either died of starvation or was devoured by wild animals.

Chief Joseph, whose Indian name was Thunder-rolling-in-the-Mountains, must be rated among the greatest Indian chiefs and warriors of this continent. He possessed splendid military capacity, as well as great ability in the management of his people. His retreat from Kamia on the Nez Percés reservation to the Bear Paw Mountains, twice crossing the Rocky Mountains, carrying with him the wounded, infirm, and the children of his people, with very insufficient supplies, through a rugged mountainous country, in all kinds of weather, covering a distance of two thousand miles, is one of the greatest achievements ever performed by an uncivilized man.

During this remarkable retreat, which lasted nearly six months, Joseph was followed by some of the ablest generals of the Civil War. He was finally brought to bay in the Bear Paw Mountains, where, after a six-days' battle, in which both sides fought with desperate bravery and persistence, he finally surrendered.

In person Joseph was tall and spare, in intellect he was a giant. He was pre-eminently a war chief; though he was not so popular with his people at first as some other chiefs, he gradually grew in the estimation of his tribe and the whites, until he became the first Indian in the Northwest. When he surrendered he did so with dignity, asking no favors for his people; but calling attention to the many alleged breaches of faith on the part of the Government, made no complaint. On one occasion he remarked that he did not blame the President for his neglect, as he had so much to attend to in looking after the whites that he could not be expected to trouble himself about anything so unimportant as an Indian. If this utterance was sincere it was magnanimous; if not, it was very sarcastic.

The highest eulogy that can be written of Joseph is that his best friends were those who fought him hardest. They learned to respect his ability and character. His language when he surrendered and resigned his freedom forever was as touching as it was dignified. He said: "I surrender because I do not wish to see the continued suffering of my people. My camp is filled with wounded, sick, and infirm; my brother has been killed in battle; my little daughter has been lost on the prairie where she ran in the confusion of the fight; my people, who have been so rich in horses and the necessaries of life, are now on the snow-covered prairie, comfortless and starving. I am within a short distance of British America, and should I care to leave my wounded behind, I can escape with my well people and cross the line, where I can be protected; but I prefer to surrender on my own ground, and the Government is at liberty to treat me personally as it may choose."

To the Shahaptin family also belonged several other large tribes. The principal in regard to numbers were the Cayuses Palooses, Umatillas, Walla Wallas and Klikatahs.

THE CAYUSES.

Of the various tribes the Cayuses were the worst of the whole. They were crafty, cunning, and troublesome, being constantly on some thieving expedition. They were notorious horse thieves, and were despised by all people in their country. The trappers and traders suffered severely from them, as they frequently stole their entire outfit, after killing many of the men when they could do so without being caught.

They were probably the meanest as well as the lowest tribe of their family, as they were constantly skulking through the mountains in small parties, and also roaming over the country in search of small bodies of Indians and whites, whom they attacked when found in a defenseless position.

When mounted they rarely used a saddle, the horse was guided by a rawhide rope around the lower jaw. The warriors, almost naked, were ready for any emergency, and could dash on a party with great rapidity, running away as quickly as they came.

Having such good mounts it was seldom that they were overtaken.

After an attack in which they killed some one, they immediately returned to their homes, when the whole tribe protected them in declaring that none of its people had been away from camp even for an hour.

They were so secretive that it was with difficulty that anything could be learned about their affairs; it was not until after their savage instincts had been reduced that a white man was permitted to have one of their women for his wife; even then they were so suspicious that he was never taken into confidence. Should anything become known about them, it was charged to the "squaw men," when some of them were sure to suffer in some way either by killing, being robbed of his entire effects, or driven away.

The Umatillas were in all respects the finest tribe of this family, not only physically but intellectually. Being surrounded by so many Indians of vicious habits and of low order of intelligence, the Umatillas did not take advantage of their ignorance and rob them, but on the contrary, did much to assist and advance them. These people did much to help the whites who first entered their country, giving them warm clothing, horses and food.

CHAPTER XXXVI.

CHARACTERISTICS AND CUSTOMS OF THE CALIFORNIA TRIBES—INDIANS
WHO TATTOOED THEIR FACES AND BODIES.

Different Linguistic Stock—Many Languages Spoken among this Group—Tribes which
went Naked—Garments of Rabbit Skins—Painting their Faces and Bodies—Personal Adornment—Slitting their Ears—The Custom of Tattooing and what it
Meant—Passing Goose Quills through the Nose—Night Watchers of the Camp—An
Indian Bath—Ingenious Ways of Catching Fish—Eating their Food Raw, Entrails
and All—A Meal of Grasshoppers—Bread Made of Dried and Pulverized Grasshoppers—Eating Portions of the Bodies of their Enemies—Money Estimate of
Human Life—Peculiar Marriage Customs—Dances and Festivities—Gambling and
Games—Treatment of the Sick—Cremating their Dead.

MARICOPA WOMAN.

PREVIOUS to the advent
of the white man in
California that region
was more densely popu-
lated by Indians than
any portion of this coun-
try. They were not of
one linguistic stock,
there being from ten to
twelve distinct lan-
guages, and double that
number of dialects
spoken among this
group.

In complexion they
were much darker than
those east of the moun-
tains. There was less
uniformity of type
among them than any
other group of Indians
in this country; some
being short and of com-
pact build, others thin
and weak; only a few
were tall and well
formed; none were fierce, and when the whites entered their country,

the Indians offered no stern resistance to them, as did those of other sections.

The mountain tribes were more warlike and physically better developed than those living in the lowlands. They were better armed and frequently fought among themselves, or made raids on their neighbors.

The Indian nations and tribes of North America resembled each other in general characteristics. Nevertheless, the influence of soil, climate, and environment, operating on them through centuries, gave to many nations as marked an individuality as may be observed among different nationalities of the civilized races.

The California Indians not only differed greatly from those who were remote from them, but differed from many of their immediate neighbors, and even differed in some respects among themselves. Living in a mild climate they were less warlike than many other Indians; their custom of living in rude habitations, and of wearing little clothing, or sometimes none, was not so much characteristic of a lower type of manhood as their inheritance of laziness. They were content simply to exist, and nothing but necessity compelled them to the least exertion.

The natives of northern California were the Yurok and Karok, who occupied the most northerly portion of the territory on the lower Klamath River, and spoke entirely different tongues. South of the Yurok, on Humbolt River were the Wishosks; these two tribes spoke languages of a common origin. Between the Wishosk and the Yuki were a Tinneh tribe, in the vicinity of the Eel and Trinity Rivers. The Yuki constituted two divisions or groups, the one embracing the region between John's Creek and the Pacific, and the other the territory south of Clear Lake.

The Yuki and the Tinneh tribes, were among the lowest and most degraded of all the California Indians, and were despised by all their neighbors. They intermarried to such an extent as to produce a mixed race, which inhabited this region, and were worse, if anything, than their ancestors.

The Pomo family also occupied a large territory as far north as the Russian River, extending inland to about the borders of Clear Lake, and as far west as the Pacific Ocean. This nation was divided into various tribes that differed but little from one another in characteristics and customs.

The Chimariko, had their home immediately south of the Karok, were few in numbers and insignificant in almost every way.

The Wintun family occupied the territory lying between Mt. Shasta and Benecia. The family was divided into two groups, the northern known as Wintuns, and the southern as Patwins. To the south and east of the south-

MAN AND WIFE—MOJAVE.

ern Wintuns lived the Maidu, and east of the northern Wintuns were the Achomawi, who extended as far east as Nevada. The Maidu family differed somewhat in their manners and customs, and even in their dialect. The further south they extended the more pronounced were their peculiarities, and the greater their superstitions.

The territory around Lake Tahoe and the Truckee River was the home of the Washo family. Between the Sierra Nevada and the Pacific, and extending southward from above San Francisco to Monterey was the territory of the Mutsun. This great family consisted of four large groups: on the east the Miook; on the south and southwest the Mutson proper; on the northwest the Olamentke, and on the north and northeast the Talatin.

To the south of the Mutsun was the Yokuts family, occupying an irregular-shaped territory into which they had been driven by the Pi-Utes. This territory stretched east and west from the Sierras to the Coast Range, and south to Tulare Lake, embracing a narrow tract of country as far as Los Angeles county. They were divided into many small tribes, forming a sort of confederacy, which acted in unison.

Each tribe regulated its own affairs, but in matters of importance councils of the chiefs of the different tribes were held. The chiefs of all the different tribes were subordinate to the head chief of the nation, but the decision of the latter was not always final, and might be overruled by a council of the subordinate chiefs. The position of head chief was hereditary, while the tribal chiefs were chosen in the usual Indian manner. Every year a great council was held at which all the chiefs were present. Councils were always presided over by the head chief, and the affairs of each tribe were presented to the council by its chief, and such measures as were deemed necessary for their common interest were agreed upon.

They were not particular about their clothing, either as to quality or quantity. The Yuroks wore a breechcloth only, though in the cold season they wore a buckskin, or a robe made of rabbit skins around them. A robe of rabbit skins was made double, with fur inside and out, and required from sixty to seventy-five skins. Among the coast tribes, garments made of seal, and other skins were often worn. The Pitt River Indians wore only a deerskin thrown over them. The men usually went bareheaded, but the women wore headgear or covering made of basket work, often gaily ornamented with feathers.

In central and southern California the men frequently went naked. The women wore an apron of deerskin or braided grass, and sometimes a garment covering the bosom and reaching to the knees. In cold weather the men often wore a deerskin about the shoulders; and the women wore a garment of skin thrown over them, in addition to a short kilt of braided grass.

The women and children of the coast tribes wore petticoats of sealskin, which were occasionally ornamented with fringe and shells. The chief's cloak reached nearly to the ground; this was the only mark of distinction in his dress or appearance. At times some of these tribes wore a gala dress, covering the body, but this was on special occasions, and was the result of vanity rather than a sense of decency. They made moccasins of braided grass to protect the feet while traveling over rough places, through brush, and sometimes bound their legs and bodies with twisted bands of hide for protection.

Both men and women painted their faces and bodies in various colors. They were fond of ear ornaments, and wore huge pendants from slits made in their ears. Some of the ornaments were from six to eight inches in length. Through the ear-holes was inserted a piece of hollow wood or bone as thick as one's finger, this was sometimes used as a needlecase; it was often decorated with glass beads and other ornaments. Bracelets and necklaces made of strings of beads and ornamented shells were also worn.

The various tribes differed in the manner of wearing their hair. Some wore it in the form of a queue, some in two twisted braids hanging down the back or over the shoulders, while others let it hang loose. Those who wore the hair loose cut it off at the shoulders, others cut it around the face; some of the tribes who plaited it wove the fibre of bark or silk grass in the plaits; although the hair was considered the greatest ornament of their persons none of them took much care of it.

Some of the men tattooed their breasts and arms, but the practice was not general among them. Occasionally they tattooed themselves by certain marks whereby they could be identified if captured.

The women tattooed their faces, breasts and arms in colors made from the juices of plants; the lines were sometimes so arranged as to indicate the personal characteristics of the person so ornamented. This, however, was only peculiar to certain tribes. The natives around Klamath Lake bedecked themselves more profusely than their neighbors, covering their bodies from the face to the waist with various colors and figures. Occasionally not only different tribes, but even families of the same tribe had their own distinctive style of tattooing and painting their faces and bodies.

Their habitations did not greatly differ. In summer they drew the bushes together to shade them from the sun. Their permanent dwellings, however, consisted of a hole dug in the ground; around this poles were set, over which a conical covering was placed. The size of the huts, or dugouts, depended on the number of inmates, which greatly varied. Habitations of this kind, as among all nomadic races, were built to meet the requirements of time and place. Some were dome shaped, like beaver houses; others were square. All bore a certain resemblance to each other in construction and arrangement.

A few tribes built more permanent dwellings, and evinced no little ingenuity in making them strong and serviceable; and all consisted of but one apartment. The sleeping places were invariably arranged in Indian fashion around the wall of the hut. Among certain tribes some of the men remained awake all night watching, while the others slept; often the guards took their weapons and joined the watchers in other lodges of the camp—all fearful of being unexpectedly attacked or surprised.

The tribes of southern California had the worst, the flimsiest, and most ill-kept dwellings of any of the Californian tribes. Those of the northern Indians were substantial and well adapted for the purposes for which they were designed, while some of the southern tribes seemed to have derived some ideas in regard to house-building from their immediate neighbors to the south, residing in what was formerly Mexican territory.

A few of the tribes bathed, or rather took an occasional plunge in the water; but this was done to cool themselves and not from a sense of cleanliness. They only moistened the dirt on their bodies, and came out of the water as filthy as they went in.

They built sweat houses of earth; these were low and small, and always located near a body of water. When taking a bath of this kind, several of them entered the sweat house, then closing the entrance, remained there until almost overcome by the intense heat; after they were nearly exhausted they rushed out and plunged into the water. Hot baths and a cold plunge were taken during the coldest weather, which did not seem to cause them inconvenience, or have any effect detrimental to the health of the bather. Sweat houses were heated by hot stones after the usual Indian custom, and were scattered all through California and Oregon.

They preferred fishing to hunting, as it required less exertion. Some of them caught fish by building closely constructed willow dams at certain places on the streams, so that the fish could not pass through; and when they swarmed at these dams, they were scooped out by means of baskets and rude drag-nets. Salmon especially were easily taken in this way by the northern tribes. When they swarmed up the rivers in spawning time, they collected in such numbers before the dams that they could be literally taken out of the water in basketfuls. Some of the tribes had fishing chiefs when they went on their fishing expeditions, and the orders of these chiefs during that time were implicitly obeyed. The coast Indians ate shellfish, seal, and stranded whales.

Their principal food consisted of acorns and nuts. These were often eaten raw, or sometimes pounded into a pulp, then made into bread; this was baked in a hole in the ground, over which hot coals were heaped.

Occasionally they ate their food raw; at other times it was half-boiled in close-woven baskets filled with water heated by hot stones. Meat was sometimes broiled or cooked in a hole in the ground, over which were placed live coals. The animal was roasted whole, just as it was killed, and entrails and all were eaten. They never washed their cooking utensils, or their hands, although they uniformly ate with their fingers. Fruits, roots, berries and vegetables formed part of their diet. The women did all the fruit gathering, the men confining their labors to hunting and fishing. Some of the more provident dried or smoked their fish and meats, and preserved roots, berries and acorns in baskets for seasons of want.

Many of the tribes were too lazy to hunt, and resorted to various devices for capturing game. What little game they secured was usually captured by traps or snares, or by running it down by relays, at which they were experts. Often brush fences or corrals were built, into which game was driven.

Deer and small game were shot with the bow and arrow, by stealing close to the animal. In chasing deer the hunter covered himself with a deer skin, with the head and horns aloft, and approached close to the herd before the ruse was discovered by the unsuspecting animals.

Grasshoppers were secured by setting fire to the grass in dry weather and driving the insects into pits prepared for the purpose. At other times they formed a line and beat the ground with sticks, driving the grasshoppers into the pit. These insects, when caught in large numbers, were cooked in holes in the ground, over which fires were built; at other times they were dried and put away for future use, and when pulverized were made into a kind of paste or cake.

Some of the tribes were deterred by superstition from eating the flesh of large animals, especially bear, as they believed that the bodies of these beasts contained the spirits of their ancestors.

For a low and ignorant people they were capable of great endurance, and could go for long intervals without food or water.

Their weapons consisted of the bow and arrow and lance. Their bows and arrows were well made, being equal to those used by any other North American Indians. The bow was made of the toughest and most elastic wood, and strengthened by being bound around with sinews. The arrows were from two to two and one-half feet in length. They were barbed with flint, volcanic glass, obsidian, or bone, and barbed so that the head would remain in the body it penetrated unless cut out. Great skill and patience were required in making some of the arrow-heads, and only those who had mastered the trade by long practice could produce them. Some of the flint and obsidian pebble heads required weeks of labor to fashion. The quiver was made of the skin of small animals. Despite their inoffensive disposition, these Indians were good fighters when put to it, and possessed all the unwincing courage and stoicism of the typical red man.

Some tribes scalped their enemies, others did not. All were possessed of the innate Indian trait of torturing prisoners. They sometimes ate portions of the bodies of captives, not from a cannibalistic impulse, but to absorb the courage of the slain. Their wars, as a usual thing, were neither bloody nor prolonged. They invariably killed the male prisoners, and made slaves of captive women and children. Among some tribes children accompanied the warriors to battle, and at intervals were sent, by both sides, into the enemies' lines to pick up and bring back the arrows. Nearly all these people fought on foot, and, unlike other Indians, they fought in extended lines and at comparatively close quarters, so that their arrows would be effective.

Some of the stronger nations or tribes compelled their weaker neighbors to pay them tribute. Other tribes made a practice of informing the enemy, either by courier or by signs, when they intended to march against them. The stealing of women was one of the most fruitful causes of war among these people. Another source of contention was the building of fishing dams in the rivers. The dams cut off the supply of fish from those further up the stream, and bloodshed was the inevitable result.

The women were skillful in plaiting grass, making baskets and other articles, and the men of certain tribes made substantial boats, but their skill in handiwork went no further. Their wealth consisted of shell money, canoes, deerskins and women. The more wives a man had the richer he was.

Shell money consisted of shells obtained on the coast, its value depending on size and shape. Shells were fashioned in the form of quills, and strung together like beads. They were, as a rule, from one to two inches in length, and about a quarter of an inch in thickness. Five perfect shells were considered to be worth about one dollar in gold or silver. Skins, furs, and rare feathers also constituted articles of exchangeable value.

Among some tribes chieftainship was hereditary, in others the chief was chosen on account of his wealth or prowess. Where there were no male descendants, the office was by some tribes conferred on the wife of the dead chief, a custom peculiar to these Indians. The wife and daughters of a chief had little power, though they were generally respected and their advice was occasionally followed.

Murder was punished by a fine, or the relatives of the victim slew the murderer. Fines, however, were not very exorbitant. The life of a woman was worth only half as much as that of a man. They were usually paid in allicochick shells, the price among certain tribes being a hundred dollars for the murder of a man, and fifty dollars for killing a woman. Some of the fines were paid in canoes or other articles of recognized value. Six canoes were considered an equivalent for a man's life.

The California Indians had no marriage ceremony. The girls were sold by their parents for such articles of value as the husband could give in exchange for them. At other times a man and woman agreed to live together, and this agreement constituted them husband and wife. A man could have as many wives as he could buy, but a woman could not have a plurality of husbands, or more than one man to whom she owed allegiance. When a difficulty occurred between two men about a woman, and they could not otherwise settle it, they fought it out, the victor claiming the female.

Wives were bought; the price was regulated by the appearance of the woman or her capacity for work. The old men who had accumulated the most wealth bought the handsomest girls; the young men who were not able to pay a high price had to content themselves with the old and ugly women. Should a man grow rich enough to buy a young wife he discarded the old one unceremoniously. Some of the coast Indians were allowed to have only one wife at a time, but they could exchange her for another as often as they wished. Adultery was severely punished and was consequently rare. Some tribes disemboweled the offending woman; among others the man who committed the offense was compelled to buy the woman; while in other tribes the outraged husband compelled the offender to exchange wives with him.

Childbirth rarely interrupted the mother in her usual avocations for more than an hour or so. When the time arrived she retired to the forest or in the vicinity of a stream, where, after the birth, she washed the newborn infant and returned to the lodge with the babe strapped to a board on her back, resuming her usual work.

They had few games or pastimes, but owing to their indolence, took little interest in them. In games of chance the winner did not exult in his success, nor did the loser manifest regret over his losses.

Both men and women often gambled away the last article of clothing in their possession, after which they went about naked, and with a satisfied air, as though owning the effects of the whole tribe.

They had dances at intervals and festivals on certain occasions, such as the season when they gathered acorns and nuts for winter, or after a successful hunt, and upon other important events. They usually danced naked. Their music was of the rudest kind, and consisted of beating on skin drums, or blowing a reed whistle.

The California Indians seemed to be subject to a greater variety of diseases than any others of the Western tribes. Their medical treatment was confined for the most part to the incantations and mummeries of the medicine men. Women doctors among some tribes were more numerous than male doctors, though among other tribes they were not tolerated.

They never mentioned the names of their dead; although they had no religious rites or beliefs, in the Indian sense, they were victims of all kinds of superstitions. Having no conception of the Great Creator, as believed in by other Indians, they imagined that the coyote or small prairie wolf was responsible for everything that existed. How they got this idea none of them could tell. They had an abundance of evil spirits, some of which were considered all-powerful, while others were limited in their capacity for evil. They had doctors and medicine men, who were supposed to be able to placate evil spirits or neutralize their powers. Only when sickness or misfortune befell them did they endeavor to propitiate evil spirits by paying homage to them. The medicine men were chosen by a competitive dance, the dancer who held out the longest being the successful candidate. No other qualifications were required for this position among the majority of the tribes.

Different mourning customs prevailed among the various tribes. The widow and the relatives of the dead lingered around the grave for days, lamenting their loss, and the widow sometimes cut off her hair in token of grief. The property of the deceased was either buried with him or left at the burial place. Their idea of heaven and the future life was purely materialistic. They believed heaven to be a place where they would enjoy all the good things they desired in their earthly life.

The dead were disposed of in various ways; some of the tribes buried them in shallow holes; others were dragged away to be eaten by dogs or wolves. The coast tribes threw the corpse into the ocean, while others placed them in trunks of trees which had been cut out sufficiently to receive the remains; these were wrapped with grass, then placed in a standing position in the timbers. Among the northern tribes bodies were covered with skins and left in a sitting posture.   The bodies of prominent men were often placed in trees, shrouded in their best raiment.

Among the more ignorant or indolent tribes, neither common warriors, women nor children received much attention after death.   A few tribes burned the bodies of the dead; these and a few Indians in Arizona were the only savages who disposed of the dead in this manner.

One of the principal vices with some was sensuality.   The females gave free rein to the indulgence of their passions at an early age, and it is difficult to describe the results of their depravity, especially in connection with the early trappers and employees of the various fur companies when visiting their country; as some of the diseases and troubles which followed cannot be written.

They were also gluttons of the most pronounced type, and ate such large quantities at times as to ren· der them unfit for anything for days; when in this condition they laid about helplessly, until starvation compelled them to again go in search of supplies.

At irregular intervals the men of some of the tribes repaired to the forest and made masks for their heads shaped like a skin-covered lodge; these were made of skins or grass; the top above the shoulders ran to a point, and the lower end reached to the waist; the remainder of their persons were naked and painted in hideous colors to make their appearances as frightful as possible.   When thus attired they made forays on their neighbors and

WARRIOR WITH PIPE TOMAHAWK.

carried away by force such females as they could seize.   The natural result of these raids was extreme bitterness and wars, which latter were frequently disasterous to both sides.

CHAPTER XXXVII.

THE COLUMBIAN GROUP—THE STORY OF AN INDIAN QUEST FOR THE WHITE MAN'S BIBLE—INDIAN ATROCITIES.

A Brave but Peaceably Inclined People—Ceremonies when Preparing for the Warpath—Imitating the Cry of Birds and Wild Animals—The War Chief—How Braves were Enlisted for War—Treatment of Women among the Different Tribes—Indian Slaves and Slavery—Staking Wives and Children on Games of Chance—A Risky Profession—Burial Ceremonies—A Vicious Tribe Called the Rogues--Why they were so named—An Expedition in Search of the White Man's Bible—Father De Smet—His Life and Labors among the Indians—The Measles among the Indians—Destruction of the Protestant·Mission—Savage Instincts Aroused—An Expedition for the Rescue of Captives.

FULL WAR COSTUME.

THE Columbian tribes possessed a fertile country where subsistence could be procured without much effort. Although nomadic they did not wander far from their central home. In nearly all their characteristics and customs they were somewhat in advance of the Indians living east of the Rocky Mountains, yet retaining the innate barbarism of the Red Man.

Their wealth consisted chiefly of horses; large herds of these were pastured in the rich valleys of their country. How they first obtained them is not known. They had a tradition that they originally obtained them from the Shoshonees, who secured them from wild herds. Some of the tribes, notably the Walla Wallas, when first visited by white men owned thousands of horses; in some places the country was literally covered with them. Among many of these tribes a man was deemed poor if he did not own fifteen or twenty horses. They were the only standard of value when used in barter. The Columbian Indians were excellent horsemen, and when forced into war handled the animals with great ability.

Though living within a comparatively restricted territory, the Oregon and Washington tribes differed in character and personal appearance. The tribes of the interior, from their pastoral life, were, when left undisturbed, generally mild and inoffensive, though when aroused they were vindictive; while the coast Indians, especially those of the north, were ferocious and treacherous. They differed no less in characteristics and customs. Almost every locality had its own tribe, that spoke a language distinct from the others.

Before starting on the warpath a grand council was held, which all the chiefs attended, and the old men of the tribes determined on the best measures to be adopted. The pipe was smoked, speeches were made by the old men and tribal chiefs, and the ceremony was concluded with a grand war dance. A field review was held; the warriors, mounted on their best horses and bedecked in all their rude ornaments, went through the manœuvres of an imaginary battle.

In dress they were not particular. Formerly they were comfortably clothed in furs and skins, but after the trade in peltries became general throughout their country, they found it difficult to procure clothing, and the poor were often unable to protect themselves adequately against the rigors of the cold winters.

Hunting and fishing were the two principal sources of subsistence. The streams furnished a plentiful supply of fish, and the woods abounded in game. The Nez Percés, who were the richest, and in many respects the most advanced, of the Oregon tribes, raised a few vegetables. The women made periodical trips and migrations to gather various kinds of roots, berries, and fruits.

Salmon and other fish were dried, then pulverized, and after being mixed with oil were laid away for winter use. Fish swarmed so abundantly in the lakes and streams that it was easy to lay in a sufficient store for the winter; yet most of the tribes were so improvident that they took little heed of the future, and frequently passed from the greatest abundance to extreme want—feasting one day and starving the next.

The Shooshwaps crossed one chain of the Rocky Mountains on their hunts, but being at war with tribes on the east could go no further. The Okinagans disguised themselves with wolf and bear skins, when hunting buffalo, and could imitate the cry of birds and beasts with wonderful effectiveness. The Nez Percés, Flatheads, Cœur d'Alênes, Spokanes, Pend d'Oreilles and other tribes hunted together; the Flatheads and the Yakimas often joined in the eastern hunt.

The office of chieftainship was hereditary, although some chiefs were chosen on account of conspicuous bravery. With the exception of the war chief they did not exercise great power. Armed with a whip, the war chief could enforce discipline when necessary by flagellation; he could not, however, compel his warriors to go upon a war expedition against their will. A war dance was therefore held, which was in reality a recruiting measure, for any brave who joined in the dance was in honor bound to go with the war party, or upon the warpath.

The Kootenais and others usually entered battle naked, sometimes not even wearing a breechcloth. Their saddles and bridles were the same as those used by other Indians, but unlike most Indians, some of them used spurs made of sharp fishbones. They were extremely cruel to their prisoners of war, keeping them for torture, which was repeated over and over again at short intervals, until death ended the victim's agony. Instead of scalping, some of the tribes cut off the forefingers of the fallen foe as evidence of the victor's prowess.

Many of the tribes used boats, some making them of birch and pine, others of logs hollowed out and sloped at the ends, and others made the more serviceable bull-boat. The Nez Percés, Cayuses, and other mountain tribes had no boats. Some tribes made rude maps of the countries they traversed on skins or the bark of trees. They believed simply in a state of future existence, when the individual would be happy or unhappy according to his merits or demerits. They distinguished readily between right and wrong, recognizing the principles of justice to a considerable degree. Adultery, homicide, theft, lying, and even minor offenses were condemned as wrong, and were punished in various ways by the different tribes, usually by fines, flogging, or the reprimand of the chief.

INDIAN BALL BAT.

Polygamy was tolerated and practiced; though it was not approved among many of the tribes, among a few it was principally confined to the chiefs. Their laxity of morals was perhaps not any worse than might be expected among a rude and ignorant people. Modesty and decency were recognized in a general way and among a few of the tribes were respected.

Some tribes had no marriage ceremonies, while among others the occasion was celebrated by feastings and rejoicings. Wives were bought, the price usually being paid in horses; it was not infrequent for betrothals to be made by parents while the parties were yet children. A Spokane wooer was compelled to consult the chief and the girl herself, as well as her parents or natural protectors before he could claim her as his wife. When a party eloped, as sometimes happened, the Indians condemned the woman as an outcast, subject to the caprice of any man in the tribe; then the girl's parents were entitled to confiscate the man's property. If the wife should die in consequence of her husband's harsh treatment the husband was disgraced, and was bound to propitiate the woman's parents or relations with additional presents. The wife could be discarded at will, and it was not uncommon for a discarded wife to be taken back by her husband.

The husband, in certain tribes, could at his wife's death recover the price paid for her. A custom prevailed among some tribes, prohibiting the husband from marrying for a year after the death of a wife. The rule was often evaded by the husband marrying just before her death, unless she died suddenly. In the Okinagan tribe the wives lived among their relatives a great part of the time, one or two of them remaining with the husband. When a Spokane married a woman of another tribe he joined her tribe, on the ground that a woman would be more useful and work better in the tribe to which she was accustomed than among strangers. Some tribes treated the women with remarkable consideration, for Indians. Most of the work was done by prisoners held by the tribes, therefore they were considered valuable property. Prisoners were generally treated well except in old age, or when disabled, then they were left to perish of want or neglect. Captives were generally regarded as slaves, and it was not uncommon for some of these tribes to engage in war for the purpose of capturing them. Children born of captives were also considered slaves.

Throughout the entire territory occupied by these Indians their habitations were much the same. Usually they lived in lodges, especially when moving about; but during the winter season those tribes that lived almost exclusively on fish, and did not wander far in search of food, built themselves huts. These were usually from fifteen to twenty-five feet long, and wide in proportion, verging into conical form at the top. Within, wooden strips or cross pieces were stretched for the purpose of drying salmon, meat, and other articles of food.

All the Oregon tribes were fond of amusements, diversions, and were inveterate gamblers. Horse racing was the chief amusement. Those in the region of the Columbia River carried the vice of gambling to excess. In horse racing they stopped at nothing. After having lost all their personal effects they staked their children or wives, and last of all, themselves. Should he lose himself, he became the slave of the winner. Sometimes a number of individuals staked their effects together, when one side or the other was sure to be beggared.

Their dancing consisted of jumping around, after the usual Indian fashion, uttering fierce yells, singing weird songs, and vigorously beating drums. They were greatly addicted to smoking after the white man taught them the use of tobacco. On all important occasions from the making up of a war party to meetings for barter and trade, the pipe was smoked continually.

Their large herds of horses were marked by cutting the ears in various ways, so that the owners could tell their own. Horses were often left without a guard, yet they rarely strayed far from the habitations of their owners, who were good, though not remarkable, horsemen. Children learned to ride when two or three years old. They also had countless numbers of dogs, which, in reality, came pretty near being tamed prairie wolves. Occasionally when traveling, they used them in carrying light burdens on travois.

All the tribes used the same kind of sweat baths as the California Indians, besides various herbs for curing disease. When these failed, they resorted to the magic of the medicine man. As he was supposed to possess the power of curing all maladies, if he lost his patient he paid the penalty with his life, provided he could not satisfactorily explain how his medicine was neutralized by that of some rival medicine man. Sometimes he bought off the indignant friends of the deceased. Few medicine men died a natural death, as they were sure to lose a patient sooner or later.

Mourning for the dead was shown by painting the face black and cutting off the hair. On special occasions they lacerated their bodies in a frightful manner, and cut out pieces of flesh, and threw them into the fire in their frantic demonstrations of grief.

All these tribes had an aversion to mentioning the names of the dead. They had various ways of disposing of the bodies of the dead, and various customs and ceremonies on these occasions. Some buried the bodies in the ground, wrapped in their clothing; others placed them in a canoe, suspended from a tree. The Okinagans bound the bodies of the dead to the trunk of a tree, in an upright position. Food and valuables were left at the burial place, and horses were killed at the spot.

The Nez Percés, Flatheads and Kootenais were among the best type of the aboriginal race found west of the Rocky Mountains.

The Klamaths embraced the Modocs, Shasta, and other tribes. The Umatillas, who were a notable tribe, were a branch of the Cayuses. The Warm Spring Indians consisted of what was called the "confederated tribes," confined mainly to middle Oregon. They were comprised of the Walla Walla and Wasco tribes, which banded together in self-defense, but did not trouble their neighbors as long as left undisturbed. In characteristics and customs they were degraded to the ordinary Indian level, and were much less advanced than the Nez Percés and other tribes.

The Umatillas, Cayuses, the Walla Wallas, and Nez Percés lived near the Columbia River about a hundred miles east of the Cascade Mountains. To the left of this range lived a tribe, vicious and treacherous, called the Rogues, who gave that name to the river where they had their homes—sometimes called the Rascal River. Their aboriginal name was the Potámeos, but, owing to their treachery and hostility toward white men, the French Canadian trappers called them the Rogues, or Rascals.

Next to the Nez Percés, the Cayuses were the most intelligent and the best disposed toward the whites. They were an inferior off-shoot of the Nez Percés, and lived on the north side of the Snake River. Next to them lived the Spokanes, also a peaceable tribe, quite intelligent for Indians, and usually willing to serve the whites who entered that territory.

The tribes that lived in the Willamette Valley, and along the basin of the Columbia River west of the Cascade Mountains, were irredeemably vicious, and the savages east of the mountains in the Dalles country were in no wise better. The country then inhabited by these people was generally avoided by settlers, owing to the hostile and treacherous disposition of the Indians.

The Umatilla branch of the Cayuses showed the strongest inclination of any of the Oregon tribes to receive the white man's civilization, which was the result of the influence exercised among them by the French Canadian trappers and *voyageurs*, and half-civilized Iroquois Indians from Canada, who had come among them and joined the tribe.

Some of the Cœur d'Alênes were among the first of the wild Indians to embrace Christianity. It came about in the following curious manner. A party of semi-civilized Iroquois from French Lower Canada made their way to the country of the Cœur d'Alênes, fraternizing with them. They told their newly-made acquaintances of the many wonders in the white man's land; how they lived; of the great things they performed; their countless numbers, and, chief of all, their manner of reaching the happy hunting ground after death. They told them that the white man had a book, a "medicine" book (the Bible), that would show every Indian the true trail to the happy hunting ground, where he would live forever in perfect bliss. After much discussion and consultation the Cœur d'Alênes determined to procure a copy of this wonderful book, and a party was organized to go in quest of it.   They had no definite objective point other than the vague East, where the Iroquois told them they could procure it.

This little band, after traveling a long distance, encountered a war party from their neighbors on the east, who attacked and killed some of them. The others escaped, and returning to their own people told them what had occurred.

Another and larger party was immediately formed to continue the search for the white man's Bible.   This party succeeded in reaching Fort Benton, where they sold enough animals and skins to pay the passage of a few of them to St. Louis on the steamboat.

Wandering about the city, they fell in with Pierre Chouteau, an old trapper of the Indian country, and by the use of the sign language told him what they wanted.   He took them to the "black gowns" priests, among whom was one Father De Smet.   They recounted to him what the Iroquois had told them, and enlisted his sympathies to such a degree that he asked and received permission from his superiors to accompany the Indians back to their country.

Father De Smet was one of the most remarkable men of his day.   A Belgian by birth, he came to the United States when a young man, and his entire after life was shaped by the Indians endeavoring to secure a copy of the Bible for their people.   The most astonishing thing in his entire career among the Indians is the fact that he lived for many years among the Blackfeet, the Cœur d'Alênes, the Flatheads, and other savage tribes without molestation.   Endowed with a singular faculty of acquiring languages, he was soon able to communicate orally and by the sign language with almost all Indian tribes with which he came in contact.   His services were subsequently enlisted by the Government, and he kept army officers and officers of the Fur Companies well informed of the true condition of affairs among the many Indians with whom he was acquainted.   When war parties were being formed, and he knew their object, or objective points, he was frequently instrumental in preventing Indian wars and bloodshed.

At the request of the Secretary of War, he accompanied the army as envoy extraordinary to the Rocky Mountain Indians on one of the longest marches ever made, covering over fifteen thousand miles.   I believe he finally died in his self-imposed service of attempting to spread Christianity among these wild people.

In 1847 occurred the first outbreak of the Oregon Indians against the whites. A party of emigrants, while passing through the Cayuse country, were attacked by the mountain fever, a disease brought on by the extremes of temperature that prevail in the mountainous regions of the West. Then the measles attacked the Indian children, soon spreading among the older people. It was in the winter season, and the Indians, ignorant and neglectful of advice, took no adequate measures to combat the disease. They noticed, however, that the whites recovered, while many of the Indians died. In addition to this the United States Government had promised to pay the Indians for their lands, but failed to keep the contract. The Indians accordingly became sullen, discontented, and finally turbulent. They thought that the whites were responsible for the death of so many of their number—an idea that was encouraged among them by some half-breeds and other unscrupulous persons.

The consequence was that the person who had charge of the Protestant Mission, a devoted man who had long served the Indians with unflagging zeal, was one night called to his door and killed by two Indians, armed with tomahawks. A tumult was precipitated by this act, and a general uprising took place, in which all of the whites attached to the Mission were slain. In this slaughter none of the atrocities usually perpetrated by Indians when inflamed by passion were wanting. The massacre lasted for days, very few of the whites escaping. Even some of the Indians who had shared the hospitality of the Mission and received its assistance, were among the most bloodthirsty of the murderers. Some of the white women were taken captive, and the horrors to which they were subjected cannot be written. Some of those who survived captivity never recovered their reason.

One of the notable features of this massacre was the fact that neither religion nor civilization had up to that time, a controlling influence on the Indian character. Some of them were "friendly," or "good Indians," having been for years regarded as sincere Christian converts. But, no sooner was the slaughter begun than, like wolves at the smell of blood, all their innate savagery was aroused, when they outdid their unconverted brethren in deeds of violence and butchery. It is but just to say, for the honor of human nature, that a few of these Indians exhibited humane instincts, and did what they could to protect the defenseless whites. Especially praiseworthy was the action of the chief of the Spokanes, who cared for those who sought his protection and sent them away in safety the following spring.

An expedition was fitted out to rescue the captives, who would doubtless have been murdered if the Indians had been hard pressed or defeated; but Mr. Ogden, of the Hudson Bay Fur Company, had in the meantime effected their release. The prisoners numbered many women and children. How near they were to death may be realized from the fact that when a messenger from Mr. McBean, the agent, arrived at the Cayuse encampment the Indian women—always the most fiendish in torturing prisoners—were assembled with knives to kill the captives. A threat from the messenger saved them. It must be admitted that the Cayuses committed these acts of atrocity under the idea of grievous wrongs, real or imaginary. They had despaired of ever getting justice from the whites.

Meantime a military expedition had been sent to punish the Cayuses, and, as usual in such cases, the innocent were killed in punishing the guilty. An Indian was shot wherever he was seen, simply because he was an Indian. This precipitated the Cayuse war. Five hundred volunteers marched from the Willamette Valley against the Cayuses, and the latter met them in about equal numbers. An Indian battle followed. The savages fought from behind trees, and other obstacles, but the volunteers, all frontiersmen, beat the Indians at their own tactics. The Palooses, who occupied neutral territory between the Spokanes, the Cayuses, and the Nez Percés, joined in the war against the whites. The result was that the lands of the Indians were confiscated, because the latter did not surrender the murderers of the whites.

SIOUX CAMP ON THE YELLOWSTONE RIVER.

CHAPTER XXXVIII.

THE GREAT INDIAN NATIONS.

Their Marked Characteristics and Radically Different Languages—The Great Algonquin Family—Their Widely Separated Tribes—Names of the Different Tribes—The Apalachees or Mobiles, Often Called the Southern Indians—Names of the Tribes—The Athabaskees—Names of the Tribes—The Lacotah or Sioux—Names of Tribes—The Shoshone Nation—Names of Tribes Constituting this Nation—The Sahaptin Family and its Tribes—The Salish Family—The Chinooks—The Haidahs—The California Tribes—The Pueblos—The Columbian Group—Names of Tribes—The Pawnees—Their Obscure Origin—The Miscellaneous Tribes, of whose Origin Little or Nothing is Known.

THE Indians of North America were divided into a number of great nations or families, each possessing marked characteristics, and speaking radically different languages.

Nearly all tribes, wherever located, could be traced to one of these nations; not that they possessed written records, or had reliable traditions concerning their origin, but because the characteristics and customs of each of the great nations were different.

The resemblance of members of the same family to one another was so marked among all, that their origin could be traced by their peculiarities or personal appearance, even if it were not betrayed by their language or dialects.

Some of the tribes of the different nations became widely separated, but so indelibly marked were they, that to one knowing Indian character and general outline, their origin could be readily told.

WOODEN LANCE
HEAD.

THE ALGONQUIN.

Among the largest and most widely spread of these nations was the Algonquin. They were first found along the St. Lawrence River, and afterward throughout the West.

They were divided into a great number of tribes. These differed greatly in characteristics and customs, some being fierce and warlike, others mild and inoffensive; some being nomadic, living by the chase; others remaining stationary. Some of the tribes of this nation were the best warriors in the great West. This is notably true of the Blackfeet, Bloods, Piegans, Crees and the Northern and Southern Cheyennes. To this nation belonged the following tribes:

Piegans,	Blackfeet,	Illinois,
Bloods,	Chippewas,	Piankashaws,
Gros Ventres of the Prairie,	Sacs and Foxes,	Kickapoos,
Kaskasias,	Ottawas,	Crees (or Abbitibi),
Keeches,	Pottowatomies,	Mohicans (or Mohegans),
Cheyennes (Northern),	Menomonees,	Abenaki,
Cheyennes (Southern),	Miamis,	Michigamis,
Lenni Lenapes,	Peorias,	Tamaronas,
Shawnees,	Wampumnaogs,	Cahokias,

New England tribes, etc.

THE APPALACHEES, OR MOBILES, SOMETIMES CALLED THE SOUTHERN INDIANS.

Another of the great Indian nations was the Appalachees.

Their original home embraced the country bounded by the Mississippi and Ohio Rivers, and from the shores of the Gulf of Mexico to the Atlantic Ocean. In the early history of our country they caused the settlers much trouble.

During the Revolutionary War some of them allied themselves with the British, fighting against the Americans. In early days some of their handiwork was skilfully executed. Specimens of Jasper, Quartz and Chalcedony cut by them are fine. This is the only nation of Indians that has increased in numbers during this century. To this family the following tribes belong:

Alabamians,	Choctaws,	Creeks,	Muscogees,
Chickasaws,	Congies,	Natchez,	Seminoles,

Cherokees.

Some of the tribes of this family who lived along the Gulf, have long been extinct, leaving no trace of themselves.

THE ATHABASKAN.

Another of the great nations of Indians, was the Athabaskan. Their original home extended from Hudson's Bay to the Pacific Ocean, on the north to the great Slave Lake, and on the south to the southern portion of the United States. Some of the tribes were found along the Pacific, from Cook's Inlet to Oregon. Other tribes occupied portions of Arizona, New Mexico, Texas and the northern portion of Old Mexico. This nation had a language of its own, but the dialects of some of the widely separated tribes differed markedly.

All the tribes, whether located in the extreme north, or the almost tropical climate of Arizona, or the mild climate of California, bore unmistakable evidence of their origin.

In stature those of the north were tall and lithe, those of the south were short but strongly formed. The tribes of this family differed greatly in intelligence. The Navajoes and Apaches, who lived in close proximity, are a striking example of this fact. The Nav-

TATTOOED WARRIOR—DECORATED BREECH CLOTH.

ajoes were mild, inoffensive, and lived in fixed habitations, cultivating the soil, raising animals, and producing some of the finest handiwork. They were monogamous, and universally kind to their females.

The Apaches were nomadic, of a low order of intelligence, savage, treacherous, brutal, and all that was bad.

Some of the northern tribes were gentle and peaceful when left undisturbed.

Other tribes of this family had peculiar superstitions, and believed that when the moon was in that phase that it presented the appearance of a man's face, that it was a deity, looking at them, reading their thoughts, and scanning their actions.

Should sickness visit them during this time, they believed it to be the work of the "man in the moon," and that they must make an offering to appease the offended deity. Other tribes believed in a multitude of deities, who watched them constantly; that when the deity on watch became tired or sleepy, another took its place. When in trouble all the members of the camp went through their mysterious rites to appease its anger. In doing this, both men and women were almost naked.

At times they awaited a rainstorm to make their medicine more effective.

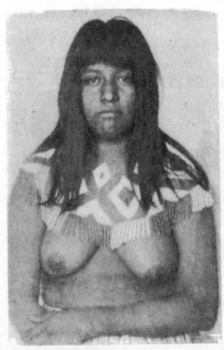

They would stand in the rain until it ceased, when they believed the penalty had been fully paid. To this nation belonged the following tribes:

Chippewayans,	Red Knives,
Horn Mountains,	Sheep Indians,
Beavers,	Sursees,
Dog-Ribs,	Brushwoods,
Hares,	Chins,
Rocky Mountains,	Mauvais Mondes,
Sikannis,	Apaches,
Kutchins,	Navajoes,
Inkaliks,	Lipans,
Taculli (or Carriers).	
Mojaves.	

MOJAVE WOMAN.

THE LACOTAH, DACOTAH, NADOWESIOUX, NADOESSI, AND LASTLY THE SIOUX.

The largest, most intelligent and warlike nation of wild Indians of this continent was the Sioux, or, as they called themselves, the Lacotah.

They had a language of their own.   It was rich in words, soft and pleasing to the ear, and could be more readily acquired than any other tongue of the aborigines of America.   There were no dialects among the tribes, of which there were a great many, all living within the hunting ground of the nation in harmony with each other.   In characteristics and customs they were the furthest advanced for Indians of all savage people of North America.   Their territory was so immense and produced such a diversity of natural food for man and beast, that both they and their animals lived well.   They were nomadic, polygamous, and some of the tribes very savage.   The following tribes belonged to this family:

Yanktons,	Osages,	Uncpapas,	Ogalalas,
Winnebagoes,	Otoes,	Two Kettles,	Tetons,
Assiniboines,	Bad Faces,	Poncas,	Missouris,
Mandans,	Omahas,	Minneconjoux,	Iowas,
Minitarees,	Sans Arcs,	Santees,	Kaws (or Kansas),
Crows,	Sissetons,	Brules,	Quaquas,
Gros Ventres,		Tribe-that-Don't-Eat-Dog, etc.	

THE SHOSHONEE NATION.

Another of the great Indian nations whose many tribes were scattered over the country from the Mississippi and Missouri Rivers, west to the Pacific, and from the boundary line between the United States and the British possessions on the north, and south into Mexico, was the Shoshone.   This nation had a language of its own, but the dialects of its widely scattered tribes differed greatly.   The Shoshones were the lowest in the order of intelligence and manner of living of any of the great families of the continent.   None of the tribes belonging to this nation rose above a low level, whether in intelligence, customs or property, so far as such a term can be applied to the effects of Indians.

They were for the most part filthy, miserable, thievish, treacherous and bloodthirsty.   To this nation belonged some of the lowest and most degraded people in the world.   Wherever found, and under what conditions soever, they had marked characteristics that plainly indicated their origin.   Their language was also of the poorest, both in vocabulary and flexibility of expression.

The Shoshones seemed to excel in nothing save in vice.   None even of the most intelligent tribes of this nation compared favorably with the most degraded tribes of some of the other nations.

In personal appearance all the various tribes of the Shoshones bore a strong resemblance to one another, from the Bannocks in the far north to the Co-

WARRIOR IN CEREMONIAL COSTUME—PREPARATORY TO A "BIG TALK."

manches in the extreme south. In stature the Shoshones were short, but of compact build. Their complexion was dark, and the characteristics and customs among all the different tribes were somewhat similar. Their possessions were few, and of small value, except among certain of the tribes, who stole or captured large numbers of horses. Their intelligence was stunted; they had no traditions extending back more than one or two generations. They cared little for the future, lived solely in the present, and only exerted themselves in supplying their daily material wants. Some of these tribes, when in war, were very fierce, and would go to any extreme to defeat their enemies. None of these people, no matter under what exigencies, were skilled in handiwork, or in the making or handling of boats. To this nation belong the following tribes:

Snakes,	Diggers,	Sampitches,	Kechi,
Bannocks,	Comanches,	Tosawees,	Kishnetela,
Utes,	Kiowas,	Cum Umhahs,	Kool-Salkara,
Pah-Utes,	Pah-Vants,	Wimmenuches,	Tukuarika,
Gosh-Utes,	Pah-Edes,	Chemehuevi,	Hokandikah.
Weber-Utes,	Washoes,	Cohuillo,	Tovarika.

THE SHAHAPTIN FAMILY.

The Shahaptin family occupied the territory lying between that of the Salish on the north and the Snakes on the south. They are tall, muscular, and well formed, especially the Nez Percés and the Walla Wallas. They were in every respect superior to the coast Indians. Their complexion was somewhat lighter than that of the surrounding tribes, and many of their young women were fairly good looking. They dressed in skins in winter, using for this purpose the hide of the buffalo, the elk and smaller animals. Their dress was profusely ornamented after Indian fashion. The men painted their faces and bodies. They wore their hair hanging loose over the shoulders. Their dwellings were constructed of poles, and covered with skins, matting or bark. The principal tribes of this family were:

Nez Perces,	Palooses,	Cayuses,	Wascoes,
Walla Wallas,	Waiilatpuans,	Umatillas,	Cascades,
Klikitats,	Molales,	Piscons,	Yakimas,
Shastas,	Scotans,	Coosas,	Alsias,
Klamaths,	Modocs,	Wal-pah-pio,	Warm Springs,
Catsops,	Tillmorocs,	Nehalins,	Cluckmans,
Calapoorias,	Rogues or Rascals, and numerous coast tribes.		

There were many other small tribes speaking the language and living in the territory of this nation.

THE SALISH FAMILY.

Another family or nation of Indians who had their home in the northwest was the Salish. Some of the tribes of this family differed greatly, and had very marked characteristics, notably the Flatheads, who flattened the heads of their children by compressing the head between two boards in the shape of the letter V. Another tribe, the Pend d'Oreilles, slit the ears, from which hung large and long pendants, made of different trinkets, sometimes reaching to the ground.

In these pendants were shells of various kinds. The women of some tribes, when a child was born, wound its legs and hips in a tight bandage in order to keep the legs straight, the hips small, to give the body the appearance of having broad shoulders. These they considered a mark of beauty. They spoke various dialects, but all derived from a common tongue.

They were not a warlike people, but when aroused were brave and skilful

warriors. To their prisoners of war they were fiendishly cruel, exercising every art and mode of ingenuity to torture their victims. In this the women were the worst. Among their methods of torture were burning the flesh with hot irons, cutting off the ears, cutting out the tongue, scooping out the eyes, pulling off the nails and other cruelties. In personal appearance they were tall and well formed, and their skins were somewhat lighter in color than the majority of Indians.

While this was a distinct family, having its own language, it was not a large one, its chief tribes being:

Salish,	Lakes,
Pend d'Oreilles,	Colvilles (or Skoyelpi),
Sans Puell,	Pisquows,
Spokanes,	Cœur d'Alênes (or Skit-
Okinagans,	shuish,
Flatheads proper,	Chaudieres,
Linkins,	Nespelum.

CHINOOKS.

Another of the great families of this continent was the Columbian group. Of these the principal was the Chinooks, the entire family being sometimes called by that name. The Chinooks had their home in the present State of Oregon, west of the Cascade Mountains, extending north of the Columbia River, and were divided into a number of tribes. Those living on the south side of the river differed markedly

UTE CHIEF—CEREMONIAL DRESS.

from those on the north, but all bore a common resemblance in appearance, language, characteristics and customs. They were small of stature, thick-set and muscular. In winter they dressed in skins, but during the heat of summer most of them went naked. Some of the women made a sort of garment from the fibre of cedar bark, or of strong grass, which was fastened around the waist, reaching to the knee. Their winter habitations were large, built of logs and thatched with bark. They lived largely on fish, there being an inexhaustible supply of salmon, which they caught. Their principal weapon was the bow and arrow, and some of the tribes made a shield or armor of the dried elk skin, which would resist an arrow. They were not a bloodthirsty people, and when they went to war did not perpetrate the cruelties so characteristic of the North American Indian in general. The captives taken during their wars were made slaves, and the families or descendants of these captives were also slaves. When one of the slaves died the body received no burial, being left on the ground to rot, or to be devoured by wild animals. They had medicine men, who were called in case of sickness. Should the patient not recover, the medicine men were sometimes killed by members of the family. There were some twenty distinct languages spoken in this group, and all were so peculiar that they could not be reduced to any form of writing, and I do not believe a white man was ever able to acquire any one. All the tribes were polygamous. When a young man bought a wife he took her to the lodge of his parents. When there were several sons, the family grew very large, but they all lived together in harmony. The master of the lodge was not always the oldest, but the most active member of the family. It was among these people that the custom of flattening the head of a child originated. Slaves were not allowed to flatten the head, as this custom was regarded as a badge of honor or distinction. The following tribes belonged to this family:

Chinooks proper,	Wilapah,	Calapoogas,
Kootenais,	Saiustklas,	Clackamas,
Kikwulit,	Katlawotsetts,	Molales.
Chilts,	Alseas,	Tlaquit.

Another family belonging to this group, but which had its own language, and was divided into a number of tribes, was the Haidah. The principal tribes were:

Haidah proper,	Massets,	Kaignaies,
Chimmesyans,	Nass, and about a dozen others.	

THE CALIFORNIA INDIANS.

One of the Indian families of the west was that known as the Californian group. They had no traditions concerning their origin or migrations, and it is difficult to classify them generally. They were divided into three somewhat distinctly marked portions, or sub-groups, namely, the northern, the central and the southern Californians. The home of these various tribes embraced the territory of the present State of California. They spoke a multitude of dialects, and differed widely from each other in a variety of ways. Those of the north were superior physically and mentally to those of the center and the south, some of the latter being among the most degraded type of humanity. Some of these people wore a scanty covering made of skins of the smaller animals, but in the warmer regions they went entirely naked. Both sexes among the various tribes tattooed their faces and bodies, and were fond of paint and the usual Indian ornamentation. Their habitations were of various types, from the log built, earth-covered hut to a mere burrow or hole in the ground. In general manners and customs they resembled the other Indians of the northwest, though there were many things peculiar to certain tribes. Some of the lower tribes could not be said to have marked characteristics or customs, and were human in nothing save in form.

This family was divided into the following tribes:

Northern Group.	Central Group.	Southern Group.
Tototins,	Mattoles,	Tulares,
Modocs,	Betunkes,	Yosemites,
Klamaths,	Loloncooks,	Cahuillos,
Euroes,	Fresnos,	Diegnos,
Tolemahs,	Pomos,	Cayotes,
Hoopahs,	Comachos,	New Rivers,
Shastas.	Kinklas.	San Luisienos.

MISCELLANEOUS TRIBES OF CALIFORNIA.

Yurok,	Karok,	Wishoska,
Wishosk,	Yuki,	Chimariko,
Wintun,	Patwin,	Maidu,
Achonrawi,	Washo,	Mutsun,
Miook,	Alamentke,	Talatin,
Yokut,	San Antonia,	Santa Barbara.

Many of these tribes were of different linguistic stock, there being as many as five to ten different languages spoken among them.

Some of the northern tribes were physically the equal of any of the Indians of the northwest, while some of the more southern were repulsive in appearance, and were inferior to the point of deformity.

PUEBLOS.

Another body of Indians were the Pueblos, or those tribes living in fixed habitations.   This was the name given by the early Spanish discoverers to all those Indians living in villages or towns, the word *pueblo* signifying town or village.   These people were not all of one stock, but were an aggre· gation of tribes, scattered throughout New Mexico and Arizona, and were partly civilized, as compared with their wilder nomadic neighbors.   Some of them claimed to be of Aztec, and others of northern origin, while many of them cannot be classified with any degree of certainty.   To this group belonged:

Pueblos Proper,	Papagos,	Pimas,	Maricopas,
Moquins,	Cosinos,	Yampais,	Cocopas,
	Zunis, and a few minor tribes.		

VARIOUS TRIBES.

West of the Mississippi and Sioux rivers, and from the British possessions on the north to Mexico on the south, were scattered a multitude of Indian tribes of whose origin little or nothing is known.   Each of these spoke its own language, and differed from the others in personal appearance, characteristics and customs.   One of the most important, in the order of numbers and intelligence, was the Pawnees.   It was claimed by some of the early frontiersmen that these people originally belonged to the Sioux.   This I do not believe, as their language bore no resemblance to that of the Sioux.   Their characteristics and customs were also different.   Their mode of cutting the hair was peculiar to themselves.   They had no reliable traditions as to their origin, and I must therefore class them with the tribes whose family origin is obscure or entirely unknown.   These people were divided into three tribes, namely:

Pawnees proper (or Pani),   Arickrees (sometimes called the Rees),
    Wichitas (or Pictured Pawnees, who tattooed themselves).

These tribes were also divided into various minor tribes.

There were other tribes or bodies of Indians scattered throughout the great West whose origin is obscure or unknown. All of these spoke a different language, had their own peculiar characteristics and customs, and each differed from the other in many noticeable ways.

Some were intelligent, others ignorant; none of these were numerous, consequently, as civilization encroached upon them they were compelled to remain stationary, and live in peace. Some of these tribes were:

Arapahoes,	Tawacamies,	Tonkaways,
Tawaccaras,	Caddoes,	Umpquas,
Ionies,	Keeches,	Wacoes.

There were also many other tribes that have long since disappeared, leaving no trace of themselves. This is especially true of tribes who lived all along the shores of the Gulf of Mexico.

TOM TOM AND ELKHORN SCRAPER.

CHAPTER XXXIX.

THE SUN DANCE OF THE SIOUX—THE GREATEST OF ALL INDIAN CERE-
MONIES—SELF-INFLICTED WOUNDS AND AGONIZING TORTURE—A
TERRIBLE ORDEAL.

The Greatest of all Indian Ceremonies— I find myself in Favor with the Indians and take
Advantage of it—Obtain Permission to Witness a Sun Dance—Assurance that I
should not be Molested—Precautionary Measures—An Animated Scene—A Moving
Mass of Animal Life—Preparations for the Dance—Selecting the Sun Pole—Awaiting the Rising of the Sun—Painted Warriors on their best Horses—A Wild Dash
around the Sun Pole—The Dance formally begun—Scenes in Camp during the First
Day—Wonderful Endurance—First Night of the Dance—Left Naked and Destitute
on the Prairie—Horrible Self-Torture—Slitting Open both Breasts—Inserting a
Lariat Through the Slits—A Dreadful Ordeal.

FACIAL PAINTING—BEAR SKIN CAP.

THE Sun Dance was not peculiar to any
one nation of Indians, but was held by
many nations under other names and in
various forms, and was usually given as
the result of a vow or solemn promise
made by the dancers who engaged in it.
One, for instance, would make a vow that
he would dance the sun dance, if some
member of his family who had been very
ill, recovered; another, after a fierce battle
in which he narrowly escaped being
captured or scalped by the enemy, would
say to his comrades, "I will dance the sun
dance because of my deliverance," while
another went through this terrible ordeal
for the sole purpose of exhibiting his courage and endurance. In this instance, the
person was generally a young man who
was anxious to gain the admiration of his
people. Another perhaps, used this method
of furthering his ambitious designs to become a chief by thus proving to his
tribe his bravery, endurance and contempt of physical pain. Hardly any
two participants, as a rule, engaged in the sun dance from exactly the same

motive.   Among some nations it partook somewhat of the nature of a religious ceremony; among others the motives of the dancers were known only to themselves.

At the time of which I write, it was exceedingly difficult for a white man to obtain permission to witness these savage rites.   I was fortunate in this respect, however, owing to the fact that I had on numerous occasions done friendly service for some of the Indian leaders with whom I had come in contact, and performed some acts of unexpected kindness toward them.

The old adage says the nearest way to a man's heart is down his throat; and I found this to be particularly true of the red men.   On several occasions I had given them a *wacpomanie* (feast), such as my means would allow me to prepare from the stores that the United States Government's Commissary Department supplied to the troops.   These feasts usually consisted of hard bread, bacon, peas, rice, hominy, coffee, etc., etc., and after being cooked by the troops such a meal was considered by the Indians a dinner fit for the gods, and gained for me great favor.

Furthermore, at the distribution of annuities to the Sioux during the time when Majors Twist and Loiree were the agents, these distributions were made in the bailiwick of Old Smoke's tribe (with whom I was well acquainted), at Bordeaux' ranch on the Platte River, near the Overland stage road some miles below the confluence of the Platte and Laramie rivers. Great dissatisfaction had prevailed among the Indians at that time in relation to the manner in which their annuities had been previously distributed to them by the agents of the Government.   In accordance with special instructions from Washington, Major Mackey, myself, and Mr. Charles E. Guerreu, an expert interpreter of the Sioux language, with a detachment of troops for protection, proceeded to this point on the day set for the distribution.   There were a great many Indians present, I should say not less than ten thousand.   Major Mackey and myself examined the articles intended for distribution to the different tribes, and the allowance to which each was entitled; we also had the original invoices in our possession to verify the correctness of the supplies.   The chief or head of each tribe then called out the names of the heads of the families for whom the supplies were intended, and the names were translated into their English equivalents by the interpreter.   Both Major Mackey and myself were determined that nothing should be left undone to ensure the delivery of everything contained in the invoices, and that the authorities at Washington should be fully apprised of the number of the recipients.   Many of the Indians expressed great satisfaction at the amount of stores received on this occasion.   This gained for me the reputation of being their friend and benefactor.

Knowing that the sun dance was to take place some few months later, and finding that I was in special favor with the Sioux, I then and there secured permission from them to witness this, the greatest of all Indian ceremonies. I had the assurance of several of their prominent chiefs and influential men that I should not be molested in any way while witnessing these savage rites. These pledges were carried out fully, although as a precautionary measure I had some troops present.

There was no stated time for holding a sun dance, and it was not of frequent occurrence. Whenever the Indians determined to perform the ceremony the announcement was heralded throughout the nation. The dance was given during the warm weather, usually in August or September, on a fixed date, which was designated by the number of nights in advance of it. For a long time previous to the celebration of the ceremony great preparations were made among the tribes who were to take part. Bands of warriors mounted on ponies, groups, and caravans bearing the old people, the food, and paraphernalia to be used on the occasion, moved from mountains and plains in every direction, for days previous to the meeting, all converging to the designated point of rendezvous.

This particular dance was held during the month of September, in the valley of the North Platte River. After a great many Indians had assembled in this beautiful place the scene was very animated. As far as the eye could reach the fertile, grassy plain around the large encampment was a moving mass of animal life. Horses and mules were everywhere picketed, or turned loose, all contentedly feeding on the luxuriant grass. Dogs were also in great abundance; although strange to each other and largely inbred with the wolves of the plains, they were not quarreling, but were ranging or lying about the camp, apparently taking no notice of each other. Many of the Indians, too, coming as they did from every quarter of their vast domain, were entire strangers to each other.

The appointed day arrived. All being in readiness, the first proceeding in the ceremony was to stake out a large circle from one hundred to one hundred and fifty feet in diameter, which was surrounded by a wall ten or twelve feet high, made of the skin coverings of lodges, the enclosure somewhat resembling a circus tent without a roof. In the center of this large enclosure was an inner circle from fifty to seventy-five feet in diameter, surrounded by rawhide ropes. This enclosure was set apart exclusively for the dancers, no one else being permitted to enter it during the ceremony.

Then followed the selection of the sun pole. This was made of the trunk of a straight tree, eight to twelve inches in diameter at the base, and from twenty-five to thirty-five feet high. The selection was made by one of the oldest women in the nation, who was especially chosen for the purpose. In this duty she was accompanied by a number of Indian maidens; as this ceremony was one of the most solemn rites known to the Indians, no female could think of joining the procession against whose virtue the slightest imputation could be cast. The bark was taken off, and the pole was securely set in the ground in the center of the dancers' enclosure. The pole had suspended from it the heads of buffaloes, skulls of bears, and other portions of animals which had been killed by some of the warriors about to participate in the dance. With the selection, preparation, and setting of the pole, the ceremonies of the first day ended.

Early on the following morning a number of old men repaired to an elevated spot in the immediate vicinity and remained there until the rising of the sun. As soon as the entire disk appeared about the horizon, these old men uttered wild yells, waved their hands, swayed their bodies, and made violent gesticulations. This was the signal to the vast throng that the anxiously awaited moment had arrived. A number of young warriors, mounted on their best horses, and fantastically painted in many colors, now dashed around the enclosure in which the pole had been placed, frantically shouting and wildly gesticulating after Indian fashion. A prayer of some kind was then offered by the old men to the newly arisen sun, when every person made a dash for the enclosure and commenced a weird chant. With this the dance was formally begun.

The dancers, eleven in number, and naked except the breech cloth, were gathered together by the master of ceremonies about one hundred and fifty yards from the tent, and, after being placed in Indian file, were thus marched into the inner enclosure, the master leading with uplifted hands, as if to command silence. Though passing through the great number of assembled Indians, the way was kept open, and absolute silence prevailed. Every one stood still, intently gazing on the dancers as they marched to the enclosure. The faces of the dancers wore a smile as they passed through the throng. After they had entered the ring the master of ceremonies made a short address to the sun and then to the sun pole. To the sun he said: "To-day we dance to you as the great giver of light and heat, who makes the snows melt, the grass and trees grow, and brings warmth to our bodies."

Having placed each in position around the sun pole, he began an address to the dancers in a loud voice, which, as interpreted by Mr. Guerreu, was substantially as follows: "To-day you dance to our Great Creator, as a sacred thank offering to him for his goodness in granting the requests you have asked. We all know your hearts are brave, and by this dance you will show that you are Lacotas, the bravest of all people. When you are through you will be loved by the Great Spirit, and be the pride of our own great people.''

Then turning to the assembled crowd he harangued them, crying out, "Lakotas, Lakotas, Lakotas, to-day you will witness the valor of our people! Those of you who have come from afar off can return, when this ordeal is over, and tell those who could not come of the strong hearts of our warriors. You can tell them of the valor of our braves. You can tell them that the prayers to our Great Creator have been heard, and will be answered.''

Turning to the musicians he indicated that everything was ready, whereupon they began a chant which did not exceed the compass of three or four notes, in which the entire assembly joined. At a given signal from the master of ceremonies the chant ceased, the musicians began to beat their tom-toms, and the dancers began to dance.

The spectators now divided into groups, or moved about at will. The young maidens and women formed in a circle outside the enclosure, and danced and skipped around it. They were encouraging by their songs and presence those within, who were about to undergo a fearful ordeal; stimulating them to sustained effort by the consciousness that their feats of endurance

ROCKY BEAR—SIOUX.

were winning the praise and admiration of the dusky beauties outside. The old women, gathered in groups, sat on the ground and talked and boasted of the prowess of those of their tribe or family that were undergoing this crucial test; while the old warriors from time to time sent encouraging yells and cries to the dancers. This was a part of the first day's proceedings. After this the dance by the young maidens and women around the enclosure ceased.

During the entire first day the Indians streamed back and forth to get a look through the opening of the enclosure at the animated scene within. The dancers jumped up and down on their toes, chanting their weird chants, their heads thrown back, and their faces turned toward the sun. As night came on, their heads were lowered to their natural position, but they continued dancing without interruption during the entire night, never for a moment ceasing the monotonous movement of their bodies, or relaxing from an erect position.

When the moon shone brightly no other light was required; otherwise fires were built from pine knots which lighted the enclosure. On this occasion small fires were built outside, around which both males and females sat, or stood, during the entire night. Here strangers became acquainted with each other, the young of both sexes admired each other's charms, and the old people told improbable stories of personal prowess, indulged in the tittle-tattle of the camp, and entertained themselves after Indian fashion generally.

Within the enclosure to the left as one entered sat the musicians, all fantastically painted and decorated, some with buffalo horns on their heads, others with small war bonnets, others with the head of a wolf, but all having headgear of some kind. The majority were naked to the waist. The dried flint hides of several large animals were stretched in full before them. Each musician had a strong stick in his hand with which he struck these hides in unison, and thus marked the time to which the dancers danced. Those who had a tom-tom beat it to the same measure. The musicians numbered from thirty to forty; and their chanting and beating of tom-toms and flint hides made a noise that was anything but grateful to the ear. On the right of the enclosure stood the friends and admirers of the dancers. On this side a passage was kept open all the time to permit the people to enter freely and witness the dance. Through this channel a constant stream of Indians passed in and out. They would enter, watch the dancers for a short time, and depart without saying a word.

The second day and night of the dance was a duplicate of the first, only that some of the musicians who had tired themselves out were replaced by others. After three days and nights of constant dancing in the manner I have described, during which time the dancers neither ate, drank, slept, nor smoked, the dancing was brought to an end about mid-day by the master of ceremonies directing the musicians to cease, whereupon the dancers also stopped.

All the Indians of the camp were now in the highest state of expectancy, for the dancers were known to possess a good supply of worldly goods, and this meant a harvest for the crowd. Short pieces of wood were now laid before the braves, each piece being marked in some way known to them.   A dancer took one of these pieces and threw it over the wall outside of the enclosure, saying, "Whoever gets this stick has such a horse" (naming the horse); seizing another stick and throwing it in the same manner, only in a different direction, he exclaimed, "Whoever gets this stick has such a horse" (naming it).   The throwing of these sticks continued until the dancer had given away all the property belonging to himself and family. This was continued by the other dancers until each one had given away his

BRAVES READY FOR THE WAR-PATH.

entire possessions.   For each article owned by the dancers, a stick was thrown by the owner.

In this way they disposed, in a short time, of their accumulations of years. They first started with their most valuable articles and continued until they finished with those of the least value.   The dancer could not tell who would come into possession of the article represented by the stick, for each was thrown in a different direction, and the Indians outside made a lively scramble for them.   After thus disposing of their property, both the dancers and their families were left destitute and almost naked, though after the dance was over such of the Indians who chose to take pity on them presented them with some articles of wearing apparel and camp equipage to enable them to start in life again.

After the dancers had disposed of their worldly wealth, the master of ceremonies stepped into the enclosure of the dancers and made a speech, inviting other warriors who had gone through the sun dance to enter the arena, naming each one who was to participate. After these had entered the circle, one of the prominent warriors stepped forward, knife in hand, and seizing a dancer, thrust the knife through the flesh of his breast to the bone, making two wounds, one where the knife entered, and the other where it came out. He then slit the breast up and down from four to six inches in length, and two to three inches in width. After both breasts were slit in this manner the warrior passed the end of a lariat rope through each wound leaving the rope trailing on the ground.

The next dancer was then seized by another one of the warriors, who had been invited into the circle. This warrior thrust his knife through the back of the dancer in the same manner, making terrible wounds, through which lariat ropes were passed. Each dancer was treated in a similar manner, some having the outside of the thighs slit and a rough piece of wood inserted through the gashes. One end of the lariat ropes which now dangled from the gaping wounds was then fastened to the sun-pole at a height of from five to ten feet from the ground. Against these lariat ropes the dancers threw themselves with terrific force, in their efforts to break away, until at last the ropes tore through the quivering flesh and set the victims free.

It required repeated efforts of the dancers to tear themselves loose from these ropes. One dancer, with a lariat rope in his back, to the end of which were fastened several buffalo heads, ran madly around the arena, dragging them after him. The skin of the back rarely ever tore out when dragging this weight.

One of the most surprising things revealed at these dances was the elasticity of human muscles and skin. The skin and muscles of the back would stretch six inches or more before the lariat broke through the flesh.

After this horrible torture had been continued for a couple of hours, the master of ceremonies gave a signal to stop; and, after haranguing the Indians present for a few minutes, the ceremony was declared at an end.

During this trying ordeal of voluntary torture the dancers never showed the slightest sign of pain or fear, but laughed a sickly laugh during the whole ceremony. They left the enclosure without congratulations of any kind, immediately sought their families and friends, and partook of food and drink for the first time since entering the arena.

The reader may naturally suppose that in many instances these tortured and mutilated people succumbed to the effects of this terrible ordeal. Such, however, was not the case. In endurance of pain the Indian was very different from his civilized brother. After going through these cruel rites the dancers never complained of their sufferings or exhibited the slightest feeling of discomfort, much less of pain. Any such demonstration would be deemed unworthy of a man who had at so severe a cost established his title to a brave. Sometimes representatives from most if not all of the tribes took part in these dances, and when they returned to their respective localities, with lacerated bodies but stout hearts, they were recognized as heroes for a time, and braves forever. No further deeds of daring or danger could, in Indian estimation, add to their renown, and no matter what happened to the brave afterward, he was never alluded to as lacking in physical courage. It was a great honor to have gone through the sun dance. It secured for the participant many tribal honors and privileges.

At one time the Government endeavored to prevent this ceremony, and I believe that Father De Smet called the attention of the authorities in Washington to its cruelty, and tried himself to prevent it, but both were unsuccessful.

Many people believe that the sun dance was given just prior to the departure of a war party, but this was not true; neither did it in any way resemble a gala day. It was a serious ceremony, and boisterous festivities were not indulged in during the performance.

At sunrise the following morning many of the families had their effects packed on their animals and travois and were ready to return from whence they came. Before the middle of the day the entire country was covered with caravans of the different tribes going in every direction, each returning to its own home.

During the entire ceremony the vast concourse of Indians quietly amused themselves in different ways. They formed into groups and feasted on their favorite meat, the dog. The young men assumed their most inviting and imposing manner, and formed the acquaintance of, and wooed young Indian girls from far-off portions of their territory. Many a young brave secured for himself, if not then, at some future time, the hand, if not the heart, of one of these dusky maidens.

Old women and young girls sat in groups amusing themselves after their own fashion. The men were dressed in their finest attire, and showed themselves to the best advantage to their neighbors. With their hair greased, done up in plaits, combed and smoothed until it shone like glass, the part in the middle freshly painted a bright carmine; their faces painted in all the colors of the rainbow; their moccasins, leggings, and robes of the newest and most elaborate pattern in their possession; holding their pipes, toma-hawks, or bows and arrows on their arms; in their hands bunches of sweet smelling grass, wild flowers, or the branches of some odoriferous tree, they would strut through the camp with such dignified pomp as only an Indian can assume, each one in his egotism believing himself to be the observed of all observers, and the most important personage of the entire assembly.

During the ceremony, no woman, old or young, did any work other than cooking and taking care of the animals. They believed that unnecessary work militated against the medicine of the dancers, and, according to their superstition, cause great injury to those going through this ordeal. During the evening and night the scenes all through the camp were picturesque and animated.

The Indians formed themselves in groups, dancing and singing to the noise of their tom-toms. At another place a warrior entertained his hearers with vulgar stories. Elsewhere a brave told his newly-made acquaint-ances of the many battles in which he had been engaged, of his hairbreadth escapes, his skill, and his wonderful deeds of daring.

In another spot a number of men sat in a circle on the ground, smoking their long pipes. Here they remained for hours smoking in perfect silence, presenting a very solemn, not to say doleful, appearance.

It is but natural to suppose that at these gatherings there was more or less trading and bartering. Such was not the case. They came solely to witness the dance or to join in its rites. Whatever amusements they had during this time were of a quiet nature. Even with the breaking up of the camp and starting of the different tribes for their homes, they did not engage in any traffic whatever; each tribe returned from whence it came in a grave, dignified, and silent manner.

Catlin states, in substance, that a most cruel ceremonial dance was occa-sionally performed by the Mandans immediately after undergoing the terri-ble ordeal of the sun dance. Six or eight of them were led out of the dance lodge with buffalo skulls and other weights still hanging from the freshly-cut slits in their flesh and dragging on the ground. The dancers were naked, and the dance was performed in the presence of the whole assembly. Rude wreaths made of willow branches were held in the dancers' hands, connecting them in a circle. At a given signal the dancers circled around and around, yelping as loudly as their exhausted condition permitted. Weak from long fasting and loss of blood they were urged on by the spec-tators. Those who fell were immediately seized by the wrists and dragged around the circle, often with their faces in the dirt, until the weights hang-ing to their flesh were disengaged, which was often done by violently tearing the flesh out. Friends and relatives stood ready to minister to each fainting victim and restore him.

NOTE.—The last instance of the performance of the sun dance among the Indians took place at Havre, Mont., June 19, 1894, despite the Government's efforts to prevent it. This barbarous ceremony was witnessed by many white people. All the newspaper correspondents who were present described it in about the same way. I give literally that published in the New York *Sun :*

"HAVRE, MONT., June 19.—The Cree sun dance has just been concluded here, after being in progress for three days. Every sheriff in the State had been instructed to prevent the dance at any hazard, but there was no interference here. Three Indians were hung up by thongs thrust into slits in their breasts, and slashed by Little Eggs, the chief. All fainted before the ordeal was over.

" A young Indian had slits cut in his shoulders, and to the inserted thongs were tied four buffalo skulls, which he dragged after him. Eighty pieces of flesh were cut from his arm, to be kept as tokens."

INDIAN WOMAN—CLOAK DECORATED WITH ELK TEETH.

CHAPTER XL.

THE SCALP DANCE AND ITS SIGNIFICANCE—GHASTLY TROPHIES OF MASSA-
CRE AND WAR—THE WAR DANCE AND ITS OBJECT—GREWSOME
TRINKETS WORN.

The Scalp Dance—Treatment of Scalps—Scalp Poles—Description of the Dance—A Strange
Place to make Love—Courting an Indian Maiden—The Scalp Dance next in Importance to the Sun Dance—Excitement of the Dancers—Telling how the Scalp was
taken—Exhibition of Trophies—The Scalp the Unmistakable Evidence of having
killed an Enemy—Indian Braggarts—Notorious Liars—The War Dance—Its Object
—Organizing a War Party—Encouraging the Braves to Join—Praying for their Safe
Return—Feasting on Dogs—Prayers of the Old Women—The Medicine Dance—
What it was and why it was held—The Medicine Bag—Nations who used it—Mystery
of the Medicine Bag—Disinclination of Indians to talk about it—Grewsome Trikets
Worn—The Fire Dance—The Snake Dance.

AFTER the return of a war party with a goodly number of scalps, the
ghastly trophies were stretched inside of small wooden hoops and attached to
poles eight to ten feet in length.   At the appointed time the Indians, both
men and women, would assemble and sit or stand in circles.   The musicians
sat or stood by themselves, and vigorously beat their tom-toms to the noise
of which the dancers kept time.   The poles to which the scalps were attached
were held high in the air.   The dancers jumped up and down on their toes,
moving slightly to the right and left, and keeping together in a circle, while
chanting the praise of the valor and skill of the captors of these bloody trophies of massacre and war.   The dance was continued during the entire
night, and all present who cared to do so had an opportunity to join in it.

Ceremonial dancing in various forms was a prominent feature in Indian
life.   They were fond of amusement of this kind and indulged their taste
in this direction upon the slightest provocation, and with a fervor worthy of
a civilized devotee of the Terpsichorean art.

The scalp dance was not a religious ceremony, but was a dance of rejoicing and festivity to which all came and enjoyed themselves after Indian
fashion.   There was always a feast—generally a dog feast—and all kinds of
devices were adopted for the entertainment of those present.   If there was
ever love-making it was at the scalp dance.   Young women on these occasions separated themselves a short distance from their natural protectors, in

order to meet a young brave. Etiquette required that they should remain standing. The robes of the two might encircle both, and love-making thus be carried on, but always under the watchful eyes of the family of the girl.

The scalp dance was regarded by the Indians as one of their greatest festivities. It afforded the braves an opportunity to exhibit the evidence of their prowess, and to indulge to the fullest extent in self-laudation. The excitement produced among both dancers and spectators on these occasions only fell short of that witnessed at a sun dance. All who attended exhausted their strength in the ceremonies. The participators mimicked the manner in which they had slain and scalped their victims, and their bloodthirsty savage passions were again inflamed, as when in the midst of deadly conflict. Those who had taken no scalps boasted of the manner in which they intended to make up for their present misfortune in the next battle, or recounted deeds of blood and daring in which they had participated on previous occasions. They related to the spectators the cause of their failure, which they invariably attributed to the malign intervention of the Bad God. When a long period had elapsed since they encountered and scalped their enemies they contented themselves with bringing out old scalps and re-enacting the scenes of their capture. The participators in a scalp dance usually prepared a speech for the occasion, and each had a self-laudatory harangue or his excuse for failure at his tongue's end.

INDIAN GIRLS—SIOUX.

There was no ceremony preceding or succeeding a scalp dance. Its object was to attest the bravery of the warriors who had performed certain deeds of valor.   This attestation could be made only by a warrior exhibiting the scalp he had taken.   The ghastly trophy was, of course, proof positive that the brave who possessed it had slain an enemy, or was the first to strike a prostrate victim.   Should the scalp be that of a white person it redounded all the more to the glory of the slayer.

No one would believe that an Indian had killed his enemy unless he produced the scalp of his victim; this was one reason why such extraordinary pains were taken to secure this evidence of their valor.   Sometimes an Indian might have been defeated and driven from the field, in that case he could not scalp the slain.   Again, a warrior might receive a wound, and be carried off by his comrades, in order to prevent his falling into the hands of his adversaries and being scalped by them.   In such cases a warrior made all kinds of representations at a scalp dance as to what he had accomplished in such a battle.   But as Indians are notorious liars, these stories were regarded by all with a great deal of suspicion.

Another dance and one that was more frequently indulged in was the war dance.   Among all the different nations and tribes the war dance was common.   It was held during the time a war party was in course of preparation, for there was no military discipline whatever among the Indians, and war parties had to be made up of volunteers.   The war dance was held prior to the departure of, or immediately after the return of a war party.   If held before, it might last from two days to two or three weeks, according as the warriors and braves volunteered to go on the warpath.   There were no formal invitations to the war dances.   Both men and women congregated at a convenient spot in the camp where the dance was to be held, and all who cared to do so joined in the ceremony.   This was continued until a sufficent number of warriors had volunteered to make a war party of the desired size. The merrymaking and festivities were continued during the afternoon and the greater part of the night.   Those who did not take part in the dance sat around in groups telling stories, or the warriors described what they intended to do when they met in battle.   The men remained on one side of the circle and the women on the other, each jumping up and down by themselves and all keeping time to the beat of the tom-tom.   The women were dressed in their best clothing, with a bunch of sweet-smelling grass, or holding a wild flower or the branch of a fragrant tree in their hands.   The men were gaily adorned but without robes or blankets.   Their faces were painted in stripes of various colors, and their bodies were painted in the same colors, though with much broader stripes.   Their hair was neatly dressed, and in every way they assumed their most attractive appearance.   Both men and women held in their hands poles to which scalps were attached.   They gave voice to howls and yells, and told each other of the valor of the braves that belonged to their families, now about to go to war, and of their ability to defeat all whom they met. Everything was done to induce the young warriors to join the party and conduct themselves as braves during the battles they might engage in.

During these dances the chief or leader who was to guide the party after it set out gave several feasts, one or two of which were dog feasts. In giving these feasts the leader hoped to gain the good will and obedience of his warriors. When the war party was completed and ready to start, those who remained behind sang songs to encourage the departing braves, and made prayers to the Great Spirit for their safe return. On these occasions the old women were loud in their lamentations, not only for warriors who had been killed in battle on former occasions, but also for those who might lose their lives while on this expedition.

Among some nations and tribes a dance called the medicine dance was indulged in at irregular intervals. In the majority of cases the medicine dance was a dance of superstition, and was held for the purpose of attracting some imaginary power.

Among the Sioux the medicine dance did not differ materially from the war dance, except that there were no scalps exhibited. It more nearly resembled a supplication to the Great Spirit, beseeching him to grant extraordinary powers. At some of these dances great numbers of Indians congregated, at others there were but few. Occasionally a brave who was ambitious to become a medicine man would go through strange manœuvres and violent bodily contortions, making wild gestures with his hands and arms, to attract the supposed medicine to him; using his best endeavors to make the spectators believe that he had been endowed by the Great Spirit, the sun, the moon, or something else, with superhuman powers. After this he might claim to be a medicine man. When but few Indians were present the dance was of short duration. When there were many it frequently lasted from one to two days, at which time nearly all joined in a prayer to the Great Spirit to bestow upon them some special favor.

Among other nations and tribes the medicine dance was conducted in other ways. Among the Blackfeet it was the dance of a few braves who desired to be known as medicine men. They congregated at a certain place at a fixed time, being naked, except for the breech cloth. They first blackened their faces and bodies, and went through the most violent contortions, gesticulating in the most absurd manner with their hands and arms, making themselves look as hideous and as much unlike human beings as possible. In this manner they sought to attract the medicine to them, and to appear to those witnessing the performance as though they were receiving mysterious powers from some unknown source that would enable them to perform miracles in keeping away or curing disease.

At the medicine dance of the Comanches a large number of them gathered on a fixed day at a certain place, each one having a small medicine bag. The dance was begun in the afternoon, and was continued late into the night. The dancers sought to draw the medicine or power from some unknown

ON THE WAR-PATH.

source to their medicine bags, which were carried away by them after the charm was believed to have entered.

All who had medicine bags danced the medicine dance; firmly believing that the medicine would enter the bags during the dance.

Often medicine dances were continued uninterruptedly for days, or until such time as the dancers believed the charm to have taken effect.

The Cheyennes had no hesitancy in speaking of the medicine bag or exhibiting it, but I do not believe they ever told what it contained. Some others had medicine charms or totems which they carried with them, or kept in their habitations, all firmly believing in their efficacy.

Many other tribes and nations had various medicine totems; some carried about their persons portions of the bodies of brave warriors whom they had slain in battle. This often consisted of bones of the fingers, toes, or the ears; charms of this nature were not hidden, but were worn conspicuously. War implements taken from the beaten enemy were also constantly carried by them, as they believed them to be very "good medicine," bears' claws and teeth were also considered particularly good luck; this is one reason why there were so many bears' claw and teeth necklaces worn among all the Indians of the West.

Some few tribes held fire dances, the object of which was known only to themselves.   First a large amount of dry wood was placed in a pile, then set on fire, and when the heat was the most intense, naked men rushed to the burning pile, and, lighting the dry bark or sticks each held in their hands

FIRE DANCE.

began skipping around the fire, yelling like demons. The dancers burning each other's bodies with their lighted torches; often the burns left great scars on the bodies of those so burned. This dance was always held during dark nights, and was continued until those going through this ceremony were completely exhausted. While it lasted the dance was very exciting, and all who witnessed, or engaged in it, were excited to wild frenzy. When it was over all disappeared in the darkness; silently going to their homes.

Some of the Moki Pueblo tribes in Arizona hold snake dances; these are religious ceremonies and supplications for rain.   The dance is a superstitious rite and usually lasts nine or ten days; during this time their priests—who direct the dance—enter the *estufas* or bake ovens and perform their mysterious rites away from the peering throng.   Clad in peculiar attires the dancers appear; their faces smeared with white clay, black lines and pigments made of charcoal or soot, are drawn and daubed in irregular places on the clay, which give the dancers a ghastly appearance; the dancers then gather in large numbers with snakes in their hands, mouths, and coiled about their necks, then shuffle about with the reptiles writhing and twisting in their efforts to free themselves.   At a signal, the priests begin shaking rattles and singing in low murmuring tones, which become louder and more weird, until at last all burst forth in fierce yells or war whoops.   This is continued until evening when the snake priests emerge from the ovens with bodies painted red, and faces blackened, with white lines drawn over the black, then all rush and seize what snakes they

SNAKE DANCERS—PUEBLOS.

can and run to the open country where the snakes are released, which terminates the weird ritual.   Some tribes of Pueblos hold sacred meat dances; for these, the chiefs select women to prepare sacraments of meat.   The women are aged wives and chosen because of their virtuous lives, but should one accept the position and her chastity be questioned and proved, she was stoned to death in the presence of the assemblage.

All of our Indians held sacred dances of some kind, after their own fashion.   The Arapahoes held their flat pipe dance, as they believed this pipe was the first thing made by the Creator.   The Gros Ventre held drum dances, claiming that the tom tom was the special gift of the Creator which enabled them to dance to him; and so on interminably.

If our wild Indians can be charged with any one universal trait, it is that of being ready and willing at all times to join in the dance, for there was no tribe which did not have dances, although many were distinctly tribal or local.

CHAPTER XLI.

ORIGIN OF THE NORTH AMERICAN INDIANS—WHERE DID THEY COME FROM
—INTERESTING THEORIES—A QUESTION NEVER SOLVED.

The Indians of North America—Ingenious Theories of their Origin—Claimed to be of
  Mongolian, African, and Hebrew Descent—Did they Descend from the Ten Lost
  Tribes of Israel?—Different Theories—Difference between the Indians and Hebrews,
  Chinamen, and Negroes—Curious Analogies—My Own Opinion—Why I think that
  the Indian was Placed here by our Great Creator—A Distinct Race—Entirely Unlike
  any other—Old-Man-Afraid-of-his-Horses' Logical Reasoning—Mountains and Rivers
  in the Moon—Did they cross Over from Asia by way of Bering's Straits?—The
  Mound Builders—Implements found in the Mounds—Their Art in Cutting Precious
  Stones—Exquisite Gold Images from their Graves—Conclusion as to the Origin of
  the Red Man.

MANY attempts have been made to explain the origin of the Indians of
North America, and no field of archæological research has been more prolific
in theories.   The fact that the New World was occupied by unknown races
of men was a revelation to the civilized nations of Europe.   When it was
known that the inhabitants were savages, and when some, in their native
barbarous costumes, were taken to Europe and exhibited as specimens of the
aboriginal people living here at that time, the question at once arose as to
their origin.   Much study and research has been given to this question, and
the problem is no nearer solution than when America was first discovered.

Many ingenious and plausible theories have been advanced on this subject.
One is that the Indians were descendants of the Mongolian race; another
that they were of African descent; and a third, which seems as plausible as
any, that they were the direct lineal descendants of the ten lost tribes of
Israel, who were carried away captive by the Assyrian king, as recorded in
the Old Testament, and ever after lost to history.

In support of the Chinese theory, the strongest point argued is the similarity in complexion and hair of the two peoples.   Both had skins of nearly
the same hue, prominent cheek bones, and coarse black hair, but here the
comparison ends.   No similarity can be traced in the language, characteristics and customs of the two races.   The Chinese have preserved, in written records, their national history, long antedating the time of Confucius
and the era of American discovery.   The Indians had no written language

and no records; and it is absurd to suppose that if people from China had come to this country by way of Bering Straits, that separate the two great continents, they would not, with their pronounced conservative characteristics, have maintained their old mode of life, clung to their religious belief and worship, and held in sacred memory their national traditions. They would unquestionably have followed up their observance of these things with the same zeal and pertinacity with which they are now retained in the Chinese Empire.

There is much less to be said in favor of the African descent theory. The ebon hue of the native full-blooded African is too many shades darker than that of the Indian to presuppose a possibility of descent from the same source. Besides, I have never seen or heard of, and I do not believe any one else has, a full-blooded Indian with kinks in his hair, that capillary peculiarity so distinctly African and so utterly unlike the long, straight, coarse hair of the American Indian. Again, the Indians almost invariably had sound teeth, which the negroes, as a class, do not have.

The theory that the Indians descended from the Hebrews is more plausible; for it cannot be denied that they were many points of resemblance between the aborigines of America and the early Israelites. So marked has been this similarity that it has arrested the attention of historians and ethnologists. There are very striking analogies between these races. For instance, some Indians, in certain ceremonies, marched under a rude ensign bearing the figure of an animal, which was selected as their distinguishing emblem, and no two tribes had the same symbol. This custom, though not universal, might have been all that remained among the Indians of a similar custom that prevailed among the Hebrews, and was handed down from their forefathers from time immemorial. Again, the Indians computed time the same as did the early Hebrews, reckoning it by moons. They calculated their travels in the same way, by days' journeys, and nights' sleeps. These analogies might be followed out at great length, but while they are curious they are by no means convincing.

After my varied experiences among many nations and tribes of Indians, and as the result of a great many conversations with the most intelligent men among them, and diligent studies on the subject, I assert without fear of logical contradiction that the North American Indian was placed on this continent, in his original entirety, by our great Creator, and that he is indigenous to this country as much so as are its animals and trees.

Our great Creator also provided subsistence for them, and the means of obtaining it. He covered this entire country with the most nutritious grasses, and placed on it large herds of antelope, elk, deer, bear, mountain

AN ARIKARA INDIAN—BELT DECORATED WITH BRASS BUTTONS—BEAR
CLAW NECKLACE.

Twenty Years Among Our Hostile Indians.

sheep, and millions of buffaloes. For this reason I again assert, all other theories to the contrary notwithstanding, that the North American Indian was placed here by his Maker.

The North American Indians look like North American Indians, and nothing else. I have never seen another race of people that resembled them in any way. Their high cheek bones, prominent noses, narrow heads, broad, strong jaws, beardless faces, hairless bodies, strong teeth, and erect forms, are peculiarities of the North American Indian alone.

Again there were more than three hundred distinct languages spoken among the aborigines of America. Each nation of Indians not only had its own language, but many customs uncommon to any other people in the world.

Their only religion was the worship of the Great Creator. Their theories of their origin extended only a short time back, and the conclusions they arrived at were somewhat logical. For example, on a bright moonlight night, while I was having a "talk" with Old-Man-Afraid-of-his-Horses, at which other Indians were present, the old chief turned to me, and through the interpreter said:

"They tell me there are mountains and rivers in the moon." I replied, "They say so." He said: "If there are mountains and rivers in the moon, there must be white men there." I asked him why he came to this conclusion. He replied, "Where there are mountains and rivers there must be beavers and otters, and where there are beavers and otters white men surely go." He arrived at this conclusion from the fact that for many years back the whites had trapped from the mouth to the source of almost every stream in his country, for beaver, otter, and other pelts. This, to my mind, seemed a logical conclusion.

The fallacy of the arguments adduced in favor of the theory that the North American Indian is a natural descendant of the lost tribes of Israel, or that he is of Mongolian or African origin, is also apparent from the fact that there is but one way by which he could reach the American continent. This was by Bering Straits. If the Indian followed this course it would have been impossible for him to have reached Ohio, where so many discoveries have recently been made, relating to the early mound builders, without leaving unmistakable evidences of his migration behind him. The mounds and ruins scattered from the Lakes to the Gulf abundantly testify that this continent has been the home of an indigenous race from time immemorial. More than ten thousand of these mounds have been found in the State of Ohio alone. Their antiquity is evidenced by the fact that the largest forest trees are found growing on them. The Indian races had no tradition concerning these mounds. Their origin is lost in the mists of antiquity, and they stand

as enduring testimony to the existence of the red man on this continent cen
turies before the white man touched these shores.

In many of the States of the West and South, including Wisconsin, Michigan, Indiana, Tennessee, Kentucky, the Carolinas, Georgia, Florida, and
Alabama, we also find relics of various nations of Indians, sometimes in
mounds, sometimes overturned by the plow, or washed to the surface by
rains. All these show that the Indians, from a remote period, possessed
the art of making articles necessary for procuring their food and material for
their clothing.

In nearly all of these mounds are found pipes of various designs and
forms, and wrought of different materials. The most of these are made of
stone or clay. It is highly probable that other kinds of material were also
used; but so ancient are these ruins that the more perishable materials have
long ago crumbled to dust. Some of the Indians living on the coast of Lake
Superior made pipes of copper by pounding the metal into the desired shape
in its raw state. Nowhere west of the Missouri River, save in a few places
in Missouri, have any mounds been discovered containing the bones and implements of the red man. Nor have I ever known of the discovery of mounds
left by the Indians in any part of the great plains of the West, North or
South. Nor have any remains of the articles and implements used by the
many nations that once inhabited that vast territory ever been brought to light.
These people, especially below the mouth of the Missouri River, did not
make use of the flint in making arrowheads, stone knives, and kindred
instruments. No specimens of pottery or articles of ornamentation, or implements of war or the chase, have been left by this primitive people west of
this great river. They seem to have been different in a variety of ways
from the people who inhabited the older States. The latter lived entirely by
the chase, have made no advancement in the mechanical arts, and had no
desire to learn, or to change or improve their condition.

It is incredible that these people could have come by the way of northeastern Asia and worked their way down to the South without leaving any
indications or signs of their progress. The mounds of the Mississippi valley,
and the proficiency attained by some Indians in mechanical arts, prove
conclusively that they occupied the North American Continent at a very
remote period. Had they come by Bering Straits they would undoubtedly,
on their way south, have left some signs of their migration.

They had no beasts of burden previous to the discovery of America by
Columbus, and their migration would have been necessarily slow before that
time. Besides, the ruins and remains of prehistoric times abundantly prove
that this continent was occupied centuries ago by a stationary people; and

YOUNG KIOWA COUPLE IN FULL DRESS.

The young woman's suit has on it five hundred and fifty elk teeth; each tooth is worth from two to ten dollars, and as each elk has but six teeth which can be used for the purpose, it required ninety-two elk to supply this number. As the animals are becoming scarce, the teeth are becoming more valuable. The young man's buckskin suit is also rare and valuable. His hair is wrapped with otter fur cut in strips and bound with bead ornaments. In a short time clothing of this kind will be but a memory, as the material from which they are made is fast disappearing.

that this people did in due course of time push south is evidenced by their articles of use and ornamentation. Among them I have seen beads and even pearls, which had been taken from graves where they had lain for centuries, with holes in them that must have required the most delicate art to execute.

Some of their articles recently found show the existence of villages and camp life. As the race migrated toward the south they seem to have developed a higher stage of civilization, and to have advanced in the mechanical arts. The implements and articles they have left behind were better made, were more symmetrical in shape, and of finer material. I have seen articles exhumed from the graves of the Aztec Indians wrought in pure gold, and of exquisite workmanship, containing from three to five hundred dollars' worth of gold. They represented various ideas and were wrought in different forms, sometimes taking that of an imaginary animal. They were symbolic of the dead, with whom these ornaments were interred, and perhaps they referred to some deed of prowess, or personal or family trait. The grotesqueness of the designs in these trinkets never detracted from their skillful and cunning workmanship.

Passing to Mexico, we find the native races enjoying a rude civilization and skilled in many of the mechanical arts. The Aztec Indians, ages before the advent of the Spanish conqueror, had learned the use of metals and were proficient in extracting gold and silver from quartz. They were also highly skilled in cutting precious stones, and in the art of ornamentation and decoration. We find to-day specimens of quartz crystal cut by this primitive people of beautiful shapes and designs; and as quartz crystal is one of the most refractory minerals known to science, necessitating great patience and skill in cutting it, it must have required ages for these people to have attained so high a degree of proficiency in this line of handiwork.

It is equally improbable that the aboriginal races of America were the descendants of persons wafted across the Atlantic to the shores of the Western Hemisphere. The time necessary for their increase and migration, as well as the diversity of the native races, on both the American continents, disprove this theory. The same reasons show that it would have been impossible for the two American continents to have been peopled by the lost tribes of Israel within the period intervening between their disappearance and the discovery of America by Columbus.

For every argument in favor of the Old-World origin of the American aborigine, a dozen can be adduced to the contrary. He was characterized not so much by his resemblance to other races or portions of the human family, as by his marked difference from all of them.

The only logical conclusion, therefore, to my mind, is that the great Creator placed the Indian here, and surrounded him with everything necessary to his existence. I also assert that the animals of this country were placed here by our Creator in their entirety.

Except on the theory that they are indigenous to the soil, it is wholly im-

TYPICAL INDIAN ENCAMPMENT.

possible to explain the presence not only of the buffalo, but of nearly all other wild animals that once existed on the American Continent. If they were not here from the beginning, how could they have reached here?

If it be argued that the American continents were at some prehistoric period united to the Old World, the difficulty arises of explaining how it is that many of the animals of America are found nowhere else on the globe. Did they migrate to this continent *en masse*, leaving no trace behind them? Neither have any fossil remains of many of these animals been found in any other part of the world.   What more conclusive proof could be adduced that they are indigenous to this country?   But even admitting that they could have come by way of Bering Straits, how could they have subsisted during their migration to warmer latitudes, as these northern wastes were entirely devoid of vegetation?   And furthermore, even if they possessed an abundance of food they must have perished of cold.   How could the cloven-hoofed animals, including the buffalo, have crossed the ice?   It is almost impossible for animals of any kind to stand on ice, to say nothing of making a long journey across its glassy fields.   Many of the animals of Central and Southern America could not live an hour unsheltered and unwarmed in our northern latitudes.   The Rocky Mountain grizzly bear, for instance, is found only within a small area in the Rocky Mountain region, and nowhere else in all the world.   Hundreds of animals from the Arctic zone to Terra del Fuego might be enumerated that exist nowhere else on earth, and of which no trace or remains have ever been found save right here on this continent, their original home.

A FEW PUEBLO IDOLS.

CHAPTER XLII.

INDIAN MASSACRES AND BATTLES—THRILLING INCIDENTS OF FRONTIER LIFE—TRAGEDIES OF THE MOUNTAINS AND PLAINS.

Indian Warfare—Attacking Field Pieces with Tomahawks—Burial of Massacred Troops—Burial of Dead Warriors—The Fetterman Massacre—Reserving the Last Shot for Themselves—How Information about this Bloody Affair was Obtained—Firing the Station with Burning Arrows—Killing a Lurking Foe—Blowing the top of an Indian's Head off—Our Battle on Tongue River—A Desperate Charge—A Troopers' Grim Remark—A Fierce Indian Battle—Two able Leaders—How they described other Battles and Massacres.

TYPICAL INDIAN—BUCKSKIN SHIRT.

FROM the troopers' point of view, Indian warfare was very unsatisfactory. First it was always necessary for troops to travel long distances before the scene of action was reached; even then the troops arrived at the battle ground in an exhausted condition.

Traveling for days, weeks, and months, over dry and arid plains, through rugged mountains, in all kinds of weather, constantly changing water, with poor and insufficient food, broke not only the health, but the spirits of the soldiers. When the Indians made a stand the troops were compelled to fight after the red man's tactics, as well as obey the orders of the officers, which made it doubly severe for the white men.

Therefore Indian warfare was usually a one-sided battle.

They rarely attacked the whites until they felt sure of defeating them. They often hovered about a camp for weeks, remaining unseen in the vicinity,

waiting for an opportune moment to strike. Their favorite time for attacking was early in the morning, just at break of day. The red men mounted
their animals, riding in a circle around the besieged party, yelling at the
top of their voices, flaunting buffalo robes, firing arrows and guns, and doing
everything possible to stampede the animals. They seldom, if ever, exposed
themselves in an upright position when mounted. They would lie on the
side of their horses away from the party attacked, and fire over or under the
animals, thus using the latter as a shield. They rarely, if ever, took
chances in killing a party of whites, if they could possibly secure their animals without doing so, unless it was a foregone conclusion that they could
kill the whole party without much risk to themselves.

There have been many complete annihilations of troops at various times by
the Sioux, notably the Grattan massacre, on the North Platte.

Lieutenant Grattan was sent from Fort Laramie with a detachment of
soldiers and two brass field howitzers, twenty-four pounders, to this rendezvous of the Indians, with instructions to hold them in check. Upon their
arrival the troops were placed in position, and the guns double-shotted, but
through an error of judgment, or a mistake of some kind, one of the guns
was fired prematurely; whereupon the Indians, who greatly outnumbered
the troops, made a rush and massacred them to the last man, with their
tomahawks, knives, lances, and bows and arrows.

Their fear of the field pieces was so great that during the fight they
rushed in, striking a blow at the guns with their tomahawks, and instantly
ran away. After a while their fears were partly allayed, when they rushed
back, again attacking the gun carriages with tomahawks, viciously hacking
the wheels in their efforts to destroy them. These field pieces were at Fort
Laramie as late as 1866 or 1867, and still bore the marks of this attack;
some of the spokes of the wheels were almost cut through, the brass pieces
themselves bearing the marks of the tomahawks in many places.

The troops killed in this unfortunate engagement were subsequently buried
on the battle ground, just as they had fallen. They were interred in their
uniforms, as soldiers usually are buried after a battle, namely, by digging
a trench or large hole in the ground into which the bodies were thrown. In
this instance the trench or grave was dug deep and covered with large stones
to prevent wild animals from preying on the remains. The last time I
passed through this region, I visited the burial place of these unfortunate
men, and found it in a fair state of preservation. The locality was a forbid-
ding and barren stretch of country, with nothing to break the monotonous
stillness save the howling of wolves at night, and the mournful wailing of
the wind.

The Indians killed by the troops in this fight were also buried here. Their relatives or friends erected posts from ten to fifteen feet in height, and made scaffolds on them, upon which they placed the dead. Some of them were deposited in the few trees in the vicinity; the bodies were wrapped in the robes they had used during life; their saddles, lariats, and firearms were placed on the scaffolds beside them. A number of their best horses were killed under their resting places. For years afterward, relatives repaired to this spot and wailed most dismally, although they had probably never seen one of the deceased during life.

I may cite the massacre of the Collins party as an illustration. Lieutenant Caspar W. Collins's command numbered about eighty men, of whom forty

or fifty were cavalry and the rest teamsters. They encountered a large Indian war party at Platte Bridge and having allowed their fire to be drawn by their cunning foes, were all massacred. The Indians captured the stores and animals, then burned the wagons and outfit.

Warriors from the Uncpapa, Ogalala, and Minneconjou Sioux perpetrated this massacre. Fort Caspar stands near this place, and was named after the given name of this unfortunate young officer, because there was already a fort on Cache La Poudre River in Colorado bearing the name of Fort Collins.

APACHE WOMEN.

Lieutenant Collins was an officer of superior ability, highly educated and expert with his pencil, having made many drawings of the Indians, and the physical features of that country. He was brave to rashness, but impetuous, and lacked discretion. He allowed the wily savages to out-general him, and paid the penalty with the lives of himself and of his entire command. When found, his men were mutilated beyond description. They were stripped of their clothing and the bodies of all were penetrated by arrows, some having over twenty driven through them. Some, though not all, of the men were scalped, and all would have been had not the Indians been anxious to get as far away from the scene as possible, fearing the approach of a body of troops that they knew were in the vicinity. After setting fire to the wagons and securing all the animals, the savages made off to the north, taking their booty to the fastnesses of the Rocky Mountains. They were never punished for this outrage, for the Government at that time did not have sufficient troops in that vicinity to pursue and chastise them. Some of the animals of Lieutenant Collins's command were subsequently captured in our battle with the Indians on the Tongue River, thus showing that the Sioux had afterward been at war with the Cheyennes and Arapahoes, as there were no Sioux at the battle of Tongue River.

Another noted massacre was that which occurred at Fort Fetterman, on La Paralle Creek, in December, 1866, when Lieutenants Fetterman and Brown were in command, in which about one hundred persons, and these two officers, lost their lives. I was credibly informed by Indians who were in that bloody affair, that Lieutenants Fetterman and Brown, seeing that the day was lost, rather than fall into the hands of the Indians and be tortured to death, grasped each other's left hands, and with pistols in their right hands simultaneously blew out each other's brains. As every white person in this affray lost his life, the only means of obtaining information of the battle was from the Indians who participated in it. I do not doubt the truth of the story of the fate of these officers, however, for it was understood by every soldier, trapper, and mountaineer, who knew the habits of the wild Indians, that he should save the last shot for himself and take his own life rather than be captured.

Not so with the Indian, however. He fired his last shot at the enemy, then made a bold dash with his lance or other weapon, standing in a defiant attitude, as if saying: "Do your worst, I am ready to die."

Another massacre was that of Lieutenant John Brown and his command, at Brown Springs, a stream tributary to the Cheyenne River which prior to his massacre had no name. Here Lieutenant Brown, with his command, after a desperate battle, were annihilated. We were never quite able to learn who perpetrated this massacre, whether the Crows or Minneconjou Sioux.

I also recall the massacre of an entire party at Sage Run, a small stream west of the stage route crossing at North Platte, thirty-five miles from the mouth of Bridger's Pass. Here the station with its corral was attacked by Indians. After besieging the party for nearly a whole day, without making an impression upon them, the Indians fixed lighted rags to their arrows, firing them into the station. As it was built of wood it caught fire, compelling the inmates to leave the burning building, when the Indians killed them all.

Shortly after this affair I was sent to protect the stage route at that place. Just above the station a vicious band of Sioux attacked us, who gave me a hot time for several hours. I received an arrow in my knee during this battle, inflicting a severe and permanent injury. A snowstorm coming on enabled my command to withdraw, for which I was thankful, for we were greatly outnumbered, and defeat for us was sure.

Our campaign to the north, along the Powder River and into the Big Horn Mountains, under General Connor, resulted in the battle of Goose Creek. The troops, numbering some eight or nine hundred, with three or four pieces of mountain howitzers, traveled a long distance north to reach this place. Colonel Cole, with his command, was to have swept around from the Yellowstone, to make a junction somewhere about the Rosebud River with the troops under General Connor. The latter discovered a large Indian trail running up Goose Creek, and started in the evening to follow it. After riding the entire night we suddenly came to an Indian village about four o'clock in the morning. It was situated in a beautiful bend of the river, which was skirted with numerous trees and thick underbrush.

We were compelled to cross a deep ravine before we could get into the valley in which the village was located. General Connor ordered me with about two hundred cavalry to cross this ravine, and draw up in front of the village. He crossed the ravine a little later with his troops, bringing them into line in front on the edge of this ravine, which brought them at right angles with my command, or on my flank. When his bugle sounded the charge, we dashed into the village, tired and exhausted as we were, dealing death on every hand. It only required a minute to start up the sleeping warriors, who outnumbered us to such an extent that it was necessary to retreat a short distance; after rallying again, the general's bugle sounded the charge for the entire command.

We went into that village as I have never seen cavalry go before or since, and the fight was something terrific. For the first half or three-quarters of an hour we used one of our howitzers so rapidly that it became heated and useless. We drove the Indians out of their camp and across the river (in which many of them lost their lives), attacking them in the foothills of the mountains on the other side. We had the advantage until about eleven o'clock in the day, having them on the run; the troops were so exhausted by this time that they were scarcely able to do anything further, when we began to retreat.   The ground was covered with dead and wounded Indians. A guide named Antoine Ladeau, a Canadian Frenchman, was riding beside me.   Pointing to a heap on the ground that looked like some buffalo skins, he said: "Do you see that Indian lying under his robe, pretending to be dead?"

INDIAN TREE GRAVE.

Whereupon Ladeau rose in his stirrups, took aim with his carbine, and sent a bullet into the lurking foe.   The Indian jumped two or three feet from the ground after being shot, and fell a corpse, one of the troopers facetiously remarking, "Be quiet after this, please," this caused a grim smile.   Returning to the village, we set it on fire, burning three or four hundred lodges and contents, and capturing six or seven hundred horses and mules.

We had in this expedition a number of Omaha Indians.   While we were on the march they were constantly in front, looking for signs.   When the battle commenced they charged into the village, fighting Indian fashion, showing their savage instincts by killing everybody they met, men, women and children.   Many of the Omahas lost their lives in this battle, for when the Indians emerged from their lodges, and saw that we were accompanied by red men they directed their attack on the Omahas.

Soon after the beginning of our retreat, when both the Indian and our own lines were wavering and the ground was being contested step by step, the troops killed a warrior, who, falling from his horse, dropped two Indian children he had been carrying.   In retreating, the Indians left the children about halfway between the two lines, where they could not be reached by either party.   After a few minutes of severe fighting, they were both unintentionally killed either by the troops or the Indians.   It was a sad sight, but one of the unavoidable incidents of this kind of warfare.

While burning this encampment, we discovered some buffalo skins on the banks of the river piled up like cotton bales, over which lodge covers were drawn.   The wind blew the coverings off, exposing the heads of one or two Indians, who, I supposed were wounded, and had gone there to conceal themselves.   One of the Omaha Indians, seeing the head of a Cheyenne just above the bales of hides, knelt down, and taking deliberate aim with his rifle, shot off the top of the Cheyenne's head; whereupon out jumped two or three more warriors who were quickly despatched by the troops.   We continued to fire the village until about three or four o'clock in the afternoon, and then started for our base of supplies, a distance of about forty miles, on Tongue River.

Notwithstanding our desperate attack and fighting this was not a complete victory for us, for after eleven o'clock we were on the retreat, followed by the Indians, who fired upon us during the entire night.   We arrived at camp about seven o'clock the next morning, more dead than alive, having a number of captives, whom General Connor returned to their people.   Never have I seen troops undergo such hardships as we experienced during the forty hours of this march and battle.

In this engagement we encountered some of the allied Cheyennes, Arapahoes, and others, numbering from twenty-five hundred to three thousand, who had for a long time previous been committing exasperating depredations on emigrant trains, overland freight trains, and the stage line, murdering travelers and settlers, throughout the entire country from the South Platte to Bridger's Pass, a distance of some three hundred miles.   In these raids, they had captured large numbers of horses and mules, as well as arms, ammunition and general stores.

The Government, realizing the serious depredations committed by these miscreants, determined to strike them a blow they would not readily forget, and the expeditions under General Connor and Colonel Cole were organized for this purpose. Had Colonel Cole succeeded in making the junction where it was originally intended, the result of the battle might have been different. Unfortunately he lost all his animals about seventy-five miles from the point of junction, and came near losing his entire command. They would all undoubtedly have perished had not General Connor come to their rescue by sending them supplies.

The command when found presented a pitiable appearance, being nearly dead from starvation, hardship, lack of boots, clothing, and the necessaries of life. They had been compelled to eat the putrid flesh of horses and mules. Had the Indians come upon them while in this condition, they might have massacred the entire command.

Probably the fiercest battle that ever took place between the Indians within the memory of white men, was that fought between a war party of Crows and Sioux. As the warriors of both were brave, well mounted and equipped, the battle was to the death. They met in the Big Horn Mountains, near the headwaters of Clark's Fork of the Missouri River. There was about an equal number on each side. The Sioux were led by their chief, Old-Man-Afraid-of-his-Horses, the Crows by their noted chief, A-ra-poo-ash. The Sioux warriors, realizing that they were about to encounter their greatest enemy and most formidable foe, blackened their faces, which in the Indian sign language was equivalent to raising the black flag, announcing no quarter.

All the warriors were mounted as usual, and it was nothing more nor less than a series of cavalry charges, fierce, impetuous and deadly. The horses were not encumbered by saddles or bridles. A lariat secured by two half hitches around the lower jaw of each horse made up his equipment. But the daring Indian riders guided their war steeds with consummate skill, and under their control the horses made forward bounds and charges, and halted or wheeled, as the case might be, with lightning rapidity. The warriors were naked with the exception of a breech cloth; bows and arrows, lances and some firearms, which, latter, however, were very limited, were their only weapons.

The repeated charges were made with a terrific yell—a wild whoop on both sides, which could be heard a long distance. For a few moments the air was clouded with whizzing arrows, and the resounding clash of lances told the fierceness of the fight.

At the first onslaught of the battle many were killed and wounded on both sides. Each side then withdrew for a short distance. When they resumed hostilities they fought with strategy, the battle lasting all day. When night came on each side was willing to retire, and in the darkness they secured as many of their wounded as possible, remaining to make an observation of the situation the following morning. The loss in killed and wounded was very great, so much so that hostilities were not resumed. Each party claimed to their own people to have been victorious.

This is the substance of this battle, as given me by the Indians of both sides; some of them when describing it, gave the most glowing descriptions of how they had fought, and what they had accomplished.

KIOWA GIRL.
N. Y. Herald.

Battles of this kind were constant between nearly all our wild Indians except, perhaps, as to the numbers engaged and the ability of the leaders.

They engaged in conflicts with their neighbors, or distant tribes, on the slightest pretext; if they had none, then some old or imagined grudge was heralded through the tribe or tribes, when a war party was organized for the warpath.

The group of Algonquin Indians located west of the great lakes and east of the Rocky Mountains, along the boundary line between the United States and the British possessions, when first known to the white man, were alone estimated to have numbered eighty thousand souls; in less than twenty-five years they did not exceed fifty thousand, and during my time among them, no one claimed more than thirty thousand in all of the tribes mentioned.

That group of the Selish nation known as the Flatheads, which embraced the Pen d'Oreilles, Cœur de Alenes, and the Kootenai, located in the Bitter Root Valley and contiguous country, when first visited by pioneers, numbered, according to them, about fifteen thousand; when I last saw them they did not exceed one-half this number, but as they were not so warlike as some others, their decrease was not so rapid. There is no nation of red men in their savage state that has not greatly diminished in numbers from constant warfare between themselves since they were first known to the white man.

CHAPTER XLIII.

THE MASSACRE OF GENERAL CANBY BY THE MODOCS—CAPTAIN JACK AND SCAR-FACED CHARLIE—INDIAN TREACHERY—PUNISHMENT OF THE MURDERERS.

Wars between the Modocs and their Neighbors—Inexperienced Agents—Surprising Captain Jack's Camp—Fight between the Modocs and the Troops—Massacre of White Settlers by the Modocs—Avenging the Massacre—Thirty Soldiers Killed, and not an Indian Injured—The Peace Commission—General Canby Chosen—Sullen and Angry Indians—Schonochin—His Hatred of the Whites—Waiting for Revenge—Ben Wright's Inhuman Massacre of the Modocs—A Bloody Day—Scar-faced Charlie—His Friendship for the Whites—Treachery Suspected—Danger Ahead—The Indians Indicted for Murder—Captain Jack's Retreat to the Lava Beds—A Conference sought with him—Falling into a Trap—Going to the Meeting Unarmed—Massacre of General Canby and his Party—Capture and Punishment of the Murderers.

LARGE WAR BONNET.

THE Modocs occupied the territory east of the Cascade Mountains, and south of the boundary line between California and Oregon. They were a comparatively insignificant tribe, but acquired prominence some years ago by their war with the Government, and the massacre of General Canby.

Their country was about forty by sixty miles in extent, a most desolate and sterile region, covered with basaltic and volcanic rock. It contained no large game, but berries, edible roots, small game, wild fowl and fish were rather plentiful; on these the Modocs subsisted. The country to the north was occupied by the Klamath and Snake Indians. With these the Modocs were sometimes at war, and most of the tribes, previous to 1865, were at war with the whites. In that year a treaty was made with the Government by which a reservation was allotted to the Klamaths, Snakes, and Modocs. The Indians ceded nearly twenty thousand square miles of territory for seventeen thousand dollars.

A few of the Snakes, and a portion of the Modocs, accepted this treaty and moved to the reservation. After remaining there for over two years they found that the Government had failed to keep its promises, whereupon the Modocs claimed that they had not sold their lands at all; that they were good lands for fishing and hunting, and intimated that they intended to return to them. They claimed that the parties who sold these lands were unauthorized to do so; were only interlopers who were thrust forward by unscrupulous and irresponsible parties in order to secure possession of this territory; and having at length consented to go on a reservation they found themselves constantly annoyed and harassed by the Klamaths.

Having complained so bitterly of the difficulties of their position, Agent Knapp ordered them removed to another location where they might not be troubled by the Klamaths. But the Modocs were opposed to another removal, and stampeded without a sign or warning. They soon turned up in their old hunting ground, in the vicinity of Lost River, but made no trouble, wishing only to be left undisturbed. Soon afterward Agent Knapp, Superintendent Huntingdon, Dr. Mackey, and Mr. Applegate had a parley at their camp and sought to induce them to return to the reservation. After many talks, extending over ten days, the greater part of the tribe returned peaceably to the reservation, where blankets and provisions were issued to them, the same as to other reservation Indians. Here they remained quiet, giving no trouble and manifesting no signs of discontent, until the following spring, when the agent stopped issuing rations to them. Pressed by hunger, they left the reserve, and hunted over the country lying between Lost River and Yreka.

Once more they were induced to take a small reservation of about six miles square, exclusively to themselves, under promise of remaining at peace with the whites. Superintendent Meacham, who always acted honestly and for what he thought the best interests of the Indians, recommended this policy to the Government; but before it could be fully and successfully carried out, a change took place in the Oregon superintendency, and a new and inexperienced agent undertook to remove the Modocs to the Klamath reservation by military force.

The officer commanding the troops at the nearest military post was applied to by the superintendent to enforce his order. This officer, with thirty-five men, set out to surprise the Modocs. After a forced march of fifty-five miles the soldiers surrounded the Modocs' camp in the early morning, and summoned them to surrender. The Indians came out of their tepees, and upon learning the mission of the soldiers they generally agreed to obey the order, though under protest, saying that they did not want to fight with the whites. While this talk was going on, one of the Indians, Scar-faced Charlie, made some menacing demonstrations, whereupon the military officer in command ordered him arrested. A fight ensued in which four Indians were killed, and some soldiers lost their lives.

The Modocs made for the nearest white settlement, where they killed all the men and boys, but spared the women and young children. Intense excitement prevailed throughout that country following this murderous raid, and the settlers demanded that vengeance be wreaked on the murderers. A military expedition was sent to punish the Modocs. At the first attack thirty soldiers were killed, and as far as could be learned not a single Indian was either killed or wounded.

The Government then sent three peace commissioners to settle the question by inducing the Indians to accept a small reservation in the vicinity of Lost River. General Canby, who had command of the forces at the time, was invested with full power to settle the difficulty. He was a man of sound judgment, of long experience, and just in his acts toward all concerned. The commissioners, under instructions from Washington, were to confer with him before taking action looking to the final settlement of the affair.

The commissioners, after consulting with General Canby, proposed that the Indians remove to Angel Island, in San Francisco Bay, until a suitable reservation could be established for them in Arizona. The interview led to to no satisfactory results; although Captain Jack's speech on the occasion was pacific, it was evident that the Modocs were in an ugly mood. There were sixty-nine warriors present at this talk. Schonochin, one of the leaders of the tribe, was especially hostile, and threw every obstacle he could in the way of an amicable settlement. His hostility to the whites may be more readily understood when we recall the fact that he was the survivor of one of the most dastardly and cold-blooded massacres that white men ever perpetrated on the Indians. Some twenty years before, Ben Wright and his followers massacred in the most treacherous manner forty-one of a party of forty-six Modocs, who, under the promises of friendship and safety, he managed to get into his power. One of the five survivors was Schonochin, then a youth. He never forgot the scenes of that bloody day, and his hatred of the white man was ever afterward unquenchable. Many of those who were murdered were members of Schonochin's family, and he was determined, if possible, to avenge their death.

When the conference ended Scar-faced Charlie asked Commissioner

CHIEF SPOTTED TAIL'S GROUP OF TIPIS

Steele, the only commissioner present, and who acted for the entire commission, to sleep in his lodge, as he anticipated trouble.   The commissioner did so, and Charlie sat beside him all night.   Were it not for this action the commissioner would certainly have been killed.   In the morning another council was held, as the Indians were menacing and ugly.

Captain Jack wore a war bonnet, and Schonochin made a vicious speech. Captain Jack also made a war speech.   The Indians finally declared that if they were allowed to remain in the Lava Beds they would live in peace with the whites.   They proposed that Mr. Meacham and Mr. Applegate should meet them the next day and shake hands with them, in ratification of their renewed friendship.   The Indians, when they made this proposition, evidently contemplated treachery.

The local authorities of Oregon had in the meantime indicted the Indians for murder; and obstacles in the way of a settlement were precipitated by speculators and others who made money out of the troubles between the Indians and whites.

Commissioners Applegate and Steele resigned in disgust; the vacancies were filled by Mr. Roseborough of Yreka, at the suggestion of General Canby.   Rev. Mr. Thomas, Agent Dyer, and General Canby himself made up the new commissioners.   Captain Jack had in the meantime reached the Lava Beds, and feeling that he was secure would make no terms whatever. He promised to remain at peace if left undisturbed, but he would not consent to a change of location.

After many unsuccessful attempts to come to terms, Captain Jack sent word that he and three or four others desired to meet the commissioners at a spot near the lake, about three-quraters of a mile from the camp.   Frank Riddle, a white man who had an Indian woman for his wife, informed General Canby of the danger he was about to incur, as one of the Modocs had told Riddle's wife that they intended to kill General Canby and the commissioners.   Mr. Meacham, who had experience of Indian ways and wiles, was unwilling to go; but when General Canby and Dr. Thomas insisted, he accompanied them.   The party went to the conference unarmed.   The meeting took place in an open space, the talk for a time being peaceful and satisfactory.   Mr. Meacham anticipated danger and kept a close eye on the movements of the Indians.   After a time the latter grew haughty and insolent, and finally, at a signal from Captain Jack, an attack was made on the party.   Captain Jack himself shot down General Canby.   Mr. Meacham was the only member of the party who escaped, but he was badly wounded.

The Indians fled to the Lava Beds, an almost inaccessible spot.   They were followed by the troops, and compelled to surrender within a month.

Captain Jack and his associates were tried by a military commission, and were found guilty of murder.   Jack and three others were hanged at Fort Klamath for their crimes.   This massacre was only another instance of the white man's injustice and bungling in dealing with the Indian, and the Indian's innate treachery in dealing with the white man.

CHAPTER XLIV.

A FRONTIER TRAGEDY—GENERAL CUSTER'S LAST FIGHT—HIS DEATH, AND
THE ANNIHILATION OF HIS ENTIRE COMMAND—NARRATIVE OF RED
HORSE, A SIOUX CHIEF.

Custer's Annihilation—The Country alive with Hostile Indians—Who was Sitting Bull?—
An Indian Camp of Ten Thousand Men, Women, and Children—Striking the
Enemy—Chief Gall—An Able Indian Leader—The Battle of the Little Big Horn—
Custer's Fatal Mistake—A Desperate and Bloody Battle—Where was General
Custer?—Discovering the Bodies of the Slain—A Pile of Empty Cartridge Shells be-
side each Corpse—Coming to the Rescue—Burying the Dead—Appearance of the
Slain—Their Pained and Terrified Expressions—Rain-in-the-Face—His Vow to Cut
Out the Heart of Captain Thomas Custer—Sitting Bull a Great Liar, a Wily Old
Rascal—My Interview with Rain-in-the-Face—An Indian Account of the Battle by
Red Horse, a Sioux Chief.

GALL—CHIEF UNCPAPA SIOUX, AND LEADER OF
BATTLE OF LITTLE BIG HORN.

No frontier tragedy excited greater horror than the annihilation of General Custer and his command in the battle of the Little Big Horn, June 25, 1876. In this bloody battle two hundred and sixty-five officers and soldiers lost their lives, and fifty-two more were wounded.

The causes which led to this battle were substantially as follows: A large number of discontented Sioux had refused to be confined within a new reservation. Notice was accordingly served upon them by the Government that unless they moved to the reservation before January 1, 1876, they would be treated as hostiles. To this notice they paid no attention. These wild bands of Indians were influenced by Sitting Bull, an impostor, who never had more than sixty lodges on whom he could depend, and by Crazy Horse, who was an able leader. These Indians roamed over an almost unknown region comprising an area of nearly ninety thousand square miles. The hostile camps contained eight or ten separate bands, each having a chief of its own. No chief was endowed with supreme authority, but in this emergency Sitting Bull was accepted by many of the Indians as their leader. From five hundred to eight hundred warriors were the most the military authorities thought the hostiles could muster, but this proved a fatal mistake, as results subsequently showed; for when Custer met the enemy he found nearly ten thousand men, women, and children, and probably not less than two thousand five hundred warriors armed with Winchester rifles and other firearms, besides Indian boys who were armed with bows and arrows.

The campaign opened in the winter, but the troops were partially defeated, and it was not until spring that they resumed the offensive in three isolated columns, the first column under General Crook, the second under General Terry, including the entire Seventh United States Cavalry, commanded by General Custer, and the third column under General Gibbon.

It was believed by the authorities that either one of these columns could defeat the Indians. The result showed how utterly mistaken the Government was in its estimate of the enemy's numbers.

The first result was that General Crook's column encountered the enemy June 17, and was so badly defeated that it was practically out of the campaign.

On the 21st of June, Terry, with Gibbon's column from the east, which had by this time united with him, was on the south bank of the Yellowstone, at the mouth of the Rosebud. Up to this time not an Indian had been seen, nor recent signs of them. The troops were in good spirits, and the officers expressed the belief that they would find no Indians, and all were sanguine that they would return to their stations by the middle of August. General Terry therefore returned with his staff to the mouth of the Tongue River. General Custer, with the left wing, proceeded to the Little Big Horn River, on the 25th, where he found Indians and gave them battle on the following day.

The Sioux were commanded by Gall, who was chief of the Uncpapa Sioux. He was a man of more than ordinary natural force and intellect.

It was he who planned and directed the battle of the Little Big Horn with the consummate skill of an able and experienced general. Gall did not enter the battle personally, but remained at a distance, directing the movements of the warriors under their respective leaders, and the result proved his ability and sagacity as a commander of men, as well as an Indian tactician. On that day he had several able lieutenants, the principal of whom were Crazy Horse, Rain-in-the-Face, and several others less notable.

Rain-in-the-Face afterward told me that the presence of the troops had been suspected by the Indians for some days previous to the attack, and after learning that Custer had divided his command into two parts, one being left far in the rear to guard, care for, and bring up the pack-train (this was composed of four companies of the Seventh Cavalry under command of Captain Benteen), and that the other eight companies under Custer were advancing rapidly in the direction of the village, they prepared to meet the troops. The Indian scouts soon afterward reported to Gall that Custer had again divided his troops, the smaller portion going in the direction of the Uncpapa camps. This was Major Reno's command, consisting of three companies of the Seventh Cavalry. As he approached the Indian village the Indian skirmishers fell back a short distance, when Gall directed a large number of warriors to surround and attack this body of troops. Here a desperate encounter took place, the troops being compelled to retreat toward the river, when another stand was made, Reno dismounting his men. Trooper number four of each set of fours remained mounted, leading the horses of the other three, and in this way all the horses were taken into the brush. After dismounting, Reno formed his troops into three sides of a rectangle, keeping the space open toward the river and the brush where the horses were. Observing this, some of the Indians crossed the river, got into position from which they could shoot, and killed a number of the horses. One of the troopers reported the situation to Major Reno. As the troops were vastly outnumbered, and would have had no chance of escaping on foot, Major Reno ordered them to retire to the horses and remount. This they did with much difficulty, as during the retreat they had to maintain their lines to keep the red men from rushing in upon them. After reaching their horses, some remained on foot fighting until the others mounted, these latter then taking up the fight until all were mounted. Major Reno, seeing that they were virtually surrounded, gave orders to charge to the ford of the river, which was a short distance away, and cross it. Here took place a desperate hand-to-hand encounter with the pursuing savages, Lieutenant McIntosh being pulled from his horse and cut to pieces. While crossing the river some of the troops were drowned. The opposite bank was steep, and the only way out was through a gap that afforded passage for but one man at a time. The Indians, seeing the helpless position of the troops, posted themselves along the bank, firing into them, killing and wounding many. After crossing, Reno led the troops to the hills a short distance away. Here they prepared to resist an attack. Meantime, Captain Benteen came up with his command and pack-train, and joined Reno. Shortly afterward a large portion of the Indians withdrew in the direction of the village. This move was by order of Gall, and was for the purpose of reinforcing the Indians who were engaged against Custer. The Indian chief also directed that a sufficient number of warriors should remain to prevent Reno's joining Custer. Reno was left in this situation for two or three hours, during which time he fortified his position. After this large numbers of Indians returned and renewed the attack, fighting the remainder of the day and far into the night. On the following morning they resumed the assault, which was continued until late in the evening, when the Indian scouts reported to Gall that a large body of troops were approaching. This was General Terry's command, and consisted of infantry, cavalry and artillery. On learning of the advance of this body of troops, the Indians immediately broke camp and started for the Canadian frontier.

But where was General Custer all this time? As not one of the troops that followed him escaped, it cannot be known from a white source just what did happen to him, and the brave soldiers who followed his lead in his last battle. While the Indians were engaged with Reno, Custer must have been in conflict with the larger body of warriors, for the reason that the village was so near, and the time that had elapsed in the fight with Reno so long, he must have reached the Indian camps at the other point and begun his disastrous battle. When Gall drew off the main body of the warriors who had been fighting Reno, to reinforce those engaged with Custer, the latter, seeing the great numbers that confronted him, must have retired to the top of the hill, where the battle was fought, and made his final stand there, as that was the method followed, whenever possible, in resisting the onslaught of the enemy in Indian warfare. After the arrival of this reinforcement Gall directed a simultaneous attack to be made on both sides of the troops, Rain-in-the-Face leading the attack on one side, and Crazy Horse on the other. The attack of the Indians was so fierce and overpowering that the troops did not have time to fortify their position, and the conformation of the battle ground was such, that there was no natural protection of which they could take immediate advantage. There could have been little or no shifting position, and the troops must have fought dismounted, as was evidenced by the fact that beside the body of each dead trooper were found many empty cartridge shells, thus showing that the troops had held the position originally occupied when the line of battle was formed. The position of the bodies when found, showed that the troops had maintained their military precision until the last man fell, and that they fought with unyielding determination.

The energy and skill with which they maintained the unequal conflict is attested by the fact that although outnumbered by at least ten to one, they killed over one-third more of the enemy than their own entire number, before death put an end to the conflict.

Of the arrival of relief for Reno's command, Captain Godfrey, who was in the battle, says :*

"About 9 : 30 A.M. a cloud of dust was observed several miles down the river. The assembly was sounded, the horses were placed in a protected situation, and camp-kettles and canteens were filled with water. An hour of suspense followed; but from the slow advance we concluded that they were our own troops. 'But whose command is it?' We looked in vain for a gray-horse troop. It could not be Custer; it must then be Crook; for, if it was Terry, Custer would be with him. Cheer after cheer was given for Crook. A white man, Harris, I think, soon came up with a note from General Terry, addressed to General Custer, dated June 26, stating that two of our Crow scouts had given information that our column had been whipped and nearly all had been killed; that he did not believe their story, but was coming with medical assistance. The scout said that he could not get to our lines the night before, as the Indians were on the alert. Very soon after this Lieutenant Bradley, Seventh Infantry, came into our lines, and asked where I was. Greeting most cordially my old friend, I immediately asked, 'Where is Custer?' He replied, 'I don't know, but I suppose he was killed, as we counted one hundred and ninety-seven dead bodies. I don't suppose any escaped.' We were simply dumfounded. This was the first intimation we had of his fate. It was hard to realize; it did seem impossible.

"General Terry and staff, and officers of General Gibbon's column soon after approached, and their coming was greeted with prolonged hearty cheers. The grave countenance of the General awed the men to silence. The officers assembled to meet their guests. There was scarcely a dry eye; hardly a word was spoken, but quivering of lips and hearty grasping of hands gave token of thankfulness for the relief and grief for the misfortune. . . .

"On the morning of the 28th we left our intrenchments to bury the dead of Custer's command. The morning was bright, and from the high bluffs we had a clear view of Custer's battlefield. We saw a large number of objects that looked like white boulders scattered over the field. Glasses were brought into requisition, and it was announced that the objects were dead bodies. Captain Weir exclaimed, 'Oh, how white they look!'

"All the bodies, except a few, were stripped of their clothing. According to my recollection nearly all were scalped or mutilated, but there was one notable exception, that of General Custer, whose face and expression were natural; he had been shot in the temple and in the left side. Many faces had a pained, almost terrified expression. It is said that Rain-in-the-Face,

* In *The Century.*

a Sioux warrior, has gloried that he had cut out and had eaten the heart and liver of one of the officers.   Other bodies were mutilated in a disgusting manner.   The bodies of Dr. Lord and Lieutenants Porter, Harrington, and Sturgis were not found, at least not recognized.   The clothing of Porter and Sturgis was found in the village, and showed that they had been killed.   We buried, according to my memoranda, two hundred and twelve bodies.   The killed of the entire command was two hundred and sixty-five, and of wounded we had fifty-two.''

Had not General Terry arrived just when he did, it is my belief that Major Reno and his command would have suffered Custer's fate, and that not a single white man would have lived to tell the tale.

Longfellow, in the accompanying poem on this battle, makes it appear that Sitting Bull led the warriors, and that Rain-in-the-Face killed General Custer.   As already stated, Sitting Bull was not present at all, and it was Captain Thomas W. Custer—General Custer's brother—whose heart Rain-in-the-Face is supposed to have cut out.

THE REVENGE OF RAIN–IN–THE–FACE.

In that desolate land and lone,
Where the Big Horn and Yellowstone
  Roar down their mountain path,
By their fires the Sioux Chiefs
Muttered their woes and griefs
  And the menace of their wrath.

" Revenge !" cried Rain-in-the-Face,
" Revenge upon all the race
  Of the White Chief with yellow hair !"
And the mountains dark and high
From their crags re-echoed the cry,
  Of his anger and despair.

In the meadow, spreading wide
By woodland and riverside
  The Indian village stood:
All was silent as a dream,
Save the rushing of the stream
  And the blue-jay in the wood.

In his war paint and his beads,
Like a bison among the reeds,
  In ambush the Sitting Bull
Lay with three thousand braves
Crouched in the clefts and caves,
  Savage, unmerciful!

Into the fatal snare
The White Chief with yellow hair
  And his three hundred men
Dashed headlong, sword in hand;
But of that gallant band
  Not one returned again.

The sudden darkness of death
Overwhelmed them like the breath
  And smoke of a furnace fire:
By the river's bank, and between
The rocks of the ravine
  They lay in their bloody attire.

But the foeman fled in the night,
And Rain-in-the-Face, in his flight,
  Uplifted high in air
As a ghastly trophy, bore
The brave heart, that beat no more,
  Of the White Chief with yellow hair.

Whose was the right and the wrong?
Sing it, O funeral song,
  With a voice that is full of tears,
And say that our broken faith
Wrought all this ruin and scathe,
  In the Year of a Hundred Years.

—Longfellow.

Rain-in-the-Face presented me with his photograph, and a printed copy of the foregoing, at the bottom of which he also wrote his name. He had a good supply of printed copies of this poem. It must not be inferred from the fact that Rain-in-the-Face wrote his name that he was an educated Indian. He had simply been taught to write his name mechanically, and that was all he could write. It was curious to note the surprising uniformity in his signatures, and the ease with which he wrote them. An expert in caligraphy could not detect the slightest difference in the crude formation of the letters. Here is a facsimile of his autograph written in my presence:

The reader may notice that the "i" in Rain is rounded, like half of the letter "n." This peculiarity was always present. He seemed to take a pride in writing his name, and repeated the operation over and over again without being asked. When I told him the name by which I was known among the Sioux, he uttered a grunt of recognition. I gave him a few trifling presents, such as I knew took the Indians' fancy, and then asked him to answer a few questions, which were substantially as follows: First, I asked him who Sitting Bull was, as I had never heard him prominently mentioned previous to the battle of the Little Big Horn. He replied that Sitting Bull was not a chief or a leader in any sense, and was not present at the battle; that he was a long distance from the conflict, and that he had gained notoriety among some white people by pretending to be the chief of the Sioux tribes then in hostility.

RAIN-IN-THE-FACE.

Sitting Bull was not an able Indian, as compared with some of the great Sioux chiefs, but being an impressive talker, a clever charlatan, and a great liar, he achieved influence among a small portion of his people for a short time during an emergency.

I asked Rain-in-the-Face if it were true that he had cut the heart out of General Custer "the white chief with yellow hair." He answered, "No!" but said that some time previous to the battle, Captain Tom Custer (the General's brother) had put him in the guard-house at Fort Abraham Lincoln, and treated him very harshly, and that he had at that time told some of the whites at the Fort that he would cut the heart out of him, if the opportunity ever presented itself. I then asked him if he had cut out the Captain's heart. To this question he made no response, but grew sullen and morose, refusing to answer any more questions for a time. Some of the white persons present who knew Indian character well, and spoke the Sioux language fluently, and had been much with Rain-in-the-Face, and with other Indian participators in the fight, told me that Rain-in-the-Face had accomplished his horrible threat, and had literally cut out Tom Custer's heart while he was yet alive. When the body was found, Captain Custer's heart had actually been cut out, but as no white man who entered the battle lived to tell of the terrible tragedy, we are compelled to take the fragmentary accounts of it, as told by the Indians, for what such stories are worth. It has even been said that Rain-in-the-Face, in his ferocity and thirst for vengeance, ate the heart, after tearing it from his victim's breast.

Never did the American trooper give a grander exhibition of his courage and fidelity than in the fatal battle of the Little Big Horn, when every man that followed Custer, from the General himself to the private soldier, went down fighting to the last. There were no wounded, no prisoners, no missing —all were killed.

The battle was in no wise an ambush, as has been erroneously stated; it was a fight in which the pursuers were attacked by the pursued with the usual result in Indian warfare, in which the troops were almost invariably outnumbered and defeated.

Had not General Custer in an ill-judged moment divided his command, the result might have been different. That he erred in this regard, no one who knows the character of Indian warfare doubts. Nor did this battle differ markedly from many other miscalled massacres in the history of our Indian wars, except by reason of the numbers engaged on both sides, and the fame General Custer had achieved.

One fact seems plain, namely, that Custer's scouts and guides in this

SITTING BULL—SIOUX.

campaign were of an inferior kind, as they did not keep the General advised of the presence or numbers of the enemy, and the dangers of the country in which he was operating. I cannot believe that a man of General Custer's military acumen and experience in Indian warfare would have divided his command if kept properly informed of his surroundings. So large a body of Indians as were in the vicinity, counting not less than two thousand lodges and probably not less than ten or twelve thousand souls, must have scoured the country for miles around in search of food for themselves and forage for their animals, and left signs everywhere of their presence and numbers that even an ordinary guide should have seen.   If Custer had had a Jim Bridger or a Jim Baker to guide his command, he never would have been trapped.

Although this was a great victory for the Indians, they won it at a terrible cost; for in addition to the large number of slain they left on the field, there must have been also a large number of wounded, many of them mor-

SITTING-BULL'S CABIN, AND THE PLACE OF HIS DEATH.

This cabin was built by the Government for Sitting Bull and his family. While resisting arrest he was killed in it by Bull-Head, an Indian Policeman.

tally, for their dead were strewn all along the route to the Canadian frontier. The Indians admit that they suffered terribly.   Not a tepee, not a family, but had to lament its slain or wounded.   Even Rain-in-the-Face, when I last saw him, was a living illustration that his people had paid dearly for their victory.   As the result of his wounds, one of his legs was stiff, and drawn up close to his body so that he could only move about on crutches and with much difficulty.

Dr. Charles E. McChesney, acting assistant surgeon United States Army, communicated to the Bureau of Ethnology at Washington a unique Indian account, both in carefully noted gesture signs and in pictographs, of the battle of the Little Big Horn.   These drawings were made, and the account which accompanied them was given by Red Horse, a Sioux chief, and a prominent actor in the battle.   His narrative, closely translated into simple English, is herewith given.   The drawings were made on rough manila paper, some of them with colored pencils.   Some of these drawings are presented in this volume, not only as specimens of Indian art, but as a contribution from the Indian standpoint to our knowledge of Custer's last fight. Here is the story of Red Horse:

"Five springs ago, I, with many Sioux Indians, took down and packed up our tipis [tepees] and moved from Cheyenne River to the Rosebud River, where we camped a few days; then took down and packed up our lodges and moved to the Little Big Horn River and pitched our lodges with the large camp of Sioux.

"The Sioux were camped on the Little Big Horn River as follows: The lodges of the Uncpapas were pitched highest up the river under a bluff. The Santee lodges were pitched next. The Ogalalas' lodges were pitched next. The Brule lodges were pitched next. The Minneconjoux lodges were pitched next. The Sans'-Arcs' lodges were pitched next. The Blackfeet lodges were pitched next. The Cheyenne lodges were pitched next. A few Arikara Indians were among the Sioux [being without lodges of their own]. Two-Kettles [a tribe of Sioux], among the other Sioux [without lodges].

"I was a Sioux chief in the council lodge. My lodge was pitched in the center of the camp. The day of the attack I and four women were a short distance from the camp digging wild turnips. Suddenly one of the women attracted my attention to a cloud of dust rising a short distance from camp. I soon saw that the soldiers were charging the camp. To the camp I and the women ran. When I arrived a person told me to hurry to the council lodge. The soldiers charged so quickly we could not talk [council]. We came out of the council lodge and talked in all directions. The Sioux mount horses, take guns, and go fight the soldiers. Women and children mount horses and go [meaning to get out of the way].

"Among the soldiers was an officer who rode a horse with four white feet. The Sioux have for a long time fought many brave men of different people, but the Sioux say this officer was the bravest man they had ever fought. I don't know whether this was General Custer or not. Many of the Sioux men that I hear talking tell me it was. I saw this officer in the fight many times, but did not see his body. It has been told me that he was killed by a Santee Indian, who took his horse. This officer wore a large-brimmed hat and a deerskin coat. This officer saved the lives of many soldiers by turning his horse and covering the retreat. Sioux say this officer was the bravest man they ever fought. I saw two officers looking alike, both having long yellowish hair.

"Before the attack the Sioux were camped on the Rosebud River. Sioux moved down a river running into the Little Big Horn River, crossed the Little Big Horn River, and camped on its west bank.

"This day [day of attack] a Sioux man started to go to Red Cloud agency, but when he had gone a short distance from camp, he saw a cloud of dust rising and turned back and said he thought a herd of buffalo was coming near the village.

"The day was hot.   In a short time the soldiers charged the camp.   [This was Major Reno's battalion of the Seventh Cavalry.]   The soldiers came on the trail made by the Sioux camp in moving, and crossed the Little Big Horn River above where the Sioux crossed, and attacked the lodges of the Uncpapas, farthest up the river.   The women and children ran down the Little Big Horn River a short distance into a ravine.   The soldiers set fire

BATTLE OF LITTLE BIG HORN—SIOUX LEAVING BATTLE GROUND—DRAWN BY RED HORSE—SIOUX.

to the lodges.   All the Sioux now charged the soldiers and drove them in confusion across the Little Big Horn River, which was very rapid, and several soldiers were drowned in it.   On a hill the soldiers stopped and the Sioux surrounded them.   A Sioux man came and said that a different party of soldiers had all the women and children prisoners.   Like a whirlwind the word went around, and the Sioux all heard it and left the soldiers on the hill and went quickly to save the women and children.

"From the hill that the soldiers were on to the place where the different soldiers [by this term Red Horse always means the battalion immediately commanded by General Custer, his mode of distinction being that they were a different body from that first encountered] were seen was level ground with the exception of a creek. Sioux thought the soldiers on the hill [*i.e.*, Reno's battalion] would charge them in rear, but when they did not the Sioux thought the soldiers on the hill were out of cartridges. As soon as we had killed all the different soldiers the Sioux all went back to kill the soldiers on the hill. All the Sioux watched around the hill until a Sioux man came and said many walking soldiers were coming near. The coming of the walking soldiers was the saving of the soldiers on the hill. Sioux cannot fight the walking soldiers [infantry] being afraid of them, so the Sioux left.

"The soldiers charged the Sioux camp about noon. The soldiers were divided, one party charging right into the camp. After driving these soldiers across the river, the Sioux charged the different soldiers [*i.e.*, Custer's] below, and drove them in confusion; these soldiers became foolish, many throwing away their guns and raising their hands, saying, 'Sioux, pity us; take us prisoners.' The Sioux did not take a single soldier prisoner, but killed all of them; none were left alive for even a few minutes. These different soldiers discharged their guns but little. I took a gun and two belts off two dead soldiers; out of one belt two cartridges were gone, out of the other five.

"The Sioux took the guns and cartridges off the dead soldiers and went to the hill on which the soldiers were, surrounded and fought them with the guns and cartridges of the dead soldiers. Had the soldiers not divided I think they would have killed many Sioux. The different soldiers [*i.e.*, Custer's battalion] that the Sioux killed made five brave stands. Once the Sioux charged right in the midst of the different soldiers and scattered them all, fighting among the soldiers hand to hand.

From the account given by Red Horse, it can readily be seen how unreliable any statements made by the Indians are, especially in relation to battles between the white and red men. As the mounds and slabs marking the graves where each trooper is buried—and they were interred where they fell—show to-day that they maintained their military formation, and also attest the bravery of each and every trooper that fell in the conflict, that "they threw their guns away and asked to be taken prisoners," as he states, is preposterous.

This battle has been the subject of much controversy and speculation between army officers, as well as writers, for the past twenty-five years; it has

DEAD SIOUX—DRAWN BY RED-HORSE SIOUX CHIEF,

Twenty Years Among Our Hostile Indians.   Page 378

been referred to as the most tragic and mysterious in the annals of our mili
tary history.

To an experienced Indian fighter there is little or no mystery surrounding
it; for the battle was fought
after the usual manner and
tactics of the red men. In all
the battles between the two
peoples during the four hundred years of American history, there are but few important victories to the credit of
the white race. The reasons
for this are fully stated in the
first chapters of this volume.

From the first settlement
of the country, warfare between the two peoples was
almost constant, and it was
not until after this fatal conflict that the Government
awoke to the situation, and
sent sufficient troops to combat the wily red men, when
and wherever found, that
they were finally subdued,
and after being defeated were
placed under proper control
and compelled to remain sta-

TYPICAL SIOUX.

tionary. Had this method been adopted by the proper authorities long
before, it would have been better for both races; certain it is that there
would not have been so great a sacrifice of life by both, especially that of
women and children.

Had the Indians been rounded up and their arms and horses taken away,
then properly housed, fed and clothed, they might have increased instead of
diminished in numbers; for the history of man shows that the progressive
increase and force out the weaker or lower races, while those who trust to
chance have little place in the struggle for existence with others who believe
in and conform to nature's laws.

CHAPTER XLV.

THE GREAT SIOUX MASSACRE—MIRACULOUS ESCAPES AND THRILLING
ADVENTURES—SUFFERINGS OF CAPTIVES.

Cause of the Massacre—War of Extermination decided upon by the Indians—They take
the Warpath—Their First Attack—Courage of a French Ferryman—His Heroic Death
—Killing of Fleeing Settlers—Hacked to Pieces with Knives—Children's Brains
Beaten Out—Burned Alive—Hung on Hooks—Sticks Driven through their Bodies—
Mutilation of the Dead—Roasting a Child Alive—Thrilling Escapes—Two Brothers
trying to Save a Sick Mother—The Settlers Rally for Defense—Holding White Prisoners—Their Extreme Suffering—Miraculous Escape of Two Brothers—Six Hundred
and Forty-four Settlers and Ninety-three Soldiers Slain.

WARRIOR, WITH GOVERNMENT MEDAL.

DURING the summer of 1863,
while our country was strain-
ing every energy in suppressing the war of the Rebellion,
there occurred in northern
Minnesota the bloodiest Indian
massacre in the history of the
North American Continent.

The Civil War at that time
absorbed the attention of the
people to the exclusion of
almost every other subject, and
the great Sioux massacre did
not make such an impression
on the public as it would had
it happened at any other time.
This massacre was distin-
guished, too, by its suddenness,
its extent, its dreadful results,
and the fact that it occurred
almost within the limits of
civilization.

A part of the Sioux had manifested a tendency to submit to the transform-
ing influences of civilization.   Churches and schools had been established in

some parts of their territory in Minnesota, and it looked as if this portion of the Sioux and their white neighbors would live thenceforth in peace.

A short time before, they had sold a large and valuable portion of their lands to the Government. They were to receive annuities, food, and necessary articles for their new mode of life, in payment for these lands. The Government kept faith with them in every respect; but the old story of robbery of the Indians by government agents, traders, and adventurers was repeated.

In this instance particularly, the robbery of the Indians was flagrant in the extreme. They were swindled on some occasions of every penny that was coming to them. In their ignorance they did not know how to seek redress; and starving men cannot afford to look for relief in a protracted or roundabout way.

They could no longer live by the chase, as civilization had driven the animals on which they subsisted far beyond their hunting grounds, and the money and rations the Government furnished them, for the most part, never reached their hands. Finally they were reduced to the necessity of living on their horses and dogs.

There were other causes which created dissatisfaction among the Sioux. Knowing that the whites were engaged in a war among themselves, wild stories were circulated among them about it. It was rumored that the armies of the Government had been destroyed; that Washington had been captured and the Great White Father taken prisoner. It was therefore natural for the Indians to suppose that they could regain their hunting ground by taking to the warpath and exterminating the whites.

Although the Indians had been in a sullen and discontented mood for some time, and rumors of danger had been afloat, the settlers believed themselves secure and took no precautions.

The outbreak occurred in a simple and unforeseen manner. A party of twenty young bucks started up the country a distance of some eighty miles to hunt. On their way a dispute arose among themselves, when some charged others with being afraid of the whites. To show that the imputation was undeserved, a few of the braves left the party and proceeded to kill several white settlers. The Sioux were asked to surrender the murderers. A great council of war was held, and the matter was debated at length. As the talk grew warm, Indian passions were aroused, and it was then and there determined to wage a war of extermination on the frontier settlers.

A number of braves, painted and accoutred for the warpath, proceeded to the dwelling of Little Crow, a semi-civilized chieftain, who spoke English, had been to Washington, knew the power of the whites, and was noted among his people for his eloquence and sound judgment.

Little Crow, was surprised at the turn affairs had taken, sought at first to dissuade the warriors from their purpose; but seeing that they were maddened and determined, and that refusal on his part would be dangerous, he suddenly arose and said: "I am with you."

The first attack was made on the Redwood Agency. The savages burst on the place unexpectedly and killed several white people. All who could escape fled in terror across the Minnesota River. The crossing was by a ferryboat, and was a slow and dangerous process, the fugitives being closely followed by a horde of infuriated savages.

The ferryman was a French Canadian, illiterate and ignorant, and seemingly incapable of doing anything higher than running his boat across the river. But in this supreme moment he proved himself a hero of the highest type. He carried the refugees across as they managed to escape to the landing, and returned, time and again, until all who were not killed had been taken to the other side.

On his last trip, the savages, maddened at the way in which he had rescued the people, fired a final shot at him and he dropped dead in his boat. He had saved over fifty people, most of them women and children, at the sacrifice of his own life.

Having finished at the agency, the Indians moved down the river, under the leadership of Cut Nose, killing twenty-five fleeing settlers on the way. The most fiendish acts of cruelty and atrocity were perpetrated. The victims in some instances were hacked to pieces; children were seized by the legs and their brains were beaten out against the wall; some were hung alive on hooks, with sticks driven through their legs, as the carcasses of slaughtered animals are suspended. The women were invariably ravished by the whole band, and then killed. The bodies of men and boys were mutilated in a manner that only fiendish ingenuity could devise. Children were fastened to doors and tables with nails driven through the hands and feet, while the savages amused themselves by throwing knives and tomahawks at them until they killed them. Sometimes houses were surrounded and the surprised inmates burned alive.

In one instance, the savages entered a settler's house where a woman was engaged in making bread. They split her head open with an axe, and then took the baby from the cradle and baked it in the oven until nearly dead, when its brains were beaten out against a wall.

Meantime, Captain March had been dispatched from Fort Ridgely to meet the marauders and come to the aid of the settlers. On his way up the river he encountered the Indians, and while parleying with them, on the other side of the river, a number crossed to where he and his little force stood and ambushed them, killing twenty at the first fire.   He himself fought his way out, losing all but nine men.   While trying to ford the stream farther down, his retreat was cut off, and he was drowned, but the nine survivors succeeded in reaching the other side in safety.

The Upper Agency on the Yellow Medicine was saved through the goodness of Other Day, a friendly Indian, who informed the garrison.

Instances of escape and thrilling adventure during the march of the savages down the river would be considered exaggeration, if found in the regulation Indian dime novel.   The instances of heroism and self-sacrifice also were striking.   In one case two brothers placed their sick mother on a mattress in a wagon, and sought to reach a place of safety.   They were pursued by the Indians and could have escaped, but would not abandon their mother, and both were killed while she was compelled to witness their murder.   The savages then set fire to the mattress, burning her to death.

All the Indians in this locality were now aroused, and their savage instincts were inflamed to the fiercest degree. They were determined on a war of extermination. They moved next on New Ulm, a town then containing about fifteen hundred inhabitants and some five hundred fugitives, who had fled before

WARRIOR WITH BEAR CLAW NECKLACE.

the advancing hostiles.   Most of the people were women and children, and the inhabitants of the place were unprepared to meet an attack.   Before the arrival of the savages, Mr. Boardman from St. Peter's, with fifteen men, reached the town, and began preparing means for defense.

With what force he could gather in the town, he moved out to the prairie after dark, and repulsed the Indians for some time.   At nine o'clock that night, Judge Flandreau, with a force of a hundred men, arrived.   After a prolonged and desperate attack, in which several lives were lost, the savages withdrew and proceeded to join Little Crow in an attack on Fort Ridgely. Sergeant Jones and a small force, with two howitzers, were sent to meet the advancing hostiles, and to save the defenseless settlers. The Indians' dread of artillery kept them at a safe distance for a time; a violent rainstorm coming on, the savages, fearing that their ammunition and arms might be rendered useless by the rain, retired to the woods, yelling and gesticulating in the usual Indian manner. Meantime the garrison had put the fort in the best condition it could for defense.

The Indians, the next morning, after a few desultory movements, abandoned the attack on the fort and resumed the easier business of murdering settlers. They continued atrocities and mutilated the bodies of the dead in the usual revolting manner. A few days afterward, Little Crow, with four hundred and fifty warriors, resumed the attack on Fort Ridgely, fighting with desperate persistence. They tried to set fire to the agency buildings by discharging fire arrows into them, and exhausted every means of surprise. For three days the garrison had been cut off, and the country felt alarmed for their safety. Failing to capture the fort, Little Crow now moved on to New Ulm again.

After the arrival of Judge Flandreau, the attack on the town had not been renewed. The approach of the Indians was marked by the smoke of the settlers' dwellings on the way. The people were as well prepared as the conditions of the situation allowed. Judge Flandreau, who now had two hundred and fifty well-armed men, left the barricades and moved out on the prairie to encounter the Indians. This was the second time that such a false move had been made. The defenders were forced to fall back behind the defenses of the town. The battle raged all day and was fought in the regular Indian fashion, a series of charges, retreats, and counter-charges. The savages retired to a safe distance during the night and renewed the attack at daybreak, but gave up the attempt to capture the town at noon, and withdrew.

Meantime, scattered bands of the hostiles were going through the settlements, murdering and burning on their way. All the male adults were killed, and the women were subjected to a worse fate before they were massacred. Even children were subjected to torture.

Two hundred inhabitants of New Ulm had gone to Mankato; their ammunition having been exhausted, their position became indefensible. The bodies of the dead, in their precipitate flight, were left unburied.

A body of fourteen hundred volunteers who had enlisted for the Civil War were now dispatched under Colonel Sibley to the relief of the Redwood Agency. On the march the most appalling sights were witnessed. The bodies of the murdered settlers were left where they had fallen, and were, in many instances, devoured by hogs and prairie wolves. Over two hundred bodies were buried by the soldiers while on this march.

Colonel Sibley, after his arrival at the fort, sent Major Brown with one hundred and sixty men to ascertain in what direction the Indians had gone. He camped at a place called Birch Cooley, admirably adapted for a surprise, where he was discovered by Little Crow. The Indians approached unexpectedly, and at the first fire most of the guard and nearly a hundred horses fell. Had the Indians charged they could have captured the entire camp, but fortunately they held off. Meantime the troops rallied behind the dead horses, the wagons, and every available object, and fought to the best advantage possible. The Indian warriors were over one thousand strong. Captain McPhail was dispatched to the fort for relief, but before going many miles he met Colonel Sibley, with his full force on the way, who had heard the firing.

As the long line of troops appeared, coming over the prairie, the Indians hurriedly withdrew. When the troops reached the scene of conflict, they found the defenders in the last stage of exhaustion, having been all day without food or water, fighting as best they could, with thirteen of their number dead and sixty wounded. It would have been impossible for them to have held out more than a few hours longer.

Little Crow, realizing the military strength opposed to him, sued for peace. He was crafty, cunning, and quick to discern the impracticability of continued resistance. He was known to be an inveterate liar, full of double-dealing and treachery, but wide-awake and shrewd. He had judgment enough to use his influence in preventing the murdering of settlers further, but the traders, whom he detested were murdered ruthlessly.

Another incident at this juncture contributed to bring about a cessation of hostilities on the part of the Indians. The tribes who lived on the upper and lower river had a dispute about the distribution of the plunder taken at the lower agency, and the breach nearly ended in a battle among themselves.

Little Crow represented that the Indians were only fighting for their rights, and although their rights had not been secured, they were, nevertheless, willing to make peace with the white people. Colonel Sibley refused to treat, except on condition of the surrender of white captives by the Indians. Little Crow, knowing that the possession of these prisoners was one of his strongest advantages in negotiating for peace, would not give them up.

About two weeks afterward Colonel Sibley marched against the Indians and defeated them at Yellow Medicine Agency, Little Crow, with two hundred of his warriors, retreating into Dakota. The others, among whom were a large number of mission Indians, who now desired peace, requested Colonel Sibley to come and take the white captives before Little Crow could return and kill them.

Colonel Sibley's forces accordingly marched to the Indian camp, where they were received by the Indians with every manifestation of delight. The wretches, who had murdered so many innocent men, women and children in the most fiendish manner, now shook hands with the soldiers, declaring that they were glad to see them, also that they had always desired to live in peace with the whites. More than two hundred captives, principally women and children, were handed over to the troops.

The sufferings of the prisoners had been extreme; some were on the verge of insanity; some told the most heartrending tales as they clasped their rescuers, weeping in rejoicing. Other captives were brought in, and all told the same tale of kindred and friends slain and outrages endured.

One incident in this campaign of massacre is especially worthy of mention—the escape of Burton Eastwick and his little brother. Burton was but ten years old and his brother five. Having escaped massacre, both started for Fort Ridgely, a distance of eighty miles. They did not know where the fort was; the elder child only knew that the soldiers were somewhere down the river.

Sometimes the elder boy carried his little brother in his arms over rough places, resting with him every now and then when he was tired out or frightened. But the two children finally reached the fort, to the surprise of the soldiers, who could scarcely believe at first they had come such a long and toilsome journey; living on berries and fruits, which they gathered on the way, having to be always on the alert to prevent being discovered by the Indians.

Besides those killed many persons were lost in wandering over the prairies, vainly endeavoring to escape. Some went mad, others died of starvation and exposure.

The Indians who surrendered were carefully guarded, and Lieutenant-Colonel Marshall was sent into Dakota, where he captured a portion of Little Crow's band.

In October the prisoners were brought to Mankato, and on the way to Fargo passed through New Ulm. All were in wagons, well secured and guarded; as they entered the town on Sunday morning, the news spread in a few moments, when the entire population turned out to attack them. The people of the town who had suffered so severely at the hands of these bloodthirsty wretches, and who had barely saved their lives, assembled with every weapon they could find at hand—guns, pistols, axes, pitchforks, and sticks, while the women filled their aprons with stones and flung them at the heads of the prisoners. One woman seized an Indian by the hair, and half dragged him out of the wagon, pounding his head with a stone, before she was taken off by the soldiers.   The soldiers in many cases were compelled to use violence in order to save the lives of the Indian prisoners.

The Indians were finally tried by a military commission, and three hundred and three of their number were condemned to be hanged, and eighteen to be imprisoned for life.   This decision was reversed by the authorities at Washington, who pardoned all but thirty-eight, who were hanged on February 26, 1863.   They died with the stoicism characteristic of the Indian, without manifesting signs of fear.

In this terrible massacre six hundred and forty-four settlers and ninety-three soldiers were slain, and the country round about had been desolated for more than two hundred miles.

After the suppression of the hostiles, isolated bands continued for some time to raid here and there, and killed thirty more whites.   Little Crow escaped capture, but retributive justice overtook the miscreant, and he paid the penalty for his atrocities with his life even before the affair was ended.   A farmer and his son were passing along the prairie when they saw two Indians picking berries in a clump of bushes.   The horrors of the massacre were fresh in the farmer's memory, and he crept stealthily within rifle shot of the Indians and fired.   One Indian jumped in the air with a yell, then dropped, and crawled along on his hands and knees through the prairie grass in the direction of his assailant, dragging his rifle with him.   When sufficiently close he fired, but harmlessly, and a bullet from the farmer's rifle put an end to him.   The other Indian in the meantime had run away.   He was afterward captured, and it was not discovered until then that the Indian who was shot was none other than the prisoner's father, Little Crow.

The results of this massacre were very disastrous, preventing for a long time further settlement of that part of the country.   With proper precaution, too, the massacre might have been prevented.   Bishop Whipple had predicted the outbreak, and on more than one occasion had warned the authorities.   He laid the blame on the Government, owing to its system of dealing with the Indians, and neglect in preventing the robbery of them by agents and traders.   For the eight hundred thousand acres of land sold to the Government, the Indians received scarcely anything.   The amount due to them was absorbed in various pretended claims, and a large portion of their annuities were stolen under similar pretexts by pirates who made fortunes by robbing both the Government and the Indian.

For every dollar of which the Indian was robbed, the Government lost ten, to say nothing of the loss of human life, the destruction of property, and the retarding, for a long time, of the progress of civilization.

CHAPTER XLVI.

THE FUR COMPANIES—HOW THEY OPERATED—HUNTERS AND TRADERS IN
THE INDIAN COUNTRY—THEIR EVERY DAY LIFE AND EXPLOITS.

The First White Men among the Wild Indians—The Hudson Bay Company—How Trading
Posts were Established fiom Ocean to Ocean—Their Maxim, "Never Trust an In-
dian"—Effect of a White Man's Fist on an Indian's Nose—Fierce Competition—Vile
Liquors Sold to the Indians—John Jacob Astor and the American Fur Company
—Hardy Trappers and Daring Frontiersmen—Danger of Trapping in a Hostile
Country—In the Wilderness for Several Years—Robbing the Indian—Twenty
Dollars' Worth of Beaver Skins for Fifty Cents—"Fire Water," why so Named—
How Indians Tested Brandy—Made of the "Hearts of Wild Cats and the Tongues
of Women"—Trappers taken by Surprise—Lying in Ambush.

CHIPPEWA IN WAR COSTUME.

THE first white men with whom the Indians of the north and northwestern parts of this continent came in contact were the trappers, hunters, and traders of the various Fur Companies. An adventurous explorer, or an enthusiastic missionary might, from time to time, penetrate into the heart of the Indian country, but they were seen by only a few of the natives in their transient passage, and rarely left a lasting impression behind them.

The first Fur Company to enter this wild region for barter and trade was the Hudson Bay Company. This association was formed during the reign of Charles II., for the purpose of importing into Great Britain furs and skins obtained from the Indians of British North America, or secured

in their territory.   The company established numerous trading posts throughout the immense region bounded east by the Altantic, west by the Pacific, north
by the Arctic ocean, and south by what is now a portion of the United States.
This company had an exclusive monopoly of the fur trade in this vast territory, and it also controlled the entire legislative, judicial, and executive
powers within those limits.

In the course of time this company developed into one of the most complete as well as tyrannical commercial systems in the world.   The native
Indians were as fierce as those of any other portion of the North American
Continent, yet the company and its officials had little difficulty with them.
This, according to the authorities of the company, was mainly attributable
to the perfect system of discipline maintained among their employees.   One
of their maxims was never to trust an Indian, no matter how friendly he
might seem or how honest he pretended to be.   In case of difficulty or trouble, employees were instructed to act with the utmost prudence and firm-
ness, to be as just as they were stern, and never to use their weapons, or kill
an Indian, except in self-defense.   Any exhibition of hostility or even arrogance was to be stopped the moment it showed itself.   The punishment for
insolence or petty offenses was to knock the Indian down at once with the
fist.   However expert the Indian might be with his knife, lance, gun, or
other weapon, he was invariably taken back by the landing of a white
man's fist on his nose.

No offense on the part of the Indians was passed unnoticed, but instead of
shooting the culprits down, or butchering them indiscriminately, the tribe
was frequently prevailed upon to send in the criminal for punishment, and
he usually got off with a reprimand, sometimes receiving a present, which
made him for the time being at least a "good Indian."   Under this system,
the company's trade prospered immensely.

After the cession of Canada, in 1763, numbers of fur traders spread over
that country and into the northwestern part of the continent, and began to
encroach on the Hudson Bay Company's territory.   These individual speculators finally combined, forming the Northwest Fur Company in 1787.
They had their headquarters at Fort William, where the directors or their
representatives met once a year.   The trade of this company was in the
region of the north.

There were many other companies engaged in this business both before
and after the amalgamation of the Hudson Bay and Northwest Companies.

Fierce competition at once sprang up between these rival companies.   Both
supplied the Indians with an abundance of intoxicating liquors, in order to

increase their trade and maintain commercial supremacy in the Indian country. The consequence was inevitable. The worst passions of both Indians and whites—many of these latter being really half-breeds—were inflamed to the fiercest degree, and great destruction of human life and property was the result. The supply of furs, too, threatened to become exhausted by the indiscriminate slaughter, even in the breeding season, of both male and female animals.

The Northwest Company had the monopoly of the fur trade of the entire region of the Northwest, and were also practically the political rulers of that great stretch of territory.

The Mackinaw Company, another rival, was subsequently established and sought to monopolize the trade to the south and southwest of the Northwest Company. Meantime, John Jacob Astor engaged in the fur trade on his own account, and obtained a charter from the legislature of New York in 1809, incorporating the American Fur Company. The rivalry of the Mackinaw Company rendering his own venture unprofitable, he and some members of the Northwest Company bought out the Mackinaw Company, and established a new one under the name of the Southwest Company, embracing part of the Northwest Company, the American Company, and probably the interests of individual traders, who had become strong. This company controlled a number of establishments within both British and American territory. Mr. Astor engaged in the trade in consequence of the treaty of 1794, which permitted commercial intercourse between Canada and the United States, and entailed the evacuation of all the posts held by the British within United States territory.

Previous to the establishment of the American Fur Company, Congress enacted a law decreeing that all fur traders in the United States territory should be American citizens, and that no foreigners should be employed in this line of business unless under bonds furnished by American employers for the proper conduct of these traders.

The central business post of the consolidated companies was near Sault Ste. Marie, on Lake Superior. The interior sub-posts extended over a vast region, running north to the fifty-ninth degree north latitude, and west as far as the Missouri River. It was found impossible to conduct the business successfully without employing some of the agents, clerks, interpreters, and boatmen of the old company, all of whom were foreigners or French Canadians. This procedure exercised an evil influence on all Indians in that region.

As already stated, when the commercial rivalry between the two British Fur Companies sprang up, both parties sold the Indians ardent spirits. Congress passed a law, after the establishment of the American Fur Company, prohibiting the sale of intoxicants to Indians, not even allowing their introduction into their country under any circumstances. But as the old employees of the Northwest Company virtually held the field of trade, this law was almost a dead letter. They were employed to secure furs, and to utilize the Indians in every way necessary for this purpose, and aimed only to make good returns to their employers. The consequence was that the Indian was debased, and all the inherent evil in his nature was awakened and set in motion.

The political influence exercised on the Indians of the Northwest was also bad. The great body of Indians in the region of the upper lakes, and extending to the source of the Mississippi, were averse to American rule. Many of them had been influenced to fight the Americans, who were frequently ambushed, surprised, and attacked in various ways and in many places, including Fort Dearborn (now Chicago), Brownstone, River Basin, Maumee, Fort Harrison, Machilimackimac, and other strongholds. The British fur traders made the Indians believe that the Americans were to be driven back to the lines of the Illinois and Ohio Rivers, an old and popular wish of the Lake Indians from early days. Large numbers of them joined the British in the war that followed, and suffered severely. Their great chief was killed; their prophet, Elksatawa, was driven into Canada; and what was worse, they were abandoned by the British after the close of the war. Many of them never came back; those who did, and those who had remained in United States territory, were discontented, sullen, and hostile. It was among these that the foreign employees of the American Fur Company traded. To their baneful influence more than to anything else may be largely ascribed the beginning of our subsequent troubles with the Indians of the Northwest.

These trappers included many of the most hardy and daring frontiersmen of those days. Their trapping expeditions were always led by one man. It was their custom to travel up the streams until they came to the mouth of a stream confluent to the one on which they were traveling, where they made camp. They then trapped to the entire source of this stream, and after securing all the beaver, otter, and other pelts possible, returned to the main stream again, moving camp to the mouth of the next stream above, going up that, and so on until they arrived at the source of the main river. Sometimes trapping parties were absent for one or two years at a time, subsisting almost entirely on meats and fish. Their only means of transportation, as a rule, were pack animals and small boats.

It may be interesting to state here that while the trappers had no bread, flour, or vegetables of any kind, they subsisted very well on the different meats which they obtained in abundance along the rivers, the flesh of the beaver being particularly sweet and nutritious, resembling much the flavor of fresh pork.

The Fur Companies were exceedingly arbitrary in dealing with their own and other men. Being far from civilization, the only law that they appealed to was force. This they used in various ways. Their traffic was highly remunerative, and the companies grew immensely wealthy. The more wealth they secured, the more arbitrary they became, frequently committing acts for which, in a civilized community, they would have been condemned and severely punished. To the employees of these companies can be traced more viciousness on the part of the North American Indians than to any other source. They did more to demoralize them than any other agency. They simply robbed the Indians of their property whenever opportunity offered. It was not uncommon for them to secure two or three choice beaver skins for a butcher knife valued at fifty or seventy-five cents, one beaver skin alone being worth in gold from four to eight dollars, according to its size and condition. The Fur Companies made all the men connected with them immensely wealthy, from John Jacob Astor down.

To offset this record, in a measure, it may be said that the Fur Companies were the first agency to send civilized persons into what was then an unknown country. They first learned the nature of the country and its inhabitants. As their trappers and hunters traveled up the streams and along nearly every river throughout this vast region, they made maps of the country, and especially of the rivers where the most valuable pelts were obtained, delivering the maps to the companies' agents. These maps were withheld by the fur companies from the general public, in order that no encroachments should be made on their rich hunting grounds.

Occasionally a party of trappers sent out by one of the companies were massacred and their goods taken by the Indians. The story of these occurrences was always exaggerated by the Fur Companies, then scattered broadcast throughout the country to show the great danger attending trapping expeditions, and the great loss entailed on the companies themselves by such massacres. This was done to prevent others from engaging in the same business. As late as 1866, these companies sent trapping expeditions throughout the western country, and all of them, even as late as this, secured large numbers of valuable pelts, although they did not trade much with the Indians. Most of the trading done with the red man was for buffalo robes, bear, deer, fox, and wolf skins. The articles traded by the companies for pelts in latter days consisted of butcher knives, red blankets, scarlet cloth, various colored paints for the Indians to decorate their faces and bodies, such as yellow ochre, carmine, vermilion, and indigo blue, small mirrors, beads, Iroquois shells, brass buttons, and other articles of small value.

When the Fur Companies first began to supply ardent liquor to the Indians in order to help their trade, the liquor was imported from England. It was the cheapest and most poisonous brand manufactured at the time, and for that reason was all the more acceptable to the Indian. When it reached the Hudson Bay territory, or the great region within which the rival fur companies traded, it was carried overland to the various posts. For convenience of transportation, casks or barrels of liquor were divided into kegs. The carriers soon learned that they could make a profit by diluting the liquor with water, when changing it from the barrels into kegs. The Indians, however, missed the powerful effects and suspected that they were being cheated. They learned how to test liquor before exchanging peltries for it. The liquor was poured on a fire, and if the fire was extinguished it was evident that the liquor was watered, and they at once pronounced it "bad." If, on the contrary, the liquor added to the flame, they knew that the alcohol had not been tampered with, and it was accepted as genuine "fire water." Hence the name "fire water," as used by the Indians, when referring to liquor. That the "fire water" supplied to the Indians of that day was comparable to the vilest stuff of present day manufacture, is illustrated by an Indian chief who had experienced its effects, and who had witnessed the sad havoc it had produced among his people. "Fire water," exclaimed this savage, "can only be distilled from the hearts of wild cats and tongues of women, it makes my people at once so fierce and so foolish."

The hunters and trappers employed by the Fur Companies were shrewd and adventurous characters. They were perfect mountaineers and frontiersmen, as much at home in the untrodden forest as in the civilization they had left behind. They learned the habits of the red man, the untamed savageness of his nature, and the danger of placing confidence in him. Hence, they were rarely taken by surprise. They were led by such men as Major Henry Vanderburgh, Jim Bridger, Jim Baker, and many others whose names will always be connected with the history of that country.

These hardy and intrepid men pursued their trade at all seasons of the year, and in the face of tremendous obstacles. They penetrated into the territory of unknown tribes, and were prepared to resist, if they could not evade, all perils and enemies. Many romances of Indian life have been written, most of them greatly exaggerated, and some of them preposterously absurd; but if the real details of some of the daring adventures of these early trappers could be written they would verify the old adage that "truth is stranger than fiction.'' Sometimes a solitary trapper was murdered by the treacherous Indians, and never heard of more. This did not prevent another trapper from starting over the same route as soon as sufficient time had elapsed to convince him that his predecessor was dead.

Their moral and physical courage have not been duly appreciated. The general goes to battle surrounded with his legions, in all the panoply of war, and if he meets disaster, he can escape under what is called a well-ordered retreat. But the trapper or hunter could not retreat, and as for fighting, he was compelled to do it all himself. Occasionally a number of trappers went together when entering the territory of a powerful and treacherous nation, such as the Blackfeet or the Crows. On these occasions they used diplomacy, and when that failed, they fought their way through, or were killed. Few of such murders have been recorded, but they were generally heralded throughout the country by the Fur Companies at the time. Occasionally an incident occurred of such a bloody or dramatic character as to become historical.

Of these one of the most noteworthy was the massacre of Major Vanderburgh and his party. They were in the employ of the American Fur Company, and hunted and trapped among Indians who had been up to that time somewhat friendly. Major Vanderburgh's party numbered about one hundred men. He was careful of their lives and distrustful of the savages, whom he knew well.

At this time there was the most intense rivalry between the many Fur Companies, each seeking by every possible means to obtain the mastery of the fur trade.

The Rocky Mountain Company was managed by two experienced and shrewd men—Fitzpatrick and Jim Bridger; while the American Fur Company had in its employ Major Henry Vanderburgh and Mr. Dripps. Vanderburgh was one of the most daring leaders in the pathless wilds of the West, and a typical American frontiersman. All of these men were courageous, enterprising, and vigilant, but Vanderburgh and Dripps lacked the experience of the others and were unacquainted with the mountain regions.

Both Bridger and Fitzpatrick had been traders and trappers for years and knew every spot of these wilds. They were impressed by the fact that the evils of competition were injuring the two companies, and endeavored to bring about a compromise that would redound to the benefit of both.

They accordingly proposed that the country should be divided into sections and allotted to each, neither intruding on the territory of the other. This sensible proposition was not accepted, and both companies continued their rivalry with increased energy.

Bridger and Fitzpatrick, acting on their experience and knowledge of the country, sought to throw Vanderburgh and Dripps on the wrong track, and to a certain extent succeeded; but what Major Vanderburgh lacked in experience he made up in intelligence, now following his rivals with irritating perseverance, and then leading them a hot chase.

Finally, in an ill-judged moment, Vanderburgh divided his party in the midst of the Indian country, Dripps going in one direction, and himself, with some fifty to seventy-five men, in another. He was in the hunting ground of the Blackfeet, and having come on a deserted Indian camp which bore traces of the precipitate flight of the savages, he unwisely followed their trail.

While the party were passing through a ravine unconscious of danger, they were suddenly startled by the yells and warwhoops of a legion of Indians who sprang from ambush and closed upon them from every side. Major Vanderburgh's horse was killed at the first onslaught, and in falling he carried the rider with him, pinioning him to the ground. Unable to extricate himself, he determined to defend his life as best he could. One of

FACIAL PAINTING—APACHE.

his party was scalped almost within an arm's length of him, most of the others were killed near the spot where he fell. He had a rifle across his saddle and two pistols in his belt; and when the savages approached to dispatch him, he raised his rifle and shot the first one dead. He then drew both pistols and emptied the last shot at the yelling red men, while still lying pinned to the ground by his horse. After firing his last shot the Blackfeet rushed in and hacked him to death with tomahawks.

A large reward was offered by the American Fur Company for the recovery of his body, but it was never found. The Indians were supposed to have burned it, and also the bodies of the rest of the party who lost their lives.   At any rate, no one ever discovered the slightest trace of the massacre, or relics of the party.   The incidents connected with the tragedy were subsequently learned from the Indians who participated in it.   The loss of Major Vander-burgh and his party was a serious blow to the American Fur Company.

In trapping for beaver and otter the trappers generally went singly, or in twos, threes, or fours.   They carried the traps and outfit on their backs.   A trapper usually carried from six to eight traps.   These were generally set in the evening and visited in the morning, when, after having reset the trap, the catch was carried to camp.

While the work was laborious and dangerous the trappers had plenty of leisure time; and as the devil always finds work for idle hands, they amused themselves in leisure hours by swindling the Indian out of his belongings. It was during these times that a trapper usually took an Indian woman for his wife, and for the time being became more Indian than the Indians themselves.   Some of the French Canadian half-breed trappers and hunters became more vicious and villainous than the savages.   They knew all the ways and habits of the Indian, and as they were more intelligent than the latter they soon combined the vices of barbarism and civilization, without the virtues of either.

Edward Umfreville, to whose book, "The Present State of Hudson's Bay," I have already referred, was a Frenchman who had been in the employ of the Fur Companies for seven years; he was also four years in the same business for himself, making eleven years which he spent among the wild Indians in the British possessions.   He saw a few nations only, and did not travel farther west than the vicinity of the Great Lakes.   His book was well and temperately written, but was severe on the management of the Fur Companies.   He declared that they did much to demoralize all Indians with whom they dealt; that they traded them at all times a vile liquor known as English brandy.   This liquor, he states, made the Indians who drank it crazy, and when in this condition all the viciousness of their nature asserted itself.   During these debauches the drunken Indians not only committed extreme acts of brutality, but, in many instances, murder also.   After having swindled the Indian out of all his pelts and other articles of value the companies drove him away by force, leaving him in a worse condition than before, for during the winter it was almost impossible for the Indians to secure food for themselves and their families, in consequence of which they suffered greatly.

The Indian of a hundred and twenty-five years ago, as he knew and described him, was in nowise different from the Indian that I knew, thus showing that during more than a century he made no material advancement, and no improvement in his mental or moral condition.

He also speaks of many nations of Indians to the far west, but does not particularize them, except the Sioux, of whom he speaks as being a nation to the west, who must have numbered "at least five hundred," thus showing that at that time no white man had penetrated the Sioux territory, for that powerful nation did not then number less than seventy-five thousand souls.

The description given by him of the attack and murder of a village of Esquimaux by a party of Indians, is without parallel. The Esquimaux were attacked while sleeping, and all were murdered in the most fiendish manner. A young Esquimau girl of about eighteen years, after having been subjected to every indignity, was pinioned to the ground by a spear driven through her body; while writhing in this position she seized Umfreville by the legs, begging him to kill her.

The Indians would not permit him to interfere, and she was left to end her miserable existence after hours of excruciating torture.

He is severe on Indian character, and states that the young were reared without restraint, and that the worst part of their vicious natures were always cultivated, also that at no time during his eleven years' experience among the Indians, did he ever know of the lash having been used by any of them.

It is evident that the author quoted, saw only the better portion of our Indian peoples, as his experiences were confined to the Algonquin nation; and during the time he was among them, they had not fallen under the demoralizing influences of the pernicious squaw men and half breeds, neither had they been contaminated by dissolute white people, nor acquired the vicious habits of civilization, nor become discontented and desperate from supposed or actual ill treatment by the whites personally, or at the hands of the government of Great Britain or the United States; but they were living the life of wild men in their original homes.

Had his experiences extended to the Comanches, Kiowas or Apaches, it is but reasonable to assume that his reports to his employers would have been more severe on Indian character than they were.

CHAPTER XLVII.

FAMOUS EXPEDITIONS INTO THE INDIAN COUNTRY—PERILOUS JOURNEYS
OVERLAND BY OX TEAMS AND PRAIRIE SCHOONERS.

Expeditions of Lieutenants Lewis and Clark—Preparations for the Journey—Their First
Winter in a Wild and Unknown Country—Assistance from Friendly Indians—Meet-
ing the Snakes—Explorations of Lieutenants Pike and Long—Capture of Lieutenant
Pike and Party—Expedition of Captain Bonneville—Battles with the Early Traders
—Gold Discoveries—The Rush to the Mines—Fremont's Expedition—The Santa Fé
Trail—Prairie Schooners—A Dangerous Trip—Excitement in the Pike's Peak
Country—An Overland Wagon Train—Waylaid by Indians—How Wagon Trains
were Corraled—Fighting against Odds—The Great American Bull-Whacker—His
Whip and Skill in Using It—An Incident on the Sweetwater River—An Aston-
ished Indian.

AFTER the acquisition by the United States of the territory of Louisiana
from the French, in the year 1803, President Jefferson and his cabinet desired to have the newly-acquired territory explored. This territory contained nearly one million square miles, and its boundaries were not only
ill-defined, but unknown. Nor had the French, the English, or the Spaniards any settled boundary line of the territory they respectively claimed in
what was then the far West. The territory of Louisiana then contained all
that portion of the country south of the British possessions, lying west of
the Mississippi River from its source to its mouth, and from the confluence
of the Sabine directly north to the Red River; thence westward along this
river to its source; thence along the Arkansas River; thence west to the
Rocky Mountains; thence north to the headwaters of the South Platte; and
thence west to the Pacific Ocean. The President decided to send an exploring party up the Mississippi River to the mouth of the Missouri, and from
thence to make an exploration of the Missouri River, and the country adjacent thereto, to its source.

Two young army officers were selected for this perilous expedition. They
were Lieutenants Lewis and Clark. Both were men of enterprise and bravery, and could be relied upon to make an accurate statement of their experiences and observations. They were sent to St. Louis, where the outfit was
secured. The party consisted of some thirty or forty soldiers and as many
civilians, mostly Frenchmen, from in and about St. Louis. One entire

winter was spent in getting the outfit ready for the long journey, which was expected to last for three or four years.   The stores were carried on one large and several smaller boats, one of which was a rowboat.   These were towed up the rivers by the men, horses, and mules; the animals were also used for hunting and other purposes.

Early in the following spring, when the ice had left the rivers, the exploring party started for this unknown region.   By the time cold weather set in they had reached the vicinity of the mouth of Wood River.   There they spent the winter in the hunting ground of the Mandan Indians.   They were more hospitable and civilized than their wild brothers further west, and treated the white party with friendly consideration.

In the spring of the following year, as soon as they could safely do so, they proceeded up the Missouri River, making further explorations of the stream and country to the land of the Snakes.   The Indians, after receiving the presents which Lieutenants Lewis and Clark gave them, showed them the passes through the mountains.   Being near the headwaters of the Missouri River the party went into camp for the winter, meantime making explorations of the surrounding country and its watercourses.   It was during this winter that they discovered the largest tributaries to the Missouri, and gave to these streams the names by which they are now known—Lewis and Clark, Jefferson, Madison, and Gallatin Forks, being named in honor of themselves and the distinguished men then at the head of the Government.

The next spring, under the guidance of some Snake Indians, the explorers were piloted through the passes of the mountains, and crossed to the headwaters of the Columbia River, making the trip to its mouth, where they remained during that winter.   Early in the following year they returned over the same route, again passing through the mountains, and arrived safely at St. Louis after an absence of three years.

The most remarkable part of this journey was that it was safely accomplished.   That the party were not all massacred by the Indians through whose territory they passed, can only be accounted for by the fact that the rivers which they traveled, formed the boundary line between different nations of hostile Indians, and that no war party happened along at that time.

To this expedition the country was greatly indebted for information regarding the newly-acquired territory along the rivers which they passed.   On returning, they made full reports to the President of their achievements and observations.

This expedition was as important in its results as it was remarkable in its execution.   For fullness and accuracy of statement in relation to the country traversed, the various tribes of Indians with whom they came in contact, the fertility of the soil, and the many resources of the region, it will always remain one of the most valuable contributions to the history of that portion of the Northwest.

After the report was published, the attention of the people of the East was attracted to the prospective wealth of our western empire. From this time onward, a steady flow of emigration set in toward the setting sun, which within half a century reached the Pacific. No similar instance of rapid development is known to history, as the settlement of the country which Lewis and Clark explored less than a century ago.

The next exploration sent out by the Government to ascertain the value and the resources of its newly-acquired inland territory, was in 1805. Lieutenant Zebulon N. Pike, with a party of twenty-five or thirty soldiers, and as many civilians, went up the Arkansas River to make an exploration of the country lying adjacent thereto. Spain claimed this country, and sent Spanish troops there, who fortified themselves and captured Lieutenant Pike and his party, holding them as prisoners. They were afterward released, and returned without having accomplished their object.

Subsequently, about 1819 or 1820, Captain S. H. Long was sent with a body of troops to make an exploration of the same territory. He, I believe, accomplished more, and returning, made a report of his observations. The two most prominent peaks in Colorado were named after these two officers, Pike's Peak and Long's Peak.

The next expedition sent into this territory was that of Captain Bonneville, of the American Fur Company. He went for the purpose of trapping, but he also made some valuable explorations. The American Fur Company, finding this country a rich harvest field, established forts and trading posts at various places that were most accessible to their trapping grounds, which were near the rivers, and in close proximity to the road which they made.

During this time an active trade was carried on by caravans between the western limit of civilization and these outposts. The company also carried large amounts of stores to trade with the Indians, as well as for the maintenance and protection of their own men. Many battles were fought between the caravans, the men at the fortifications, and the Indians. For a long time the latter had possession of the country and prevented communication between these fortifications and civilization. The country at that time was a source of great profit to the Fur Company, as the rivers and streams were filled with all kinds of fur-bearing animals.

Gradually settlers crept in, and as the country became more or less in-

INDIAN HUNTER—PAINTED HORSE—TYPICAL BRIDLE.

habited, Overland route travelers were less and less molested. It was by this route that the first travelers went overland to Santa Fé and California. After this the prairie schooner (a large wagon having a canvas top to protect travelers and goods from the weather), with its ox-teams, capable of carrying several tons, traveled from civilization to these posts.

The Indians resisted the encroachment of the white men with all their power, capturing and destroying many entire trains and their contents, and killing every one connected with them; but as the business was exceedingly remunerative, men would risk any danger to engage in it.

The difficulties encountered by the pioneers were almost insurmountable, but they persevered in the face of great odds, stimulated by the attraction of the fabulous wealth of rich gold and silver mines that were said to exist in the far West.

Previous to 1847 few white men had gone west of the Missouri River. From that time onward, however, the tide of adventurous travel began for what was known as the Pike's Peak country. Prospecting for gold and silver was largely carried on in that region, and the stories of the mineral wealth which this territory contained, when reported in the East, gave a wonderful impetus to western settlement.

The gold discoveries of the Pike's Peak country resulted in greatly increasing the tide of emigration over this vast stretch of territory; and the adventurous and intrepid people who composed the caravans and encountered the dangers and difficulties of the routes, were naturally calculated to bring a spirit of enterprise into the new land. They embraced all sorts of characters, but as each and all were bent on seeking fortunes or bettering their condition, it resulted in the rapid settlement of the country. These new settlers were men of daring and enterprise, and soon established numerous villages and communities, with lines of communication between them. As the settlements grew the frontier lines were strengthened. The red man was driven back and forced to recognize the undisputed right of all people to travel from one point to another through his country without molestation.

The next exploration of the western country was that undertaken by Colonel John C. Fremont. The object of his expedition was to discover, if possible, a route along the Platte Valley, and through the mountains to Salt Lake and California. This expedition consisted of sixty soldiers and civilians, and a sufficient number of six-mule teams to carry the outfit. It was the best equipped of any expedition sent out by the Government. The party discovered and made what was afterward the Overland Route through this valley, and through the mountains by way of South Pass. This was the most direct and accessible route between the western borders of civilization and the Pacific coast, and was afterward traveled by the Mormons, the Overland Stage, and the Pony Express.

After this route became known, there followed during the summer months, an almost endless stream of horse, mule, and ox-teams traveling over it, some of which were composed of freighters, and others of prospecters, miners, or settlers.   The trains were frequently attacked by bands of hostile Indians, and sometimes were entirely annihilated, as the bones of the dead which were left to bleach in the sun, where the wolves had drawn them after eating the flesh, bore ghastly testimony.   It was afterward found necessary by the military to organize these trains so that they could, to a certain extent, protect themselves.   The wagons were detained until there were about fifty in number, with a sufficient force of able-bodied fighting men in the company to afford protection.   A captain was appointed from among the travelers by the military commander of the post at which the train was organized.   This captain received a written document from the military, giving him absolute command of the train, with authority to detail the men of his train to stand guard over their animals while grazing, and over the camp at night.   A company organized in this way proceeded with some sort of discipline and with a good prospect of reaching the next military post.   Upon its arrival the captain of the train reported to the military commander, who demanded to know if he had kept sufficient guard over his animals and trains by day and night, and if his men were obedient, and did their duty promptly.   If not, the commanding officer of the troops read a severe lecture to the delinquent or disobedient individual, or replaced him by another man, when the train resumed its journey.   This was purely arbitrary on the part of the military, but it had become an absolute necessity to compel travelers to exercise at least ordinary precaution for their own safety.   Frequently, when an attack was made on an unprotected train by Indians, the military were compelled to go to that point and relieve the distressed party, often having to care for of a number of wounded until they recovered or died.

After the action of the military in organizing the wagons into companies, fewer were attacked and destroyed by the Indians.   The wagons of the companies thus organized traveled close together, and the men were always in a position to defend themselves.   After a few of these companies had been attacked, and had beaten off the Indians with severe loss, the latter found that the travelers were generally able to take care of themselves, and a knowledge of this fact soon spread among them, when the attacks became less frequent.

An ox-train fully equipped for crossing the country consisted of from twenty to twenty-five large ox-wagons, each drawn by from six to twelve yoke of cattle, with a number of extra oxen to supply the place of those that might become disabled.   There was also an extra wagon which carried the outfit and provisions for the trainmen.   These wagons extended a long distance over the prairie and along the mountain roads, and were easy prey for Indians lying in ambush to attack them.   The trains made several stops each day; at each stop the wagons were formed into a pear-shaped corral, the pole of each wagon pointing outward, and the hub of the fore wheel of the next wagon set close to the hind wheel of the wagon just ahead of it. The wagons were so placed as to form an enclosure sufficiently large to hold the entire number of animals belonging to the train.   Indians rarely attacked a train when in corral.   It was a means of fortification that enabled the trainmen to defend themselves and their animals against great odds. When trains were attacked while moving, they immediately went into corral, and if the corral could be formed in time the Indians usually retired. Sometimes trains were kept in corral by an attacking party for days at a time.   The entire number of animals for one of these large ox-trains, including extras, sometimes amounted to from three hundred to three hundred and fifty cattle, and the number of trainmen required sometimes from forty to fifty.   The heavily-laden wagons were capable of making from twelve to fifteen miles a day.   It required weeks and sometimes months for these slow trains to move between far distant points, across this immense territory.

Each wagon had its own ox-driver, or, as they were called, "bull-whackers."   The whip used by the bull-whackers had a short staff not over one and one-half or two feet in length, to this was fastened the lash, which was from fifteen to twenty-five feet in length, being very thick a few feet from the end of the staff and tapering down to a fine point.   This was dragged behind them on the ground, at full length, and in the hands of a good driver it was a terrible instrument of punishment.   The bull-whacker could take the staff in his two hands and giving the lash one or two skillful twirls around his head, then with a blow strike an ox on any spot he aimed at, cutting the hide through as if with a knife.

An instance occurred on the Sweetwater River near the Devil's Gap, which will illustrate the bull-whacker's skill in the use of his whip.   A train of ox-wagons while passing this point stopped as usual to rest.   Some Indians who had been watching the train at a distance, at length made up their minds to visit it.   One loafer Indian, more inquisitive than he should have been, mounted the pole of the wagon, and, as usual, began taking things therefrom.   At last he came to the bag that contained the ox-driver's outfit this the Indian was proceeding to appropriate to his own use.   The teamster, who had been watching him, concluded not to be robbed. Stepping back to the right distance the driver gave his whip two or three rapid twirls around his head and aimed a blow at the Indian's back. The Indian was naked, except his breechcloth, and the end of the lash struck him just below the shoulder blade, cutting a gash, ten to twelve inches in length, straight down his back. The whip cut entirely through the flesh to the bone for the whole length, and could not have been more neatly done with a sharp knife. The Indian gave a howl, dropped the bag, jumped to the ground, and, mad with pain and rage, prepared to attack the bull-whacker. The latter immediately placed his whip in position again, preparing to strike. Seeing this, and having a painful realization of what he had just received, the Indian retreated.

This act came near costing the lives of the entire train. My command happened to arrive shortly afterward, or there might have been serious trouble. We had great difficulty in patching up peace between the Indians and the trainmen, which was done by presenting them such articles as the trainmen and military could spare.

Ox-teams were used in these trains because the animals were patient and faithful, could draw heavy loads, and readily subsist on the grasses along the route. Moreover, Indians could not stampede them, and did not look upon them with such envious eyes as they did on the fine horses and mules that were afterward used in this service.

It required but a short time for the enterprising mining towns of the far West to discover that transportation by ox-teams was entirely too slow, when four and six-horses or mule teams superseded them. On these fine teams the red men made repeated attacks, often capturing the animals of the entire trains; nevertheless, horse and mule trains continued in this service until the completion of the Union Pacific Railroad.

Almost from the discovery until the present time, the country owes its advancement and improvement to trains drawn by animals, whether the slow but sure ox teams with their immense loads, to the patient and faithful mule teams, or the more rapid and tractable horse trains of wagons stretching miles across the treeless plains, or winding snake-like through interminable cañons or over rugged mountains carrying succor and supplies to distant mining camps, frontier towns and settlements.

CHAPTER XLVIII.

THE AMERICAN TROOPER AS AN INDIAN FIGHTER—PERILOUS SERVICE—
SCOUTING FOR INDIANS.

Fighting Indians with Cannon—Their Amazement at and Dread of Shells—An Inscrutable
Mystery—Fighting them after their own Fashion—The best Soldiers in the World
—Hand-to-Hand Conflict with the Indians—Fighting on Foot—Keeping with the
Command—Blowing their own Brains Out—As Mild as a Child but as full of Fight
as a Tiger—Fighting Indians Day by Day—Sleepless Nights—On a Scout—How the
Trooper Slept at Night—A Duel between two Soldiers—A Sad Incident—After the
Duel—Toes, Fingers, and Hands Frozen—Animals Frozen to Death—Unwelcome
Night Visitors—Grizzly Bears in Camp—The Despised Wolves—Cunning and Dan-
gerous Animals—Eating Boots and Saddles—Eating their Companions Alive—
Horses and Mules Crazed by Fright.

OF all the services required of the trooper in the military service of the
United States, there was none that could compare with, or even approach,
that which was required of him in fighting hostile Indians. It was a service so unlike any other that history fails to furnish a comparison.

It was necessary that the soldiers should fight these wily savages after
their own peculiar mode of warfare, on their own ground, and at their own
time. Preparations could not be made in advance for these fights, and the
troops had to be in readiness to act on the aggressive or defensive at a
moment's notice. They had to be ready to accept defeat, and to protect
themselves instantly under all circumstances; otherwise massacre and annihilation, which so often occurred, were sure to follow.

In Indian fighting, the cavalry alone were nearly always used, for infantry could not reach the scene in time to give the savages battle. Artillery
was rarely used, and when it was, small field pieces, or mountain howitzers
only were called into requisition. These howitzers were light and could be
drawn by two horses or mules, and when in the mountains could be carried
on the back of pack animals. But even these were usually of little effectiveness; for in an Indian fight the conflict was constantly changing from one
point to another with great rapidity, and by the time the pieces were unlim-
bered and placed in position the scene of the battle might be removed some
distance. When the Indians discovered that the troops had field pieces and
were using shell or case shot, they quickly retreated behind a hill or the
most convenient shelter, remaining there until the guns became silent.

They were greatly surprised that the troops could fire a shot which would drop among them, and after remaining quiet for a short time suddenly explode with such disastrous results.

To be good Indian fighters the troops had not only to act independently, and fight after Indian fashion, as well as secure every advantage possible, but had also to preserve their military cohesion, and obey the commands of their officers according to military tactics.   Each trooper was expected to act at once as an individual, as well as a part of the whole command.   When fighting Indians he should be a mixture of white man and Indian together; he must have the courage of the Indian, and the coolness and judgment of the white man.   It was absolutely necessary that he never be out generaled by the wily red men, and under no circumstances must he permit his ammunition and strength to be wasted without effect. Should it be necessary at any time for him to engage in a hand-to-hand conflict with one or more of the savages, he must do so without hesitation or command.   It was also of vital importance that he be a good shot; for his entire supply of ammunition was generally on his person, and he was supposed to make every shot tell.   He should also possess great endurance and ability to go for a long time without food, water, or sleep. It was essential that he be an experienced horseman, and know just when to use the bit and spur, as every move made in battle against the warriors was the result of some manœuvre on their part, and had to be met instantly by the trooper.

In fighting Indians it was often necessary for the troops to pursue and overtake them in order to give them battle; and when the Indians allowed themselves to be overtaken they were generally ready for the fight, and in such strong position that the troops were at a great disadvantage.

After traveling a long distance, and undergoing great hardships, the troops generally arrived at the battle ground in an exhausted condition, both men and animals being much reduced in strength from lack of sufficient rest and food.   Hence they were necessarily at a great disadvantage and were handicapped from the start.   Again, the red man had two or three fresh horses with which to fight, whereas the trooper had but one, which was often jaded or worn out when the time and place to fight were at hand.   Should his horse become disabled or be killed, the trooper must keep with the remainder of the command, fighting on foot, and under no circumstances permit himself to become separated from it; if he did, there was but one thing left for him, namely, to blow out his brains, for it was tacitly understood by all troopers that they must never allow themselves to be captured alive by Indians.

In no other military service in the world were soldiers called upon to undergo the hardships that the American troopers did in Indian campaigns; but thanks to the advance of civilization these campaigns are now things of the past.

Our Civil War demonstrated the fact, beyond all question, that the American can be taken from almost any walk in civilized life and made into the best soldier, in the shortest time, of any man in the world. The average American is so intelligent, and has such a high sense of duty, that he has been known in many instances during our Civil War to be equal, as a soldier, to the most hardened campaigner, in less than sixty days. Recruits who had been in service not more than two weeks, have been known to conduct themselves in battle with the greatest self-possession, obeying every command as promptly as though having seen years of service.

The most important requirement to make an efficient soldier of an American, is to teach him to cook properly. No matter how good his rations may be, if not properly cooked, disease is sure to follow; the sick must be cared for by the able-bodied, which reduces the fighting force. Every soldier must take his turn in cooking for his mess; first commencing as a scullion for a week, the following week he is second cook, the next raises him to the dignity of chief cook. Should he not properly fulfil this important position, the members of his mess, and officers are liable to make it uncomfortable for him.

In well-conducted armies it is the duty of the company officers to attend each meal of the troops, and see that the food has been properly prepared.

Every boy, no matter what his station in life may be, should be taught the art of cooking, for upon this not only his health, but his finances are kept in good condition.

The American soldier enters the army voluntarily, and at once applies himself to become proficient in his new profession; he is subordinate, yet independent; he is docile, yet courageous; he is as mild as a child, and as full of fight as a tiger. There are no requirements asked of him that he is not always ready to comply with; exposure and privations have no terrors for him. His officers are not compelled to drive him continually, but is himself anxious to become a leader.

There is no army in the world in which the officers and soldiers are in such close touch as in ours. The military discipline is perfect; but there is no starched stiffness on the part of the officers toward their men, and no lack of confidence in their officers on the part of the soldiers. Both are voluntarily doing their duty, and each instinctively understands the other. Again, in our army the superiority of the officers to the men of their command is purely military. The soldier knows and feels this. He knows that officers hold their places by virtue of authority, obtained by capacity for their position; not as in the armies of the Old World, by virtue of so-called noble lineage, social caste, or wealth. Hence in our army there is not, as a rule, arrogance or superciliousness on the part of an officer toward a soldier, or enmity or jealousy on the part of a soldier toward an officer.

To see the American trooper on the plains in a hostile Indian country, after interminable marches, wearied and reduced by exposure, protracted work, and insufficient food, with his worn-out rusty uniform, one would at first glance write him down as a slouchy kind of soldier. And this judgment would be correct if one compared him to the gayly bedizened and dashing French hussar, the prim and strait-laced British cavalry man, or the precise and machine-like German Ulhan, when on a field review. But wait, and you will see in the American trooper something that can never be seen in any other. The bugle sounds; and these apparently ungraceful troopers, after long marches, and a few hours of sleep, perhaps on the wet prairie or on the snow-covered ground, will swing into their saddles with a motion that dazzles the eye by its mechanical precision. There they sit motionless; and scanning their faces one will observe that unmistakable look of intelligence which is not the result of discipline, but of education, and which is so noticeably absent in the automatic soldiers of the Old World. When the bugle sounds again mark the soldierly ease and elegant grace with which these troopers dash off, though they have been weeks on the march, half-starved meanwhile, fighting Indians day by day, passing sleepless nights, enduring every kind of weather and privations, undaunted by pitiless frosts and snows, the dust of the great plains, or the terrible thirst of the desolate alkali deserts, and one must say, in view of their great endurance, their ever cheerful readiness and easy but perfect discipline, that American soldiers are the best in the world. It is owing to these qualifications that we had in them such excellent Indian fighters. And I venture to say that nowhere in the armies of the Old World could a body of troops be selected, of equal numbers, who would compare at all favorably with them in Indian campaigns.

In the Indian country, when a detachment of cavalry went on a scouting expedition, the men were always reduced to light marching order. Neither the officers, troops, nor guides were provided with shelter of any kind. Sometimes, if the scout was to be a long one, they might have an extra shirt, a towel, a piece of common soap and a tooth brush, but these were the limit of extra baggage. Their beds consisted of the saddle blanket and a rubber poncho spread on the ground. Sometimes two or three troopers bunked together at night, and if the weather was clear two ponchos were placed on the ground, thus having two or three blankets with which to cover themselves. In this way they secured the best shelter possible under the circum-

MOTHER AND CHILD—CAPE MADE OF IROQUOIS SHELLS.

stances. When camp was made for the night, everything was left as comfortable and secure as possible, and the most favorable position was selected to prevent annoyance from unwelcome visitors of all kinds.

Among the many hardships borne by the American soldier at that time, was the neglect of the Government to furnish suitable clothing for those stationed in different latitudes. For those serving in Texas in an almost tropical region the clothing was the same, both in quality and quantity, as that issued to the troops stationed in the cold regions on the borders of the British possessions. There were no warm gloves, wraps, or coverings for the neck or ears furnished to the troops during long winter campaigns; neither were there extra supplies of blankets nor an extra quantity of rations. The clothing and rations were the same the year round; during winter campaigns against the Indians both men and animals often suffered from an insufficient supply of both food and clothing. At night, when near the enemy, no fires could be built, and when the cold was severe, the suffering of the troops and animals was intense. On these campaigns the men's fingers and hands were frequently frozen, and it was not uncommon for the animals to freeze to death where they were fastened. The poor beasts were compelled to live on grass, which they could only obtain by pawing away the snow that covered it. In Texas, during the extreme heat of summer, with the same regulation clothing, both troops and animals suffered greatly from the heat. Even the medical supplies furnished by the Government for campaigns were limited, consisting only of a few articles such as each officer could administer to his men. The hardships endured by the troops engaged in fighting the Indians were thus greatly multiplied. When transportation was furnished for a campaign it was always limited in amount. The consequence was, that in a short time the pack animals broke down, or their backs became a mass of sores, thus compelling the command to abandon a portion of its limited supplies.

The one thing that was never neglected for an instant by the troops in this wild country, was their arms. No matter how severe the weather, these were always protected and kept in good firing condition. When sleeping on the ground in water or snow the arms always received first attention, and were stowed away in the best possible manner to protect them. The first thing a trooper did, on awakening, was to buckle his belt with his pistols on it around his waist, and then sling his carbine (attaching it to a strap over his shoulder). This done, he immediately examined his arms, and put them in the best firing condition, for on these his life depended. Arms were not only used as a protection against the enemy, but also in procuring food.

On an Indian campaign, when pack mules were used, the supply of commissary stores was limited. The command lived largely on the wild meats of the country, and these were secured by the troops themselves. This was done by selecting the best hunter each day to secure game when any was discovered in the vicinity of the camp.

On rare occasions misunderstandings and quarrels occurred among the troops, but they were almost always settled amicably. I recall an instance, though, a sad one, that deserves notice, as illustrating the quickness and expertness of the American soldier in the use of his arms. Some troopers were playing cards on a poncho spread on the ground. Two of them quarreled over the game, one drew his revolver and shot his comrade through the top of the shoulder. The other immediately drew his pistol, remarking, "Ah, you wanted to wing me, did you?" whereupon he fired at his comrade's right elbow, shattering it to pieces; down went his right arm, the six-shooter falling to the ground. Quick as thought the wounded man drew the other revolver from the holster with the left hand and fired with intent to kill. The bullet made a severe scalp wound. Again his antagonist fired at the other elbow of his friend, breaking the joint, which put an end to the firing. The man with his two elbows shattered remarked, "You have made a fine soldier of me." To which his comrade replied, "That was the only way I had to stop you, for if you had killed me you would have been sorry for it all your life." The army surgeon in dressing the wounded man's arms, set the right arm at right angles across his body, and the left almost straight; in this position they remained during the rest of his life. The trouble began and ended in shorter time than it takes to tell; both men were devoted friends before and after the occurrence.

Another trouble that men and animals had to contend with in the elevated portions of that country was the rarity of the atmosphere. It required some time to become accustomed to the thin air of those high altitudes. Those who were not accustomed to it constantly complained of being unable to get their breath. They could not undergo severe physical exertion without becoming greatly distressed, and it usually required from eighteen months to two years before this was overcome.

Another foe was the Rocky Mountain fever. This was a peculiar form of low fever that attacked those not accustomed to the mountain air and prostrated them for a long time. After partly recovering from it, it often assailed the patient again and again, sometimes attacking him in the feet. When this occurred the patient could not bear even the weight of a sheet on any portion of his feet, as he was in constant pain. The feet often swelled to almost double their natural size, and as recovery was slow, a trooper once taken with this disease was unfit for service for a long time.

It frequently happened that the camp was disturbed by other than human enemies. When fresh meat had been cooked, visits were to be expected from all sorts of carnivorous animals. Sometimes a grizzly bear made his appearance, seizing and carrying off the carcass of an antelope, deer or piece of buffalo. If he could be driven from camp without firing a shot it was always done, for should a shot be fired in the death like stillness which prevailed at all times in that country, it could be heard for a long distance and might disclose to the hostiles the whereabouts of the troops.

The regular visitors in every camp were wolves, both gray and coyote. The latter were skulking beasts and sitting at a safe distance from the camp, would utter such unearthly howls that one not accustomed to hearing them imagined from the noise of three or four that there were hundreds present. Should there be from fifteen to twenty gathered about the camp, their howls prevented the troops from sleeping that night. They were cunning thieves and arrant cowards, and were justly despised by every person in that country. With the setting in of cold weather these famished animals became very bold, and coming into camp would eat a pair of boots, the leather of a saddle, or anything they could find to appease their voracious appetites.

PRAIRIE WOLVES—COYOTES.

The large gray wolf was another and more dangerous animal. He was a cunning, skulking thief, and approached the camp by stealth, carrying away whatever he could get hold of. In winter, when these animals were great sufferers from hunger, they became very vicious, and a pack of them often attacked cattle and horses, killing and devouring them. At times old hunters and trappers shot one of the pack, when the rest, crazed by the smell of blood, proceeded to eat their companion alive.

The skins of both kinds of wolves were sent East and made into clothing, robes, mats, or ornaments. Could some of my readers who delight in having wolf skins around them, know the habits of these miserable animals, I fancy they would discard them at once; for the dirty beasts crawled into the carcass of an animal which had been dead for a long time, and once inside of it, rolled over and over in the putrid mass, saturating their hair as much as possible with the filthy and rotten inside of the dead animal. It was not uncommon for one accustomed to it, to locate the presence of these animals by their disgusting odor.

The most important trouble for troops to guard against was a stampede of the animals, as the Indians always tried to effect this by surprising and frightening them when tied or picketed.

The stampede of a large number of animals was a frightful thing. When once a herd of horses and mules became thoroughly frightened they seemed

GRAY WOLF.

to lose their senses, and became entirely unmanageable. In their flight they ran over anything that lay in their path. They did not seem for an instant to recognize any obstacle in their way. They often ran over an embankment, or up against it, nearly dashing themselves to pieces; or rushed wildly into a stream and drowned; or into the mud and mire and became hopelessly swamped. The farther they ran the more frightened they became. The only way to stop a stampede was to cause the animals to run in a circle; in this way they ran until exhausted or cooled down.

The frontier in its original meaning was always a shifting line, long, broad and a very stern reality, full of countless difficulties, perils from savage Indians and the elements, and it was constantly changing, advancing and receding, according to the resistance made by the red men, or as the settlers became disheartened and left. The number of troops stationed there were few, poorly equipped and mounted, and the military posts were widely separated. The cavalry and infantry were strung out in thin were widely separated. The cavalry and infantry were strung out in thin lines from the British possessions to the Rio Grande or stationed at remote posts over this vast terri-tory, entirely isolated from civilization and assistance in the hour of need. The duty of the military was to hold the savages in check and pave the way for civil-ization's advance. The na-ture of these tasks was ar-duous, and the duties were trying to both men and animals. If some of the desperate struggles made by tiny garrisons or scout-ing parties against over-whelming numbers of mer-ciless foes had been written they might appear over-drawn, and yet not have been half told. The terri-ble winter at Valley Forge or the charge at Balaklava has been equalled, if not surpassed, many times by the American trooper on the frontier; here he has done many heroic and use-ful things for which he has never received recognition. The soldier is not a talking machine, nor given to her-alding his acts through the public prints, nor com-plaining of the hardships and privations during long winter campaigns against

BUCKSKIN SUIT ORNAMENTED WITH FINE BEADWORK.— NEZ PERCE.

savage Indians; but is content to do his duty at whatever cost to himself.

CHAPTER XLIX.

THE OVERLAND STAGE—DESPERADOES AND ROAD AGENTS—AN INDIAN ATTACK THAT COVERED TWELVE HUNDRED MILES.

The Overland Stage Line—How the Line was Operated—A Hundred Miles in Twenty-four Hours—Its Extraordinary Service—Prey for Indians and Road Agents—Frequent Raids on the Stage Stations—Looting the Stages—Road Agents—Jules Bevi and his Tragic Death—Killed by the Noted Desperado, Alfred Slade—Cutting Off his Victim's Ears—Nailing One of them to the Door—Dangling the Other from his Watch Chain—The Worst White Man in that Country—His Misdeeds—His Visit to my Camp—A Heeded Warning—In the Hands of the Vigilantes—Execution of Slade and his two Comrades—Dying like Cowards—A Massacre that Extended Twelve Hundred Miles—The Wonderful Mirage.

THE authorities at Washington had been urgently appealed to for an overland mail service to the Pacific Coast, and this stage line was the result. Tho Overland Stage Line was started about 1859.

The eastern end of the line began at St. Joseph, Missouri, and ran to Sacramento, California, a distance of nearly two thousand miles. About twenty-five days were required to make the trip. At first the service was semi-monthly, then weekly, then semi-weekly, then tri-weekly, and after coming under Ben Holiday's management was made daily.

The stages were what was known as thorough brace coaches, strong, durable and well suited for this service and built in Concord, N. H., these were drawn by four, six, or eight good horses or mules. Each stage had a boot in front and rear for baggage and mail, the express and mail matter being always carried in the front boot under the feet of the driver. From nine to twelve persons could be accommodated inside, while four could ride outside on the deck and two with the driver.

The stations were usually from five to ten miles apart. A team running from one station to another with its stage constituted its daily work. At each station a number of men were kept to guard the place, take care of the animals, and assist in hitching and unhitching the teams on arrival. The stages ran on schedule time; the people at the stations knew about when to expect them, and had everything in readiness to prevent delay and enable them to change horses with the utmost celerity. The driver rarely left his box while a change was being made, but when all was in readiness the reins were passed quickly to him, a start was made at once, and the horses were forced to their utmost until the next station was reached, when the same scene of hurried change was re-enacted.

The stages ran night and day, covering a hundred miles each twenty-four hours, which in these days of modern travel does not seem a long distance,

OVERLAND STAGE.
Reproduced by permission of J. B. Lippincott & Co., Philadelphia.

but in those days with a heavily loaded stage, hindered by frequent and unavoidable delays, bad roads through mountain passes, swollen streams, and other obstacles, it was regarded as extraordinary service. The ordinary day's work of a driver covered a distance of from fifty to sixty miles, and in making this journey from five to six teams were used. He went up the route one day and came down the next. His drive was made continuously, whether by day or night, and he was expected to reach his destination as nearly as possible on schedule time. A good stage driver was not only an expert reinsman, but also a man of courage, coolness, and judgment. The road was unbroken, in places very rough, with abrupt turns, deep gullies and washouts.

In the winter when snows were deep the teams frequently became exhausted, or the driver lost his way. Then the stage was abandoned, and the driver and as many of the passengers as could mount the animals did so, going to the nearest station; but when lost they could, by following the trail, return to the station whence they came. When the snow was very blinding those on foot were instructed by the driver to take hold of an animal's tail and hold on until the station was reached. On one occasion, during a blinding snowstorm, when going through Bridger's pass, the horses arrived at the foot of a hill in an exhausted condition. The driver requested the passengers to get out of the stage and walk to the top of the hill. This they refused to do. Before they realized what had happened, the driver left the box, unhitched the team, and mounting one horse and leading the others, was on his way back to the last station, leaving the coach and passengers in the snow. When they realized the situation there was consternation among them. The driver on arriving at the station reported what had occurred, whereupon the men hitched up twelve fresh animals and brought the passengers in. The latter could not have returned alone as the blizzard was blinding. It sometimes happened that stages became lost in a blizzard, remaining out twenty-four or thirty-six hours before they were able to proceed.

The arrival of the stage coach at military posts, trading posts, and ranches, was a matter of great moment, and much excitement usually prevailed while the team was being changed. The journey across the country was very exhausting as the passengers could only sleep while sitting very close together and in cramped positions.

As was to be expected, the stages were great prey for the Indians, and robbers, who were known in that country as "road agents." After capturing the stage and killing its occupants, the Indians secured the arms, clothing, and animals of the victims, and made off; while the road agents, after holding up the stage, robbing the passengers of their valuables, and securing as much express matter as they could manage, permitted the looted stage to resume its journey.

The stations were usually situated in isolated places and were exposed to attacks from the Indians who frequently raided them, securing all the animals, thus seriously crippling the service. The raids were of frequent occurrence and had much to do with hastening the demand for modern means of travel.

At first stages were accompanied by outriders, or, as they were termed, "whippers-in." These men rode a horse alongside the team and vigorously whipped the leaders, to urge them to their greatest speed. Whippers-in were of great service in case of attack from Indians or road agents, all being heavily armed and well mounted, could do much to defend the stage.

Along the road originally traveled by the Overland Stage, were many strange freaks of nature.   From Cottonwood Creek to Court House Rock on the North Platte, during warm weather, when the sun was strong, there was a strange phenomenon called the mirage.   This phantom is very deceiving, for in looking into the distance, through the heated air, there are plainly seen immense herds of elk, with large antlers, grazing, walking or running by turns.   They no sooner disappear than will arise in their place beautiful forests of every kind, to be succeeded in a moment by war parties of Indians with flowing headdress, mounted on fine horses.   These, like the elk, seemed to be standing, walking or running, or making movements, as though in drill.   Great cities and castles also presented themselves, only to vanish like the rest.   I have, when traveling over these plains, in the intense heat, asked those riding beside me what they observed in the mirage.   Their reply generally accorded with what I had seen.   The eye is deceived in a thousand ways by the wonderful transformations of this curious phenomenon, which vary according to the atmospheric conditions, so that a person passing over the same spot at different times will scarcely ever see two similar scenes.   No satisfactory explanation of the cause, so far as I know, has ever been given of it.   My own opinion, and that of almost every person with whom I have conversed, and who are familiar with this curious phantom, is that it is the result of the action of the heat on the ground, and on the vegetation which it decomposes, thus causing an evaporation which produces the illusion.

Where this phenomenon is most marked is on the upland prairie between the crossing of the South Platte and Court House Rock on the North Platte. Here the atmosphere is clear, and looking forward, Laramie Peak is seen so plainly that it does not appear more than five or six miles distant, when in reality, from this point to its base is fully one hundred and twenty-five miles.   Every clear day this spectacle may be observed while crossing this plateau, during the heated portion of the day.   This is the only spot, to my knowledge, in the Great West where this phenomenon appears.

When the Mormons first crossed the plains, about 1847, they, in a manner, paved the way for the Overland Stage Route.   They passed up the Platte River as far as the present town of Julesburg, Colorado—which reminds me that the name of this town is connected with a tragedy, which is worth relating.   Some time after the Mormons passed through this vicinity, a Frenchman named Jules Bevi built and maintained a trading post there for the purpose of trading with Indians, trappers and others.   After the

Overland Stage was started, it passed over the same route traveled by the Mormons, and Bevi's ranch was made a stage station. The stage company had in its employ some desperate characters, for the work was extremely perilous. Among them was a man named Alfred Slade, who was superintendent of the division, which ran from Fort Kearney west to South Pass, and passed by Bevi's ranch. Slade, with some of his comrades, all of them intoxicated, entered Bevi's house and murdered him in the most brutal manner. Slade cut off Bevi's ears, nailed one of them to the door of his victim's ranch, and attached the other to his watch chain. For this brutal crime Slade and his companions were denounced by all the whites in that region. It was from this incident that the present town of Julesburg derived its name—after Jules Bevi.

Slade was probably the worst white man in that country at the time. He was a desperate villain of the meanest kind, and the armed escort he invariably had with him were as thoroughly bad as their leader. He and his party committed many cold-blooded murders, and terrorized the people of that whole section.

About this time the route of the stage line was changed, and ran from Julesburg up the South Platte to Denver, thence under Pike's Peak and Long's Peak, crossing Cache La Poudre River, thence to Virginia Dale, a most beautiful spot, surrounded on either side by almost perpendicular mountains. Here Slade had his headquarters, and lived with his wife. From this beautiful place he and his desperadoes started on their nefarious expeditions.

On one occasion Slade and his party, while drunk, came into my camp on the Laramie Plains. Knowing the man as I did, and the desperate characters with him, I simply said: "Slade, as long as you are in my camp I want you and your party to conduct yourselves in a peaceful and gentlemanly manner. You know that the troops have no love for you, or your party, and the first trouble you make I shall turn them loose on you, and every one of you will be wiped from the face of the earth." It is enough to say that they conducted themselves as I requested, and soon left.

Shortly after this Slade was discharged or left the Overland Stage Line; he and his followers drifted into Montana, where he bought a ranch near Virginia City, to which place he frequently resorted with his crew, and, as usual, terrorized the town. But his reputation had preceded him, and the Vigilantes concluded to mete out to him the same kind of justice he had given to others. One morning when he, with two of his companions, rode into Virginia City, the Vigilantes were in readiness, and at an opportune moment covered them with their guns, compelling them to throw up their hands, and then disarmed them. Slade, knowing the temper of the men he was dealing with, tried to reason with them. His request that he be permitted to send a note to his wife was the only one the Vigilantes complied with. After the departure of the messenger with the note, nooses were adjusted around the necks of Slade and his two comrades, and they were hanged. Soon after this Mrs. Slade appeared on her horse, hoping to save the life of her husband; but she arrived too late, and after viewing the bodies she rode away. Slade and his two comrades died as they had lived, without friends, and in their last extremity begging like cowards for their lives. Not long afterward, Mrs. Slade sold her ranch and left the country for parts unknown, as Slade had perpetrated a great many robberies, it is supposed that she carried with her much wealth.

From what I have already said in previous chapters it will be remembered that each nation or tribe of Indians did not roam over the entire country. Yet, strange as it may seem, an alliance was once made between almost every Indian nation who had their hunting grounds adjacent to or near the Overland Stage road, from the Missouri River to Salt Lake City. Every nation or tribe along this entire distance selected from its forces all the available warriors possible, and during the latter part of August, 1864, made a simultaneous attack on the stages, overland travelers , and all defenseless ranchmen, for a distance of about twelve hundred miles. At that time the stage road was covered with wagon trains almost from one end to the other, and scarcely a train escaped this attack. In some of the trains all of the people were massacred, men, women and children, and their animals and stores carried away. This was the greatest piece of concerted action among the Indian nations that was ever known. For a long time afterward the transportation and ranch interests were completely paralyzed. Even the overland stages carrying the United States mail were compelled to stop until the government could send forces strong enough to protect the line.

This massacre demonstrated the strength and ability of these savage people. For a long time afterward the road was unmolested for the reason that the Indians had secured so much plunder that they could live at ease until more was required. In this massacre millions of dollars worth of property was destroyed or carried away, and the entire emigration to the West over this road was closed for the year.

In this massacre were the Brule Sioux, who had their hunting ground farthest to the east of any tribe of wild Indians, the Ogalalas, Bad Faces, the Tribe-that-don't-eat-Dog, Minneconjoux and other Sioux tribes. The Cheyennes and Arapahoes from as far south as the Araknsas River, were also known to have taken part in the attack. The Utes, Snakes, and Crows, with probably some other nations or tribes, also joined in it.

CHAPTER L.

THE PONY EXPRESS—A DANGEROUS SERVICE IN A DANGEROUS COUNTRY
—WONDERFUL ENDURANCE AND DARING FEATS OF THE RIDERS.

Riding on Horseback from the Missouri River to the Pacific Ocean in Ten Days—A Buck-
ing Pony—A Vicious Beast—Bleeding from the Nose, Mouth, Eyes, and Ears—
Courage and Daring of Pony Express Riders—Running the Gauntlet for Hundreds
of Miles among Hostile Indians and Murderous Road Agents—Exhaustion of the
Riders—Unable to Dismount—Incidents and Experiences—Riding Night and Day—
The Fastest and Longest Ride ever made—Wonderful Endurance—How the News
of Abraham Lincoln's Inauguration was carried across the Continent—Taking a
Dead Man's Place—Dangers by the way—Pursued—Safe at last—Physical Strain of
Long Horseback Riding—A Personal Experience—My Escort—A Never-to-be-for-
gotten Ride—A Country alive with Wild and Frenzied Warriors—The Electric
Telegraph.

THE Overland Stage proved too slow as a means of communication between the East and the Pacific Slope. At first the stage reduced the time
from long months required by ox-teams, to twenty-five days, and it was in
turn beaten by the Pony Express, which carried letters and small express
parcels through in ten days.

The Pony Express was started in 1859, and ran between St. Joseph,
Missouri, and Sacramento, California. It was not a passenger service, but
was established for the special purpose of carrying light express matter,
funds, special letters, etc. The weight carried by each horse was limited
to twenty-five pounds.

The horses used in this service were of small size, usually bronco or wild
horses, intractable and vicious, but having a tender mouth they obeyed the bit
and spur promptly. To saddle and bridle one of them usually required the
united efforts of two or three men. After being caught, a blanket was
placed over the animal's head covering the eyes; while thus blindfolded the
beast was saddled and bridled.

As soon as the rider was firmly seated in his saddle he put the rowels of
his large Mexican spurs securely through the hair cinch (this was woven
open for that puprose) to prevent the animal from throwing him. When all
was in readiness the rider yelled to the men who were holding the blindfolded horse to let it go; whereupon the blanket was suddenly pulled from

its head, and the animal was left to the control of the rider. The beast at once began "bucking" in the most furious manner. Bucking was peculiar to these animals. The operation consisted of suddenly humping its back like a cat in the presence of a beligerent dog, at the same time lowering and thrusting its head between its fore legs, its tail thrust between its hind legs, and all four legs as stiff as if they had no joints in them. In this manner the pony made astonishingly rapid jumps sideways, backward, forward, and in every other way possible, using its utmost endeavor to throw the rider. Some of them, at times, seized the rider's leg with their teeth, holding it as in a vise, in their vicious rage making a strange noise through the nose and mouth. Sometimes they bucked so furiously that the rider bled from his nose, mouth, eyes and ears. After the beast was satisfied that it was impossible to get rid of the burden on his back, it apparently came to its senses and all at once ran off at full speed. The rider then applied both whip and spur and away they went at a mad pace to the next station.

The saddles used were Mexican, were very comfortable for the rider, and well adapted for this service, being prepared at the cantle to hold and carry the bags or pouch containing the express matter. A man can ride a longer distance on one of these saddles without injury to himself, than on any other saddle in use. As the riders bore a large portion of the weight of their bodies on the stirrups, the latter were made of wood, with broad treads for the soles of the feet. Some riders hugged their horses so tightly with the thighs that they rubbed the hair off the animal under the skirt of the saddle. The saddle bags used for carrying the express matter were two small leathern pouches, hung on both sides of the cantle of the saddle. They were sealed and locked at one end of the route, and were not opened until reaching their destination.

There were about two hundred stations along the line, requiring six hundred horses, about one hundred riders, and from five to six hundred other men were employed in maintaining the equipment, supplying fuel, forage, and other necessaries.

The qualifications for a Pony Express rider in those days were expert horsemanship, undaunted courage, and sound judgment. The route was through a country infested by roving bands of wild and murderous Indians, as well as by desperate road agents whose sole object was plunder and who did not hesitate to commit murder on the slightest pretext. From the latter the rider had as much to fear as from the savages.

Almost the entire distance between the two ends of the line was constantly raided by war parties of Indians who were at all times ready to resist all efforts to wrench from them the control of, or the making of roads through their hunting grounds. Besides, the whole country was subject to blinding snowstorms and blizzards during the winter; and in summer its dry, parched, long, weary road, its ragged sandhills, rugged mountains, long brown plains, and peculiar watercourses made it lonesome and dangerous beyond description. The many remains of wagons and human bones that were strewn by the roadside all through that country were sufficient to send a shudder through the frame of the stoutest-hearted traveler.

The Pony Express horses were compelled to carry their riders and express matter from station to station on regular schedule time, which was very fast. The rider, therefore, had to ride with judgment; for should he go too rapidly at first, he was liable to exhaust the strength of his mount before he had gone over his route. It was necessary at all times that the animal should have enough strength, not only to cover his route, but to carry himself and rider out of any danger they might encounter. After riding a few miles the rider noted the condition of his horse, when, if all right, he put spurs to him, urging him at the top of his speed to the next station. The horses usually arrived at the station in an exhausted condition. The distance between the stations which a horse was compelled to cover was usually from ten to twelve miles. Sometimes the distance was shorter or longer, depending upon a suitable place for the station, which whenever possible was located where wood, water and grass were to be had.

The men in charge of the stations always had a number of horses in readiness for the arrival of the rider. While the latter was getting a hasty bite to eat, the men hurriedly removed the saddle and equipment to a fresh horse, which the rider mounted in the manner already described. After its usual bucking, the horse with its load started for the next station. It was not uncommon for riders when near the end of their route to arrive so much exhausted as to be unable to dismount. In such cases the station men took rider, saddle, and trappings, lifting them bodily from one horse to another, when the rider continued to the next station. The distance covered by each rider from one end of his route to the other was usually from forty to sixty miles. He was compelled to ride night and day, sick or well, and in all kinds of weather. Each rider usually rode from four to six horses in going over his route.

I have heard these riders talk among themselves of thrilling experiences while riding over their routes on dark and stormy nights, with practically no road to follow or mark to guide them, compelled to make their way as best they could. They continually expected to run upon a prowling band of Indians, be held up by road agents, or fall into a deep gully or swollen stream, and were always haunted by the fear of dangers that might cost their lives.

Nor were these dangers altogether imaginary, for many a Pony Express rider paid the penalty of his daring with his life.

Sometimes it snowed for twenty-four hours consecutively, covering. the earth to a depth of two or three feet. The wind, rising to a gale, blew the snow into the ravines, filling them up flush with the plains. Should a rider be so unfortunate as to lose his way in one of these terrific and blinding snow-storms, he was liable to lose his life by falling over a precipice, landing on the top of a tree, in a river, or at the bottom of a deep ravine. I have known riders to fall over a precipice with their horses, landing at the bottom of a deep ravine in snow many feet deep; and in the terrible struggle that followed under the snow, the horses broke the arms or legs of the riders, sometimes killing them.

The Pony Express did not continue more than twelve or eighteen months. It was a financial failure, although for each letter weighing half an ounce, going over the route, from ten to fifteen dollars was charged. Even at this high price the enterprise did not pay. The letters were written on tissue paper, were very light, and a large number of them were carried in each pouch.

President Buchanan's last message to Congress in December, 1860, was carried from the Missouri River to Sacramento, California, a distance of about two thousand miles, in a little less than eight days; and President Lincoln's inaugural address, March, 1861, was carried over the same route in seven days and seventeen hours. When the tremendous obstacles that had to be surmounted are taken into consideration, such as rains, snows, storms, swollen rivers, hostile Indians, road agents, and real dangers of almost every kind and on every hand, together with the terrific strain on men and horses in going over these trackless wilds, one can scarcely realize, in these days of fast express trains and luxurious parlor cars, the feats of wonderful endurance performed by these hardy and daring riders.

It would be invidious to single out particular instances of daring and endurance where all did their duty so well. But I recall one feat of riding in this service which I think is worthy of mention, for it has never been equaled before or since. A rider named F. X. Aubrey covered a distance of eight hundred miles in five days and thirteen hours. During this time he stopped only for the shortest rest. On reaching the end of his route he found that the rider who was to take his place had been killed by Indians. Nothing remained for him but to take the dead man's route. He anticipated the difficulties ahead, though he knew that it was equally dangerous to remain where he was or to turn back. The country at that time swarmed with many bands of Indians on the warpath, and Aubrey was pursued by them from one point to another. He was compelled to leave the road and strike around the mountains and hills to keep in hiding from the hostiles, sometimes leading one horse, which, when the one he rode was exhausted, he mounted and continued his journey. He made his way successfully over the route and brought his express pouches through in safety. Aubrey was a man of small stature and light weight, as all Pony Express riders were required to be; he was the impersonation of grit, endurance and fearlessness. This ride came near killing him. For months after he was scarcely able to walk.

The mental and physical strain of a long horseback ride, with the knowledge that at each step one was likely to encounter overwhelming numbers of murderous Indians, and that he was liable to meet death at their hands in its most horrible form, can hardly be realized by one who has not experienced it. I recall an instance in my own experience that I shall never forget. I was detailed to carry important messages from Deer Creek to Fort Laramie, a distance of about one hundred and twenty-five miles. It was of the utmost importance that the despatches should be delivered in the shortest possible time, as they contained a request for troops to relieve a party in distress. I had an escort of nine picked cavalrymen, and our mounts, and equipments were of the best. Each was heavily armed, having two six-shooting Colt's revolvers in the holsters of our belts, a breech-loading carbine slung over our shoulders, and sixty rounds of ammunition. As there was at this time a general uprising of the Indians throughout this vicinity, the country through which we passed was swarming with roving bands of frenzied hostiles, all intent on murder. Almost from the start, and along the entire route, we saw numerous signs of Indians, sometimes indicating only a few, and at other times a considerable number. Although we kept the sharpest lookout we failed to see Indians during the first ninety miles of our journey. The road lay through a broken and mountainous country, affording excellent ambush for these bloodthirsty wretches, as we approached each rock or hill we expected to be attacked at almost any moment. Our nerves were strained to the utmost tension, and our horses seemed to partake of our feeling, for they were startled at the slightest unusual noise. A crow sitting on the ground seemed to my overwrought imagination like a veritable Indian. A crackling in the bush, the snapping of a twig, or the moving of a stone by my horse's foot, as we rode rapidly, along, sent a shudder through me.

On approaching a place called Le Bonte's Camp—a beautiful spot in a bend of the North Platte, where the Indians were accustomed to camp, the place being well wooded and watered and affording abundant game—we expected to encounter the savages. For two or three miles before reaching this locality we dismounted, leading our horses in order to rest them. On nearing the spot we remounted and prepared to run the gauntlet, passing through at a sharp trot. Much to our surprise and relief we saw no Indians, but plenty of signs showing that they were in the immediate neighborhood. From this point on, the road led through a limestone formation that was covered with a growth of small cedar trees. Here we again brought our horses to a settled pace, sparing them as best we could until we arrived in the open country. When about fifteen miles from the fort we discovered signs that were fresh and pronounced, whereupon we dismounted, leading our horses for about a mile. Suddenly some Indians appeared off to our right, scattered in ones and twos, when we at once remounted. They had doubtless been watching us for some time. I saw that they contemplated an attack, but hoped to be able to keep them at a safe distance until we reached the stage station a few miles below. On arriving there we found it had been abandoned. We thereupon urged our horses to a sharp trot, and soon discovered that the Indians' horses were tired also, for they could not twist and turn them in their usual rapid manner.

In a short time the savages, who now seemed to grow more numerous, came nearer, and it was not long before one of the warriors approached within rifle shot. I immediately ordered a halt, and directed one of the men who was a fine shot to bring down the Indian's horse by shooting it through the shoulder. This he did and the Indian was left afoot. Soon after the reds divided and were on both sides of us. When one came too near I ordered a halt, directing a trooper to shoot the Indian's horse, being careful not to kill the Indian, as I knew that would precipitate an attack that might cost us our lives. Within a short time we had killed three or four horses, leaving the warriors on foot; and as we were approaching the hills situated two or three miles from the garrison, the Indians, seeing they were about to lose their advantage, closed in upon us.

Instead of firing singly as before I now ordered all hands to put all the lead possible into both horses and Indians. This we did with such effect that several more beasts and riders were brought down. In a last desperate attempt the savages sought to surround us entirely, and prevent our reaching the hilltop. Urging our tired horses to a sharp gallop, and firing when we could, we succeeded in maintaining the distance betweeen ourselves and pursuers; shortly after getting over the hills, cavalry hastened to meet us from the garrison, where the firing had been heard. The Indians now abandoned the pursuit, and gathering together retreated over the hill. They numbered between thirty and forty.

We knew from experience how to cover the distance with the least distress to ourselves and horses, and the ride was made in thirty-two consecutive hours. On arriving at our destination I do not believe there was a man in the party who could have gone ten miles farther.

After reaching the fort and resting, the reaction from the prolonged strain, both mental and physical, set in. My knees began to swell until they became nearly twice their natural size, and I was so physically shaken up and exhausted that I could not walk without difficulty for weeks. Some of my men were unable to leave the hospital for a long time; and some of the horses were so badly used up that they were never again fit for service.

After the discontinuance of the Pony Express it was found necessary that telegraphic communication be had between the people of the Atlantic and Pacific states. Many projects were originated by which this object could be accomplished, and many influential firms and telegraphic companies were appealed to for money and means to secure this mode of communication.

It was not until the project was brought to the notice of the Creightons, who had built telegraph lines in Ohio and elsewhere that this line was built. Having fully imbued the Creightons with the practicability and financial success of such a line, they were induced to undertake it. Having spent large amounts of money and much time in securing the necessary material and equipment, some time, about 1861 or 1862 they commenced its construction along the route formerly traveled by the Pony Express. In constructing this line they had many fine mule teams. These teams consisted of two, four, and six large Kentucky mules to each wagon. In this way telegraph wire, poles, insulators, and other material necessary to build the telegraph line over the entire route were transported. The telegraph poles for the first seven hundred miles were brought a long distance, as the country through which the line passed was without timber. It required a great deal of courage to construct this line, although they accomplished it and had it in full operation within a year after they began. The line was well constructed, and was the natural outgrowth of the requirements of civilization.

A strange coincidence, and one that probably prevented the destruction of the overland telegraph, happened near Beauvais' ranch, about nine miles below Fort Laramie. When the men were constructing the line in that locality, some of Old Smoke's tribe, who where friendly with the white men, made inquiries as to what it was. They were informed that the telegraph could talk long distances, and if they injured it in any way, it would tell the great father in Washington, which would make him very angry. Three Frenchmen, Beauvais, Bissinette and Bordeaux, were Indian traders, and had Indian women for their wives, which circumstance made the Indians more friendly to them, if such a thing could be. Mr. Beauvais was a large, intelligent and courageous gentleman, for whom the Indians who were at all friendly had great respect. He told them if they did not believe that the telegraph could speak instantaneously for a long distance, he should prove it. When the line was finished as far west as the Platte Bridge, some Indians belonging to the Minneconjoux tribe (the others were Ogalala Sioux) were in the office at or near his ranch. They held a conversation over the telegraph wire with others at Platte Bridge, and agreed to meet near Le Bonte's camp, a distance of about one hundred and twenty five miles. When they met and compared notes, they were fully satisfied of the ability of the telegraph to talk at long distances. Another incident happened in this connection. Some Indians tore down a portion of the telegraph, using the wires for making trinkets for themselves. It chanced that smallpox broke out among these Indians, and almost annihilated the whole of them. After this they had a profound respect for the telegraph, and it was not molested further by them, as they believed the wire was the cause of the disease.

GROUP OF ALBINO INDIANS—ZUNIS.

CHAPTER LI.

WILD HORSES—WHERE THEY CAME FROM—HOW THEY WERE CAPTURED AND SUBDUED.

Wild Horses—First Known in America in 1518—Indians' Astonishment at first seeing a Horse and Rider—The Wild Horse's Struggle for Existence during the Cold Winter —Indian's Mode of Securing them—Their Cruelty to them—Their Great Abundance in Early Days—The White Man's Method of Securing them—" Creasing "—Walking them down—From Twenty-four to Thirty-six Hours Necessary to Accomplish it— Difficulty in Breaking them.

PREVIOUS to the discovery of the New World domestic animals were unknown to the Indians. The first known importation of horses to this continent was made in 1518. When Cortez invaded Mexico the Indians looked with wonder and astonishment on the Spanish cavaliers. When they first saw a man riding a horse they imagined that horse and man were one animal.

During and after the conquest many horses escaped to the wilds, where they multiplied, and in time large herds of them in their wild state spread over the territory of Mexico and the prairies and mountains of the entire North American continent. They have been captured as far north as the Great Slave Lake, where the Indians at first killed them for food.

The herds of wild horses that roamed in the far north in winter when deep snows covered the ground had a severe struggle for existence. They became greatly weakened from insufficient food; when the watercourses and ponds were frozen, and the ground was bare of snow, they became almost frantic from thirst. When in this condition they were easily secured by the Indians.

Nearly all the tribes of the Shoshone nation captured them with the lasso, while on foot. Their favorite method, however, was to mount a fleet horse, and with a lasso approach the wild horses as near as possible without alarming them; then suddenly dashing into the herd they selected one of the best animals, throwing the lasso with unerring aim over its neck, securing the other end firmly to the saddle and following the fleeing wild horse, slowly slacking the pace of the trained horse until the lasso became firmly stretched between the two animals. The noose around the wild horse's neck was then gradually tightened until the animal was choked sufficiently to cause it to fall. The Indian then dismounted and quickly tied the front feet of the wild animal together, leaving it in this position until it had exhausted itself in efforts to regain its freedom. He then gradually approached, until he could touch it, when he placed the lasso around the animal's lower jaw. In this position the wild horse was completely at the mercy of its captor. The animal once in the Indian's possession was treated with great cruelty until it was broken. Some of the wild horses were very obstinate, and it was necessary to almost kill them before they could be subdued and made tractable.

In summer when grass was plenty, it required an extraordinarily good horse to enable an Indian to overtake a drove of wild horses, for the mounted horse was compelled to carry the rider and his trappings, while the wild horse was entirely free, fresh, and in good condition.

In the entire country along the foothills of the Rocky Mountains, from the Great Slave Lake as far south as the central portion of Mexico, wild horses were found in great abundance. The white men and trappers secured them in various ways, one of which was by "creasing." This was done by shooting the animal through the grizzly part of the neck, just in front of the withers, and a few inches below the mane. If well done, the shot gave the horse a shock sufficient to throw it down, where it laid stunned for a few minutes. While thus dazed, the hunter ran quickly to it and tied the animal's fore or hind legs together until it was sufficiently subdued; or he fastened a lasso around the animal's neck and lower jaw, making it fast to the saddle of his own horse. In this manner the wild horse could be securely held until it was taken to camp, where it was afterward broken.

Another mode of capturing them was to walk them down. In doing this it was necessary to have a party of mounted men, numbering from ten to twenty, according to the size of the wild herd. When a herd was seen, one or two mounted men approached it cautiously, and when near enough they endeavored to cause the animals to move in a circle. Great care was required to prevent them from running or stampeding. The mounted men kept them constantly on the walk, never for an instant permitting them to stop even long enough to bite the grass, and above all, preventing them from getting water. After the animals had been kept moving in this way for two or three hours, another mounted man appeared on the scene, to assist the first one. In the course of another hour, two other mounted men carefully approached to relieve the first two men, who with their horses gradually dropped out and returned to camp for rest and refreshment. After three or four hours of constant walking without food or water, the wild animals became dazed, and if not frightened could easily be kept moving in a circle. After some twenty-four to thirty-six hours of continuous walking in this manner, the men approached the herd with lariat ropes, catching one at a time, holding it until the herd had walked a short distance away, then, after placing the lasso around its lower jaw, they led it, plunging and fighting, to camp, where it was securely tied by the neck to a tree, or to a broken animal.

The majority of wild horses were stubborn and it required much patience to train them without breaking their spirit. The stallions were particularly vicious and difficult to break. They sometimes attacked a man with their teeth, almost tearing him to pieces. From start to finish the work of capturing them in any way was difficult and fatiguing.

The Indians did not understand the science of making a gelding; consequently they and the stallions were at constant war; every time one of these horses was to be used, he had to be subdued, and the longer rest the animal had the more difficult the task.

After capture, wild horses rarely, if ever, became tractable. It was necessary to break them to each morning's work. If the animal was to be ridden, one foreleg was tied up, and the saddle was securely fastened on its back, and after the bridle was placed over its head, its leg was let down. A lasso was then fastened about its neck, and the animal was turned loose and allowed to buck until exhausted. If it was to be used in harness, its leg was tied up as before, the harness put on, the animal turned loose, when the usual bucking was indulged in. After it had been tired out, the horse was hitched to the vehicle and ready for work. These animals were small in stature, very hardy, though not tough. For sharp, quick work they compared favorably with domestic horses.

It was from these wild herds that nearly all the horses used by the Pony Express, and some by the overland stages, were obtained, and they were of great service to both of these enterprises.

Nearly all the horses employed on the cattle ranges of the entire West and Southwest were of broncho stock, and were well suited for this service, as they could readily subsist on the grass and were at home everywhere.

They were superior to the large horses in chasing or rounding up cattle, for they were sure-footed, and could turn, halt, and be off instantly, and being courageous, the cowboys could ride them close to a vicious bovine and depend on his horse holding the animal after he lassooed it.

These animals were inexpensive, a good one rarely costing more than twenty-five or thirty dollars.

CHAPTER LII.

KILLING BUFFALOES—AN EXCITING AND DANGEROUS SPORT — " BUCK AGUE"—GREEN SPORTSMEN—PERSONAL EXPERIENCES AND REMINIS-CENCES.

Millions of Buffaloes—Indispensable to the Indians—How Wolves Attacked and Killed them—Why did they always cross in Front of a Railroad Train?—Buffalo Gnats—Stinging the Animals to Fury—Buffalo Chips—The only Fuel on the Plains—Guests Deceived—Eaten Alive by Wolves—The Latter's Unearthly Howls—Excitement of a Buffalo Hunt—A Thrilling Spectacle—Horses as Buffalo Hunters—Dashing into the Herd—A Shower of Stones and Earth—Dangerous Sport for a Verdant—Shoot-ing the Animal through the Ears—Inexperienced Hunters—Teaching them to Hunt—Shooting his own Horse—An Astonished Sportsman—Danger of being Trampled to Death—Buck Ague—Its Effects.

YEARS ago buffalo herds were numerous and large, and covered almost the entire country west of the Mississippi River, to the eastern chain of the Rocky Mountains. I am inclined to give full credit to the stories of their enormous numbers. To persons not accustomed to seeing them in herds, the surprising statements as to their numbers thirty or forty years ago may seem to be overdrawn; but, as I know them, I cannot remember any statement that exaggerated the number of these huge beasts that roamed over the western country, in the early part of my experience there. The artillery at Fort Kearney actually fired into them to keep them out of the fort. I have traveled for months at a time and never been out of sight of their countless numbers.

In Kansas, where the buffalo grass was plentiful, their numbers were incalculable. As far the eye could reach in every direction was a solid mov-ing mass of buffaloes, as the plains were literally black with them. Soon after the Union Pacific Railroad was opened its trains were detained for hours while waiting for buffalo herds to cross the railroad tracks. At first, the engineers thought they could rush the trains through the herds with impunity, but they soon discovered that the only way was to let the animals take their own time in crossing.

They were not always assembled in close, compact herds, but were fre-quently scattered while feeding on the prairies, after the manner of domestic cattle. Forty years ago it would have been impossible to estimate their number even approximately, but there were millions of them; and it is difficult to realize that they have now become nearly extinct.

Formerly the buffaloes ranged over the greater part of the American continent. They were migratory, and their wandering habits were well understood by the Indians. They claimed to know of four kinds; the common buffaloes found on the plains, mountain buffaloes, wood buffaloes, and beaver buffaloes. I have not seen all these varieties, but the Indian accounts of them may be correct, as the different kinds of robes in their possession seemed to testify.

The new coat of the buffalo was dark brown in color; later it grew paler, and when the hair was shed, the coat, especially of the young animals, become a dark brownish red. The cows had one calf at a birth, which was usually dropped during May or June. At birth the color of the calf was a bright yellow, with a pale red stripe covering its backbone, this stripe gradually changed to the natural color with age. The robe was at its best in the fall or winter when the buffalo had its full winter coat. Occasionally a buffalo robe was seen in the silk. These robes were as beautiful as they were rare. The hair was fine and of a dark rich color, as glossy as the finest silk, and as soft as velvet. There was no shaggy mane on these robes, every part of the skin being covered with hair resembling the coat of the finest horse.

Years ago the buffaloes supplied nearly all the food of the North American Indians; especially for those living west of the Mississippi River and east of the Rocky Mountains. These great animals roamed as far north as the Saskatchewan River, in Canada, and as far south as Mexico. Millions of them were slaughtered every year for the sustenance of the Indans occupying this vast territory. They supplied them not only with food, but furnished them with robes and hides for clothing and dwellings. Many of the tools used by them were made from its hide, horns and bones. The hide of the bulls was tanned and used for lodge covers. When dried in the sun, after the hair was taken off, it become as hard as flint; this was used for soles of moccasins, belts, and other purposes. It was also used to keep dampness and cold out of their beds, being laid on the ground and the rest of the bedding placed on top of it. The rawhide was cut into strands and braided into ropes. The green hide was converted into kettles in which they boiled their meat, and it was also used in making canoes. The tough, thick hide of the neck of the bull made battle shields that were proof against arrows and lances. The Indians, in short, allowed no part of the buffalo to go to waste. The brains were used in tanning skins; the bones were boiled; the extract was used as a soup; the marrow was eaten; and the entrails were also eaten either cooked or raw. There was no sweeter meat than that of a fine barren cow, or young bull, the most desirable part being the muscle lying on both sides of the animal's withers. This was called the hump. The liver and tongue were of fine flavor. No one ever thought of telling the number of buffaloes he had killed, unless able to produce the tongues, and the number of these told their own story.

The Indians were not alone in pursuit of the buffaloes. Wolves, both gray and coyote, frequently attacked the old bulls for their meat. A number of wolves would single out an old bull, when one or two attacked him in the rear, and with their sharp teeth, cut his hamstring, bringing him down on his haunches. This accomplished, they at once proceeded to eat their victim alive. When a pack of wolves attacked a buffalo, they set up a yell that was unearthly. Their noise did not seem to frighten these old monarchs, but they formed themselves in a circle, preparing for battle, in which some were sure to be killed. When grazing along the foot-hills of the mountains and thus attacked, and one of their number lay prostrate surrounded by hungry wolves, a grizzly bear sometimes made his appearance and with one stroke of his paw cleared every wolf from their prey. Then they sat at a respectful distance from the carcass of the animal, licking their jaws, and whining like whipped dogs; but not until bruin had finished his meal and taken his departure, would these skulking animals again attack the carcass.

These great animals were migratory, not from inclination, but from necessity. When the ground in the far north was covered with snow and ice, it was impossible for them to reach their food, and when the rivers were frozen over, they were compelled to eat snow to quench their thirst. It was distressing to see them on the ice of a frozen river endeavoring to get water. They slipped and fell in all manner of ways. Sometimes falling into an air-hole in the ice; one after another falling or being pushed into the water and drowned.

The buffaloes were peculiar in one respect. If they attempted to cross a road upon which was a moving wagon train, body of troops, or a railway train, they all invariably crossed in front, never breaking and crossing at the rear. When alarmed and running, their heads were always down, and they kept as close together as possible. While moving in this manner those in front were unable to stop, even if they had the desire to do so, those in the rear forcing them irresistibly on; should a herd be suddenly frightened and start to run over a precipice, all of them rushed over before they could stop, and when found their bodies were one mass of bloody jelly, unfit for food. The Indians, knowing that these animals were valuable to them, were careful not to kill more than were required for their needs.

Late in the summer and fall when buffalo gnats were abundant, they annoyed these great animals beyond endurance. The buffalo gnat was a small black fly and looked like a black bead. It settled on the buffaloes, burying itself in the thick hair and hide, driving them almost frantic, sometimes eating great sores on them. Buffalo "wallows" were depressions in the land caused by the animals wallowing in the dirt, trying to free themselves from the countless gnats that were torturing them. When the first telegraph line was erected over the plains the poles were frequently thrown down from some unaccountable cause; it was subsequently discovered that this was done by the buffaloes rubbing against them to scratch themselves in their efforts to allay the irritation caused by the gnats. An experiment was made of driving heavy spikes in the poles to keep the animals away, but this only attracted them all the more.

Under ordinary circumstances buffaloes were stupidly dull and inoffensive animals, spending their time in eating and sleeping, fighting gnats during the day, and seldom going far from water, of which they required large quantities.

I am of the opinion that if care had been taken in domesticating the buffaloes they would have become a valuable acquisition to our food supply, and furnished robes for use in the northern latitudes during cold weather.

It was not uncommon along the borders of civilization to find domestic cattle running wild with buffalo herds. These cattle, after they had been with the buffaloes for a short time, became much more ferocious and wild than the buffaloes themselves.

When the buffaloes shed their long hair, which turned to a dirty brown in the spring, they presehted a singular appearance, the old loose hair hanging in patches and mats over their bodies.

One of the most useful products of the buffaloes, along the woodless course of the Overland wagon road, was the buffalo "chip." This was the dried dung of the buffaloes, and was composed of the woody fiber of the grass which the animals had eaten. After lying in the sun these chips became dry, and were the only article on this long road which could be collected and used for fuel. They made a hot fire, with only a small flame. Without buffalo chips it is difficult to conceive how travelers and plainsmen could have secured fuel for cooking purposes, for there was absolutely no other fuel in that country. Perhaps fastidious people would revolt at having their meals cooked over such a fire, with the wind blowing and covering the eatables with the ashes and dust from the burning embers.

But hunger is the best sauce; and as a cook once said in my hearing, to some gentlemen who were with us on a hunting expedition, who asked what time dinner would be ready: "Dinner in this camp is always served promptly at six o'clock, except on three occasions, when it is earlier, when it is later or when we don't dine at all," so in early days it would have been the latter alternative to everybody on the plains but for buffalo chips.

It seems incomprehensible that the millions of buffaloes that once roamed over the vast plains should have almost entirely disappeared, and that our government should not have taken steps to prevent hunters and others from wantonly killing these valuable beasts for their hides alone (which brought only three or four dollars each,) leaving the carcasses to rot where they had been slain. South Park was filled with buffaloes. It was well watered, had suitable grass for their subsistence, was well proctected from the elements, and, at small expense, large numbers of these great animals could have been maintained there.

Once while on a hunting expedition in Texas, a party of gentlemen from the East joined us, and, as domestic cattle were plentiful, and could be had for the killing; we always had in our wagons a good supply of fine beef. After killing some buffaloes one afternoon, and bringing the meat into camp, I asked my guests if they desired some of it for dinner. They said no; that the beef they had been eating was good enough for them, and politely insisted that they wanted no buffalo meat on the bill of fare. I said no more, but called the cook, who was a son of Ham, and said, in their hearing: "Professor, I want for my dinner the finest and juicest piece of buffalo hump that you can find; for the rest of the party you may cook some of the prime beef in the wagons,"—at the same instant giving him the wink. He replied, "All right, sah." That evening at dinner, my guests did not cease to comment on the fine flavor of the beef they were eating, and to disparage the dry meat of the buffalo which they supposed I was eating. Dinner over, I said to them: "I noticed that you particularly liked the beef you had for dinner; permit me to say that I did not enjoy mine as much as you did yours, for I dined off a piece of beef and you feasted on the hump of a buffalo." It did not require persuasion afterward to induce them to eat buffalo hump.

On approaching a herd of buffaloes the old bulls were always encountered first. They formed a sort of fringe around the great brown surging mass, and were usually scattered in groups or singly at a distance of from a hundred yards to half a mile from the body of the herd, from which they had been driven and kept at a distance by the young bulls, after the latter had attained full growth and strength. Hence when buffaloes were attacked by wolves, it was the old bulls on the outer edge that met the attack. Their ostracism resulted in forming a guard for the rest of the herd. When the herd was frightened or stampeded, however, the old bulls mingled with them in their flight. At times groups of these ex-monarchs abandoned the herd entirely, wandering away by themselves.

When young bulls attacked the old ones they were no match for the latter in single combat. When a young bull attacked one of these sturdy old fellows and defeated, other young bulls came to the assistance of the beaten animal, a desperate and ferocious combat was sure to take place. The fight sometimes lasting for hours, and in the furious encounter the young bulls were often disabled or mortally wounded. The old bulls were sometimes of enormous size and strength, and fought with great ferocity. It was only after the fiercest and most protracted encounter that they would relinquish leadership among the herd, leaving the places to their younger rivals. During these combats both the young and old bulls fought until both fell exhausted. In this condition, with blood pouring from many wounds, tongues hanging from their mouths, panting and gasping for breath, they continued the battle. The ground fought over in these encounters showed the fierceness of the struggle, being torn up for rods around and covered with blood and tufts of hair. Sometimes one or two bulls might lie prostrate mortally wounded; at other times, with a broken leg, or having lost both eyes, they remained on the scene of carnage presenting a pitiable sight, and in this condition were frequently eaten alive by wolves, bears, and other carnivorous animals. It did not take long after blood had been drawn before the keen-scented scavengers made their appearance in large numbers, particularly wolves. They quietly sat or stood in circles by daylight, around the scene of battle, and at the first opportunity one of the bolder or hungrier made a dash for its victim. If successful, it was but a short time before the carcass was literally covered by these snarling beasts. If the battles were at night, especially when the weather was sharp and cold, the wolves set up an unearthly howl, and soon there were countless numbers of them on the spot waiting an opportunity to appease their voracious appetites.

The killing of an old bull was a perilous undertaking. When a number of old bulls discovered the hunter, they prepared for battle, their heads down, and their eyes glowing like balls of fire. At the first shot they either ran away or charged the attacking party. An old buffalo bull when wounded was a very dangerous animal, and used every effort in his power to reach his pursuers. I have seen them with blood running from their noses, scarcely able to move, stand and tear the ground with their sharp hoofs, their tails erect in the air, doing their utmost to induce the pursuer to come near enough for attack, and until life had left them it was dangerous to go near the furious beasts.

The excitement of a buffalo hunt, in which I often participated during my long sojourn in the Indian country, will always remain with me a vivid and pleasing memory. To see the Indians on their fleet ponies, in swift pursuit of those shaggy-maned monarchs of the prairies, was, to me, a spectacle more thrilling than the fiercest bull fight in the pent-up amphitheatres of Spain. To be a participant in the hunt was still more thrilling, an experience never to be forgotten; and so fascinating that the more it was indulged in the keener grew the enjoyment, until finally it became a passion. The space for the hunt was as limitless as the prairies. In the eagerness of the chase every muscle quivered, every nerve was at its fullest tension, every faculty was keenly on the alert, and the excitement brought with it the glow of health and the vigor of youth. It was magnificent outdoor sport. The long rides, the exhilaration of the exercise, and deep draughts of pure air, made this sport one of the most fascinating that could be indulged in.

When on a buffalo chase only the best horses were used. It was necessary that the animal selected should have not only great courage and speed, but intelligence enough to carry its rider without guidance after the killing once began. When the firing began the reins were dropped over the pommel of the saddle, and not touched again by the rider until he was through firing. The horse was expected to jump over a rock or hole of his own accord, as well as to avoid all obstacles in the way.

After approaching the herd as near as possible, without being discovered, the hunting party dashed into it. The buffaloes, now thoroughly alarmed, first wildly stared, then crowding together, with heads down and tails up rushed at a mad pace from their pursuers, the small herds joining the others in their flight until they formed an immense solid black mass fleeing across the prairie. In their flight, when the ground was dry, they raised great clouds of dust which could be seen for miles. This was exceedingly trying for both men and horses. The eyes, nose, and mouth of both soon became filled with dust, and when dampened by the moist breath formed a sticky mud, not only disagreeable in itself, but creating intense thirst.

Should the ground be soft or wet both rider and horse were covered with the wet earth, which the buffaloes, in their flight, threw back with great force from their sharp hoofs into the faces of horse and rider. It required a horse of courage to withstand the constant rain of clods of earth on breast, flanks, face, nostrils and eyes.

When buffaloes were once frightened and started to run, or were stampeded, they kept close together, forming a compact mass. Should one stumble or fall, many others stumbled over their prostrate comrade before it could rise, and often could not get up at all. The hunter had to avoid groups of fallen and stumbling buffaloes, for should he get into them his horse might also fall, and both it and the rider be severely injured if not trampled to death.

Buffalo hunting was a science that had to be learned. To those not accustomed to it, it was dangerous sport. The inexperienced hunter was always doing what he should not do, sometimes wounding his horse, or that of a comrade, or wounding or killing himself or some one else. A man might be ever so good a hunter for other game, and yet be the veriest bungler in hunting buffaloes.

In killing these animals the hunter rode bodly into the fleeing herd, his horse running only as fast as the buffaloes. Then selecting the animal desired, he fired directly behind the fore shoulder, as this was the tenderest place, and a shot entering at this point was most likely to strike a vital part. This threw the buffalo down, and after the hunter had exhausted his ammunition, or had shot a sufficient number, he returned and killed those he had already wounded that were left lying on the prairie. When in the chase and shooting these animals, it was necessary at all times to have one or two buffaloes between the rider and the animal selected to be shot, for if this precaution was not taken the wounded buffalo was liable to fall in front of the horse of the hunter, or strike the animal next to it a severe blow with its horns. It was useless to fire at the head of one of these huge beasts, for no ordinary bullet would penetrate its thick skull; yet, I have seen an experienced buffalo hunter shoot a buffalo in the ear, killing it instantly. The animals selected to be killed were usually barren cows, young bulls, or heifers, as the meat of the old bulls was strong in flavor and stringy, although it was used as food by the Indians.

We frequently had visits from distinguished visitors who desired to learn something of the life of this wild country. On several occasions, I, with my command, escorted them on a general hunt for antelope, elk, deer, buffalo, and sometimes bears. When a herd of buffaloes was discovered, a detail of eight or ten of the best troopers in the command were chosen for the chase, selecting those who were good shots, and expert riders.

When any of the civilians cared to accompany us on a buffalo hunt the first request made of them was to disarm themselves, this was sure to excite their indignation and was invariably followed by the question, "Why do you ask us to disarm? We can't kill buffalo without weapons." The invariable reply was that it was more important that they should not kill or wound themselves, or any of the troops. We then started for the chase, I directing each civilian to ride close to one of the troopers, and selecting one of the verdants to accompany me. We always kept the civilians on our right, as the firing was usually to the left with a carbine, and to the right with a pistol.

On a hunt near Fort Phantom Hill, in Texas, after having taken a party through their first chase, I consented that on the next some of them might accompany us armed. One of the gentlemen had a Colt's army revolver, and was mounted on a fine horse. We had scarcely entered the herd before I heard a shot, and looking in that direction, saw a horse falling, the rider going heels over head through the air. The rider in his excitement had placed the pistol between the ears of the animal, and fired a bullet into its brain. I assisted the rider to his feet, but he was so confused that he could scarcely speak. In reply to my inquiry as to why he had shot his horse, he said, after some hesitation, that it was incomprehensible to him, unless he was so excited that he did not know what he was doing.

Fear seemed to take possession of every one making his first attack on these animals. The experience of all plainsmen, mountaineers, and army officers, when initiating new men in the buffalo hunt, was, that they became very nervous and excited when coming up with the herd, and were seized with what was known as "buck ague." When once seized with buck ague, inexperienced hunters trembled as though suffering from a violent attack of chills; and seemed to lose control of themselves, and were liable to discharge their arms unconsciously in every direction.

During the chase it frequently occurred that the buffaloes, when frightened, and running at the top of their speed, squeezed so close together that they crushed the legs of the hunter against his horse. On such occasions it was necessary that the experienced hunter should exercise control over the novice and force him to ride as rapidly as the running buffaloes; for, should he attempt to stop his horse, he might be run down by those pressing relentlessly forward in his rear.

I have often been compelled to strike the back of a buffalo with my carbine in order to drive it away to prevent my horse from being thrown. After we had expended all our ammunition, or had killed enough buffaloes, it was not uncommon to find ourselves in the center of a great herd of these animals a mile or more in diameter. The effort then was to withdraw. This was accomplished by slacking the pace of the horses gradually, until the herd ran past, for if we attempted to stop at once, the buffaloes, in their mad rush, might throw our horses down and trample us to death. It often required half an hour's run to get out of a great herd.

The horse that I rode on many hunts had great speed, and possessed more courage and intelligence than any horse I have ever seen. He was a perfect buffalo hunter, and seemed to enjoy the chase as much as I. While I was sometimes frightened at the position in which we found ourselves, this horse, with the reins lying over the pommel of the saddle, and without guidance whatever, would run only as fast as the buffaloes surrounding him. When he came to a small depression or ravine he cleared it with a jump. If passing through small timber, he would always leave sufficient room between a bush or tree so that neither of us might be injured. He seemed to enjoy the sport so much that with every shot I fired, frightening the buffaloes more and more, he only increased his speed sufficiently to hold his position in the herd, never for an instant losing his head or temper.

BUFFALO BULL—*Herd of Hon. John H. Starin.*

In a report of the Department of the Interior, dated at Washington, D. C., July 1, 1902, the Recapitulation says: The number of buffaloes running wild in United States, 30; in Canada, 570; in captivity in United States, 664; in Canada, 30; in Australia, 12; Belgium, France and Holland, 14; Germany, 46; Russia, 2, and in England, 26, and in captivity in other countries, 100, making a total of 1,494. In speaking of the great changes which have taken place in the fauna of America, the report says of the buffaloes: "The fate of the bison, or American buffalo, is typical of them all. 'Whether we consider this noble animal,' says Audubon, 'as an object of the chase or as an article of food for man, it is decidedly the most important of all our American contemporary quadrupeds.'

"At the middle of the last century this animal pastured in Pennsylvania and Virginia, and even at the close of the century ranged over the whole Mississippi Valley and farther west wherever pasturage was to be found. At the present time a few hundred survivors represent the millions of the last century."

CHAPTER LIII.

WILD ANIMALS AND REPTILES OF THE PLAINS AND MOUNTAINS—THE DEADLY RATTLESNAKE AND ITS HABITS—FUR-BEARING ANIMALS AND THEIR WAYS.

The Rattlesnake—Its Deadly Bite—Its One Good Trait—Its Sickening Odor—Coiling for a Spring—Manner of Striking—How Deer Killed the Rattler—The Rattler's Only Redeeming Quality—How the Peccary and Hog Killed Snakes—How the Blacksnake Killed the Rattler—The Pisano or Road Runner—Its Method of Killing Rattlers— The Bull-Whacker's Method—The Prairie Dog and its Habitation—What it Lived on—Its Domicile Invaded by Rattlers and Screech Owls—The Antelope and its Habits—Its Fatal Curiosity—The Elk—The Moose—Use of his Flag Horns—The Black-Tailed Deer—The White-Tailed Deer—The Beaver—A Born Architect—Their Beds—A Sagacious and Industrious Animal—Gnawing Feet off to Gain their Freedom —The Otter.

THE Overland road, (after being changed) from Denver west, passed near the foothills of the Snowy Range of the Rocky Mountains whose summits are covered with perpetual snow. Hidden among these mountains are the most beautiful glens, parks, and streams that can be imagined. Here the elk and flaghorn moose were numerous, also black and white tailed deer, as well as black, cinnamon, and grizzly bears, and mountain lions. On the plains below, on either side of this range, were found antelope in countless numbers.

On the tops of the mountains lived the mountain sheep, the meat of which was the finest of any animal in this region. Here also the feathered tribe thrived in great variety; geese, ducks, California quail (a beautiful species, with a tuft on the head like a peacock, but without the song of the familiar Bob White), pinnated grouse, prairie chickens, and pine cock were in great abundance. The latter lived on pine cones, and its meat tasted strongly of the resin contained in them.

Our esteemed friend, the rattlesnake, also flourished in all this region. I call him our "esteemed friend" because all who knew him had great respect for this venomous reptile, always allowing ample space and treating him with due consideration. It was rarely, if ever, that anything except the hog survived the bite of one of the death-dealing rattlers. They made their homes generally among the stones, sometimes in the habitations of prairie dogs, and were usually from one foot to four feet in length. Of the truth of the statement that for each year of a rattler's life a rattle was added to his tail, I have my doubts; for I have frequently seen large rattlers, probably three inches in diameter, and three or four feet in length, having only a few rattles, while others only an inch in diameter and two to three feet in length, with fifteen and sixteen rattles on their tails were common.

The rattlesnake has one good quality when alive, *i.e.*, if you gave him a chance he always notifies you not to come too near.   If alarmed and angry he immediately coils, and in the center of his coil the end of his tail with the rattles on it stands erect, with these rattles he makes a peculiar noise that

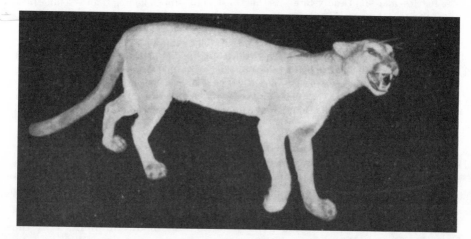

MOUNTAIN LION.

once heard is never forgotten.   At the same time he emits an odor from his mouth that is so sickening as to cause any living thing near to pause.   The rattler cannot strike except when coiled, and when he does so, he uncoils so quickly that the eye cannot follow the movement.   He can only spring about three-quarters the length of his body.   The upper jaw being almost vertical, the two fangs standing at almost right angles to it.   With these he strikes the object aimed at, injecting the poison at the same time.   When at rest, the fangs, which work as if on hinges, lie close along the upper jaw, the points turned backward.   The fangs are connected with the sac that contains the poison.   After striking, he immediately resumes his coiled position and prepares for another stroke.   The rattlesnake is an enemy to all living things, and nearly all things of flesh and blood are enemies of his.

It was interesting to watch deer kill rattlesnakes.   The deer would run from the side of a hill, and when close to the snake crossed their feet in the shape of the letter X, landing with a bound on the body of the snake, and springing away before he had time to coil and strike.   Deer never jumped on a rattler when he was coiled.

The hog, and the peccary, which is a species of the hog, both of which were numerous in Texas and Mexico, were also great enemies of the rattle-

RATTLE SNAKES AT REST.
Supplied by " Cosmopolitan Magazine," April, 1899.

snake.   Both killed the rattlers with their teeth.   The venom of the reptile does not seem to have a bad effect on either of these two animals.   A hog will never seek its dinner elsewhere while he can scent a rattler.   Many stories are told of the hog's invulnerability to poison, how he will turn his cheek to the snake, letting it strike repeatedly until the serpent exhausts its poison, and other preposterous tales.   The plain truth is: a hog will seize the rattler, or any other snake, place his forefoot on it, tear it to pieces, then eat it, and seem all the better for the meal. In the case of the rattler the hog scents the reptile, and appears to delight in nosing it out of the ground. Farmers know that in fields and places where hogs are turned loose the rattler soon disappears.

One of the greatest enemies of the rattler is the blacksnake. The latter is the more powerful, and by far the more agile. The rattler is sluggish in its movements, and is quick only when striking from its coil. Then it is so swift that scarce any living thing can evade it. Whenever these two species

RATTLESNAKE PREPARING TO STRIKE.
Supplied by " Cosmopolitan Magazine," April, 1899.

of snakes meet, there is sure to be a fight, and to the death. The rattler is almost invariably the victim. It knows by instinct that the blacksnake is its deadly enemy, and at once prepares for battle. Why the blacksnake has such an antipathy to the rattlesnake, no scientist, so far as I know, has ever satisfactorily explained. But of that antipathy, anybody who has spent a short time among the lignum-vitæ woods of Texas, where both of these species of snakes abound, cannot doubt. When the two snakes meet the rattler coils at once, and the blacksnake, instinctively knowing the venomous quality of its hated enemy, keeps at a safe distance. It is curious to witness the tactics of the combatants as they begin the strife. In the opening rounds the blacksnake is always the aggressor; but it maintains the scriptural reputation of the wisdom and subtlety of the serpent, for it tries to baffle and confuse its enemy and defers the final struggle as long as possible, though the rattler is far from being its equal in strength.

The physical construction of the two snakes are quite different, and each fights in its natural way. The rattler coils, with head erect, ready to spring. It does not try to get away, for its enemy is animated lightning, and would embrace it in its coils in a flash. The blacksnake is a constrictor, and not venomous, depending on its rapidity of movement to daze and seize its enemy. It sweeps around the rattler in a circle, its head erect and a few inches above the ground, while the rattler tries to follow it, with eyes aglow, its head in striking position, its fangs set, and its rattles in constant motion. Quicker and quicker the long, lithe, black fellow sweeps around until it seems to be a gleaming hoop of black, all the time keeping at safe distance. This movement is continued until the rattler becomes dazed in its effort to follow with its eyes its circling foe. At length the rattler droops its head, and then with a dart so swift that the eye cannot follow it, the blacksnake springs upon its victim, and seizing the rattler just behind the jaws, holds with the tenacity of a bulldog. Should it miss or lose its hold, it is sure to be bitten, which would be fatal. In a second the rattler is enveloped in its folds and the blacksnake proceeds to crush the life out of its victim. Both reptiles now lie motionless for a time, save that the constricting coils of the blacksnake may be noticed pressing its foe tighter and tighter. After a while the tail of the blacksnake gradually uncoils as if cautiously feeling whether or not its victim is yet alive. When satisfied that the rattler is dead, the blacksnake unloosens its coil, lets go the dead snake's neck, and then glides off through the grass or into the bushes as if in the exultation of a duty well performed. The blacksnake does not eat the rattler; but kills him from pure hatred.

Another enemy of the rattler is the pisano, or chaparral cock, commonly known as the road runner. This is a beautiful species of bird, symmetrical in form, somewhat on the lines of the mocking bird, and about the size of an English pheasant. Its legs are black, long, and very fine, its tail long and thin, its beak about the three inches in length, is straight, and very sharp-pointed. Its wings are small, and while it can only fly a short distance, it uses them to help itself in running. It runs so rapidly with the aid of its wings that neither a dog nor a fleet horse can overtake it, and it frequently runs in advance of travelers on the road for long distances. This queer bird seems to have a natural antipathy to the rattlesnake. It will take a dried portion of the thorny cactus, and holding it in its beak, boldly approach the snake, extend its wings, and cause the reptile to strike. When striking the bird holds its bill in such a way that while the wing is withdrawn with the rapidity of a flash the rattler receives the thorns in the mouth. After striking the thorns once or twice, the reptile's mouth is lacerated and his venom is so expended that he becomes prostrated and refuses to strike again, no matter how tantalized or angered. Then the pisano proceeds to pick his eyes out with his long sharp beak, leaving the reptile to die.

In addition to the natural enemies of this venomous reptile the human family also destroys it. Mule-whackers, bull-whackers, and stage-drivers stand at a safe distance from a rattlesnake, cause it to coil, and then strike its head off with one blow of their long whip lashes.

Much has been written on the rattlesnake's power to charm, and the question has given rise to many discussions among naturalists and scientists. These discussions, as a matter of fact, hinge on scientific technicalties or quibbles. The snake may, according to these learned men, "charm" or "fascinate" its victim, or it may not. The truth is that nature has provided the snake with a means of securing its prey or food as she has all other living things of creation. Nature never made a living thing but she made another to destroy it, and furnished it the means to do so. Now the snake, instead of pursuing its prey, allures it. Instead of "charming" or "fascinating" it, it paralyzes it with fright. It is the intense hypnotism of fear that causes the bird to drop from a limb, or the rabbit to sit trembling in terror until seized.

PRAIRIE DOGS.

The prairie dog is a little animal that flourished on the plains, and is peculiar in its habits. Its towns were numerous throughout the West. Prairie dog towns were sometimes from half to three-quarters of a mile across, and covered with countless hillocks made from the dirt dug from the holes. On a bright sunny day the dogs could be seen running in every direction. On the hillocks a number of the little animals were perched as if standing guard, and if alarmed, they made a barking noise, and disappeared in their holes. After a short time they again put their heads above ground, and if the danger remained they barked and disappeared. The ground in and about their towns was entirely bare of grass, showing that they lived on grass and its roots.   They doubtless also ate earth worms and other small living things.   I do not know why this little animal was called a dog, as it in nowise resembles one; but I suppose it received its name from the peculiar snappy, barking noise it makes when stationed on guard at the entrance of its habitation.   Neither did its meat resemble that of the dog, but looked and tasted more like pork.   The prairie dog was difficult to secure for, when shot, it nearly always fell into its hole.

Rattlesnakes and the prairie owl—a small species of the screech owl that lived on the prairie—often made their abode in prairie dogs' holes.   Some persons (one a representative of the Smithsonian Institution at Washington, who accompanied us for a short time) thought, after careful observation, that the prairie dog, prairie owl, and the rattlesnake lived together in har-

PRAIRIE DOGS.

mony.   My theory is that the rattlesnake took forcible possession of the prairie dog's hole, and was an intruder of the worst sort, and from which the occupant of the home always fled.   It not only dispossessed the little animal of its home, but whenever possible, devoured its young.   The owl was also a rank intruder, thrusting itself into the prairie dog's retreat to escape the light of the sun during the day.   My opinion is that the owl also was in great fear of the rattler.

THE ANTELOPE.

The antelope was the most plentiful of all small game on the plains and in the foothills of the mountains.   It rarely entered the timber, but was found on the hillsides where grass was abundant, or on the open plain where it could see everything likely to approach or attack it. In winter they were found in vast herds always near the foothills of the mountains. I have seen, at the foot of the Rocky Mountains, and in the Black Hills, during a snowstorm, hundreds of thousands of antelopes in a single herd. These animals had one or two young at a birth, and as soon as they were born could run as rapidly as the mother. The antelope had great curiosity, which often cost its life. A piece of red cloth, or a flag, if held up, attracted its attention, and as long as it remained quiet antelopes approached from all quarters to learn its meaning. While they were to the windward

THE ANTELOPE.

they approached near, and could be easily killed. Their sense of smell was very acute, and they readily detected the presence of man if the wind was in the right direction. Their meat was among the best that could be obtained in that country, being tender, nutritious, and of fine flavor, one could subsist on it for a long time without anything else. Its skin was of small value, being tender, thin, and porous, but the Indians used it for varous purposes after tanning. The horn stood erect from the head, straight, and spike-like, for ten or twelve inches, its short and sharp end turned backward. It was the fleetest of any animal in that country.   An antelope could outrun the swiftest greyhound.   I have seen an antelope, with its foreleg broken by a shot, chased by one of these dogs, run away with ease; its foreleg flopping over its back at every jump.

The manner of killing them was to approach through a ravine, if this could be done; for if they were in the hills, and became alarmed, they immediately ran up the first valley they came to, ascending a hill, and then stop to make an observation.   The hunter going up the valley next to it, getting if possible to the top of the ridge before the antelope, when he could usually secure one or two.

THE ELK.

The elk was found during the entire year in great abundance in the Black Hills, or near them.   During the breeding season, or when the antler was in velvet, the buck elk was aggressive and often attacked a man without hesitation.   Their gait was a trot, the animal never going at a gallop until tired or wounded.   When they broke into a gallop they could be easily captured or killed.   When going through the timber the head was elevated until the antlers laid upon their backs, forming a wedge to enable them to get through the brush, for it was impossible for them to penetrate thick brush with antlers erect.   The antlers of a full-grown buck elk measured from four to six feet ̓n length, and from three to five feet in width.   With the antlers laid on their backs, their eyes looking skyward, they could not see their way, and would run over anything in their path.   The cry of a wounded elk was much like that of a child.   Just below the eyes were two smooth places, and in the mating season the animal called its mate by uttering a shrill sound through these.   By imitating this noise, hunters called the elk near enough to shoot them.   The hide was coarse, spongy, and of little value.   When dried in the sun it became as hard as flint.   The Indians used this flint hide for soles of moccasins, and other purposes, and when tanned. for covering lodges, making saddle girths, and the coarser articles of horse equipment.   The meat of the elk was coarse and dry, like that of a mule, although when jerked and well dried, it could be eaten, but like the meat of a mule it was not eaten from choice but from necessity.   They bred but once a year, and had one or two young at a birth.   After the birth of the young the buck was particularly ferocious, and if approached often killed its offspring.

THE MOOSE.

The moose was also found in that country, but not in such numbers as the elk.   It belonged to the same family and closely resembled it, except that it had a flaghorn with which it shoveled away the snow in order to obtain food during the winter.

The black-tailed deer was also plentiful, it was found in the mountains,

ROCKY MOUNTAIN BUCK.

and timber along the streams.   Its meat was fine and nutritious.   The hide was of but little value.   They did not go in herds, except in cold weather. They had two fawns at a birth, which were born in the spring, and the young could run as fast as their mother, immediately after birth.   The same may be said of the white-tailed deer, which was easily killed.   Its meat was coarse, dry, and unpalatable, but its hide was the best of the entire family.

MOUNTAIN SHEEP.

The mountain sheep was a peculiar animal, having the habits of the chamois, living only on the highest peaks of the mountains. The horns of the bucks were immense; it is claimed by some hunters that the buck when pursued jumped from a precipice, and landed on its horns instead of feet. This I do not believe, for the females had no horns, besides Nature does not provide such marked advantages for the male portion of any of the animal kingdom. They did not in any way resemble our domestic sheep, either in habits or appearance. The hair was straight and thick, of a dirty gray, and was useless for any purposes of manufacture. In size they were larger than the common goat, which they somewhat resembled in appearance. They were exceedingly nimble and sure-footed, and jumped with great rapidity from crag to crag when pursued by the mountain lion and other carnivorous beasts. The home of this animal seemed to be among barren rocks, where little vegetation grew. Yet when secured by the hunter they were always fat and in good condition. There was no water where they roamed, but snow was perpetual in the valleys below them, and this supplied the necessary drink. They went in herds numbering from one to two hundred. Living as they did in such isolated places, it was exceedingly difficult to find or kill them.

THE BEAVER.

The beaver was found throughout this entire country in all the rivers in which they could live. I make this exception because some of the rivers were so filled with alkaline matter and other impurities, that no animal life could exist in them. To these animals we are more indebted for early discoveries in this region than to any other cause. It was the beaver that gave rise to the formation of the various fur companies, who organized expeditions for their capture. Their skins at that time brought in the market twenty dollars each in gold.

This animal is worthy of note on account of its remarkable intelligence and curious habits. They assembled on the banks of clear-flowing streams on which was situated a growth of cottonwood timber, and with their sharp cutting teeth, two of which are in the upper and two in the lower jaw, cut down a tree a foot and a half in diameter, in a short time, taking out chips with their teeth, four or five inches in length and two or three inches in breadth, the result of their labor being equal to the work of the best woodsman with a sharp axe. They always fell the tree in the direction of the stream, so that as much of it would fall into the water as possible, and they could cut down the entire forest along the river bank in a short time.

When the trees were felled it did not take them long to cut them in lengths sufficient for use in building dams across the river.   Then with their tails and paws the beaver moved the logs into the stream, placing them in position, much the same as an engineer would in building a dam that was expected to sustain the pressure of a large body of water.   Beaver dams were built in crescent shape, the crescent being up the streams, and were built in the fall of the year.   These animals built dams in the mountain streams that were sometimes twenty feet in height, forming a pond above the dam twenty feet deep, and from ten to a hundred feet in width, the dams being so securely constructed that they withstood the severe freshets of spring.   In the pond above the dam they stored cottonwood, on which they partly subsisted during the winter.

Their habitations were in the ground, or bank, near the river, and were built a sufficient distance to protect them from encroachment either by water or their natural enemies (the principal of which was man).   The mouth of the tunnel leading to the beaver's home was deep down in the water of the pond above the dam.   It was then dug upward above the level of the water, when it made a sharp turn downward, going below the water level.   Again it made a turn upward, going above the surface until it reached the bank where it had its home.   Its habitation was the most ingenious in construction that can be imagined.   The beds were located on the sides so that one or two beavers could lie comfortably in a bed.   The animal required a bed of considerable length, for a full-grown beaver, tail and all, was from four to five feet in length.   Its tail was from one foot to eighteen inches long, and was unlike the tail of another animal, being stiff, so that it required a special place for its reception to enable its owner to lie comfortably.

The beaver's tail, next to its cutting teeth, was its greatest tool.   It was its means for transporting logs, dirt, and heavy substances, it was also used as a hoe, trowel, and broom.

The beaver was the most affectionate of animals, as well as one of the most knowing, and being fond of playing with their young in the water, it was interesting to watch them unobserved.   They indulged in all sorts of antics with their young, turning somersaults, swimming with great rapidity, jumping out of the water and then diving head first, cutting such capers as only a beaver can.   Trappers in olden days used to lie for hours watching them in their sportive moods, and then shoot them at a favorable opportunity.

The manner of trapping the beaver was by means of an ordinary trap, patterned like the modern steel rat-trap, only stronger and without teeth in its jaws. A heavy chain was attached to it, this was fastened to a stone, a tree, or a stick firmly driven into the ground. The trapper entered the stream some distance above where he intended to place his trap, and waded to the spot he had selected for it. He thus prevented these intelligent animals from scenting his trail. After setting his trap at the bottom of the pond, he placed near it a stick of sufficient length to reach above the surface of the water. On the exposed end of this stick was tied dried castor of the beaver, this had a strong musky smell, resembling that of the musk deer. As soon as the beaver appeared above the water and scented the castor it immediately swam to the stick; then following it with his nose to the bottom was caught in the trap by one of its legs. The smell of the castor seemed to cause this wily animal to lose all sense of its surroundings. If the beaver did not drown, it would sometimes gnaw its foot off to escape.

The foot of the beaver was webbed and was used for swimming. They also had nails with which they scratched the earth in a similar manner of the mole or badger. Their meat was juicy and resembled fresh pork. They were exceedingly wild, and their sense of smell was very acute. At the slightest approach of danger they dove deep into the pond, rarely if ever, entering the tunnel leading to their home, if there was the slightest chance of being observed. The beaver was as much at home on land as in the water, and when on the ground was in constant motion. However, it never strayed far from the water.

THE OTTER.

The otter was perhaps the most valuable of all the fur-bearing animals of America, on account of the richness and fineness of its fur. This animal measured about two and one-half feet from its nose to the root of its tail. It lived almost exclusively on fish, but when hungry it ate frogs, snakes, and other small animals. It was admirably adapted by nature for pursuing and catching fish. Its body was lithe, and its toes so broadly webbed that it was able to propel itself with great speed through the water. The tail was long, and was used as a rudder to direct its movements in the water; while its short, powerful legs were so loosely jointed that the animal could turn them in almost any direction with ease. The hair on its body and limbs was of two kinds; a close, fine soft fur, lying next to the skin protected the animal against heat and cold; the other composed of long, shining, coarse hair, permitted the animal to glide easily through the water. Its teeth were very sharp and strong, and when diving for fish it rarely missed its prey. In color it varied somewhat, but was generally of a rich brown, intermixed with whitish gray.

The otter made its habitation along the banks of rivers and streams, generally in some natural crevice, or deserted excavation. If these could not be found, it made a hole for itself. The entrance to the holes or burrows were always below the surface of the water. When alarmed, the mother otter with her young plunged into the stream, taking refuge amid the vegetation, or anything that afforded shelter; but as they could not remain under water for a great length of time, they often came to the surface for air. This they did by putting their noses above the surface, filling their lungs, then disappearing again.

The otter was a remarkable fighter and could defeat almost any animal of its size. In fighting a dog, it required but a short time to cut the flesh of its opponent to shreds with its sharp teeth. They were prolific, and had from three to five young at a birth. The young made their appearance early in spring, about March or April, and at first were nursed by the mother, but were soon turned adrift to obtain their own living. They were extremely fond of play, both young and old went to an inclined bank of a river, sliding into the stream on their wet bodies. The trappers called these places "otter slides." At the bottom of the slides he placed his traps into which the otter plunged, becoming prisoners. Like the beaver, when caught in traps it would sometimes gnaw off its foot to regain its freedom.

The beaver and otter were the most sought after by the different fur companies of all the animals in that great country. About the same means were employed in capturing them, and both were trapped for at the same time. The otter did not go to the ponds like the beaver, but was found almost everywhere. The meat of the otter was never considered a palatable dish. As it lived on fish largely, its flesh had a strong, fishy flavor. These animals were prized only for their fine fur. In the early days the otter was found in great abundance, but in latter years became scarce.

Among the Indians their pelts were much prized. They used them for making medicine bags, pouches, and articles of ornament. Having only limited means for capturing them, and the otter was so wary that it was difficult for the red men to secure them at all. When they did, it was usually at an otter slide, where they waited for days at a time, patiently watching for an opportunity to shoot them. Then, if they did not kill it instantly, the animal disappeared in the water, dragging itself off to its hole, where it died. After death the others dragged the remains into the stream to float away with the current.

CHAPTER LIV.

BEARS AND THEIR WAYS—ADVENTURES WITH GRIZZLIES—AN EXCITING
FIGHT AND A RACE FOR LIFE.

The Black Bear—Its Home, Habits and Food—Fondness for Honey—Tenacity of Life
—The Bear as a Boxer—How Indians Secured Them—Four Bears Equal to One
Scalp—Tearing out the Entrails of a Dog at one Blow—The Cinnamon Bear—Its
Peculiarities—A Puzzle to Naturalists—The Grizzly Bear—The Largest and Most
Formidable Bear in Existence—Its Awkward Gait—Why the Grizzly was called
"Sambo"—Avoided by Mountaineers—Indians Killing a Grizzly—A Memorable
Fight With a Grizzly—Starting Him Up in the Underbrush—An Exciting
Time—An Enraged Bear—The Fight On—A Race for Life—A Narrow Escape—
Tormented by Dogs—Fourteen Bullets in Sambo's Body—Killed at Last.

ALTHOUGH the bear family is at home in many parts of the world, there
are but three varieties indigenous to our country, viz.: the black, the cinnamon, and the grizzly.

Of these the black bear was the most common, and was smaller in size
than the cinnamon or grizzly, usually weighing from two to four hundred
pounds. Its coat was soft and the fur thick and long. It is clumsy in appearance, with a thick-set body, short, stout legs, though it is active and
vigilant and had great strength it could scarcely be called a ferocious animal, for it always avoided man. It changed its haunts with the seasons, in
the spring living on roots and juicy plants found in the vicinity of streams,
ponds, and lakes, during summer spending most of its time in the underbrush, where it fed on berries, bugs, frogs, and such small animals as it
could procure. In the fall it sought higher ground, and fed on wild fruits,
acorns, and nuts. It is extremely fond of honey, and in its rambles
through the woods, being an excellent climber, it never passed a bee tree
without robbing it of its store of sweets. Although living for the most part
on vegetable food, it was also carnivorous; but it would not eat meat which
was tainted, unless pressed by hunger. Notwithstanding its clumsy gait it
could run rapidly, and when closely pursued would, whenever possible,
take to a tree. It is also a good swimmer, crossing rivers with ease. Its
cubs were dropped in the spring, and were as frolicsome as kittens in their
play. By the time cold weather set in, the cubs had attained fully two-
thirds of their growth, and when hibernating were fat and in good condition
to remain in a torpid state until the return of spring.

When hibernating, these animals generally hid themselves in the hollow of an old tree, or in caves and crevices, where they remained undisturbed until spring. Sometimes the heavy snows and ice imprisoned them until long after the usual time for making their appearance.

When an Indian secured a bear he regarded it as a great prize; first, for its skin, which made a beautiful robe; next, for its claws and teeth, which were used as ornaments; next, for its meat, which was the red man's pork, and with him was a dainty dish; and last, though not least, is the fact that when an Indian had killed four bears it was considered equal to taking an enemy's scalp. This was considered by them equal to counting a coup.

The black bear was to a certain extent migratory in its habits, and before very severe winters set in they sometimes moved southward in large numbers. It was sagacious in escaping the hunter, but when wounded would, like all the bear family, fight to the death. It was dexterous in the use of its forepaws, and when fighting it stood on its hind legs boxing after the manner of an athlete. With one blow of its sharp claws it could tear out the entrails of a dog. All the bear family have very strong jaws, with which they can crush any small animal.

The cinnamon bear in form and size, as well as in its habits, much resembled its cousin, the black bear. It was larger, however, more fierce and dangerous when molested; but, like most of the bear family, it was comparatively harmless if let alone. The larger specimens of this animal measure from nose to tail over five and a half feet, and in height a little over three feet. It lived largely on berries, roots, and vegetable food, though it by no means disdained flesh when it could get it. It never voluntarily attacked man, but retired on seeing him; but, if cornered or wounded, it was about as ugly a customer and gritty a fighter as could be found.

Its hair was softer and thicker than that of the black bear; under it the fur was finer in texture and considerably longer. Naturalists are generally agreed that the cinnamon is not a different specie of bear, but is a distinct variety. The idea once prevalent that it was a cross between the grizzly and the black bear, has long since been rejected. It was sometimes known as the silver-tip bear, on account of the silvery color of the hair at the extremity of its stunted tail. It has never been found near the seacoast, or in any place far removed from the vicinity of the Rocky Mountains. It is also a northern animal, not being found as far south as Texas. Its natural habitat was west and north of the Missouri River, in the direction of the cold and barren regions of the northwest. It is found in no other part of the world. Its existence was unknown to naturalists until the advent in that region of the fur trappers and hunters. They purchased a bear's skin from the Indians, which was of a pale reddish brown; this the Indians said was from an animal entirely distinct from the grizzly bear. This led to inquiry as to the different species or varieties of bears in that region. The Indians showed the different kinds of bear skins they had, and persisted in saying that there were three kinds of bears in their territory, viz.: the grizzly, the extremities of whose hair were of a white or frosty color; the black bear, and another bear, having white hairs in his light reddish-brown coat.

The cinnamon bear had long been known to the trappers and fur traders before white settlers entered that territory, and the skins of these animals, on account of the fineness of the fur, were much sought after and were more valuable than those of the black bear.

The grizzly bear was the largest and most formidable of any of the bear family whose habitat was in the West, sometimes attaining the length of nine feet and weighing ten to twelve hundred pounds. Specimens have been shown weighing as high as eighteen hundred, and even two thousand pounds. Its habitat were about the same as that of the cinnamon bear.

The coat of this animal was of a dirty brown, or grizzly gray, whence it derived its name. Its claws were long and large, measuring seven or eight inches, sharp and gouge-shaped, and were used with terrible effect in striking down or tearing its prey. They were also of great efficiency in digging for roots. With its sharp claws the grizzly would at one blow tear the entrails from a buffalo, ox, or horse. Like its cousins, it was a great boxer, and used its forepaws with tremendous effect when in battle. In moving, it had a shambling, clumsy, gait, its head constantly swaying from side to side. Its color ranged from brown to nearly black, and sometimes to almost white. It confined itself exclusively to the Rocky Mountain regions and the plains adjacent thereto, where the grizzly made its haunts, the black and the cinnamon bears were scarce. From this I conclude that it was constantly at war with the other two members of the family. All other animals retreated from the presence of this ferocious beast.

The grizzly bear may be called the king of American wild beasts, for it occupied the same relation to the wild beasts of North America that the lion does to those of Africa, or the tiger to those of Asia. In fact, I believe that neither of these latter would be a match in combat with it, for, unlike them, it not only had jaws that were large and powerful enough to crush almost any animal at one bite, but with its chisel-like claws it could tear open the hide of the largest animal at a single blow.

Next to taking the scalp of an enemy, the Indians considered the killing of a grizzly bear their greatest feat. They greatly prized the long claws, the large, sharp teeth, and great warm robe. They wore the claws as ornaments around their necks, and were fond of boasting of their battles and hair-breadth escapes in killing this powerful beast. When the Indians knew that a grizzly bear was in their vicinity, the men, mounted their best horses and armed with their best arms, went in parties to give it battle.

Among the mountaineers and plainsmen the grizzly was known as Sambo, a name given to it because of the resemblance of its hind foot to that of a negro. The old mountaineers and plainsmen, unless they were a strong party, gave Sambo a wide berth. The meat was unfit for human food, being rank, strong, tough, and stringy, especially in an old one, but the flesh of the cubs of three or four months could be eaten if it was allowed to hang in the open air for several days. The cub of a grizzly bear, no matter at how early an age it was captured, could neither be tamed nor trusted.

At the foot of Medicine Bow Mountain, on a creek of that name, I once had a few well-mounted cavalrymen, half a dozen Indians, and a pack of good hunting dogs. Three or four of the dogs were greyhounds, two or three were fox hounds, and the remainder were common-bred animals. I sent a few of the troops with some of the dogs into the thicket to start a grizzly, for they were plentiful there at that time. In a short time after entering the dense underbrush the fox hounds set up their yell, and Sambo soon appeared in the open where we gave him battle. After he had received one or two flesh wounds, he became furious and made an attack on one of the Indians. The latter was mounted on a good horse and fled at the top of his speed, all hands and the dogs following at full cry.

In attempting to escape from the bear, the Indian rode his horse up the smooth side of a butte for almost half a mile, until nearing the top and knowing that he must go over a precipice or turn back, he chose the latter alternative. As soon as he turned, the grizzly turned also, when the whole party of pursuers scattered in every direction. The Indian, knowing the character of the grizzly, ran his horse down the face of the butte with all his speed, lashing him at every jump. The bear was so close to him that at almost every leap he struck with one of his fore paws at the horse. Finding that he could not outrun the bear down the hill, the Indian opened his blanket and threw it in the bear's face, completely blinding him for a few seconds. Bruin made short work of the blanket and was soon in pursuit of his intended victim again. Seeing the Indian's perilous situation, I directed some of the troops to open fire on the grizzly. Some of the bullets must have passed close to the Indian, for he yelled at the top of his voice, while making directly for a creek a short distance from the bottom of the butte. On reaching the water, the bear plunged in to cool himself, and the Indian made his escape. Then began the real fight.

While the bear was in the creek, one of the greyhounds came too near him and the bear with a stroke as swift as lightning hit him in the side with its paw, and with its sharp claws tore out the dog's entrails, killing him on the spot.   After this we fought the bear out of the water on to the plain where for two hours, we had some royal sport.   The greyhounds showed their great value and peculiar cunning in fighting it.   They would never get near its paws, but at every opportunity one of them jumped at and snapped the bear's hips, springing away instantly, while another then repeated the operation. When the grizzly turned to strike its tormenter, a dog from the other side made a snap at it in the same way.   In this manner the bear was kept turning from one side to the other constantly, and not permitted to get away. After a fight of two hours, we succeeded in killing it, some twelve or fourteen bullets had been fired into its body.   No animal ever fought with more ferocity than that bear.   It was particularly annoyed by the arrows the Indians fired into it, and grabbed the shaft of the arrow with its mouth, standing on its hind legs, fighting the stick as though fighting the enemy. It was a fine specimen and weighed about eleven hundred pounds.

After the death of Bruin, every Indian in the party made a mad rush for the carcass, and, jumping from their horses, each made an effort to be the first to strike it with his hands.   There was great excitement, much loud talk, and wild gesticulations among them.   Upon making inquiries as to what the row meant, I found they were wrangling among themselves as to who was entitled to the honor of striking the carcass first, and were also contending as to who should have the claws, the teeth and skin.

INDIAN DRAWING ON A TANNED DEER SKIN.

CHAPTER LV.

JIM BRIDGER, FAMOUS SCOUT, GUIDE, FRONTIERSMAN, AND INDIAN FIGHTER
—PERSONAL EXPERIENCES WITH HIM.

A Typical Frontiersman—Trapper, and Famous Indian Fighter—An Unerring Guide—
His Skill as a Trailer—The Man who Trained Kit Carson—Bridger's Wit and Humor
—Some Characteristic Anecdotes—The Invisible Mountain—A Thrilling and Fatal
Adventure—Telling the Story of his own Death—Bridger's Strange Manner of Liv-
ing—Unable to Read, but could Quote from Shakespeare—A High-Priced Book—
Bridger at the Battle of Powder River—" A Mean Camp "—His Visit to the Presi-
dent—What Bridger thought of Him—A Gang of Desperadoes Discomfited—My
Winter with Him—His Queer Habits—Going to Bed at all Hours—Cooking his
Meals in the Middle of the Night—Singing "Injun"—Bridger in Battle with the
Utes, Killing and Scalping a Ute in a Hand-to-Hand Conflict—Challenging an
Arapahoe—What Followed.

DURING my long and varied experiences in the pathless wilds of the West,
it was my good fortune to have met some of the most noted trappers, mountaineers, plainsmen, frontiersmen, and guides in that country, and to have
been associated with them in various ways. Many of these men were famous throughout that country. They were as much a part of its wild life as were
the savage Indians, wild animals, mountains, rivers, and forests, some of them
were of invaluable service to the pioneers who first entered that unknown
region, as well as to the army, in guiding the troops when in pursuit of the
savages. I think, therefore, a brief sketch of the most noted of these will
not be uninteresting to my intellectual reader.

James Bridger, or, as he was familiarly spoken of in that country, "Old
Jim Bridger," was the most efficient guide, mountaineer, plainsman, trapper and Indian fighter that ever lived in the Far West. He knew more of
that country and all things within its borders than any one who ever lived.
He had been a trapper for various Fur Companies, and had trapped on his
own account for many years, long before the foot of a white settler entered
that territory, having trapped from the mouth to the source of nearly all its
rivers and streams. Although Bridger had little or no education, he could,
with a piece of charcoal or a stick, scratch on the ground or any smooth surface a map of the whole western country that was much more correct than
those made at that time by skilled topographical engineers, with all their
scientific instruments. I have seen Bridger look at a printed map, and

point out its defects at sight.   His experience in that country was not confined to a few nations and tribes of Indians.   He knew more about them, their habits, customs, and characters, than any man who ever lived in all that region.   On no occasion would he trust an Indian.   His disgust for them knew no bounds.   He called them "sarpints," "varmints," and "pizen." He maintained that a rattlesnake was of some good, but that an Indian was good for nothing.   He prided himself on the fact that in anything the "sarpints" (meaning the Indians, not the rattlesnake) did, he (Bridger) could outdo them.   He was a marvelous trailer—unquestionably the most expert that ever lived.   Even when old, and with dimmed eyesight, he could run a trail, when mounted, as fast as his horse could carry him.

The trappers, when trapping, as a rule, took but little notice of the watercourses, cañons, foothills or mountains.   Bridger, on the other hand, was careful to note the lay of all these, and this habit of keen observation and the knowledge it brought subsequently served him well when guiding expeditions through the pathless western wilds.   He noticed every feature of the country, especially its configuration, and possessing, as he did, a retentive memory, he could invariably recall all landmarks with unerring accuracy, even though he had not seen them for years.

Bridger hardly knew his birthplace.   He was scarcely able to write his name, although his wonderful memory and natural abilities served him so well that he was much respected by army officers and by the authorities at Washington, as well as by all whites with whom he came in contact.   The Indians also learned to respect and fear him.   When an important military expedition was planned, Bridger's services were secured whenever possible. The most important man on these campaigns was the guide, for on him everything depended, even the very existence of the command.   Should he lead into ambush, or where there was no water or fuel, the command might perish.   The majority of the guides in that country at that time were brave and in the front when marching, until Indians were sighted or the trail became very pronounced, when they were somehow generally found in the rear.   Not so with Bridger.   He was always at the front.   It was necessary at all times for the guide to be acquainted with, and on the lookout for traps laid by wily savages, and to know how to guard against them to prevent the troops from being outgeneraled.   While Bridger had ample caution, he had the courage of a lion.   In that country, in opposing the cunning savage, an army of deer led by a lion was worth more than an army of lions led by a deer, and Bridger was the leader.

Bridger was an old man when I last saw him, about seventy-six years of age, and a great sufferer from goitre, brought on by the long use of snow water. In some of his many engagements with the red men he received three arrow wounds in his back, and was in consequence unable to straighten himself without suffering great pain. He was also badly ruptured, and I could scarcely understand how he rode a horse at all. Yet with all his bodily infirmities he was cheerful and ready to do valiant service at all times. The government appreciated his services so highly that he frequently received twenty-five dollars per day, his rations, horse, arms and quarters, while in its service. It was Bridger who first brought Kit Carson to the notice of General John C. Fremont, who made Carson famous. I have seen Carson take his orders and instructions from Bridger as a soldier does from his commanding officer. Some of the most skillful guides and famous mountaineers in the western country were trained by Bridger.

Bridger was first employed by the Rocky Mountain Fur Company when a boy but eleven or twelve years old, and, after working for this and other Fur Companies, he was given charge of a trapping party, which position he retained until he engaged in the same business for himself, at which he amassed quite a fortune.

Fort Bridger, situated on Ham's Fork, a branch of Green River, Wyoming, was originally established by him as a trading post, and was, at the time of its establishment, probably the farthest outpost occupied by a white man. Here Bridger kept supplies, and traded with the Utes and other tribes of Indians who occupied or visited that country. It was not until after the Mormons established Salt Lake City, and their destroying angels, known as the "Danites," became prominent for their mysterious deeds of violence and murder, that Bridger was compelled to leave this place. They had a particular dislike of him, and he would certainly have felt their vengeance and probably lost his life had he remained much longer.

Bridger was much sought after by emigrants crossing the plains, for his reputation as a guide and Indian fighter was well known. The pilgrims annoyed him with all sorts of questions, which often compelled the old man to beat a retreat, yet he had a streak of humor, and gave them a ghost story every now and then. Some of these stories were unique. He had a quick and surprisingly vivid imagination, and reeled off story after story with a spontaneity that was astonishing. He told these stories, too, with a solemn gravity that was intensely amusing. I know that I am largely indebted to him for often keeping up my spirits when they were at a low ebb. I always knew something good was coming when he began to tell a story, but never dared to smile until the climax was reached, for that would have spoiled it all.

"Is there anything remarkable to be seen about here?" an inquisitive pilgrim asked him one day.

"W-a-l-l," he replied, in a peculiar drawling tone, which he generally assumed in telling stories, in order to gain time to give his imagination fuller play, "There's a cur'ous mountain a few miles off'n the road, to the north of here, but the doggon'd trouble is you can't see the blamed thing."

"A mountain and can't see it—that's curious," interrupted the pilgrim. "How large is it?"

"Wall, I should say it's nigh onto three miles in circumference at the base, but its height is unknown," continued Bridger with imperturbable gravity.

"Is it so high you can't see the top of it?" inquired the puzzled traveler.

"That's what I say, stranger; you can't see the base of it either. Didn't you ever hear of the Crystal Mountain?"

"I never did."

"Wall, I'll tell you what it is. It's a mountain of crystal rock, an' so clear that the most powerful field glasses can't see it, much less the naked eye. You'll wonder, p'r'aps, how a thing that can't be seen no how wus ever discovered. It came about in this way. You see, a lot of bones an the carcasses of animals an' birds wus found scattered all around the base. You see they ran or flew against this invisible rock and jest killed themselves dead. You kin feel the rock an' that's all. You can't see it. It's a good many miles high, for everlastin' quantities of birds' bones are jest piled up all around the base of it."

On another occasion he told one of these persistent questioners the story of a gold mine, which he said was not far from the Overland road.

"Why, the gold's so plentiful," said Bridger, "that all that's necessary to secure it is to jest pick it up. Great nuggets of the purest gold are scattered all over the ground. There's no diggin' to be done, or rock-crushin' machines an' siftin' required. You orter to stop over and fill your pockets; you'll find it mighty useful on your journey. Anybody who's in want of gold need only go there an' load himself."

"Do you mean to say that it is free to anybody?" asked the traveler.

"Free as the air we breathe," said Bridger.

"How can we get there?" one of the listening crowd ventured to inquire.

"*Hire a buggy*—easiest thing in the world," answered Bridger.

The joke was that a buggy could not be had nearer than six hundred miles.

Another story of this strange and eccentric character:

"You must have had some curious adventures with, and hairbreadth escapes from the Indians, during your long life among them," observed one of a party of a dozen or more, who had been relentlessly plying him with questions.

"Yes, I've hed a few," he responded reflectively, "and I never to my dyin' day shall forget one in perticlar."

The crowd manifested an eager desire to hear the story. I will not undertake to give his words, but no story was ever more graphically told, and no throng of listeners ever followed a story's detail with more intense interest. He was on horseback and alone. He had been suddenly surprised by a party of six Indians, and putting spurs to his horse sought to escape. The Indians, mounted on fleet ponies, quickly followed in pursuit. His only weapon was a six-shooter. The moment the leading Indian came within shooting distance, he turned in his saddle and gave him a shot. His shot always meant a dead Indian. In this way he picked off five of the Indians, but the last one kept up the pursuit relentlessly and refused to be shaken off.

"We wus nearin' the edge of a deep and wide gorge," said Bridger. "No horse could leap over that awful chasm an' a fall to the bottom meant sartin death. I turned my horse suddint an' the Injun was upon me. We both fired to once, an' both horses wus killed. We now engaged in á han'-to-han' conflict with butcher knives. He wus a powerful Injun—tallest I ever see. It wus a long and fierce struggle. One moment I hed the best of it, an' the next the odds wus agin me. Finally——"

Here Bridger paused as if to get breath.

"How did it end?" at length asked one of his breathless listeners, anxiously.

"*The Injun killed me,*" he replied with slow deliberation. The climax freed him from further questioning by that party.

While on a visit to St. Louis, one of his old mountaineer friends of the American Fur Company met him on the street, and greeting him, said: "Jim, wh..t are you doing here?" With an oath he answered, "I'm trying to find my way out of these —— cañons;" adding, "This is the meanest camp I ever struck in my life. I have met more'n a thousand men in the last hour, and nary one of 'em has asked me to come to his lodge and have something to eat."

When on a visit to Washington, he was introduced to the President. After staring at him in amazement for a few moments, Bridger turned to the member of Congress who had introduced him, and said, "Looks jest like any other man, don't he?" He had expected to see in the President a superhuman person, and was much astonished to find that he looked very much like other people.

While his trading post flourished at Fort Bridger he was supposed to have a large amount of money in his possession. Some desperadoes entered his house one night for the purpose of robbing him. Bridger, awakening from

his sleep, quickly said, "What are you lookin' for?" One of the desperadoes answered, "We are looking for your money." Bridger replied,
"Wait jest a minute an' I'll git up and help you." This disconcerted the
robbers, and knowing their man concluded not to wait until he "got up,"
but "got" themselves.

The wagon trains crossing the plains at that time were very numerous,
and usually before leaving the starting points along the Missouri River,
the emigrants bought little guide books for ten cents, giving the location of
good water and grass along the road. Hence it frequently happened that
camp was made at night where not a spear of grass was to be found for the
horses and cattle, it having been consumed by the thousands that had
camped there before. Then the travelers called on Bridger and asked him
where the next good camping place was. The information was cheerfully
given, and the travelers immediately turned to their guide books, and not
finding mention of the locality would accuse Bridger of deceiving them,
which was very annoying, and did not increase his regard for the pilgrims.
Sometimes he would sit for hours and act as if deaf and dumb, in order to
put a stop to the silly questions of travelers.

I occupied the same quarters with him one whole winter, where I had
ample opportunity to study his character and learn his peculiar ways and
manner of living. He never did anything until he felt so inclined. For
instance, if he grew sleepy in the afternoon, say by three, four, or five
o'clock, he went to bed, and when he awoke, say in four, five or six hours
afterward, he would rise, make a fire, roast meat, eat it, and sing "Injun,"
to use his own term, the rest of the night. If he had a tin pan, he turned it
bottom side up, and with a stick, beat on the bottom, making a noise like
the Indian tom-tom. He never ate until he was hungry, and, as he lived
largely on meats, he was thin and spare, although strong and wiry. His
manner of living during this winter did not coincide with my habits or
ideas, by any means, so I tried to entertain him every afternoon and keep
him awake until nine or ten o'clock in the evening. My first effort was in
reading to him. A copy of "Hiawatha," was found among the troops,
which I read to him as long as he permitted it. He would sit bent over, his
long legs crossed, his gaunt hands and arms clasping his knees, and listen to
the reading attentively, until a passage was reached in which Longfellow
portrayed an imaginary Indian, when Bridger, after a period of uneasy
wriggling on his seat, arose very wrathy, and swearing that the whole story
was a lie, that he would listen to no more of it, and that "no such Injun
ever lived." This happened over and over again. After a while I quieted
him, and began reading again, but after a short time he was sure to stop

me, swearing that he would not listen any longer to such infernal lies. However, I managed to entertain him in this way for two or three weeks, during which time I secured a reasonable amount of sleep out of each twenty-four hours.

Bridger became very much interested in this reading, and asked which was the best book that had ever been written. I told him that Shakespeare's was supposed to be the greatest book. Thereupon he made a journey to the main road, and lay in wait for a wagon train, and bought a copy from some emigrants, paying for it with a yoke of cattle, which at that time could have been sold for one hundred and twenty-five dollars. He hired a German boy, from one of the wagon trains, at forty dollars a month, to read to him. The boy was a good reader, and Bridger took great interest in the reading, listening most attentively for hours at a time. Occasionally he got the thread of the story so mixed that he would swear a blue streak, then compel the young man to stop, turn back, and re-read a page or two, until he could get the story straightened out. This continued until he became so hopelessly involved in reading "Richard the Third" that he declared he "wouldn't listen any more to the talk of any man who wus mean enough to kill his mother." That ended our reading of Shakespeare, much to my disgust, for I was again doomed to be kept awake at all hours of the night by his aboriginal habits. After that it was amusing to hear Bridger quote Shakespeare. He could give quotation after quotation, and was always ready to do so. Sometimes he seasoned them with a broad oath, so ingeniously inserted as to make it appear to the listener that Shakespeare himself had used the same language.

During that winter Bridger's suit of buckskin clothing (and it was all he had) became infested with vermin, and in despair he at last asked me how he could get rid of them. I told him that if he would take off his buckskin jacket and breeches and wrap himself in a buffalo robe, I would undertake to rid his clothing of the pests. He thereupon took his clothing off, and turned it inside out. After spreading the garments on the ground, I poured a ridge of powder down all the seams of the suit, and touching it off burned the vermin, but the process also burned the buckskin clothing badly. On the seams of the leggings I had sprinkled so much powder that it burnt the garments to charred leather. They were drawn up short at the seams, and after being turned, each leg curled up until it looked like a half-moon. Bridger looked at me for an instant in great disgust, and with a big oath said, "I'm goin' to kill you for that." I was afraid he would make his threat good, for he was certainly very indignant. I laughed at him, and taking hold of the leggings stretched them into the best shape possible, but the leather was burned to brittleness, and the breeches broke at the slightest touch. Bridger did not forgive me for this for two or three days, during which time he was compelled to go about in a buffalo robe until another buckskin suit could be procured. Every time he saw his ruined suit he blessed me, saying, "The next time you want to rid me an' my clo's of varmints don't you do it with a doggon'd train of gunpowder."

An instance of Bridger's courage happened under my own observation. While scouting in the South Park he was our guide; we also had with us some Arapahoe Indians, and a white man who had an Arapahoe woman for his wife.

After a sharp engagement with a war party of Indians, who greatly outnumbered us, we were compelled to withdraw to the hillside. As soon as the Indians saw our position a number of warriors dismounted and hid themselves in the bushes and tall grasses; from this concealment they began firing upon us. I did not consider it advisable, for the time being, to separate the command and send a party to charge into the ambush. Bridger all this time was growing restless, and at last challenged an Arapahoe to go into the copse with him and attack the Indians hand to hand. The Indian refused and Bridger abused him soundly by means of the sign language. The Indian at last grasped Bridger by the hand, and the two started. It was not long before I heard the report of a six-shooter, and in a few minutes Bridger returned holding in his hand the scalp of a warrior covered with warm blood; he found an Indian in the brush and before the latter had time to move had killed him. The Arapahoe not returning, I was satisfied that his earthly career was ended, or that a worse fate was in store for him. I determined to burn the tall, dry grass, and ordered the white man with the Indian wife to send one of the Arapahoe Indians to set it on fire; they all refused, until Bridger ridiculed them so unmercifully that the whole party accompanied him, and the grass was fired. It burned rapidly, and it was not long before the fierce flames disclosed a great many Indians hidden in the underbrush. When the command opened fire upon them, they ran in every direction; but soon returned with their mounted warriors ready to resume the fight. Bridger insisted that under no circumstances must we leave our present position, as there were at least two or three Indians to one of us. In a short time they made an attack, but we had the advantage of high ground and could anticipate every movement they made. Bridger picked off the first Indian who got within range of his deadly rifle, and the best shots among the troopers also used their Spencer carbines with effect. The Indians were thus prevented from getting near us, and after a few hours of this kind of fighting they withdrew.

Bridger was chief guide and scout on our Powder River expedition. When we arrived in the vicinity of Rosebud River, Bridger informed the officers that we were near a large body of Indians, and that they had large numbers of newly stolen animals, giving their numbers. This he did from the marks of the animals' shoes, as the horses and mules of the Indians are never shod. When we entered this battle everything he said was found to be correct.

An instance of Bridger's wit occurred on the expedition. While encamped under the Big Horn Mountains one night, when all was quiet, an officer asked him why this chain was called "Big Horn Mountains." Bridger turned his face to the mountains and saw the new moon standing on end, and half hidden by the summit of the mountain. Bridger said, with his usual gravity, "Look, don't you see the horn on the mountains, that's why."

During the winter we roomed together Bridger told me many interesting stories of early life, one of which was that of killing a mule. It is well known that during the night when everything is still, animals will approach a fire, their eyes shining like fireballs; the hunters then aimed directly between the eyes and fired, which was sure to kill. This mode of killing animals was common among all hunters of the plains and mountains, and was known as "flashing." When a young man Bridger was trapping with a party on Green River; during the night he heard a noise, and looking in the direction whence it came, saw a pair of eyes flash, and taking deadly aim with his rifle, fired. Going to the spot where he expected to find a deer, or elk, that he had killed, to his horror he found that he had shot a fine mule between the eyes, killing it instantly. For this mule Bridger was compelled to work two years without one cent of pay.

CHAPTER LVI.

A FAMOUS FRONTIERSMAN, TRAPPER, SCOUT AND GUIDE—A WHITE MAN
WHO HAD A SNAKE WOMAN AND LIVED THE INDIAN LIFE
MANY YEARS—HIS ADVENTURES AND EXPLOITS.

Jim Baker a Noted Character—Wanders into the Snake Tribe—Lives With a Snake
Woman and Adopts the Clothing and the Life of the Snakes—A Desperate Fight
with Indians—Fleeced by Gamblers—His Fortitude—Adventures with a Party of
Miners—Discovers Gold—Attacked by Indians—Fighting Indians Step by Step for
a Hundred Miles—The Killed and Wounded—His Deadly Rifle—Hatred of the Mormons—A Perilous Journey—Concealed by Day and Traveling by Night.

TRUE mountaineers and frontiersmen, possessed the important qualities of
courage, coolness, perseverance and physical endurance. Of the few white
men who visited this almost unknown territory at that time, few remained
longer than the time it took them to get away; those who remained per-
manently did so for various reasons. Some of them built ranches, around
which they erected stockades for protection as well as for corraling their
animals in case of attack. At these ranches they established trading posts
for the purpose of trading with Indians. Nearly all of these "ranchmen" had
one or more Indian women for their wives.

It was not uncommon for frontiersmen who had Indian women for their
wives by whom they had children, to remain among the tribes to which their
wives belonged. Of this class was Jim Baker, who became noted throughout the entire northwest. He was originally employed by the American
Fur Company, and in his early days was sent by them to the headwaters of
the Missouri River. Subsequently he wandered into the Snake tribe of
Indians, and secured according to Indian custom, a Snake women for his
wife, by whom he had several children.

Baker possessed all the qualities, both mental and physical, of the typical
frontiersman. In a short time after he had married into this tribe, he adopted
the clothing and life of the red man, and soon became an adept in the
ways of the savages. His mental faculties seemed exactly suited to this
kind of life. He could follow the trail of almost any animal that had
walked over the ground at the top speed of a fleet horse. His marksmanship
with rifle or pistol was unerring, and as he depended upon these weapons for
subsistence, was in constant practice.

In throwing the lariat he was very skilful.   As there were large numbers of wild horses in his immediate vicinity, he rode into the herds, lassoing as many as he needed, always selecting the best.   In this way he kept a large supply of horses on hand at all times.

From his early experience with the fur companies in trapping in the numerous streams in that region from the mouth to their source, Baker became familiar with the watercourses, the cañons of the mountains, and the geography of the country; hence he was much sought after as a guide through this pathless region.

Baker, with some Ute Indians, piloted an expedition from Salt Lake to the headwaters of the Arkansas River, during 1856 or 1857.   On this campaign the commanding officer compelled Baker to dress himself in the clothing of the white man.   Baker said with an oath that it was "the first time in many winters that he had worn such an outfit," and when he was through he declared that it would be "the last time that store clothes would decorate his body."

Baker often buried himself in the wilderness for one and two years at a time, and after securing a large number of pelts, he returned to civilization and converted his accumulations into cash, when he invariably went on a wild spree.   On one of these occasions he visited a gambling house, having with him his accumulations of three or four years.   He played against the game until his last dollar was gone, and then discovered that he had been robbed by the gamblers.   After looking the sporting gentlemen over, and studying their faces for an instant, as if determining what to do, he realized the desperate characters of the men, and the folly of attempting to recover any of his money.   He said, as he turned to leave, "Well, easy come, easy go!" This so pleased the gamblers that they made inquiry as to who he was; after learning that it was Jim Baker, they gave him sufficient money to pay his way back to his own country, where he could suffer and toil for many moons to again accumulate sufficient for another debauch.

Once when crossing a swollen stream on a flat boat, he got into an altercation with one of the boatmen, who, after a few words, struck Baker a severe blow on the head with a stanchion, knocking him into the stream.   After being fished out, he braced himself up, looked at his assailant, and remarked coolly to his friends: "That fellow came mighty near getting the best of me, didn't he?"

When the gold fever broke out prospectors and miners swarmed to that country in search of the precious metal.   One of these parties met Baker, and knowing his qualifications as a trailer and mountaineer, induced him to join them.   Baker led the party up a valley, prospecting all the way, but found no evidences of gold or silver.

They crossed the summit of the mountains, prospecting down the valley on the other side. Coming to a plateau, where camp was made, Baker, as was his custom, immediately started to reconnoiter. He soon came to a place covered with bright, shining yellow metal. He at once filled his pockets and rushing back to camp, excitedly yelled: "Here we are, boys! I've found a place where there is gold enough to make clinkers to supply the world." After showing the contents of his pockets, one of the party, who was an expert miner, quietly said: "Baker, you old fool, this is only pyrites of iron." Baker paused for a moment and said: "What a great thing we have lost then!" and at once began to make "medicine." One of the party who was looking at him in his ridiculous posture, asked him what he was doing. He replied that if he only had his old woman with him to help him to make the right medicine, he "could turn the pirates of iron into pure gold."

His companion said: "Well, further down this valley, we may strike a rich find yet." Baker, well knowing the character of the country significantly replied: "If you do, you may run against some more pirates, but they won't be like these, they will be the Palous, the Cœur d' Alenes, the Spokanes, the Pah-Utes, or worse, them pirates of Mormons."

Curiously enough, it turned out as Baker predicted. The party was shortly afterward attacked by Indians, and some of the miners killed.

Baker, well understanding the methods and wiles of the savages, retreated with his party to a supposed place of safety, but the savages followed up their trail, and came upon them suddenly. Baker rushed from his hiding-place and despatched two of the most advanced with his six-shooter. This so demoralized the rest of the Indians that they fled in confusion. Baker and his party reported to the authorities the killing of their comrades, and Colonel Steptoe, with his comanmd, was sent to avenge the murder of these men.

This unfortunate affair was one of the causes that precipitated the war between the troops and the allied forces of the Palooses, Cœur d' Alenes, Spokanes, and probably other Indian tribes.

The troops being greatly outnumbered, were defeated in the onslaught, and compelled to retreat. During the retreat, they were harassed at every step, and compelled to fight the savages every inch of the way. During the day they fought from hastily thrown-up breastworks, and such natural shelter as they could secure. When darkness fell, they retreated as far as possible. Here they made a stand, throwing up earthworks, and when darkness again came on, resumed their retreat until they finally reached the Snake River, over one hundred miles distant from the scene of the attack. Here, with the aid of some Nez Perces they crossed. From the suddenness of the attack, the premeditated treachery, and the overconfidence of the savages, it was obvious to Colonel Steptoe and his officers that their assailants were instigated and supported by the Mormons, a suspicion subsequently found to be true.

During this retreat of nearly one hundred and ten miles the troops lost several officers and many men, some of whom were killed outright, among the latter being the brave Captain Taylor.

It might naturally be supposed that the loss of these officers and men had a depressing effect on the survivors; on the contrary, it stimulated them to greater effort. As their numbers grew smaller, and their ammunition grew less, they stood closer together, fighting with increased energy. The soldiers were also hampered in carrying their wounded.

In one of these desperate stands, Baker seeing a number of the enemy approaching, called to an officer near him, who, I think was Lieutenant Gaston, to allow him to advance from his position with fifteen soldiers to attack this detached body. Baker sallied forth, leading the attack. They were met by one of the chiefs at the head of a large number of the enemy. This chief was a skilful warrior and leader, whose Indian name was Pow-ti-mine, but was called by the Mormons "Vincent." A desperate conflict ensued. Baker seeing that they were greatly outnumbered, advanced only a short distance, and called upon the troops to kneel, take good aim and make every shot tell. The troops' fire was so hot, that it held the Indians in check for a time.

Soon Lieutenant Gaston fell mortally wounded, and was left on the field, the troops being unable to carry him away. Baker seeing that further resistance was useless, directed the troops to retire as best they could to the main body of the command. On reaching it, they discovered that but seven of the fifteen were left. During the retreat Baker was the last man to leave every point of vantage, and he used his muzzle-loading Hawkins rifle with deadly effect. After joining the main body of the troops, and observing the few that were left, he said with his usual oath, "that pace was hotter than my old woman's frying-pan. I don't want to get into any place like that any more."

In this battle the Cœur d' Alenes were led by Mil-kap-si, one of their chiefs, whom Baker knew well, and had met on former occasions. It was this chief, who on meeting Baker afterward, told him who the allied party consisted of, and gave their numbers, from which it was learned that the Mormons were the real instigators of the war.

After this affair Baker returned alone through the mountains to the Snake country, a distance of over two hundred miles. On this journey he was compelled to pass through the country of the hostiles, and was constantly in danger of falling in with bands of roving Indians.   Baker always claimed that this was the most perilous journey of his life.   Were it not for his knowledge as a frontiersman, he could not have accomplished it.   He lived on game, and frequently, when in the neighborhood of hostile Indians, was reduced to the verge of starvation, not daring to fire his rifle, lest its sound should betray his presence.   At other times he was forced to remain in concealment all day, and to travel only by night.   He finally reached the Snake country.   This is his own story in brief as he gave it to me.

BARK HOUSE—SAC AND FOX.

INDEX.